HABITS OF MIND
The Experimental College Program at Berkeley

Katherine Bernhardi Trow

Institute of Governmental Studies Press
University of California, Berkeley
1998

©1998 by the Regents of the University of California. All rights reserved.
Printed in the United States of America.

Library of Congress Cataloging-In-Publication Data
Trow, Katherine.
      Habits of mind / Katherine Trow.
         p. cm.
      Includes bibliographical references.
      ISBN 0-87772-380-X
      1. University of California, Berkeley. Experimental College Program--History. 2. Tussman, Joseph. 3. Meiklejohn, Alexander, 1872-1964. I. Title.
LD743.T76 1998
378.794'67--dc21   98-6238
                                                                       CIP

For Martin

Sarah, Peter, and Paul

"The American college must rediscover and renew its commitment to its fundamental purpose . . . for society and for the individual, to develop our rational powers, to heighten sensitivity to and awareness of fundamental human problems, to cultivate and strengthen the habits . . . the practices, and the spirit of reasoning together. . . . "

"But the problem is not simply to free the student from the traditional routine and turn him loose. It is, rather, to establish a ritual that will support and encourage the development of a set of intellectual habits consistent with a reasonable, effective, and continuous use of the mind."

—Joseph Tussman
Experiment at Berkeley

"Being in the Program gave you the opportunity to think and reflect and it got to be a habit."

"It built a habit of conversation, of civilized discourse, talking seriously about serious subjects, on your own . . . "

"It educated us, taught us how to read things, how to learn for ourselves, how to think about it. Well, I take that back, it didn't teach us how to do it, it got us into the habit of doing it."

—former Experimental College Program students

"A teacher affects eternity; no one can tell where his influence stops."
—Henry Adams

ACKNOWLEDGMENTS

The study of the long-term effects of the Tussman Experimental College Program and the writing of this book, which reports its results, were aided in countless ways by many colleagues and friends in the higher education community both here and abroad. Among those who have offered encouragement and support from the very beginning, I particularly want to mention David Riesman, whose expressions of interest and enthusiasm helped to give me confidence from the start, Tony Becher, whose timely personal and material support allowed me to complete the exploratory study upon which the major study was based, and Zelda Gamson who has been a steadfast supporter all along. Neil Smelser read several drafts and reports, and both he and Oliver Fulton made suggestions that helped substantially to improve early drafts. Clark Kerr, Arnold Leiman, Thorsten Nybom, Sigbrit Franke, A. H. Halsey, Torsten Husén, Patrick Hayashi, Benson Snyder, and the late Joe Katz among others were kind enough to read and comment on proposals, project reports, and drafts of the book at various stages. Nathan Glazer, Tom Popkowitz, Michael Burrage, Barbara Leigh Smith, Martin Kramer, James Perkins, Maurice Kogan, and Svante Lindqvist also made useful suggestions and have been helpful in a variety of ways.

Grants from the Fund for the Improvement of Postsecondary Education (FIPSE) helped support the study and publication of the book. Equally importantly, Director Charles Karelis's vote of confidence in the project offered moral support at crucial times. David Holmes, Sandra Newkirk, Cari Foreman, Frank Frankfort, and David Johnson are others on the FIPSE staff whose help was valuable to the success of the proposals.

At the University of California, Berkeley, Janet Ruyle deftly wove her way between two dinosaur bureaucracies as she administered the original grant at the Center for Studies in Higher Education, and later Jeri Foushée at International and Area Studies managed the whole second grant process and administration with great expertise. My chief assistant, Georgina Edwards handled a variety of tasks related to the project with impressive skill. Marian Gade was on hand at the Center to answer questions about higher education, and Bill Roberts kindly dug out materials from the University archives. Bob McCarthy at the Survey Research Center did the data processing. I also appreciate the help of Susan Sullivan at the Center for Studies in Higher Education, and in the closing stages while abroad, the staffs at the Center for Research and Development in Higher Education, Hokkaido University, and the Sapporo Guest House, Sapporo, Japan.

The choice of the Institute of Governmental Studies Press as publisher has proved to be a particularly fortuitous one—Jerry Lubenow handled it all with professional ease, friendliness, and good humor. It was truly a pleasure to work with Jerry, Maria Wolf, and Pat Ramirez.

I am also in debt to Susan Cerny of the Berkeley Architectural Heritage Association (BAHA) for providing information about the historical significance of the Ernest Coxhead building, which the Program occupied, to Anthony Bruce at BAHA for help in finding pictures of the house, and to Mary Hardy of Seigel & Strain Architects who generously lent me original drawings of the building. And to Olivia Masson who granted permission to use the photograph of the House.

Perhaps my greatest obligation is to the 40 former Program students, who by necessity must go unnamed, who gave their time and their recollections, and recounted to me the meaning for them of this unique experience in their educational lives. Their intensive, candid interviews formed the empirical basis of this book. I am also deeply indebted to Joe Tussman whose writings and speeches about his Experimental College Program and the educational principles upon which it was founded were the inspiration for this study. He willingly gave his time to answer endless questions about the Program and to give me important background information. Adrian Marriage provided helpful insights into the operation of the Program from a second-cycle faculty perspective; Arthur Lipow gave me his views of teaching in the first cycle. Robert Suczek graciously shared with me findings from his early study of Program students.

Because it is customary, Martin Trow's name comes last on this list, although by rights it should come first. He has given his expert help and advice on all phases of this project. Over and above this essential practical assistance, he has served as my Muse, offering encouragement and inspiration at countless times. For all of this I shall be eternally grateful.

CONTENTS

Introduction   1

I. THE BEGINNINGS

1. The Experiment at Berkeley   7

II. THE PLAN

2. How Students Came to Apply and Why   27
3. The Faculty   37
4. The House   75
5. Educational Features   83

III. THE RESULTS

6. The Major Impact on the Lives of its Participants   133
7. The Educational Effects   181
8. The Vocational Effects   227

IV. STUDENT DEVELOPMENT

9. The Role of Development   241
10. Teaching and Learning   263
11. Community   295
12. Politics and the Program   321
13. Authority in the Program   351

V. THE LESSONS LEARNED

14. Summary, Implications, and Conclusions   387

References   417
Appendix A: Academic Senate Report   425
Appendix B: The Reading List   449
Appendix C: Time Table of Major Political Events   453

Appendix D: Invitational Letter   455
Appendix E: Interview Questions   459
Appendix F: Methodology and Survey Findings   463
Appendix G: College Attitude Study Questionnaire   473
Appendix H: Interview Invitational Letter   477

Index   479

About the Author   483

ILLUSTRATIONS

All photographs appear after page 76.

Figure 1   The House on Hearst Street designed by Ernest Coxhead.

Figure 2   Program faculty meeting.

Figure 3   Joseph Tussman, founder of the Experimental College Program at Berkeley.

Figure 4   Lecture in Northgate Hall.

Figure 5   Same lecture showing all faculty members in attendance.

Figure 6   Program students in the House lounge.

Figure 7   Faculty-led seminar in the House.

Photo of the House reprinted with permission from *The Buildings of Berkeley*, Robert Bernhardi, The Holmes Book Company, 1975. Other photographs by Ted Streshinsky of Photo 20-20.

Introduction

Back in the middle sixties on the campus of the University of California, Berkeley, at about the same time as the Free Speech Movement that was to spread rapidly to other campuses throughout the country and the world, another quieter but equally radical educational event was taking place. Extraordinary in its own right, it was set in the midst of the hubbub and furor of the student revolution, and sometimes confused with it, although it was in no way part of it. It was an experiment in curricular reform called the Experimental College Program, led by Professor Joseph Tussman, then chairman of the philosophy department at Berkeley, and was modeled after Alexander Meiklejohn's Experimental College at the University of Wisconsin. A similar program at San Jose State University at about the same time was short-lived (Cadwallader 1984); another called Vico College at SUNY-Buffalo, modeled in part on the Tussman program in the early seventies, survived about 10 years. The program or parts of it have been adapted by other institutions in the U.S. and Canada, and the many learning communities now spread over the U.S. owe their pedagogical inspiration, in whole or in part, to the Meiklejohn/Tussman plan. Ironically, Tussman's Experimental College Program (hereafter the Program) did not take permanent hold on its own campus for reasons having to do with problems of staffing rather than with the Program itself. It opened in the fall of 1965, continued for two, two-year cycles, and ended in 1969.

Tussman's plan for the Program was unique in its purpose, particularly for a large, public research university, unique in its curricular design, and unique in its pedagogical approach. Its purpose was to offer students a "moral" education, an education for responsible citizenship, to develop what Tussman called a "political vocation." The curriculum of the Program was based on a study of "culture in crisis" from four different historical periods: Greece during the Peloponnesian Wars, seventeenth-century England, America during the Federalist period, and contemporary America. The pedagogical structure did away with courses consisting instead of a coherent, integrated program of lectures, seminars and tutorials covering virtually the whole of the students' first two undergraduate years in the setting of a learning community in which five or six faculty members read the syllabus together with 150 students. The Program was housed in one building, allowing all Program activities except the large lecture meeting to be conducted in one place and with much informal contact and discussion among faculty, among faculty and students, and among students.

This was a bold plan indeed, bold even for a time noted for educational innovation, and it attracted national attention through articles in *Time*[1] and *Mademoiselle*[2] magazines among others. It was considered a failure by some in the educational community at the time because it was discontinued after four years.[3] Yet before long, evidence began to surface contradicting these early assumptions. In a review of curriculum highlights for the decade spanning the late sixties and early seventies, Arthur Levine found that "very few of the Program's faculty or alumni can be located who do not highly praise its idea (Levine 1978)." Could it be that contemporary judgments came too soon, were subject to hearsay, jealousy, or political bias, and were misleading? Could a small program conducted a quarter of a century ago, focused on citizenship and using a "Euro-centered"

---

[1]"Intellectual Immersion at Berkeley," *Time* (March 15, 1968): 78.

[2]Eric Peterson, "The Program Has Helped Me Know That I Don't Know: A Report on the Berkeley Experiment." *Mademoiselle*, August, 1969, p. 261.

[3]The reason for its discontinuation was not, however, as Peter Dale Scott has stated, that it "failed to demonstrate to its academic colleagues that any of its experimental curricular innovations should be made permanent"; nor had it "foundered" because "the faculty and students . . . could not agree on what [its] unity should be (Scott 1989)," as will be discussed in later chapters.

Introduction

curriculum, that lasted only four years be relevant to the world of higher education today?

Before we can answer these questions we need to know more about the Program and how it worked, how it was conceived and executed, and how it affected those who participated in it. We need to know more about its unique pedagogic structure that departed so dramatically from customary undergraduate education in the first two years, and about the impact of that approach on learning. We need to know about the kinds of students who applied to the Program and why, and about the faculty who taught in it. Were there any other aspects of the Program, apart from its pedagogic features, that made it special? Was it a good program for all its students, and if not, why not? And what difference did it make that it took place in Berkeley in the '60s?

Above all, did the Program have any notable effects on the lives of its participants, on their subsequent education, their jobs, and careers? We will look at the delayed effects of this program of instruction on its former students two decades or more after they left it. At the same time, this study will explore the question of whether any judgment of a comprehensive educational program of this kind can properly be made on the testimony of students at the time they leave it.

To answer these questions about the Experimental College Program and about its short- and long-term effects, we turn to its former students who will be the best judges of its value to them then and throughout their lives. The reports of 40 former participants of their experiences there, and of its influence on their lives since leaving college, provide the major source of evidence for this study of the impact of this special experimental program.

The book has five parts. The first describes the origins of the Program as it related to Meiklejohn's original Experimental College at Wisconsin, Tussman's purpose and plan behind his vision of the Experimental Program, its content and structure, and its chances for success at Berkeley.

The second is an account of the Program at Berkeley, how and why students came to apply to the Program, the curricular content of the Program, and the pedagogical methods it employed.

The third, examines the impact that the Program had on the lives of its former participants—its effects on their subsequent education and careers, and how its educational content and methods shaped that impact.

The fourth looks at how student ethical and intellectual development was effected by the Program and its pedagogical features, and how different aspects of the developmental process influenced the effects the Program had on its students.

And in the fifth, we take another look at judgments of the Program's successes and failures, its replications, and its implications for improvements in current higher education, in teaching, curriculum, and research.

THE BEGINNINGS

CHAPTER 1

The Experiment at Berkeley

THE ORIGINS OF THE PROGRAM, ITS PURPOSE AND ITS EDUCATIONAL STRUCTURE

The story of the Experimental College Program, or Tussman College as it came to be called at the time, begins at the University of Wisconsin in the late twenties with Alexander Meiklejohn. Meiklejohn, a former president of Amherst College and an educational reformer of wide influence throughout his lifetime, was brought to the University of Wisconsin in 1926 to found the Experimental College there based on principles Tussman later embodied in the Experimental College Program at Berkeley. The Experimental College at Wisconsin lasted until 1932, when it folded for a variety of reasons, mainly the lack of enough faculty support "with the total structure of the University education seemingly threatened by the questioning, the controversy, the sheer exhilaration, camaraderie, and freedom generated by the Experimental College."[1] Joseph Tussman studied with Meiklejohn at Wisconsin in the late thirties, although he had not been a student in the Experimental College there. Still, he carried with him Meiklejohn's vision of this radically different conception of undergraduate

---

[1] Cynthia Brown, et al., "Alternative Education: Trends and Future Implications," in *Against the Current: Reform and Experimentation in Higher Education*, ed. Jones, Richard M., and Barbara Leigh Smith, (Cambridge, Massachusetts: Schenkman Publishing Co., 1984).

education, his "moral education" for "political vocation," throughout his teaching career at Syracuse and Wesleyan until he arrived (for the second time) to teach philosophy on the Berkeley campus in 1963.

Tussman introduced a proposal for his version of the Program on the Berkeley campus in 1964. His plan for the Program was not connected in any way with the Free Speech Movement (FSM), even though some FSM leaders might have embraced the idea of the Program as alternative education when it was first introduced. But because it was an alternative to the first two years of the regular undergraduate program, and because it was presented to administrators and faculty in the spring of 1965, soon after the take-over of Sproul Hall Plaza by student radicals in December of 1964, it was commonly viewed as having been a response to the FSM, a misapprehension that persists among many to this day. Nothing could be further from the truth. Instead of an open-ended, student-designed, "do-it-yourself" program, as might have been advocated by the FSM, this new program focused on a required curriculum designed by its founder and its faculty to cover the entire first two undergraduate years without change and without student input. Similar perhaps at first glance to FSM rhetoric, it had at its core the concept of freedom, but freedom in an entirely different relationship to authority than that of the FSM.

The Experimental College Program at Berkeley has been described by Professor Tussman in four publications: the first, a report to the Berkeley division of the Academic Senate published just as the second year of the Program was beginning;[2] the second, a fuller account in a book titled *Experiment at Berkeley*, (Tussman, 1969), finished in the fall of 1968, the middle of the fourth year of the Program; the third, a set of reflections in essay form about the rise and fall of the Program titled "A Venture in Educational Reform: A Partial View" (Tussman, 1988); the fourth, *The Beleaguered College*,[3] published in 1997, a more wide-ranging view of the Program. In his first book *Experiment at Berkeley,* and later in his

---

[2]Report of the Executive Committee, Faculty of the College of Letters and Science, University of California, Berkeley, 1966-67. Included here as Appendix A.

[3]Joseph Tussman, *The Beleaguered College: Essays on Educational Reform* (Berkeley, Calif.: Institute of Governmental Studies Press, University of California, 1997).

reflections, Professor Tussman describes his purpose and his plan for the Experimental College Program. The following is a distillation of the ideas he presents in his books, the essay, and in his report to the Berkeley Division of the Academic Senate. The quotations used are from these earlier sources.

In simplest terms, the primary purpose of the Program was to teach undergraduate students in their first two years of college to become responsible citizens in a democratic society. According to Tussman, democracy imposes on everyone a political vocation, and this vocation demands a special education; since everyone in a democracy is to share in the ruling function, that is, government, everyone then needs to share in the education that was reserved, in elitist societies, for the ruling class.

There were two parts central to his plan: one, the curriculum, or educational content; and two, the pedagogical methods, or the process by which the curriculum was to be taught. The purpose of the Program as Tussman saw it was to "lead the student into a broad and sustained examination of the 'moral' dimensions of the situation in which [the student] and we find ourselves. The curriculum is a concrete plan for doing that" (1969, 50). The curriculum then was not a course either in "Western Civilization" or in "Great Books," but was instead about "great problems," "about times of cultural crises throughout history, periods that produced a rich and varied literature in which powerful minds grappled with fundamental human problems." Inspired by Meiklejohns' Athens-to-America "moral curriculum" but expanded to include other works, the Program curriculum focused on Greece during the Peloponnesian Wars with readings that included the *Iliad* and the *Odyssey*, the writings of Herodotus, Thucydides, Plato, and Sophocles; on seventeenth-century England with readings including *King Lear, Paradise Lost*, Hobbes' *Leviathan,* and the King James Bible; eighteenth- and nineteenth-century America with the *Federalist Papers* and Henry Adams; and contemporary America including Marx, Freud, and the autobiographies of Lincoln Steffens and Malcolm X. (A more complete list is presented in Appendix B.) It was neither historical, though readings clustered around these four historical periods, nor disciplinary, though at times it drew heavily on a philosophical perspective. Neither was it meant to be interdisciplinary, but since it drew from a variety of perspectives—history, philosophy, political science, literature, and others—it was often mistaken for an interdisciplinary program. Instead, it was independent of all these common curricular characteristics—a fact sometimes difficult to grasp by faculty outside the Program and students within it.

The faculty were to read these works together with students, think about them, discuss them. Students were largely unfamiliar with the readings; faculty were unfamiliar with some of them. But that was in keeping with the principles of the community of scholars that the Program fostered, where faculty and students were to read the works together. "We begin cold," Tussman says in his book, "with the *Iliad*, but everything after that is read in a steadily thickening context of insights, questions, ideas . . . a growing sense of relation and inter-connection as we progress" (1969, 59).

Although the curriculum might be labeled elitist, this was most emphatically not an elitist honors program. Letters explaining the Program and inviting students to apply were sent by the dean of the College of Letters and Science to all freshmen entering Berkeley during the summers of 1965 and 1967, then the names of 150 students were chosen at random from the 300 or so applicants. (Names were actually pulled from two hats, one for women and one for men, since Tussman and his faculty wanted equal numbers of men and women students in the Program.) Tussman wanted as "typical [a] group as we could get" since he judged the curriculum to be "suitable for anyone and everyone faced with the necessity of living his life in today's world."

Pedagogically, the Program differed radically in most ways from the first two years of the regular undergraduate program at Berkeley (called there the "lower division"). There were to be lectures in the Program, but they were only one part of the pedagogical structure, and they went beyond the purpose they served in regular lower division classes. Lectures, held twice a week for the entire student body with all faculty present, were sometimes led by individual faculty, sometimes by faculty together in panels, and occasionally by guest lecturers brought in from the campus or surrounding community. Their main function was to "stimulate and deepen the reading process . . . to sharpen and deepen the issues or problems latent in the reading" (1969, 88). While there might be some discussion during lectures, discussion was to be conducted mainly in the seminars, of which there came to be two types. The first was a small seminar of 10 to 15 students with a faculty member present. The second, a feature of the second two-year cycle, was the same seminar group without a faculty member present, the idea being for students to learn to conduct seminars themselves.

There were no exams and no grades other than pass-fail in the Program. In order to track students' intellectual development, papers were assigned every two weeks, to be read by faculty and discussed with the students in individual tutorials. In addition to the papers, students were asked to write each day, for at least 15 minutes, in journals, keeping track of their thoughts on the readings, lectures, seminars, and discussions. The faculty-student ratio (24 to one at the beginning and about 15 to one after roughly one-third of the enrolled students in each cycle eventually left the Program) was similar to that in the rest of the university, but conditions of life and study in the Program allowed for informal discussion to take place between faculty and students.

The Program's particular brand of team teaching was not to be an easy ride for faculty. Giving up their customary solitary lectures on subjects they knew well, they were to teach sometimes unfamiliar material together. Lecturing in front of the entire group exposed them to the scrutiny of their colleagues, a new experience for most of them. Instead of their customary practice in their regular university classes of assigning readings and every so often giving objective examinations usually graded by teaching assistants, faculty were required to pay close attention to students' intellectual development in tutorials and small seminars, and in careful reading of the writing assignments.

CHANCES FOR SUCCESS

In summary, that was the purpose, the plan, and the structure of the Program: to replace the usual set of unrelated beginning lecture classes for first- and second-year students with an integrated two-year program (satisfying social science and humanities breadth requirements) with a coherent "Athens-to-America," "moral" curriculum chosen by faculty to educate students for their place in a democratic society through close student-faculty relations in a learning community without exams and grades but with communal lectures, small seminars, papers, and tutorials instead. It was a worthy sounding experiment, staffed with first-class scholars and teachers at a first-class university. Why then was it not renewed after its second cycle?

The chances of such a program surviving at the time in the large, public research university in which it was set were influenced by several factors likely to bear on the outcome: (1) the kind of educational reform that the

Program represented, (2) the campus in which it was to be conducted, (3) the political implications of the climate on the campus during the years in which it functioned, (4) the place occupied by its students in the developmental life cycle.

1. Tussman's views of undergraduate educational reform center both on the purpose of the lower division and on the educational process by which these first two years are conducted. He contends that the first two undergraduate years at research universities such as Berkeley are an educational wasteland. He argues that the lower division has become simply a holding period for the upper division when students begin study in their major fields and has lost its sense of an independent mission, that of initiation into the privileges and responsibilities of society.[4] He believes the current system of a set of loosely organized, mostly unrelated courses that constitute the first two undergraduate years, or first program, are a wasted opportunity and should be converted to programs with coherence and integration and an organizing principle different from that on which the second program, the upper division, with its emphasis on majors, is based. He favors the Program for the first two lower division years over the course, or set of courses, because it can be coherently organized around a theme, although, he says, not necessarily the one he chose for the Experimental College Program.

---

[4]The "missionary" spirit of colleges of higher education has a long history in the United States going all the way back to the first college ever proposed in the new colony. The plans for Henrico College on the James River in Virginia, entrusted by the Virginia Company in 1619 as an endowment for an English university with a residential college for Indians, had the purpose of educating natives to become fit for conversion to Christianity. But they were never realized because of financial difficulties, the Indian uprising in 1622, and the dissolution of the Virginia Company in 1624. Other plans for including a "moral" curriculum at both William and Mary College and Dartmouth College for the education of Indians also failed although the host universities survived (Axtell 1985, 179-364). And somewhat ironically, the city of Berkeley itself was named by one of the university's founders for the Bishop of Cloyne who became a patron of American colleges (particularly Yale) after he was forced to abandon his own dream of founding a college in Bermuda, which he had hoped would "strengthen Protestantism in America . . . and save the souls of Indians and slaves" (McArdle 1983, 4).

His plan, and Meiklejohn's before him, represent what Gerald Grant and David Riesman call "neo-classic telic reform," that is, "a restoration of the classical curriculum with new intensity and purity and dominated by a moral imperative (Grant and Riesman 1978, 15-20)." It was an attempt "not only to change the university but to set forth new ideals," and is distinguishable from what they call "popular reform" which merely "brings about a general loosening of the curriculum." They view the chances of success for "telic" reforms, which threaten the basic conceptions of undergraduate education, to be much smaller than for "popular" reforms, which do not require a "radical reorientation of institutional goals" (*ibid.*, 179.) Tussman's reform was not only based on a radically different conception of lower division studies, it necessitated radically new and personally more demanding ways of teaching for members of the Berkeley faculty who were to staff the Experimental College Program. From this standpoint alone, the Program design was bold and risky.

2. The place Tussman chose for his experiment was not a new institution establishing its separate identity along experimental lines from the very beginning, as was, for instance, the University of California at Santa Cruz or Evergreen College in the State of Washington, which later adopted and adapted the Meiklejohn-Tussman scheme. Nor was it a small liberal arts college dedicated from its beginning to principles of educational reform, such as St. John's. The University of California, Berkeley, is a large, well-established, highly respected, and well-known public university with roots in the middle nineteenth century—the flagship university of what many believe to be the finest public university system in the world, and widely recognized as one of the best two or three research universities in the country. It has become famous not for its undergraduate teaching, but for its top-rated research faculty, many of them Nobel Laureates, and for its very strong graduate and professional schools and departments, many of them consistently rated first in the country.[5]

Long before 1965, the lower division at Berkeley had become a vehicle by which to introduce students to the academic disciplines, requiring them

---

[5]That is not to say the faculty noted for research and scholarship do not make outstanding lecturers—a great many do. But the teaching emphasis at Berkeley had been toward training graduate students rather than teaching undergraduates, even more in 1965 than today.

to fulfill requirements for entrance to the upper division major by taking a prescribed set of undergraduate lecture courses. Some of the large beginning lecture and laboratory courses in the sciences had become sorting places aimed at weeding out weaker students before they progressed too far in major fields where academic excellence would be demanded of them. Perhaps these conditions on their own present a strong argument in favor of curricular and pedagogical reform, but at the same time, they most certainly did not go against the grain of established pedagogical practices and the common educational ethos of large, public research universities in the U.S.

3. Much has been written about the student revolution of the sixties both at the time (for instance, Heirich 1971; Lipset 1965; Searle 1971) and more recently now that 25- and 30-year anniversaries are being observed (Gitlin 1987; Goines 1993; Rorabaugh 1989). Although the particular relationship between the Program and its political setting will be discussed later, it will suffice to say here that the campus was in political turmoil for a decade beginning from the early sixties and covering the time the Program was in operation. (A timetable of crucial events during that period is included as Appendix C.) Nonetheless, it is worth noting some historical facts at this point.

Tussman began negotiations over the Experimental College Program with the university administration and had developed a concrete proposal for it by the spring of 1964, before the first rumblings of campus demonstrations were felt toward the end of that summer, and well before the eruption of the Free Speech Movement in that fall and winter. However, negotiations were not completed until the spring of 1965, invitational letters were not sent to incoming freshmen until the summer of 1965, and the Program was not ready to open until that fall. By that time, Berkeley had been made famous throughout the world by, among other events, the take-over of Sproul Hall by student activists in December of 1964. This is the time when the most prominent of the movement's leaders, Mario Savio, in an often-quoted speech, exhorted students to "put your bodies upon the gears and upon the wheels, upon the levers, upon all the apparatus [of the University] and . . . make it stop. And you've got to indicate to the people who run it, to the people who own it, that unless you're free, the machines will be prevented from working at all" (Heirich 1971, 271-72).

Prospective students applying to Berkeley for the 1965-66 academic year would almost certainly have become aware, at least by the time they applied to the Program during the summer of 1965, of the political mobilization of the campus, and the spirit of revolt against the educational status quo which it had come to represent. The invitational letter contained terminology that, if not read too closely and if the references to expectations of hard work on the part of students were overlooked, might have been interpreted as having been written in response to student demands for more individualized and intimate undergraduate education. The words "flexible" and "flexibility," for instance, are used three times in the letter; it states that "its essential feature is that it abandons the course system"; and the "spirit" of the Program is described as "informal." (The letter is reproduced as Appendix D.) It would be understandable if some applicants to the Program had assumed that the Program was part of the revolution, rather than based, as it actually was, on premises totally contrary to it—the inherent inability of beginning students to wisely choose their own course programs.[6]

Tussman said "the crux [of the Program] is freedom. Liberal education aims at the free mind. Every aspect and device of the Experimental Program is intended to serve that end" (1969, 29-30). But this kind of freedom did not mean the absence of restraints as the Free Speech Movement defined freedom; Tussman's concept of freedom was based on qualities of "strength and wisdom," defining the free man as "one who has the power to achieve what is indeed good." And since Tussman held that neither minds nor students are made free by being left alone, to allow students to choose to study only what interests them is to "pander" to their "accidental" interests and to allow the college to evade its responsibility for educational planning. He argued instead for a fixed curriculum chosen by faculty, experienced scholars, and teachers who could guide students toward the goals of the Program.

In addition to adhering to a concept of freedom that restricted students to a curriculum chosen by faculty and not by them, Tussman expected in students a kind of educational "docility." He did not define docility as submissiveness, but rather as teachability (1969, 32-33). This invitation to turn oneself over to and trust in a faculty-run program certainly did not square with one of the popular slogans of the time, "Don't trust anyone over

---

[6]Even some of the Berkeley academic community had erroneous impressions of what the Program was all about. One of the regents of the university wanted to vote against it, claiming it was "really going to be a course in revolution, taught by Marxists" (Heirich 1971, 378).

thirty!" Tussman describes teachability in his book as "[A] spiritual relaxedness, a looseness which comes from faith, hope, love, trust, confidence—a sense that something good is going on and that one wants to, and can join in." While "spiritual" and "love" were part of the lexicon of the times, "docility" certainly was not.

4. Beginning college students in the United States, ages 17, 18, 19, span the stages of late adolescence and early adulthood. Their contemporaries who do not choose to attend college generally enter the work force or the military, and some marry and begin to raise families; college students are, for the most part, not expected for at least another four years to take up those responsibilities of adulthood. More and more students today are "mature" students, having left school at one stage or another to work or to raise families and are now returning to either begin or to finish their college degrees. This was less common in the middle sixties than it is today. Whether they were living at home, in dorms or cooperatives or fraternity or sorority houses, or off campus in apartments, or were working full or part time, students proceeded with the normal developmental tasks of separation and individuation. College offers students a kind of half-way house between dependence and independence, and students at Berkeley, as elsewhere, often spend their first year under the protection and convenience of dormitory or fraternity/sorority life, then go on to their own independent living arrangements. The dissolution of the old *in loco parentis* mandate to colleges to take care of students' moral and physical as well as educational development, in part a consequence of the student rebellion, allowed undergraduates freedoms they might not ordinarily find at home.

While students were not meant to actually live in the House (the former fraternity house that served as a physical location for the Program), the Program offered them more of a "home away from home" in many ways than was available to ordinary Berkeley undergraduates. Even if not formally in residence there, students were still to have free use of the House, available to them at all times, day and night. Faculty or staff were generally not around in the evenings to enforce rules, allowing some students to use the House for whatever purposes they wished. This arrangement allowed some of the freedoms of adulthood to an even greater degree than life in dorms or fraternity or sorority houses where more social control was practiced under the authority of adults or older students in residence. (See Chapter 4, The House.)

Faculty and staff of the Program were there to teach and to lead, not to enforce rules, but, as educational authorities, they could serve as symbols of adult authority nonetheless. Close relations were encouraged with faculty members, who were all male, and those relations included argument and debate. The only woman staff member, except for one woman teaching assistant the first year, was the Program secretary, and students often sought her out as a source of advice. And so in some ways, factors in the make-up of the Program encouraged its symbolism as a surrogate home complete with multiple surrogate parents. Just at the time of the Program's existence, the war in Vietnam was becoming America's great "cultural crisis," so that in a program based on what must have appeared to some to be authoritarian principles, emphasizing moral choices in difficult times, particularly times of war, and encouraging discussion and debate, it would be reasonable to expect some students would transfer some of their idealism about these issues and their growing needs for independence and self-assertion to the Program and its personnel.

Reviewing these four major factors most likely to affect the outcome of Tussman's "Experiment at Berkeley," we begin to see why the kind of telic reform it represents, as Grant and Riesman define it, challenging accepted educational practices at large research universities and making heavy demands on faculty, generally does not enjoy a high rate of success. Had the Experimental College Program been the popular type of educational reform, loosening rather than tightening the curriculum choices for students or making life easier rather than more difficult for faculty, it might have been more attractive to both Berkeley administration and faculty and stood a greater chance of becoming institutionalized. Hearsay or general descriptions of the Program probably led many students to believe it was of the popular type of reform, which then might result in many of them leaving after they discovered the true nature of the curriculum and what was expected of them. However, the faculty of this university whose success, promotion, and salary depended primarily on research achievement and very little or not at all on teaching would know immediately that any kind of program based on telic reform would require a good deal of professional and perhaps personal sacrifice, which not many of them could be expected to make.

From what I could learn about how the administration viewed the Experimental College Program, it is clear it was content that it appeared at the time to help satisfy the cries for reform of undergraduate teaching both from students on the campus and from legislators in Sacramento. In the view of the Berkeley administration as well as the Academic Senate, any innovative undergraduate program, led by a senior Berkeley faculty member and within reasonable cost limits could be approved. Martin Meyerson, who was acting chancellor at Berkeley when the Program was approved, although he thought Tussman to be a serious and respected senior professor who would not cause a "scandal," saw the Program as only one of what he hoped would be many innovative approaches to undergraduate teaching.[7] And the Program after all, by being both small and experimental and not proposing, at first, to become a permanent part of the University, was not seen as threatening to the established order on the campus. Serious and not scandalous, small and not institutionalized, it was tentatively allowed to take its place among several alternative undergraduate programs on the Berkeley campus. Lost in the midst of the educational, social, and political chaos at Berkeley, its unique contribution to undergraduate curriculum reform was not evaluated or generally recognized at the time.

Related to the type of educational reform the Program represented is the setting in which it took place. The fact that it went against the long-established and not visibly unsuccessful educational tradition of viewing the first two undergraduate years as preparation for the upper division major, and therefore as the time for completing requirements for that major, placed another obstacle in the way of its success on a campus noted for its strong and successful academic departments. While it would appeal to some students because it fulfilled all lower division requirements for the social sciences and humanities, it would not appeal to others who wanted to sample courses in various departments before choosing a major. And the timing of the experiment, thrust as it was into the most politically, socially, and educationally disruptive times on colleges campuses anywhere in recent memory, may have helped initially to smooth its way toward acceptance by the administration and faculty, although that was a short-term gain. When eventually it was discovered by students that Tussman's conception of freedom involved responsibility, and his idea of teachability included hard work and a certain degree of docility on their part—not the kind of educational reform endorsed by the Free Speech Movement—they were

---

[7]Martin Meyerson, personal communication, June 1993.

bound to realize the Program was not the *laissez-faire*, do-it-yourself arrangement for which many of them were looking.

Added to that, these "subjects" in Tussman's "experiment" were late adolescents prone to carry over generational conflicts about separation and individuation from their parents to available faculty in their colleges and universities—and Program faculty were meant to be highly available. Operating in a house all of its own in an informal and almost family-like setting further encouraged the transference of the dependence-independence theme they were struggling with developmentally. Since the Program emphasized discussion and debate, no one had to feel shy about questioning and challenging authority as represented by these faculty members close at hand, who not only expected but encouraged argument. While that aspect of the Program appealed to some students, it turned off others wishing for more independence from all adults.

ANOTHER LOOK AT THE EXPERIMENTAL COLLEGE PROGRAM

So Tussman was taking many chances when he attempted to establish such a radically different approach to the first two years of undergraduate education in a large, public research university. In his reflective essay, he raises the question of why the Program failed, or if it did not fail as an educational venture, why it failed to become a permanent part of the university, a very different question altogether. But there is a larger, underlying question he does not raise or attempt to answer, and that is: how do we go about judging the success or failure of such educational experiments? What criteria are we to use? Are they to be judged solely by whether they survive to become permanent parts of the universities that initially make only a temporary commitment? Are we to accept Tussman's assessments of the Program's failures? And is the Experimental College Program to be judged a failure just because it lasted only two cycles? Are there records of faculty or student evaluations done at any time? Were any studies done at the time, or since? What else do we have to go on? Tussman's enthusiasm, dedication, hard work, and charisma, aided by faculty and student effort, propelled the Program for four years, "graduating" roughly 200 students into Berkeley's upper division. Its purpose was noble, its teaching methods unique for its time, its curriculum classical.

Can it be, as Tussman states in his essay, that it "disappeared without a trace"?

The Experimental College Program did not survive long enough to be reviewed by a committee appointed by the Academic Senate, as did other educational experiments of the time, such as the Collegiate Seminar Program, commonly known as Strawberry Creek College.[8] Student evaluations were not commonly conducted on the Berkeley campus at the time, as they are now, and none were conducted by or for the Program. The only study of any part of the Program was one undertaken by staff members of the psychiatry department at Cowell Hospital, who had become involved with the Program as observers through one of the faculty during the first cycle. That study (Suczek 1972) was an attempt to compare personality development of first-year Program participants with first-year students in the regular lower division program in 1965-66, but ended up abandoning its original research design (hence the title, *The Best Laid Plans*) in favor of gathering information from students through small group discussions with them.

But there exists another potentially rich, previously untapped source of information about how the Program actually worked, and what the consequences were for students who participated in it, that is, its former students. Twenty years after completing the Program, former students are in a position to look back at the Program from the vantage of greater maturity. Since the sixties and early seventies was a period of great political and social turmoil particularly on the Berkeley campus, looking at the Program with some objectivity might have been difficult for students at the time or soon afterwards. Now that the dust had settled, former participants in the Program might be able to see it with clearer vision. And no one could speak with better authority than they about what effects the Program had on them at the time, and whether any of these have been long-lasting effects. In light of the Program's long-range goals, it would be logical to assume it might take time for its full effects to be realized.

---

[8]Strawberry Creek College, although an example of popular reform, did not survive for long either. "Report to the Chancellor of the *Ad Hoc* Committee on the Collegiate Seminar Program," June 1979.

The Experiment at Berkeley

There is a small tradition of long-range studies of the effects of higher education. Theodore Newcomb did a follow-up study in the early fifties of Bennington students he first surveyed in the thirties (Newcomb 1967) to which D. F. Alwin has recently added a study of political attitudes over 50 years using the same subjects (Alwin et. al 1991). An eight-year follow-up survey of students who attended SUNY-Buffalo deals mainly with satisfaction in a number of different current life situations (Hoelke 1977). Benson Snyder has interviewed former MIT students whom he studied in the sixties (Snyder 1971, 1990). And Dr. Sigbrit Franke at Umeå University in Sweden has been conducting a long-term (10 years or more) study of the effects of university training on the attitudes of professionals (Hult, 1990).[9] Whatever their other merits, none of these studies attempted an assessment of the long-term effects of curricular reform. What can Program graduates tell us about the Program and its effects on their lives then and now? Can they shed light on the effectiveness of the Program and help us to learn about its relevance to undergraduate educational policy?

During the spring and summer of 1989, I interviewed intensively 40 former Berkeley students who had completed the Experimental College Program 20 or 22 years earlier. (A description of the interviews and the selection process can be found in Appendix F.) Analysis of these interviews provides us with a picture of how the Program operated as seen by these 40 participants, the difference it made to them then, and how they viewed its effects on them now. They tell us what the major impact of the Program has been on their lives, its other rewards and benefits, what they learned in the Program, and what academic skills they acquired there as well as how the Program made them feel about themselves academically. We find out what the transition was like from the Program to the regular university program in the upper division, and how these participants saw themselves as compared to other university students who had not been in the Program. We learn about the various features of the Program, the lectures, seminars, tutorials, the House; whether these former students found the various features effective, and which had the most impact on them; what they thought of the faculty and what is was like to study and learn in a community of scholars. They tell us if they had any regrets about being in

---

[9]For descriptions of other alumni studies of the effects of college on its graduates, see Pascarella and Terenzini, 1991.

the Program, would they do it again, and what changes they would like to see made in such a program. Piecing together what these informants have to say about their participation in the Program at Berkeley in the late sixties and how they have come to view it since gives us their view of this extraordinary experiment in higher education and its meaning for them then and now.

Looking at its beginnings in 1965 we have the setting for an unusual kind of academic drama. The scene is the campus of one of the world's most prestigious public research universities in the middle and late sixties, just at the time when the war in Vietnam is growing increasingly unpopular on the campus as well as nation-wide and when a powerful student revolution is bursting onto the scene, alongside a larger cultural revolution involving civil rights and civil disobedience, sexual freedom, women's liberation and the lure and increasing availability of all kinds of psychedelic drugs. The stage is a handsome old fraternity house, devoid of all but the most utilitarian furniture but attractive nonetheless, and the actors are respected faculty members and beginning university students on their way to becoming adults, who could be—in their own words—eager, bored, excited, confused, rebellious, dependent, independent, trusting, sincere, elated, afraid, naive—and who could be imperceptive and insightful, ignorant and knowing in turn. The play itself, set in this particular time and place, tells the story of how its cast of characters acted out Tussman's and Meiklejohn's grand plan of "neo-classic telic reform," this daring attempt to establish a learning community with a cohesive and integrated curriculum going back to the Greeks, Shakespeare, the Bible, all to provide students with a "moral education" and a "political vocation." We can now turn to the story of how the Program unfolded. Here we start to find answers to the questions raised in the Introduction: what difference did the Program make in the lives of its former participants, and what that might mean to undergraduate educational practices today.

It is the story of how a particularly intense form of higher education can have strong, long-lasting effects on students exposed to it, effects that grow rather than diminish over time, effects that are often not realized until some time has passed. Even though the experiment was conducted in the mid-sixties, it has relevance today in its substitution of a coherent program for the unrelated series of undergraduate survey courses commonly resulting from the domination of the modular system in the first two undergraduate years. Its creation of a cooperative learning community of faculty and students can serve as a model for the kind of closer relations with teachers that students at large universities often seek. It is a demonstration of how a unified program, open to students from all kinds of backgrounds and with all kinds of interests, can become a center serving academic, social, and personal needs. Open to average as well as above average students, it can provide challenges to students that encourage them to stretch toward new levels of intellectual development.

As testimony from participants in the study unfolds, evidence emerges of the advantages a program of this kind can offer undergraduates, not only in their collegiate years, but well beyond. And out of this evidence, insights emerge for teachers and administrators who seek creative ways of improving undergraduate education, particularly the first two undergraduate years. In itself, this testimony presents a fascinating account of an important experiment in curricular and pedagogical reform whose full story has never been told.

THE PLAN

CHAPTER 2

How Students Came to Apply and Why

THE INVITATIONAL LETTER

In order to understand the meaning of the Program for its former participants, it will be helpful to first learn something more about the conditions under which they had applied to the Program. The letter sent to all entering freshmen during the summers of 1965 and 1967 was a straight-forward description of the structure of the Program, with its departure from the course system in favor of the study of significant themes and problems. The letter outlined the curriculum without mentioning specific readings. It included detailed information about just which requirements the Program satisfied,[1] and the outside courses students were expected to take, preferably in foreign languages in order to fill that requirement, and a caveat to those interested in majoring in science to the effect that the Program would not meet science requirements for a major. The letter also mentioned the experimental nature of the Program, the fact that hard work was expected of faculty and students alike, and that it was not an honors program but meant to enroll a representative group of students. The only requirement for acceptance to the Program was that

---

[1] Its 48 units of credit satisfied the reading and composition, social science, and humanities requirements of the College of Letters and Science, leaving the language and natural science requirements to be satisfied outside the Program. See "A Technical Note on Academic Bookkeeping" in Appendix A.

students would have met the Subject A requirement, the entering examination in reading and writing that approximately half of the entering students pass each year, so that they would not have to take the noncredit course in English composition. (While this requirement was meant to exclude students who would have to add the burden of another course to their schedule, as the Program was meant to occupy most of the student's time for the first two years, it also probably served, unintentionally or not, to screen out students less well prepared for college work in reading and writing.) The application form asked for a high school grade-point average, S.A.T. scores, and plans for major or career, but since the selection of admittees was done randomly, these facts and figures were not used as screening devices, although some students might have thought they were simply because they had been asked for them. (The letter and application form are included here as Appendix D.)

Nowhere in the letter was to be found any mention of Tussman's larger purpose behind the design of the Program. Although several participants stated that the letter gave an accurate picture of what they could expect from the Program ("a small group, a lot of teacher/student contact, learning about these great books"), there was no mention of the "moral" curriculum, or the political vocation underpinning its design, and there was no talk of educating citizens as the ruling class in a democracy—the focus was instead on the structure of the Program. The simple list of the main themes of the curriculum—Greece during the Peloponnesian Wars, 17th-century England, the period of the adoption of the U.S. Constitution, and contemporary America—together with the description of how the Program was to be conducted would have offered few clues to the prospective student as to the underlying rationale of the Program, or even much about its purpose, to replace the "educational wasteland" of the lower division with an integrated, coherent program of purposeful, moral education.

According to Tussman, some 325 or so students applied for admission to the Program during the summer of 1965; the number of applicants was slightly lower for 1967. These applicants represented roughly 10 percent of the entering freshmen classes at Berkeley those two years. According to participants, not everyone who was admitted to the Program during each cycle received the letter; several participants said they heard of the Program through word of mouth after they arrived to register at Berkeley. Not everyone who applied to the Program, either during the summer or after school started in the fall, had received the letter. A few said they had never received the letter or had thrown it away or ignored it until friends interested in the Program reminded them of it. A few had been told about the Program by high school advisors, or in one case, by a friend whose parents knew Tussman. And some, although still entering as freshmen in the fall, had been accepted at other U.C. campuses and came to Berkeley as transfers and were not on the summer list of entering freshmen. Two participants from the Bay Area who attended advanced placement classes at Berkeley as high school students did not receive letters either. The expectations of several students, then, depended on what other people had told them about the Program. Although the educational structure of the Program as it differed from the rest of the University would have been clear to everyone whether or not they had received the letter, other aspects of the Program, such as "hard work," the "representativeness" of the student body, etc., would not necessarily have been apparent to entering students who had not seen the letter.

THE APPEAL OF THE PROGRAM TO ITS APPLICANTS

Participants were asked during the interview why they had applied to the Program. Of the several characteristics of the Program they gave as most appealing, its small size in relationship to the larger university and its low faculty-student ratio were mentioned most frequently by the participants. A quarter of them specifically mentioned the low faculty-student ratio or attention they would get from faculty; a few the fact that they would get to know the same group of students over the two-year period.[2] According to one woman, "it seemed like the best of both worlds for me . . . I wanted to experience 'the world' by being at Berkeley, but I was somewhat intimidated by the big size . . . my experience at a small girls' [private high] school showed me that I excelled much better in a small, more personal environment."[3] To another woman, a resident of the Bay

---

[2]The numbers in the study are too small to merit a quantitative approach, so figures are reported for the most part in qualitative terms.

[3]The following quotes, and all subsequent quotes from the interviews used throughout the book have been edited in two ways. First for readability: "ums," "uhs," repetitions and countless "you knows" have been deleted. Second, in the interests of confidentiality: any personal information that would allow the

Area, who had attended a small, parochial girls' high school, the size was also important.

> The size of it impressed me. I was sixteen when I entered college, so I wasn't about to leave home to go someplace . . . and the University of California is a fairly overwhelming experience, so this was a kind of a gentler, kinder way to be exposed to university level studies without the overwhelming aspect of the mass . . . I still don't do well in those kind of big situations.

Men also found the size appealing. This man was from a large, suburban high school in southern California:

> It was smaller and it sounded like we'd have a lot of contact with professors and there would be this small student body. I was going away to school, and I was scared to death and it seemed like a very nice, small unit to become part of.

The "best of both worlds" aspect of the small Program set in the large, prestigious university was a theme repeated by several participants who mentioned that they had either applied to and been rejected, or wished they could have afforded to apply to small, liberal arts colleges, such as Stanford, University of the Pacific, Pitzer, Reed, Antioch, Swarthmore, Oberlin, St. John's, Barnard, Columbia, and unspecified colleges in the East, out of reach of parental financing. As one woman put it, "This Program might offer some of the things that I'd been looking for at Reed . . . small, intensive, intellectual groups where ideas would be discussed." The fact that the university as a whole offered all of its students a first-class education at a prestigious university, publicly subsidized, was not lost on either the applicants or their parents. The size and character of the Program offered students a way to get a liberal education for two years in an

---

participants to be identified has been omitted. Occasionally identifying information has been changed or disguised in order to protect confidentiality. Each quote is used only once, unless otherwise noted. Since the principal object of the study is to tell the story of the Program through the eyes of its participants, I have tried throughout the book to present enough of their own words to allow readers to come to their own interpretations of evidence presented in the interviews.

intensive, private-school atmosphere closely attended to by outstanding faculty and costing no more than a public university education. To some, it must have appeared not only the best of both worlds, or the "frosting on the cake" as another put it, but a great educational bargain at that.

Parental influences on participants' decisions to apply to the Program ranged from those parents who did not take any active part at all in the decision, to those who were supportive, to those who were interested and encouraging, to the one participant who said his parents were so enthusiastic about it they filled out and sent in the application for him themselves since it had arrived while he was traveling in Europe. No parents of participants in this study were openly opposed to their youngsters entering the Program, although one man said he later found out after completing the Program that his father had not wanted him to participate in the Program or even to attend Berkeley, but to attend a university closer to home and to major in pre-med. Some parents voiced slight misgivings, but they were very few. One woman from the Bay Area said, "My mom was a little suspicious because she felt that I should be taking regular kinds of things—math, science, English—[but][4] she basically trusted me to do whatever I did over there." A father of one participant thought that not getting grades might go against his son. More mothers than fathers were reported by these participants, both men and women, to have taken an active role in encouraging them to apply to the Program. Two mothers living in the Bay Area went to talk directly to Tussman. Several parents had been Berkeley alumni, felt positive about their experiences there, and passed on their enthusiasm to their sons and daughters. Two people from the first cycle had been urged to apply to the Program by high school advisors; one by a Berkeley graduate student volunteering in a local high school who was to become a teaching assistant in the Program (later referred to as Mr. I).

In response to a question about what had appealed to them about the Program, the 40 participants gave a total of 95 attractive characteristics of the Program. One third of the participants, twice as many men as women,

---

[4]When the taped interviews were unclear or incomplete, the author has supplied words or phrases in brackets in order to clarify the meaning of the quotes.

found the experimental, alternative, novel nature of the Program interesting and appealing.[5]

An awareness of their being in a crucial developmental stage in some respects, and how the Program related to that, was mentioned by a few participants. The man quoted above who liked the small size of the Program also said,

> I fancied myself a little eccentric in high school so I thought, 'Well, this is just up my alley.' My psychological style was forming, whatever that means. I liked to believe that I could not be like other kids and that's why this was very attractive to me.

A third of the participants, twice as many men as women, were attracted by the curriculum, the "Greeks," or "Great Books." Several said they wanted a good education, or they wanted to be developed educationally. The notion of development was taken further by one man, who had previously thought of taking a pre-med program:

> As a high school senior, I started getting these first ideas of how I don't want to limit my life, just get sort of cubbyholed into one idea. I want to be developed, that's the appeal the Program had to me. Here's a place to get a high quality, affordable education. I always considered myself sort of an intellectual, and I didn't want to be limited to something like medicine.

The fact that the Program was structured to meet most lower division requirements appealed to a half dozen participants—some who weren't sure what they wanted out of college wanted to have the Program's structure for their first two years at Berkeley in order to avoid having to make decisions about what courses to take. A few appreciated its integrated nature; some having all their general education requirements met; others found the absence of grades and exams appealing. A few welcomed the writing they would be required to do in the Program; others its exclusive quality. A few

---

[5]In reporting the results of this study, when there were substantial differences between either of the two cycles, or between men and women, in their responses to questions in the interviews, they will be noted throughout. Otherwise, it can be assumed there were no significant differences between either of these groups.

thought the Program would tie in with their political concerns, as indeed some had mentioned the political atmosphere on the campus as having drawn them to Berkeley in the first place. And one participant mentioned the quality of the teaching in the Program as attractive to him:

> What appealed to me about the Program was first, a very close interaction between students and faculty, and the best faculty. To get full professors, who didn't have to play all the tenure bull shit games and could afford to concentrate on the students . . . the thought of being in close contact with people that had been Nobel Prize nominees, and heads of their various departments was a challenge, something I really wanted to do. . . . And I perceived the Tussman Program of being the creme of the creme, and I wanted to self-select myself for that.

Of those four characteristics of the Program mentioned most often as appealing to participants in the study—its size (26 responses), its experimental nature (14), its curriculum (12), and its low faculty-student ratio (8)—both the size and the low faculty-student ratio appealed to men and women and first and second cycle students equally. The experimental nature of the Program appealed to three times as many first cycle participants as second (one possible explanation being that perhaps that by the second cycle the Program was viewed as not quite so novel and tentative) and to more than twice as many men as women. The curriculum was a greater drawing card for men than women, particularly in the second cycle, by a ratio of two to one. (Other differences between men and women in their responses to the question about the major impact of the study will be discussed in Chapter 6.) Equal numbers of men and women found the size and low faculty-student ratio attractive. Apart from the major appeal of its small size, a variety of characteristics of the Program appealed to students. This is just one aspect of the diversity that characterized the Program in many ways, and from which it drew a great deal of its strength.

WERE APPLICANTS RISK-TAKERS?

Despite the experimental nature of the Program, it should not be assumed that an educational experiment such as this one would appeal largely to students who were risk-takers. Actually it was quite the opposite for many in this group of 40 former Program students. As one woman put it, "It was a safe, safe move. I'm not a big risk-taker. I'm very conservative, and I chose it because it seemed safe." Just a few participants said they felt they were taking any risks at all, and those risks were minimum. One of them said that although

> [going to college] was stepping into the unknown . . . [the Program] was less of a risk than picking out classes on my own. It was a kind of a comfort zone to me. It looked to me like I would be getting more assistance than I was going to [have] in the broader college.

Two men thought that not having grades might handicap them when they tried to get into their major field or into graduate school, but one of them reasoned that he could earn good grades in the upper division and establish a good grade point average there, which he did. The grading issue worked both ways—not being graded in the Program could also be viewed as a protection from getting lower grades as beginning students in large, competitive undergraduate courses. In spite of not being graded, another man had worried some about the possibility he might fail in this program by losing the anonymity of the large lecture class: "There's a difference between being one student out of five hundred watching your professor over a T.V. monitor as opposed to being there in front of the head of the Department of Philosophy, challenging you." But that threat to his self-esteem did not materialize in the Program—it was for him instead, he said, a continuous "high."

Two people had some concern that the Program might not prepare them for whatever major they would eventually choose, or that they would miss out on some kind of "basic training" as one put it. But since these two people did not know what it was they would end up doing anyway, they thought this kind of risk was not great for them. A few people thought there might be a risk in the very experimental nature of the Program, which meant its students were "guinea pigs" and that after starting in the Program it might have "fallen apart . . . they could have found they couldn't run it, that it's possible for these kinds of things to flop."

But from interviews with participants who completed the Program, there emerged no sense that any of them felt they were taking serious risks by entering the Program. It is possible, of course, that the Program did attract students with dare-devilish attitudes who did see entering the Program as a substantial risk and wanted to gamble on an unproven alternative program. But if students with this kind of motivation did enter the Program, they might have been likely to drop out, since it did demand serious attention to serious matters over the course of its two-year period. What does become apparent is that Program students—that is, the ones we interviewed for this study—were on the whole an academically confident group who saw little, if any, risk at all in participating in it. (Some of the basis for the self-confidence of Program applicants—higher high school grades than other UCB entering freshmen, more with private school backgrounds, more mothers who were college graduates—are discussed in Appendix F.)

CHAPTER 3

The Faculty

We know now about the purpose and plan behind Tussman's Experimental College Program, the special time and place in which the experiment took place, and something about the kind of student who was applying to the Program and why. To complete the cast of characters, we now need to know about the people who were to teach in the Program. This chapter describes first- and second-cycle faculty and how they were selected, the teaching assistants during the first year of the first cycle, why they were introduced and then discontinued, interfaculty relations and how they effected students, how students responded to faculty availability and faculty diversity, differences between first and second cycle faculty, and the impact on students of their unity or lack of it.

FIRST-CYCLE FACULTY

Tussman's task of finding faculty to staff the first cycle of the Program was by no means an easy one. Aiming for a student-faculty ratio of about 25:1 in order to keep the cost of the Program in line with the rest of the university,[1] he needed five colleagues to join him. They needed to be

---

[1] Since the entire student-faculty ratio at the university at the time was 17.6:1, the Program with a 25:1 ratio could be viewed as actually less expensive than the university as a whole. The 17.6:1 figure, however, included the very low graduate student-faculty ratio and so was somewhat misleading. In any event, after about

tenured Berkeley faculty whose respectability, he felt, would make up for the "sketchiness of the proposal." But they also needed to be "bold or reckless enough" to enter into this educational experiment not governed by the usual disciplinary rules. They needed to be good teachers, judged presumably by their reputations in large lecture classes and graduate seminars. They supposedly had no prior experience in team teaching, including Tussman. In a university known for the strength of its research faculty and graduate departments, he had then to find five strong teachers, respectable, tenured faculty who were able to leave their research and departmental responsibilities for two years, who could temporarily abandon the lecture course and the graduate seminar, and who were brave enough or confident enough of their careers to want to join Tussman in his plan to revolutionize the way the beginning freshmen and sophomores were taught in the lower division. The real risk takers in the Program, it seems, were the faculty rather than the students.

After a difficult search he finally found two tenured faculty who could commit themselves to the two years of the Program (one a lawyer, the other a mathematical engineer), and two who could commit themselves to one year only (a political scientist and a poet from the rhetoric department) and who would need to be replaced before the second year began. In place of the sixth member, they decided to "settle for," in Tussman's words, a group of five graduate teaching assistants, who remained in the Program for only the first year for reasons discussed below. Thus the Program began in the fall of 1965 with five faculty members and five teaching assistants. In the fall of 1966 three new faculty members (two sociologists and one from the philosophy department of a Canadian university) were added to replace the two who dropped out and the set of five teaching assistants who were not asked to return.

Altogether then, eight faculty members and five teaching assistants participated in the first two-year cycle of the Program. While all professors attended and participated in the lectures and whatever informal discussions took place around the House, each student was assigned to a different

---

a third of the enrolled students left the Program, the ratio eventually was reduced to about 15:1. That figure corresponds with the 14.5:1 student-faculty ratio that existed prior to Governor Reagan's intervention in the mid '60s that forced the ratio to increase to 17.6:1, which is still in effect.

professor for the seminar and the tutorials each semester. There was a switch from the semester to the quarter system throughout the entire campus after the first year, meaning that each of the first-cycle students would have been assigned to a total of five of the entire number of eight faculty teaching in the Program that first cycle. (This was not the case in the second cycle where no faculty left between the first and second years, so each student would have been assigned ordinarily to each of the six faculty over the two-year period.)

Of the four first-cycle professors who are remembered most vividly by participants, two of them left after the first year. Participants had most to say, and the most positive things to say, about four of the eight first-cycle faculty. The remaining four faculty were rather more shadowy figures, and participants do not remember them as well as the others. These more prominent ones will be referred to here as Professors A, B, C, and D, and the remaining four as Professors E, F, G, and H. Some typical general comments were (from a woman who couldn't overcome her difficulty in speaking with faculty): "I admired them, I liked them, I think I felt in awe of them." One man said: "I feel those guys gave us a lot . . . they really knocked themselves out. That's the memory I have. To be available for all of us as much as they were must have taken a commitment on their part." In talking about the less prominent faculty, one woman said:

> I think there were some sort of noodle head professors . . . I think there were some soft spots. . . . [Professor A] was very charismatic and very inspiring, [but] I don't think everyone quite cut the mustard. . . . The material . . . was really fertile soil, I just don't know if it was always tilled or hoed expertly.

Another man gives a description of the differences among faculty: Some of them were absolutely outstanding, just brilliant guys. . . . Some of them took me to the bushes and beat the crap out of me intellectually. . . . Others, in a sense, were like burnt out shells . . . [they] were disappointing. . . . " The faculty conferences were for this man the most exciting part of the Program:

> I had some real interesting ones with [Professor A]—he was a fascinating character. I remember most of them with him because they tended to be confrontational. He was confrontational and I was pretty confronta-

tional. . . . I saw them all as, I won't say classic gladiator matches, but very close to it. . . . [Professor A] was to me a juggernaut. Without question, the guy was absolutely brilliant.

And the positive relations he experienced with Program faculty were not repeated in later college years except for his doctoral program, "because faculty [in the regular undergraduate program] don't get close to their students."

Another man, who apparently brought with him to the Program some negative expectations about relations with faculty, talked about the individual conferences with them as "pretty favorable . . . I was actually surprised that I wasn't too threatened, they were easy and congenial men to deal with . . . probably they were most helpful psychologically in just being able to relate to a male who would actually listen. . . ."

Participants had more to say about Professor A than any other faculty member: "Easy person to talk to, very accessible and I really liked that," according to one woman. A man said of him,

> He would ask these endless sort of rhetorical questions and he'd get you thinking. That's a good teacher. Not somebody [an anthropology professor in an outside class in the regular university] who just reports on bones. . . . I sure remember getting turned on to Hobbes. . . . A big book like the *Leviathan* would have been very intimidating to me, and it would have taken something to get me interested in something like that . . . I suspect it was [Professor A].

Another participant spoke of his personality: "I greatly admired [Professor A]. He was a presence and a force that had a tremendous impact I think on everybody, but definitely on me. . . . I remember feeling impressed and welcomed at the same time."

Another man remembered him differently:

> I remember [Professor A] quite well because his personality and his ego sometimes were very high profile. . . . I have a bit of a hard time making a connection with him on a personal level. He was best for me in the lecture room when I was one of 100 or 150 students because he had a great grasp of the material and whatever his personal prejudices were, points of view were, he was a balanced enough person to be able to present a wide range of views about things and he was very good in that

context. . . . The Program as I experienced it, and this may be a necessity of getting it launched, getting it to happen at all, was dominated by his personality. And to the detriment of the Program at times. I think if he could have gotten out of his own way, he would have been fine because he was really a capable and bright guy.

By contrast, another participant made this distinction: "I didn't admire him intellectually, but I did like him a lot as a person." Another says, "I didn't always agree with what he said [but] I felt like he was always fair and very open. He was trying very hard to make it work, even though I thought that other people didn't see him that way, somehow I think I saw him that way."

Professors B and C also received favorable comments. "I sure remember just being amazed listening to [Professor B]. And of course [Professor C]. . . . I took a speech class from him after the Program and loved it." A few other participants also mention taking courses from Program faculty, including Professor D, in the upper division. Professor B was also described as "the one who stood out most for me. . . . I liked the way he would engage things . . . his way of expressing himself was very interesting. I mean it would engage you, and get your attention . . . he had these rhetorical skills in delivery, in content, in organization." And, in contrast, "[Professor F] just didn't speak as much as the others, he just wasn't as vocal." And so while A was given the most attention by participants, they did not each view him in exactly the same way, nor did they always agree on the characteristics of the others. Clearly, about half of the faculty stood out from the others, even though two of those were there only one year.

Certainly one of the most unusual aspects of this Program, set as it was in a large, public university, was the relationship of the faculty to their students. Stepping out of their customary roles as solitary lecturers, and as paper and exam graders (or the supervisors of the teaching assistants who did the grading), they assumed new and different duties, and consequently are remembered by the former students in the Program who were interviewed for the study as being very different from regular university teachers. One man said, "I remember feeling very comfortable with the professors and not like, 'this is my teacher who's going to be grading me and judging me'." One almost has the sense of a kind of collegial relationship between faculty and students, rare if not unheard of for lower division students. This same former student goes on to say, "You would say 'good morning' and they'd remember who you were from the day before which I don't really remember at all with any of the following two years of my education. . . . I don't remember any relationships at all with any teachers or teaching assistants after the Tussman Program." Another participant reported:

> I'd go do the [outside] science classes and tell my other friends about what we were doing and they were overwhelmed and awed and jealous. I thought it was great. We really did have close contacts. You know, we'd call the professors 'Joe' and recognize them on the street or whatever and they'd respond to you, and in some of the classes here [in the regular university] unfortunately, you could see professors on the stage but you wouldn't recognize them on the street because you had seen them from so far away you really didn't know what they looked like . . . that didn't happen in the Program. I appreciated that . . . that was a real positive aspect of it.

The climate conducive to debate established by the faculty in the Program allowed for the kind of intellectual give and take not found in the usual lecture class:

> I really liked [Professor B] an awful lot; I didn't always agree with [Professor A] as much as [Professor B] but I really admired his leadership and he made the Program much more interesting because . . . I remember having arguments with him, and I don't think I ever had any arguments with other professors until I was in graduate school.

While participants remember faculty in both positive and negative ways, each one made positive comments about at least one professor, including all but one of the less vividly remembered ones. For every professor a participant might remember as having not been easy to connect with, there was at least one professor, and often more than one, who was. The diversity of available faculty, then, played an important role in the faculty's collective effort to reach and to have an impact on their students.

Several participants specifically remembered favorable comments some particular professor had made on a paper, and those comments appeared to have a lasting positive effect on how the student viewed themselves in regards to their academic potential. And in one instance, a professor encouraged a student not to leave school when he was considering dropping out at the end of the first year of the Program. Not only did he then finish the Program and graduate from Berkeley, he progressed academically to near completion of a Ph.D. at the time of the interview. He credits that incident with possibly saving his life, since he feels he would otherwise have been drafted and sent to Vietnam.

The House played an important part in providing the right setting for informality, as one woman says:

> I remember talking individually with faculty much more than I ever did other times just because, I think, of the House more than anything. I spent a lot of time at the House . . . they'd be around then . . . coffee . . . or they'd be in their office; it was much more a casual kind of an interaction with the faculty than I'd experienced later in my other classes at Berkeley.

Interestingly, she doesn't remember having any individual conferences with faculty, only this informal contact.

Not everyone reports taking advantage of the availability of the faculty to establish any kind of close relationship. One man said, "I didn't have any, what I consider relationships with faculty other than the most superficial kind you have when you come in and discuss something perfunctory." Half of the women participants in this first-cycle group expressed a wish for closer contact with faculty, but at the same time could not bring themselves to make that contact, in spite of the recognized availability of faculty. One said,

> I always felt like I could approach the faculty. I just felt like I had, I guess, nothing important enough to approach them with, some new brilliant idea or something. And I had a hard time thinking of them in any other terms. I had an easier time thinking of *them* that way than I did my outside class teacher, but I had a real hard time, thinking, they were always authority figures and you were not to bother them. That was the way I was raised, and I had a lot of trouble changing that, it took time. . . . It wasn't that they were unapproachable. . . . I saw other people do it, and I knew that they were perfectly willing to listen to people. I guess it was nice knowing that I could, but I just *couldn't*. It wasn't them, it was me. . . . It was one of the things I sort of regretted when I left.

Another woman describes her lack of confidence in relating to faculty.

> I don't remember striking up any particular relationship with any one faculty member. And probably that would have been the most helpful to me.... I wish that I had had the confidence then to make better use of the opportunity that I had.... My recollection is that they were easily accessible.... I remember feeling nervous and scared when I went in which I think said probably more about me as an eighteen-year-old than their attitudes. I remember going over papers, talking about ideas.... I don't think I realized what a wonderful opportunity that is for a student, and I don't recall that I made the most of it.

More regrets from another woman:

> It should have been an opportunity to have a closer relationship with the professors and the T.A.s [teaching assistants]—for some reason that never panned out for me. I'm sure a lot of it has to do with the fact that I was very shy and afraid and somewhat intimidated by everybody.... I kind of regret that I sort of ended up feeling like a very tiny part of a big school even though I was in this—something that was supposed to sort of avoid that feeling.... we had to have conferences at least once a quarter, and that was the only time I ever talked ... one-to-one to anybody.

Another woman expressed regret that she had not been able to "ally" herself with one of the people who were being "offered up" because it would have been a more enriching experience if someone had "taken me under their wing a little bit." It seemed to her that they were all assigned a particular professor but that there were no regular assigned times for meeting with them individually, and that there should have been more of "an exchange, a seeking out of us . . . regular appointments, conference times." (Regular scheduling of student-faculty conferences did not take place until the second cycle.)

And yet in spite of feeling she had not taken advantage of the availability of faculty in the Program, this former student was able to profit later on from attitudes learned during the Program. She reported that in upper division history seminars,

> I remember a number of professors that we had small groups with, with whom I did establish relationships. Maybe it just took me a while to learn how to do that. Maybe I did figure it out because I do remember participating fully, much more fully than I had in the first two years and feeling confident . . . maybe it was my experience in the Tussman

The Faculty

Program that made me feel that way. Because when I look back on the history seminars and the times we had with a number of the history professors, I remember feeling very much like, "I can do this. This is no problem."

So maybe, I've never thought about it before, but I remember myself in the Tussman Program very differently than I remember myself as an upper division history student. I think there must have been [some effect from the Program]. If nothing else then, by osmosis; I realized somewhere in my unconscious that, "this is how you're going to get what's going on, this how you're going to make the most use of it. . . . " I can remember very specific history seminars that were really quite similar to the Tussman Program, but I wasn't similar anymore, I had grown.

Another woman longed for closer faculty contact, while at the same time acknowledging she may not have been ready for it, or fully receptive to it.

I never went for any help or any guidance [even though] there was a real feeling of a warm, nurturing place. . . . I expected to be kind of left alone, and that's pretty much what happened . . . nobody really sought me out. In retrospect, it makes me feel a little abandoned. When I think about it now, I see myself as just sort of flailing around and I guess I'm just a little disappointed nobody recognized that. . . . In retrospect I think I would have appreciated some more sort of seeking out . . . someone in some kind of knowledgeable position sort of overseeing these little fledgling kind of tadpoles . . . could have offered [us] a little bit more guidance. . . . It's possible that I just sort of blanked and I wasn't receptive to that. I'm not saying that it wasn't offered. But I know it didn't come to me or I didn't hear it.

The poignancy of this young woman's dilemma is underscored by the restrictions placed on students by the popular attitudes towards authority they held at the time. She went on to say:

I felt as if I cheated myself, 'cause I just plain didn't know. There was no one to tell me. . . . I am sure there were lots of student orientation classes going on, but at that point the administration was the enemy and therefore we did not go to the standard freshmen orientation kind of stuff.

From their testimony, it becomes clear that for many participants from the first cycle of the Program, particularly women, it was not easy or in some cases possible for them to take advantage of the opportunity to establish closer relationships with faculty, although the faculty were perceived as available and welcoming. Not being able to overcome the obstacles in their paths—shyness, difficulties in approaching authority figures—however, did not prevent at least some of them from eventually learning how to more effectively relate to faculty. Even if that learning was to be applied only later in the upper division, it was an educational gain of some importance.

TEACHING ASSISTANTS AND UNINTENDED CONSEQUENCES

Another feature of the Program during that first cycle that might have functioned as an obstacle to closer student-faculty relationships, although it was never intended to do so, was the use of teaching assistants during the first year. Not part of Tussman's original plan, he acquiesced to their inclusion at the urging of some of the faculty when he had trouble finding a sixth teacher. Slightly over half of the people interviewed from the first cycle mentioned the teaching assistants. Most did not remember anything about them, but for others they were very much like faculty. "My memory is they played a very similar role in my connection with the Program. It was sort of 10 of them, not five and five." Another said, "They were all like friends. They were real approachable. . . . " And their influence could be considerable. One woman remembers writing a paper on women's views of a particular aspect of the curriculum and being told by the teaching assistant who read it that it was a "powerful feminist statement." Although she had not intended it as such, she was flattered.

This teaching assistant was the one mentioned most often. (Actually, in all the interviews, only two others were mentioned at all, and those two by only a few participants—one for having become a nationally recognized writer in recent years and another for being the only woman "faculty member" in the Program.) Therefore "Mr. I" as he shall be called here, stands out above all the other teaching assistants. One participant described him as "real enthusiastic. He really believed in stuff and he was very verbal and able to express himself about it and got you fired up. . . . " Another said, "He was very enjoyable, very likable, very stimulating." Describing his influence in the classroom one woman said,

> One of the people who had a big impact on me at the time was [Mr. I]. I think he made those intellectual pursuits very exciting. . . . I just thought he was incredible. . . . I can remember we had a class where we listened to Bob Dylan records and he tried to interpret what they really meant. . . . I thought he was so profound thinking of those kinds of things. . . . I really liked the way he made us think. . . . I did see him attempting often to link [the curriculum] to something we could relate to.

Another participant who had been assigned to this particular teaching assistant was impressed by him, found him very articulate, very intellectual, but didn't remember "feeling at all close to him . . . I remember feeling pretty intimidated by him."

To another participant, who remembers only Mr. I of all the teaching assistants, Mr. I became a companion in an extracurricular activity in the arts which was later to become this participant's livelihood. The involvement of the teaching assistants in the lives of the students outside the Program was remembered by one man:

> I remember lots of parties that were essentially Program people. I remember going out and doing things, social, cultural events with the T.A.s . . . and there's also the whole fabric of activity which extended well beyond the formal setting, at least for me . . . it helped build community. . . . [They were] older and at least in some way committed to an academic way of life, but they were close enough in age to us that they could be like peers . . . I think they provided a very valuable model.

But another participant took an opposite stand:

> I think it probably is better to just have professors, if what you're trying to do is give people a sense of professors having contact with students. . . . I mean they're going to encounter enough T.A.s in these other situations, what they won't encounter necessarily is professors in such intimacy, and that probably would be good.

Teaching assistants did seem to represent for at least some of these students a sort of buffer between them and faculty that could diffuse somewhat the influence of faculty and interfered with what the Program was originally intended to accomplish in the way of close faculty-student relationships. It is possible to imagine students turning more readily to faculty had teaching assistants not been present to offer easier access as well as after hours sociability that was for the most part outside the boundaries of student-faculty relations. (There are some suggestions that did happen in the second cycle, but socialization between faculty and students did not reach the same levels as first-cycle participants with teaching assistants. A few second-cycle participants reported some extracurricular associations with faculty—a tennis game or two, a lunch, etc., initiated by both faculty and students, but apparently this was the extent of their socialization.)

As in the case of Mr. I, teaching assistants had the potential of becoming loose cannons, unknown and unpredictable factors in carrying out a plan of the Program that had not included them from the beginning. It was Mr. I who precipitated the faculty's decision not to rehire the teaching assistants after he openly undermined the authority of teachers in the Program. According to Tussman, Mr. I was "a pretentious militant," and, predicting that "he would be uncontrollable and destructive," was against taking him on in the first place. The fact that he was a leader in the FSM might have made it appear to students that he was fired for his political views, rather than for subverting faculty authority.

It is not surprising then that the participant who spent so much time with teaching assistants outside the Program "lost some confidence in the Program" after what he thought of as the "purge" when the teaching assistants left after the first year. "I guess they were all tossed out to get rid of [Mr. I]." The effects of their departure were for him "fewer people, instructors in the Program to talk to. You could pretty much talk to all the T.A.s because they had time. You were lucky if you could talk with one professor." But apparently he did not try and then fail to be able to talk to faculty—he simply found the teaching assistants "generally more available and made themselves more available informally."

The departure of both the teaching assistants and two of the faculty was also noted by another man:

> I wished they'd kept the TA's . . . some of the people who left [including faculty] were valued by the students . . . so there's this feeling of coming up against authority in a way we didn't like. . . . I didn't like that the faculty had changed, and I felt . . . tricked. I would have liked to have

known more of what was happening, why they left, what was going on behind the scenes.... What's going on here? Why are all these changes happening? And who's not pleasing who? ... What are the undercurrents ... the friction involved in these changes ... There was some speculation about that.

As indicated by the comments quoted above, some of the teaching assistants, and Mr. I in particular, became involved with students both academically and socially, to mixed effects. On one hand, the teaching assistants could be viewed as a bridge between faculty and students, more approachable because of closeness in age and experience and probably freer with their time, not having the professional and family commitments that faculty had. On the other hand, their closeness to students could stand in the way of closeness between faculty and students if students found it easier to seek them out rather than faculty, diluting to some degree the benefit of having faculty as available to students as they were in this program.

The teaching assistants may have served to some extent as role models, in the sense of demonstrating that young people just recently having been undergraduates themselves could deal with the academic content of the curriculum and could lead seminars and discussion groups, formally and informally. They were available socially, which the faculty evidently were not, since no participant from the first cycle mentions any social contact with faculty, and they may have made faculty seem inaccessible by contrast. This was certainly a crucial difference between regular faculty and teaching assistants. While one participant reported the favorable effects for him of enjoying cultural events with teaching assistants, other participants referred to a tragic event that occurred at a party of teaching assistants and Program students where a student was severely and permanently injured. There have been allegations that drugs were involved. The proselytizing of a younger generation of students by older students is not unique to the Program, and exists wherever they come into contact; older students "turn on" younger students to drugs, sex, music, photography, literature, and other favorite activities. They have been known to encourage attitudes and behavior antithetical to adults in authority, and this would certainly have presented a strong temptation at that time of intense anti-authority feelings on the part of students. As Tussman reports, all faculty came eventually to feel their authority undermined by the teaching assistants and voted unanimously not to reappoint them for a second year. It appears that the inclusion of teaching assistants in the Program was of mixed benefit at best, and probably held more opportunity for harm than good for the aims of the Program in this first, rather chaotic year.

This ambiguous aspect of the Program in the first cycle—the inclusion of unplanned for, nonfaculty personnel—contributed in another way to the occurrence of some events that were not in the best interests of students or staff in the Program and that were not part of the Program's design. In addition to the teaching assistants, some of whom were hired on the recommendation of just one faculty member rather than by consensus of the group, another outside person was brought into the Program by a single faculty member (Professor B), without a review of the entire faculty, for the supposed purpose of making an evaluation of the Program. Dr. Z was an administrator of one of the mental health clinics on the campus, and therefore a University employee, but he was not a staff member of the Program. The precise role this "observer" was to play in the Program was vague to the three participants who remembered him, yet he appeared to have a definite, if negative, impact on at least some of the students. One says, "He wasn't a high profile figure . . . it was in later years I heard that he had been studying the Program. . . . I became fascinated later to wonder what his role was in evaluating and assessing the Program." Two other participants remember some distinctly negative characteristics:

> He was a maniac—a very disturbing influence . . . toward the end, he got really self-indulgent and smug and as a psychiatrist he did something very awful to one of the people in this little group who went to him, very frightened . . . and professionally he was kind of irresponsible, and also just mean spirited. . . . He was parasitic. He'd float around, and he'd observe. There was a sense that he felt entitled to look into our fishbowl and I don't think he contributed very much.

Another participant was more specific in reporting the effect this particular undefined nonfaculty member had both in the Program and later:

> The only other thing I remember about the lectures was [Dr. Z] sitting off to the side, sort of looking like he was cogitating all the time. . . . I thought it was kind of weird that they had arranged for a psychiatrist to sort of follow through the Program. And we were supposed to trust this person who, as it turns out was probably completely untrustworthy. . . . I'm not sure that I believed that things were kept

confidential. . . . I did at one point go to see him because . . . I was obviously very unhappy . . . I don't think the man helped me. In fact, he made my life a whole lot worse. . . . The Program was no different from the rest of the campus. It's just one of those situations where you have these older guys who take advantage of younger people who don't know whether they're coming or going . . . it's taken me a lot of years to be clear about that.

This participant declined to describe those interactions with Dr. Z in further detail, but it is obvious that they were perceived as harmful, and that, significantly, it took some time to come to terms with this. A review of the conditions that made this regrettable event possible involves learning more about faculty selection and faculty relationships, an aspect of the Program that had various and sometimes deep impacts on the students.

Tussman describes his process for selecting faculty in both his essay and his book, and the criteria were very different for the two cycles. Faculty for the first cycle were chosen on the basis of their teaching reputations at Berkeley, although teaching in the Program required different approaches and demanded different skills than teaching in the regular university. And one of those approaches was team rather than individual teaching, so that what might have worked in large lecture classes or even graduate seminars would not necessarily work in the Program. Team teaching in the Program required cooperation certainly, and a willingness to share with four or five colleagues both the rewards of the spotlight and also of the master-apprentice relationship with students—rewards that had previously been theirs alone. If these professors had been acclaimed for their teaching abilities, they had earned their reputations in the classroom or lecture hall by themselves. Presumably none had ever been part of a collective teaching effort, or if they had, were not chosen for that reason. In the Program, skills and techniques helpful to individual classroom performance did not necessarily work, or at best were not sufficient. The scholarship and research that led to their recognition in the university and provided the basis of their lectures and seminars were no longer pertinent (except for Tussman who did use the subject matter of the Program in his writings).

Leadership in the Program was ambiguous at first. Tussman had studied with Meiklejohn at Wisconsin, was familiar with how he had run the Experimental College there, and it was Tussman's vision to try a version of it at Berkeley. He had done the ground work and won approval from the administration. But, he apparently did not expect to have to actually direct the Program—that it would not need any kind of formal leader but would become a kind of faculty co-op. That proved to be untrue, and he says that in time "as if by general consent, without comment, I was left in charge." Since leadership of the Program was unclear from the beginning, the differing degrees of familiarity with, commitment to, and execution of the design of the Program and its curriculum by the five faculty members undoubtedly led to some differences in interpretation and to some of the ensuing conflicts among faculty members.

FIRST-CYCLE FACULTY RELATIONS AND THEIR SURPRISING EFFECTS ON STUDENTS

The conflictual nature of interfaculty relations during the first cycle has been described by Tussman. The precise source, nature, and extent of these conflicts are not possible to determine from his incomplete account—it would be necessary to hear from all faculty for a full understanding of the situation—but according to Tussman, tensions were there from the start and soon became a "battle of vanities." It is not the purpose of this study to make judgments about the adequacy or effectiveness of any single faculty member teaching in the Program, but rather to understand the way in which the faculty as a whole had an impact on their students. This was an experimental program on its maiden voyage in the first year of its first cycle. Mistakes were made, and improvements were made. But one of the most interesting findings of the study has been the discovery of the unintended consequences of these conflicts among faculty that undoubtedly made teaching in the Program difficult and contentious at times—that is the effect they had on students.

The Program made unusual demands on its faculty. First, faculty members were expected to teach, that is to lecture, publicly, in the company of colleagues, rather than *in camera* as in the usual classroom situation, although seminars and tutorials were conducted that way. This form of team-teaching in the Program theoretically has the advantage of reducing the temptation for the teacher to "perform" for an audience of students rather than to teach, and for all teachers to focus together on what students were learning, rather than on individual faculty performances. It was an individualized program for students rather than for faculty. In order for this approach to be successful, faculty members have to work closely together. Unfortunately, this level of cooperation was not achieved during the first cycle. Disagreements and personality clashes were evident from the beginning, with Professors A and B the primary protagonists, barely able, as Tussman says, to "tolerate each other's presence." In his reflections, he describes B's public challenge to him at the first lecture. "The [lectures] . . . fell apart because . . . of faculty resistance to perform without shining . . . Some faculty members became 'cult' or coterie figures. . . . " In dramatic contrast to the second cycle, where faculty met for weekly dinners to discuss the curriculum and regularly to discuss student progress, Tussman's attempts to draw the entire first-cycle faculty together failed completely, and communication among them must have been casual and haphazard. It was in the context of this intense antagonism and lack of communication particularly between A and B that Dr. Z, an associate of B, was allowed access to students in the Program. It is quite possible that Tussman and other faculty, even B, were unaware of all of Z's activities and of his relations with students since he only came to be connected with the Program through B in a peripheral fashion.

Students report variously on their reactions to disagreements, arguments, and debates among faculty members. To one of two former students from the first cycle who said they would not repeat the Program, the antagonism between the two primary figures was particularly disturbing:

> I was incredibly unhappy about that . . . it was always kind of exciting and it was always kind of frightening. . . . I remember these two men sort of standing up there shouting at each other . . . sort of like Leviathans up there on the stage. . . . We didn't learn conflict resolution, compromise, acceptance of other people's point of view. No. We learned there was one point of view . . . and if you didn't agree with it, then get . . . out of here. [There was] this camp and that camp. . . . Who knew who had the right point of view?

To a question about whether this conflict was ever discussed with the faculty, the response was:

> No . . . I can't imagine that either one of those men would have wanted to hear what I had to say about it. They certainly didn't seem like they did, anyway. . . . These two people . . . had a lot of power . . . they can make you or break you if they want to, in some sense . . . if they really

didn't like . . . your points of view, they could black ball you . . . make it difficult for you to do things. . . . It's kind of hard to speak out when you don't know what people might do with that kind of information. . . . They were very flawed people and they wanted us to not know. . . . I don't think they were honest . . . I didn't admire someone like that. . . . All I was experiencing was the emotional experience, 'cause that's my tune in . . . other people obviously don't, but I very powerfully tune in there.

But other people had vastly different reactions to these disagreements among faculty. One participant said the lectures could be

very, very exciting . . . more exciting than most classrooms are going to get . . . because a large lecture is only going to get as exciting as a professor can make it in his or her lecture, and no matter how exciting that's going to be, I don't think that level of excitement can match the kind of excitement that can happen when you see two or three good minds going at each other.

Some saw the "fights" as a gain:

I think that was part of the benefit, getting to see these guys [in this case, Professor A and Mr. I] . . . they were no dummies and if they disagreed they had real strong reasons and I think that was the value, getting to hear people with good strong thinking discussing things with each other. And I would call it more discussions than fights.

Another former student's reaction to faculty disagreements was even more positive, and had the biggest impact for her of any feature of the Program:

The main thing I remember about the Program was [Professor A and Professor B] in this sort of eloquent private biff over whether it's the man and his human experience that should be understood, or if you should just look at the idea, like a symphony. You look into the symphony, it doesn't matter if the composer was a paraplegic leper, you just judge the ideas . . . that intellectually was the most vivid remnant of the whole program, that kind of discourse, and feeling the real earnestness and the authenticity of these two men as teachers and thinkers. . . . It was wonderful because it was a perpetual dialectic . . . I never did jump down on one side or the other . . . [but] it was memorable.

Most people who mentioned these disagreements, debates, or "biffs" felt comfortable with not taking sides, saw them as valuable parts of the Program, and were stimulated by them rather than turned off, as was the first participant quoted above. (It may be of some significance, however, that all three people who would not want to repeat the Program reacted with various degrees of negativity to these disagreements, rather than viewing them as beneficial or enjoyable.)

It was this rather unusual set of circumstances—frequent and public faculty disagreements, the leaving at the end of the first year of two of the more prominent faculty including the one most openly opposed to Tussman (although prearranged according to Tussman, this had never been announced to the students), and the decision to not renew the contracts of the teaching assistants for the second year of the Program—which set the stage for speculations and conjectures that these events were all connected. The fact that none of these events were discussed openly with students created a climate of ambiguity within which students were left free to try to explain them as best they could. It may have been difficult to imagine presenting these faculty differences and the unanimous decision to terminate the teaching assistants to students in a way that did not make students privy to personality conflicts and force them into taking sides. Still, it would have been helpful if students had been informed sometime before the end of the first year that two of the faculty were to be there only the first year. In a program built around the benefits of close, continuing faculty-student contacts, it is understandable that students could feel the sudden unexplained absence of faculty in the middle of the Program as unsettling. It would also have been helpful if the unanimous decision about teaching assistants had been presented that way—as a unanimous decision—rather than forcing Tussman to announce the decision alone without reference to any agreement or support from the rest of the faculty as he describes it in his reflections, and leaving students to surmise it was solely his decision.

Not surprisingly, the dissatisfaction surrounding what some students experienced as a loss was then connected to the ever-present, overriding issue of the time, that of authority. As one former student quoted earlier said, he felt "tricked" by the removal of the teaching assistants and had a "feeling of coming up against authority in a way we didn't like." For this one student, at any rate, the issue of authority became connected to a "philosophical bias" in the Program that then became more evident to him in the following year, but that had its value to him:

... a philosophical thrust concerning political obligation, duties of citizens ... and there was a lot of antagonism to that. There was the sense that, gee, you didn't *know* that something was being kind of shoved down our throats. ... It's just that we didn't enter knowing that there was a specific point of view which was going to be espoused. I kind of liked it, it gave me something to bump up against, but I remember the feeling that there was a lot of, among some people, antagonism to this ... and the rivalry between [Professor A] and [Professor B] ... there was a sense that maybe people weren't following the party line.

The man who called the departures of teaching assistants "the purge" went on to assert that students in the second cycle were then "screened" for some sort of compliance and connected the teaching assistants' leaving with that of the faculty who left under one explanation: "I assumed that was the next stage in the progressive tightening up of the Program and focusing it more toward Tussman's intellectual goals." Actually there is no evidence that there was any "screening" for political views (or screening for anything else other than the subject A exam), since students were selected randomly for the second cycle as well as the first. Nor was there evidence that any student was dropped because of political differences with faculty. It is possible that some students who did not like the political "message" of the Program as they saw it, the "moral curriculum" aimed at education for responsible citizenship, and viewed it as too conservative, may simply have stopped doing their work and therefore were asked to leave. The fact that these students were not complying with that requirement of the Program might have not been apparent to other students. If a student did not turn in papers, only the faculty need be aware of it. What is clear is that some students were suspicious of the motives of Tussman and remaining faculty members when some faculty, all the teaching assistants, and some students left the Program.

All these elements were present at the time of the changes at the end of the first year: the role played by Mr. I in subverting the authority of the faculty was the last straw leading to the contracts of the teaching assistants not being renewed. Authority was a central issue in the Program; there was an unstated philosophical point of view of the "political vocation" that lay at the heart of the Program's design; there were disagreements among faculty about this philosophical/political commitment, and down-right antagonism between at least two of them. The fact that two faculty members who left at the end of the first year had signed on for only one year, and the fact that the decision about teaching assistants had been unanimous despite faculty dissension on other matters were either unknown or overlooked. Although the philosophical point of view behind the Program was a legitimate teaching goal, it had never been presented openly to students. (In his essay, Tussman says he tried to "lead the student into the experience of relaxed, enjoyable immersion, a sustained involvement of mind, in a great work whose significance is far from obvious. . . . This is . . . one of those familiar situations in which it is futile to try to explain to someone why he should be doing something until after he has done it.") It is understandable that in the minds of some students, all this became intertwined with resentment of "authority," an issue imbued with much passion in this place at this time.

It should be noted that not all students reacted so strongly as those quoted above. Most participants did not refer to the teaching assistants and two faculty members leaving at the end of the first year. One participant said, "I never was very interested in that row," although he felt that the "row" itself diluted some of his enthusiasm about and commitment to the Program. Another former student, who as a matter of fact had enjoyed some extracurricular activities with Mr. I, didn't seem to notice the absence of the teaching assistants the second year, at least he had no recollection of their leaving. Thus it appears that this series of events involving authority and authority figures was interpreted variously by students according to their positions in relationship to these issues. (Issues of authority and politics in the Program will be discussed further in later chapters.)

SECOND-CYCLE FACULTY: GETTING IT RIGHT

Since the structure, curriculum, and most of the features of the Program remained the same from the first cycle to the second, by far the sharpest differences between the two had to do with the composition of the faculty, how they were chosen, and their relationships to Tussman. As Tussman reports, the second-cycle faculty, mostly former students of his, were chosen primarily because of his friendships with them going back to their student days rather than, as in the case of most of the first-cycle faculty, his familiarity with them as colleagues and their reputations as Berkeley teachers. His method of selecting second-cycle faculty undoubtedly resulted in a group of teachers certainly more familiar with him and his views and probably more in sympathy with his purpose as well as more comfortable with his style. All first-cycle faculty were teachers at Berkeley, with the exception of two who came in the second year from other colleges; all faculty besides Tussman in the second cycle came from other colleges and universities. All but one were philosophers; one had a degree in sociology from a British university. Unlike the first cycle where there was a 50 percent turnover between the first and second year, all the faculty remained in the Program for both years of the second cycle. There appeared to be none of the divisiveness, rancor, and bitterness of the first cycle, with the exception of one of the second-cycle faculty who apparently was not in agreement with the others on some of the basic philosophy behind the Program and on how the lectures should be conducted. Rather than leaving the Program, he withdrew from participation in the lectures but continued to meet with his students in seminars and tutorials.

Additionally, there were two important differences between the two cycles in the manner in which teaching was carried out. To begin with, there were no teaching assistants included at any time during the second cycle. That meant that the task of teaching the curriculum of the Program fell entirely to the faculty with no assistance or interference from graduate students. It also meant that second-cycle students did not experience the loss at the end of the first year, under clouded circumstances, of a group of young people closer to them in age. The second important difference had to do with the tutorials where faculty met one-to-one with their students to discuss their papers and their participation in the Program. Somewhere around the middle of the first year in the second cycle, faculty began to schedule tutorials with students on a regular basis. Up to that point they had been carried out on an unscheduled basis, although either faculty or students could request them at any time. This meant that now all students had regular tutorials, not just the ones who were eager or self-confident enough to request them. It also meant that faculty uniformly had more personal contact with students.

As a group, the faculty drew many favorable comments from these participants. Pointing out the benefits of their diverse characteristics, one woman recalled,

> I liked them all, they all had different points of view and characteristics and things that they emphasized. I admired them all for different reasons. I remember [them all]. . . . I came to like them as people. I mean, they

were very available in the House, you know, sitting on the sofa, if you lingered, they were there, they would linger, they wouldn't just dart out. . . . I'm sure they had other responsibilities, probably publishing and stuff, and their own things, families. I remember most of them as being very accessible.

Also speaking to their diversity, one man said,

I really enjoyed the company of many of the professors. I enjoyed different things about them. Whether I got to know them well I can't say, but I did get to spend some time with several of them in different contexts. . . . They all had something to tell me I felt . . . I learned something from each one of them. They were pretty vivid types . . . they . . . provided a lot of stuff for me, a lot of nourishment, a lot of sustenance.

Another woman emphasized their diversity.

Each one of them really related to students in their own particular way. They were very diverse. They definitely each had their own teaching styles. I think some were more comfortable, perhaps, with the Program than others.

In describing how faculty demonstrated respect for students in the Program, one man said,

the professors participated and took us as we were . . . they agreed to show up and speak with us about the material that was [sometimes] new to some of them . . . they were there talking with us, and making serious inquiry into issues. . . . I have recollections of having various degrees of affection, of how I was touched by each one of these men in various ways.

Another man, echoing this appreciation of the ways in which faculty related to students, said,

In general I . . . admired them all . . . because they were approachable, open and not absent-minded professor types. They were not aloof. They were sincere and open and they treated us very much more as equals than I might have expected.

More men than women in this group of former students reported that they had related easily to the faculty. One woman explained,

> I couldn't relate to them personally too well. I didn't have a lot of anxieties about it, they just felt like they were from a different world a little bit. I mean, used a different approach, a different language. And some I felt I had more respect for than others—I felt more comfortable learning from than others, but I didn't run into problems or anything.

Talking to faculty "at their level" was intimidating to one woman. According to another,

> I thought they were approachable, some more than others. I think I still felt intimidated by these professors who sounded so brilliant in their lectures—I probably felt a bit intimidated to approach them. . . . I was so taken with what these brilliant professors are saying that, it was almost like, "how could I have any thoughts of my own after hearing them?" It's very difficult to listen critically when you're hearing these people you put on a pedestal speak.

Another woman who had "expected to have more frequent meetings in a small group situation" than she actually found in the Program said,

> I wasn't a real assertive person, to go and make those kinds of requests. So I would tend to fall back more into the background and be more shy. If someone wasn't scheduling something for me, I wouldn't necessarily go and schedule something for myself. . . . I felt friendly towards the faculty but I never really made any close intellectual or otherwise friendships with any of the faculty members. I know some kids really did have a connection with some, but I didn't. It's what I wanted. I don't think I was ready or really wanted that. It just happens. Just personalities.

And in explaining how such close faculty attention to students was not always easy to accept, one woman said,

> [I]t's like being a beginner in something and having the master teach, where one of his students could teach you as well. You feel like you might be wasting his time and that maybe one of his students should be teaching you first and then when you really kind of have all the basics a

little more, then you go and chat with him. You don't want to waste his time. I can see the reason for T.A.s and that whole set up. Maybe there's a sort of in-between ground where you get a little of both.... And that's sort of a compromise between the usual lower division where all you see is the professor way in the distance and then you mostly just communicate with the T.A. I'd like to have that, his students teaching me, but then every now and then a direct one-on-one contact—a little bit of both rather than just meeting with him.

The notion some students held that they might not "deserve" this close faculty attention to their work was mentioned by other participants, as well, including some who saw it as an obstacle to overcome. One man who reported not being "real close to any of the faculty in a personal sense" had to struggle to find the right balance in his relationships with them, but eventually he succeeded.

It was always definitely a student-professor relationship. I liked a few of them as people, but I always felt like I was coming right out of high school into college and still felt that . . . dealing in a tutorial situation was a little bit intimidating, because it's not a peer relationship. [I had to learn how] to stick to my guns on topics and not be intimidated by a teacher. I felt like in high school it was like you're agreeing with the faculty, the teacher, or if you disagree, the subject is closed. There's no further discussion. Whereas here, you were expected to have a dialogue about that and that's hard to learn.

It took a little bit of getting used to—[but] it was rewarding. Some of the faculty was more encouraging about it—kind of prodded you when you disagreed or would play devil's advocate . . . and that kind of opened up the discussion. After awhile you'd go, "Aha, okay, it's okay to talk if I disagree and express a different point of view." I think that was important because when you are eighteen or nineteen years old and dealing with faculty that's in their forties and fifties, it's not an equal relationship. It sort of needs some guidance to make that happen. Some of them felt more comfortable with talking one-on-one with nineteen year olds than others did about intellectual things.

According to testimony of these former students, the benefits of closer relationships with faculty in the Program were academic rather than social. In defining the quality of student-faculty interaction, one woman observed, "One doesn't necessarily have to have a friendship with these people but have a feeling of communication, good communication." One man credits the faculty with creating a

> very warm and supportive environment. I mean, you could ask silly questions, just shallow, silly questions and whatever, and people would take you seriously. Professors would respond, and they must have thought we were idiots from some of the things we asked.

It was these qualities in the teaching relationship—support, encouragement, respect—that faculty were able to demonstrate to students and that these participants recognized were more important and more relevant to learning than social or personal relationships might have been.

The bitter debates in the first cycle between some of the faculty that arose from the competitive struggle for the minds of the students, for their allegiances was gone in the second cycle, replaced by a more productive kind of disagreement among faculty over issues raised by the curriculum. Tussman says in his reflections that, "The basic agreement on fundamentals in the second group made possible a vigorous running disagreement on almost everything else," and released him from his previous role as "Program defender." The weekly faculty dinner seminar that was one of the casualties of the first cycle succeeded in the second where faculty "argued for four or five hours" over the material they were reading in the Program. These arguments carried over to lectures and seminars and were put to pedagogical use. One man describes how it worked:

> The lectures were indispensable in the whole Program because that way different points of debate or different points of view could be brought up to the whole group, argued, presented and then brought back to the seminar group.... [The disagreements in the lecture] provided grist for the mill. You could go in, listen to these pretty smart guys who know what they are talking about. They'd argue sometimes, there'd always be some, not always, but often there would be debate.... [Then] somebody could come into the small seminar group and say, "Well, what did you think about what he said?" And that would give a good point of departure for a continuing debate or some more discussion.

A woman testifies to the significant effect of these debates.

I wasn't prepared for as many disagreements that they had between themselves. That was fascinating—I loved it. It was an eye opener to me. In high school you have one teacher who has one point of view, and that's the way you learn. To be involved in seeing adults disagree, have pretty strong disagreements a lot of times about the interpretation of this or that, was fascinating to me. And the different teaching styles were fascinating to me. It just lit a light bulb over my head, that there are different points of view, that there are a lot of right answers to the same question, that everything is not black and white, right or wrong, there is a lot of gray area. It's not a math question anymore, you know, it's not two plus two only equals four. There [are] a lot of possibilities out there.

Not every student was able to profit from these debates. One woman saw them as

> just having a personality thing among them . . . not directed to the audience . . . directed to one another. There's a way of having a debate or an argument that takes into account the listener so that the listener is enriched or trained or educated. Then there's a way to have a debate where it's just a position that you have that you want to put forward and it's really between you and the other person and the listener—the student is left wondering where they fit in all this. I can remember it seemed like as we got further along it got more pronounced, into the second year. I think I started cutting lectures . . . maybe I wanted tests or something, I don't know (laughs).

As with the first cycle, a few professors stood out more vividly than the others in the second cycle. In addition to Professor J, the only faculty member to remain with the Program after the first cycle, three other professors were mentioned most often, K, L, and M, while the remaining two, N and O, were mentioned less often. All in all, participants from the second cycle had more specific comments to make about all six professors than did participants from the first cycle about their eight professors and five teaching assistants. If sheer number of comments is any indication, faculty in the second cycle seemed to have more of a total impact one way or another on students than in the first cycle. Possible explanations lay in the fact that there were simply fewer of them to draw the attention of students; the fact that tutorials were regularly scheduled during the second cycle, ensuring regular and equal exposure to all faculty teaching in the Program; and the fact that all second-cycle faculty were present (for seminars and tutorials at any rate) for the entire two years. And there were no teaching assistants in the second cycle to serve as buffers between faculty and students.

Participants from the second cycle made more comments about Professor J than any of the others, as did participants from the first cycle. While he was the instigator and leader of the Program, he would have had no more exposure to students than the other faculty. However, his impact was stronger. One woman says, "I remember mostly Professor [J's] lectures. I think probably he was the one who had an effect on me just from listening to him at the lectures." Another woman said while she "greatly admired most of the faculty . . . people in general had unbelievable admiration for Professor [J]. He was absolutely brilliant." Another woman said of him,

> I think everybody really related to Professor [J]. He's just a wonderful, enthusiastic person and . . . his whole kind of joy for life . . . he was *so* enthusiastic about the Program. He was very much of a diplomat . . . he tried to keep everybody on an even keel. I've great respect for him just as a person. He was very, very warm and open and available, accessible.

Another woman related well to him.

> I can't imagine the Program having operated the way it did without him there as a personality. I liked him. I felt comfortable with him. He was very overpowering to a lot of people and I know some students had a lot of trouble with him—he was a very strong personality—but I never felt really uncomfortable with him. My memory is . . . of this really shiny eminence. I saw a couple of the other faculty as a little weaker but I don't know in absolute terms [if they were]. If [the other faculty] had been seen without him around them, they might have looked different to me.

He certainly had the ability to outshine the other faculty. J also stood above the other faculty for another woman. "I greatly admired Dr. [J]. I don't even remember too much about the other professors. I don't even remember how many more there were." Some women remember J as being "intimidating," even if they did admire him.

Many men from the second cycle also liked and admired him. Said one, "I certainly had great respect for Professor [J]. He was the authority figure, and I thought he was very interesting, stimulating, challenging to understand at times." In speaking of his admiration for J, one man said, "It was *his* program. No one called it the Experimental College, everybody called it by his name (the Tussman College)." Another said, "I would definitely single out [J] in appreciating his effort and tribulations in putting the whole Program together." One man spoke of the difference between J and the other professors:

> I admired Professor [J]. I thought he was a great thinker. . . . It wasn't so much the Program, it was Professor [J]. There were the other professors, but [J] was way above them. He was on a different plateau. They were like disciples of him.

One man described his teaching abilities:

> [J] was a teacher. He would make jokes about things, like if we could force men to be free we would. Just delighting in the paradoxes and watching our befuddled minds try to figure out what he was really talking about or how to figure out a way around it. He was a bit of a bully . . . or maybe not a bully, he just [likes] a good fight. Good argument. Not the shouting part of it but the context part of it. I'm afraid most of us weren't even close to being able to argue with him. He would sit here in the House with a program in his mind and get a little frustrated because things weren't going—we weren't "getting it."
>
> Here in the seminars—how good they were, I think, depended a lot on how able the professor was to draw students out. Some were much better at it than others. [Professor J's] style was almost papal, or Socratic. Without any seeming effort, he could direct a seminar and pull people through it and you went through his hoops. It was almost like a drillmaster.

Another man spoke of J's influence on him:

> He took a kindly interest in me. . . . I recall that sometime after the Program was over, I met up with a guy who also had been in the Program. We chatted a bit, and he said, "You're talking just like [J]."

Professor J's ability to influence his students sometimes had consequences they felt were not so positive, and he was not always seen by students as "kindly." One participant referred to an instance early in the second cycle when he felt humiliated by J during one of the group meetings by the response J made to a question he had asked.

> The effect that it had on me was that I didn't open my mouth for two years in the general assemblies that we had, the weekly or bi-weekly lectures. I never made a comment again. [J] was just brutal, and that was it. I shut down. It was a tough, painful thing.

The relationship was not a static one, however, and did come to a kind of resolution by the end of the Program when this man and J achieved a sort of rapprochement during a tutorial. He described it as

> a kind of wonderful moment with him . . . he let down this authoritarian pose he took . . . because he believed that kids had to have discipline . . . but there was a side of him that I saw that was a forgiving father, and it was pretty moving to me. . . . I felt a little vindication, some real appreciation, and it meant a lot. To me that sort of turn-around at the end meant more than the kind of empty praise that you might get from people who are just tossing off compliments. . . . I had a real father/son transference with him, and that's never uncomplicated.

And yet this man could still identify with Professor J, although he called their relationship an "enmeshment."

The presence of an abundance of affect in this particular faculty-student relationship was clear, and the impact of the Program on this participant was strong and positive, even with this personally wounding experience. While his relationship with J was "problematic," at the same time he had a "very special relationship" with another faculty member, K, who was "willing to think about and talk about psychological stuff whereas the other guys were not. . . . He was the first person in my life who saw the kind of mind that I had and appreciated it." He went on to describe seeing K after the Program, as well as two other professors. Next to Professor J, Professor K was mentioned most frequently by participants. He was described as "sympathetic," "eloquent," an "impressive" lecturer, "fascinating," the "most intellectual and most articulate of the faculty." According to one man,

> He had his footing from the beginning [compared to some of the others who took awhile] maybe because he came out of an English system where

they do . . . tutorials. He was able to challenge you, to get you to talk and think, and think on your feet.

K was respected and admired by many of them, although one participant said, "he got pretty disinterested at times—if you weren't talking about something that was really of interest, he'd let you know right away . . . he cut it off." Another woman found him "very haughty and well versed," and that he was the only faculty member with whom she felt "uncomfortable," as if she were being "put down," although she admitted feeling "scared," and "maybe too reticent or too shy." Another woman said she was "totally tongue-tied whenever he was around," and that he noticed that. She said she could not explain to him that she (and several other women in the Program) "had quite a crush on him. We just thought he was the bee's knees—this terrific English accent—and he was just so worldly and sophisticated—sophistication personified."

One man said,

> He seemed like a real academic . . . I always thought he was way above us. I was always a little daunted. I was afraid of going into his tutorials or seminars, sort of feeling very inadequate. I think he was a bit aloof. I don't think he was good at mingling with the students. He maintained that professorial distance.

But two participants reported that K loosened up somewhat toward the end of the second year, dropping the more formal title of "Mr." and getting to a first-name basis with some of them. In spite of what some saw as his aloofness" or "professorial distance," some former students stayed in touch with him after the end of the Program, and some reported visiting him after graduation. It is important to note that without "mingling" with Program students, he did establish relationships with them that were meaningful and helpful to them and sometimes lasted after the Program ended.

He was also willing to engage students in discussions about how they were carrying out the work of the Program, and hold them to its requirements. One woman reported that after she had missed a lecture of his because of a strike on campus, he called her into his office and in the course of discussing her absence, questioned her methods of political protest, resulting in a fierce argument between them. After what she described as a "terrible row," he persuaded her of the validity of his views.

A light bulb went on in my head, and I said "maybe you're right." Then we developed this incredible affection for one another based on the fact that I could listen. And so it was a forum—it was a place where you could actually work out the issue for yourself, with some support. I appreciated the fact that I wasn't just at loose—trying to figure this all out by myself, but there was some opportunity for dialogue and for dealing with it, even though we weren't allowed to bring it to the classroom. I thought that was wrong, and I argued that it was wrong, [but] we still were dealing with it all the time.

(The day-to-day protests and demonstrations were apparently not to be discussed in lectures and seminars, with faculty wishing to focus instead on philosophical and moral issues underlying the conflict over the Vietnam War.)

The fact that most second-cycle faculty came from backgrounds in philosophy seemed to cut both ways for students. On the one hand, one woman distinguished K as the one faculty member who used ridicule and mild humiliation in his comments on her paper from the others who she thought were "pretty humble philosopher-kings." On the other hand, another woman criticized the whole faculty for their "strong, Platonic slant . . . I think there was a very real philosopher-king attitude on the part of these men. . . . If we were reading the Bible, we were doing it from the standpoint of Plato." And in a comment about the lectures in the Program, another woman observed, "I think some of the professors were wonderful. I think that was a real advantage for us as undergraduates to have six professors and no T.A.s. . . . I loved listening to [them] lecture on philosophy."

Tussman refers in his recollections to the "battle of the vanities" between faculty during the first cycle. It might be expected therefore that in the second cycle, with faculty chosen not from a group of Berkeley faculty "stars" but from a supposedly more congenial group of friends and former students, these conflicts would have disappeared. While it was true that the bitter, rancorous disputes between Tussman and some of the other faculty in the first cycle were not repeated in the second, and according to his reflections, the spirit of competition among faculty was absent from the Program in the second cycle, one faculty member in the second cycle, K, was not in agreement about how the Program was to be conducted. According to one man,

> [L] seemed to bridle at the axiom of the Program that we will read these books out of their original context, without much historical background or secondary research. I think he communicated to me that that really wasn't right, and that in fact he was going to get secondary sources to surround this work with.

L had hired this student to do some library work for him looking up secondary sources.

> Right away I saw something going on that seemed to be not exactly what we'd all agreed to . . . but I thought, "Well, he knows better than I." . . . He began to get very angry at [J] and I think at the other professors and . . . at the whole set-up and he wouldn't come to meetings. He began to miss things, not to do his job . . . and our relationship didn't last for more than a few months. He sort of basically dropped out, in the last, claiming bad health.

Some of the other participants thought "[L] was not generally respected," "had his own agenda," "was controversial," "wanted to be on our side, whatever that was." One man described him as living

> out on the very fringes of the faculty, like he really wasn't part of the central unit. He was off doing his own stuff, was the impression we got. He got himself into a kind of sappy emotionalism, I thought, about students. He really wanted you to know that [he really felt for you] for all the trials and tribulations that were going on campus, the demonstrations, the war and stuff. He's one of those liberal kind of guys and I just didn't buy it. I just didn't see him as an effective fellow. I thought of these other, sort of colder, more hard-hearted guys as being more professional about things.

In a letter to the man quoted earlier who reported being humiliated by J during a lecture, L seemed to take the student's side. This man said of L: "he was sweet and he offered you support, but yet you didn't respect him, so you were not in his camp, so to speak." One man who had taken L to lunch early in the first year, found him to be "likable," but also a

> little bit of a fifth wheel with the rest of the teachers because he was a liberal, I mean a real liberal, a kind of bleeding heart, gushy type liberal. Kind of off to the left of the rest of them. Now that I look back on it, they

were all pretty liberal . . . philosophically, but L was liberal personally, too. He didn't seem to fit in that well and [the other faculty] really creamed him at one of those [all-Program] lectures. I mean, they just crucified him. I remember kind of agreeing with some of the stuff he was saying, and feeling that they were unfair to him. Maybe I felt sorry for him, and said, "Well, why don't we go to lunch?"

(This event shocked other students in the cooperative where this student lived since no teachers had ever appeared there in the dining commons among the students.)

Professor L did have his supporters. Whatever his personal qualities, and the basis of his disagreements with J and other faculty, he apparently tapped into the strong feelings of anti-authority harbored by some students. One man said, "[L] became a sort of symbol of freedom and of antistructure, anti-Tussman overall. I had a lot of warm feelings towards him." Another man said he had "identified with him for awhile." One woman described him as "sincere" and another remembered Professor L as "the one who went the extra mile with the comments on the punctuation and grammar and so I respected him for that."

One woman spoke at length about L's situation in the Program and the painful feelings it evoked for some of the students.

Probably some of the students had really bad feelings about [L] because he kind of dropped out . . . of lecturing at some point in the second year. . . . He continued to conduct his seminars and to meet his students, and he attended the lectures. But he didn't participate at a collegial level the way the other five did, and it caused a great rift. Among professors, mostly. It was very painful. It happened, from my perspective, in large part because those six men were not equal. They weren't all able to hold their own with [J] so well. . . . [L] was a soft, sweet sort of guy, and not a combative sort of guy. And in that sense he couldn't hold his own. And it was a difficult situation to be in, for students, because [J] could be intimidating to us. . . .

There was actually to some extent a kind of polarization between the [followers of J] and the [followers of L]. We had a play at the end of the two years which was an enactment of that. Somebody wrote it—a West Side Story kind of play—and we put it on, and it was a clearing of the air. But what it enacted was this rift, the people that sided with [L] philosophically and the people that sided with [J] philosophically. And painful—it was painful not to have L lecturing. . . . I [don't mean] to overemphasize it . . . I think that most of us were able to deal with it . . . I dealt with it by having him two quarters in a row. . . . You were supposed to have one each quarter. . . .

He was here, he had students in his seminar and he did tutorials and read papers, but it meant that if you didn't have him for a [tutorial and seminar] professor, you didn't really get much input from him because he wasn't commenting on the material as a whole, or to the students as a whole. . . . It was a loss. . . . I came to greatly admire [L] personally, I guess, more than academically, and I still see quite a lot of him.

The fourth professor mentioned most by participants appeared to have the capacity to reach students, too, in a more personal sense but not in ways that polarized and divided them as L had done. Comments about him were generally favorable: "[M] and I became friends. The kids regarded [M] with some humor. You know, this Jesuit priest who we found kind of funny, but with respect"; "I remember [M], who I liked, and felt very comfortable with"; "[M] . . . made a point of being friends with us. Having been a Jesuit priest and a youth director and so forth, I guess he had the skills to do some of that"; "There was a knot of us who . . . took over this house and more or less lived here and we . . . considered it our house and the faculty had offices upstairs, and they would come through from time to time. And [M] didn't have any real personal life, 'cause he's in the Jesuits, and they live right down here on God Hill (the location of several theological colleges adjacent to the Northside of the campus), so he was without another home, so we . . . would interact with him a little more on a personal level than with the other guys"; "[M] I got to know pretty well—he and I were fellow Catholics, and he helped me get a room in the place he was living"; "[M] I admired . . . probably because I've had a warped view of what people brought up in the Catholic educational system would be like and I didn't know that Catholics could have such a broad world view that he did. It was a worthwhile experience, knowing him"; "[M] was always really focused and always really tried to do his best to make a tutorial challenging and interesting—he was just a funny guy—he kept an index card of every thought he ever had which was sort of odd but it was always interesting 'cause he would come up with a lot of interesting concepts and ideas"; "He . . . put a tremendous amount of energy into helping kids out—just a very, very wonderful person"; "[M] was a nice man, easy to talk to, down to earth—I don't think he was a brilliant speaker, in retrospect."

The remaining two faculty were given less attention by participants in their recollections. These were all the comments from the 20 second-cycle participants about one of them, Professor N: "And somebody named [N] made very little impression on me"; "Although [N] was a very warm, giving person I didn't feel that he intellectually was quite up to the others"; "The only one I do remember well, was [N] . . . everybody thought he was a dud. He wasn't a very good lecturer, and he wasn't very good in tutorials or seminars. . . . I remember people identifying him as probably one of the weak links." But another reported, "I had good [tutorial] sessions with [N]."

The sixth professor (O) was mentioned more frequently than N in the accounts of these former students, and his impressions on them were even more contradictory: "When I connected [in tutorials] it was with [O]"; "I had good sessions with [O]." In contrast were these comments: "I didn't get a real good feel for [O] ever. He was stolid, and sort of quiet and—it seems to me the quarter that I was in his seminar we had a large seminar and it got kind of unwieldy. . . . "; "And [O] was someone who was pretty much treated with disrespect by the students. He really seemed to be a little bit out of place overall"; "I found [O] frustrating in tutorial. It seemed like a running joke within the group that he seemed like sort of an insurance salesman, both in tutorial and in seminar. I mean we never sort of got to the bottom of where he was coming from."

In spite of appealing to a few of these participants, O apparently struck several students as ineffectual, and he could also be confrontational. One woman, inspired by the tolerance faculty displayed for each others' opinions, felt O did not respect the opinions she held that differed from his, and that in tutorials "was very critical—it was not a two-way conversation, which is what I had assumed that tutorials were supposed to be. He ran it his way, and whatever you had to say that wasn't to his liking, he just said, 'No, that's not right.' He was doing this to a lot of people at the time." However, when she wrote to him explaining her objections, he apologized, and was "quite nice to me after that." The whole experience left her feeling positive, and she thought that her letter had "resolved the issue," although the feeling remained with her that the students' points of view needed to be respected and that "I can't say I was very encouraged by that particular professor." Yet her anecdote illustrates the remarkable atmosphere created in the Program where students could feel free to criticize faculty, and apparently faculty could receive that criticism with civility.

The comments about N and O taken together illustrate the striking diversity of faculty appeal to students—both of these two professors connected with some students quite effectively and not at all with others. Every teacher in the Program, at least in this second cycle, related well to some students, but not to every one who was interviewed for the study. In the same way there seemed to be "something for everyone" in the Program as a whole, as we shall see in later chapters on the Program's educational features, there was at least "someone for everyone," that is, at least one faculty member able to reach a particular student, and in some cases there were several. Despite what some students perceived to be these two "weak links" in the teaching abilities of the faculty, the others were strong enough to compensate. No participant faulted the entire faculty for the shortcomings of one or two.

FIRST- AND SECOND-CYCLE CONTRASTS

The second-cycle faculty presented to their students a much different face than did the first cycle. As we have observed, rather than representing the range of disciplines in the first cycle that included philosophy, literature, sociology, math/engineering, law, and political science, the second cycle teachers were mostly philosophers. In spite of this, there were more comments about the value of the diversity of faculty in the second cycle, suggesting that it wasn't the range of different disciplines that faculty represented that offered Program students a desirable degree of variety, but rather the differences in personality and teaching approaches that this group of mainly philosophers displayed.

With the exception of Professor L's differences with the purposes and methods of the Program, they were united in their approach to teaching and apparently had no major quarrels with its leader. In spite of L's disagreements with Tussman and others and his withdrawal from the public lectures, he remained with the Program throughout the whole two years to meet his seminars and tutorials and therefore to have some impact on his students.

What becomes apparent from a comparison of these statements of first- and second-cycle participants is that during the second cycle Tussman became much more efficacious in implementing his ideas. He drew more positive comments from participants about the way he taught and about his relationships with them, and he was able to run a tauter ship all around—in fact, the ship seemed to run itself, according to his memoirs. Even though he again had serious disagreements with one faculty member, those disagreements were confined to that teacher alone and did not spread to other faculty as it did during the first cycle. When serious disagreement did appear in either cycle, however, it tended to polarize some students into "us and them" camps of Tussman and anti-Tussman supporters. These students (who did not represent the majority of participants in the study, but only a few) were drawn into taking sides when they experienced dissension among faculty.

Yet from comments made by participants it appears that the discomfort, even anguish, some of them felt about this split in faculty unity and about how one teacher was perceived to be treated by the others was contained during the second cycle, and represented only one part of their experience in the Program. Even those students who were upset by faculty disagreement found expression for their feelings both informally and in the final student production at the end of the cycle (the skit lampooning the faculty referred to earlier), which one said led to a "clearing of the air." It did not appear, then, that this one instance of faculty dissent during the second cycle seriously interfered with students getting from the rest of the Program what it had to offer them in the way that it might have in the first cycle.

In exchanging regular tenured Berkeley faculty in the first cycle, some of them decidedly opposed to his viewpoint, for friends and former students in the second, who for the most part agreed with him, Tussman made way for a much more effectively run program. Jeopardized in this trade-off, however, was the prospect that the Program could continue on the Berkeley campus using tenured faculty. The "no department, no tenure" rule at Berkeley presented a formidable threat to carrying the Program into the future. The factor contributing to the dramatic improvement in unified teaching, ironically, then compromised the institutionalization of the experiment.

CHAPTER 4

The House

Accounts of the purpose and plan of the Program, about the kind of students attracted to it, and about the two sets of faculty who taught in its two cycles, form only part of the picture of this experiment. One of the most crucial aspects of the Program, both in its design and in the way it was carried out, was its physical location. Like Meiklejohn at Wisconsin, Tussman wanted the Program at Berkeley to be housed in a separate place on the campus, a place reserved entirely and exclusively for the Program. But unlike Meiklejohn's Experimental College, the Tussman College was not to be residential. Tussman did not want the problems of co-educational living, and he thought that Program students should not be so isolated from other students in the university. (As it turned out, most of the participants in the study who expressed an opinion on this matter agreed with him; a few did not, and in the interests of strengthening the feeling of community in the Program, wished that Program students would have been able to live in the House as well as meeting and studying there.)

Tussman begins his reflections by describing the House as he remembers it, imbued with all his ambivalent feelings about the Program. In his book, he refers to the House as "an almost ideal home. It provides us with faculty offices, seminar rooms, study hall, and commons room. . . . Our reports in process have hinted that the house, in addition to its constructive significance, has been a more or less constant source of anxiety. It has been the island on which we have lived our own variations of the *Lord of the Flies*. It has provided a stage for the display of the roles of the guardian, the passive, the heedless, the predator. It has been the scene of both constructive and destructive energy . . . " (Tussman 1971, 128). Participants in the study, however, remember it with virtually unalloyed pleasure.[1]

In spite of the paucity and shabbiness of its furnishings, it was an attractive, comfortable, and inviting space. As a fraternity house, it had been designed for the use of students; when the Program took it over, the kitchen was kept and chapter rooms were converted to lounges and study rooms, student bedrooms to faculty offices. In contrast to the more traditional classroom/office buildings on campus, it made a place for students to relax, to engage in discussions, to read, to study, to play music—to congregate for purposes other than to listen to lectures. Whether Program students used the House frequently, as some did, or not, it was there to serve as a home for the Program, for students as well as for faculty. It physically marked the Program as a separate entity, distinct from other parts of the campus, and it belonged just to the Program community.

STUDENTS' VIEWS OF THE HOUSE

The House was a particularly successful and important part of the Program from the point of view of students. Participants were almost unanimous in expressing their appreciation of the House. While a few reported feeling neutral about it, a few that they lived too far away to make much use of it even if they appreciated it, the rest were pleased to have had the use of the House to meet for discussions, for socialization, for studying, playing music, cooking dinners over the weekends. Some commuters who lived at home with their parents were especially glad to have a place on the campus to call their own. Comments ranged from appreciative to enthusiastic: "I liked it"; "Oh, God, I really liked that house"; "It was great"; "It was

---

[1] The House had been purchased by the university along with a string of others on Gayley Road (Fraternity Row as it was once called) in the sixties and seventies as membership in fraternities and sororities dwindled and their houses came up for sale. Their original designs as living and meeting places make them ideal settings for research institutes and small programs such as this. Unfortunately, the foresightedness of one campus administration was not passed on to successive ones, as one after another of these old university-owned brown-shingled houses is being allowed to fall into disrepair and eventually to be destroyed, as was the Kappa Sigma house recently.

Figure 1   The House on Hearst Street designed by Ernest Coxhead.

Figure 2   Program faculty meeting.

Figure 3   Joseph Tussman, founder of the Experimental College Program at Berkeley.

Figure 4   Lecture in Northgate Hall.

Figure 5   Same lecture showing all faculty members in attendance.

Figure 6   Program students in the House lounge.

Figure 7   Faculty-led seminar in the House.

great, I loved it there; it was a wonderful, wonderful part of the experience"; "I particularly loved that building"; "It was wonderful; it was cozy and welcoming and warm"; "It was charming and cozy"; "It was funky, comfortable and convenient"; "It held a very special place in my heart"; "The House was a *critical* aspect of the whole Program for people who really were involved in the totality of the Program. It's where we hung out. I almost lived my entire second year there"; "People would be there working and you could talk . . . that ability to interact, the sense of community you don't often get in the University—so I'd say it was critical"; "It made you feel at ease and receptive to whatever was happening." Several people said they still drive by the House to look at it; some point it out to their children as they drive by; one says he always shows it to out-of-town visitors.

THE ARCHITECTURAL SIGNIFICANCE OF THE HOUSE

The appreciation of the House focused on several of its aspects: its architectural and aesthetic qualities; its function as a community center and as a home away from home; its physical locus of the learning community that the Program fostered. Architecturally, the House is of some significance. Built in 1893 at the corner of Hearst and Leroy Avenues on the northern edge of the campus for the Beta Theta Pi fraternity, it was designed by Ernest Coxhead, a pioneering architect who had come from England to the Bay Area. In the Tudor Revival style, "it is exaggeratedly asymmetrical and deliberately designed to look like an accretion of separate parts . . . its profile an assemblage of parts treated with subtle differences, like a small medieval village." (Cerny 1990.) It is not a box divided into rooms, but each room is separate and a different part of the building—"the rooms defining the building rather than the other way around" (Cerny *ibid.*). Mary Hardy (1997) explains its design:

> The original building was designed as four interlocking blocks, each housing a distinct function, and each individually articulated on the exterior. The blocks staggered slightly in plan and varied in height and roof form, and in finish materials. The resulting composition suggested a cluster of vernacular buildings vaguely English and medieval in character, built over time.

Robert Bernhardi (1985), in *The Buildings of Berkeley*, said that both Ernest and Almeric Coxhead, his brother and architectural partner, were "noted for designing charming, warm interiors and finely honed ornamental details." It is difficult to exaggerate its attractiveness to students whose dormitories and classrooms were usually never more than squares and rectangles in basically characterless modern blocks. The features of the House include fireplaces and window seats, dormers and leaded windows, rooms of different sizes and shapes connected by warren-like passageways—quite untypical of the modern dormitories or classrooms on the rest of the campus. It is an example of the "First Bay Tradition," a new direction in architectural design begun in San Francisco about 1890 with origins in the Arts and Crafts Movement in England, an expression of the same desire to return to a more natural lifestyle in revolt against the impersonal mass-production of the Industrial Revolution (Cerny *ibid.*). It is one of the few buildings near the campus of this style to survive the Berkeley fire of 1923, and the more recent razing of historical buildings by the university in order to build parking lots and access roads to construction sites. It represents a rare surviving architectural link between the old brown shingle buildings on the northern edge of the campus just across the street, the Naval Architecture Building and Northgate Hall, and the residential brown shingles on the northside of the campus (Cerny 1992). It is no wonder so many students "loved" the house and felt it to be warm, cozy, and welcoming.

HOW STUDENTS USED THE HOUSE

Apart from the aesthetic pleasures to be found there, the House offered students in the Experimental College Program other advantages. Several participants stressed the importance to them of having their own place to come to on the campus, a place not used by others. This was another manifestation of the "specialness" of the Program that reinforced for some their sense of being a member of an "elite" group. The House had practical value for Program students as well. One woman, who had been a commuter, said,

> It was like you *had* a place instead of going from [one place to another]. The only other times I ever had a place, I suppose, was in science lab where you were given a drawer or something like that. It's like having a

locker—I felt like there was a hole, there was a place to belong, and there were other people who belonged to that place. It wasn't just as if you used it from nine to ten o'clock and then the rest of the time it belonged to somebody else.

Another commuter spoke of how easy it was to become lost in the crowd on the Berkeley campus particularly in the first overwhelming year, but that the House "just took that right away. I never felt any of that." It was not only commuters who found a home away from home in the House. One sorority member, with a sorority house of her own to live in, instead spent most of her time at the Program House. A man reported, "It was fun to go to this funky old building and [just] sit." Other participants spoke of the value of finding solitude there—a rare commodity on the Berkeley campus.

The House also provided its students another experience unusual for the Berkeley campus: "A sense of place, of being an institution . . . it was more than a bunch of people in classrooms. You could expect to find people there. It was not like trying to hunt up a T.A. in Dwinelle [one of several large, impersonal buildings on the Berkeley campus]." "A centering place, kind of akin to a community center," as another put it. But it was a community center not just in the social sense. One man said, "You could always find somebody there who was reading the same stuff and thinking about the same things that you were." It is difficult to imagine the Program establishing the sense in its students that they were part of a community of scholars without having the House, or something like it, as a physical location along with their sharing the common curriculum.

If there was any dissatisfaction at all with the House on the part of participants, it was in its use for social purposes. Without any kind of adult authority constantly present to regulate the use of the House, it was sometimes taken over by one group or another for social and recreational purposes not to the liking of other students. "It had a certain cliquish social aspect to it among certain students whose social lives revolved around it that I didn't feel akin to," one put it. One member of one of the cliques described himself as being

> quite possessive about it. Myself and maybe a half a dozen other people. We got a big load of firewood . . . we put together a couple of communal

dinners and spaghetti feeds. . . . A knot of us took over, considered it our house.

The groups habitually using the House were described by other participants as the "long-haired radical type"; as more of a "literary crowd" that put out a poetry journal. Not all students fit into these groups, however, and some of the participants said they did not feel comfortable socially in the House, although they liked the House and were appreciative of its other functions. The "counter-culture hang-out" that Professor Tussman describes was attested to by some of the participants: "Some of us were pigs," admitted one; another, although she "loved" the House, called it a "junky heap." Since the sixties were an age of heightened experimentation with both sex and drugs, and since students had keys to the building, it is not surprising that some of them used the House for these purposes. A few participants talked about using the House as if it were their own in which to conduct romantic liaisons; a few talked of some drug dealing from time to time in the upper floors of the House far away from where ordinary Program business was conducted.

And yet, in spite of the use some students made of the House as a place to make statements about authority and individuality in ways that disgusted some faculty and turned off other students, the House was nonetheless an important agent helping to generate a sense of identity for all students, for both those who used the House socially and those who did not. It was a "centering place," a place they could truly call their own that was not used by any other group in the university. Apart from whatever "juvenile" use it was put to socially by some students, the House could still provide the serious community of scholars, teachers, and students with a physical location. (That is not to suggest that students who could behave in a juvenile fashion from time to time could not also be serious about what they were learning.)

The place chosen for the Program, then, could hardly have been more conducive to its successful functioning from the point of view of students.[2]

---

[2] As the dean of the newly established Graduate School of Public Policy, Aaron Wildavsky, another gifted educator, insisted on being assigned the House as its home after it was vacated by the Tussman Program in 1969 on the grounds that it provided an excellent environment for learning.

The House

A house manager, as Tussman suggests, could have helped to regulate student use after hours, and this would have been an improvement. Other than that, there were no complaints from participants about the House to dilute the appreciation it called forth. While not strictly a pedagogical feature, the House allowed the pedagogical features of the Program to be more fully realized.

CHAPTER 5

Educational Features

The picture of how the plan, the people, and the place as we have described them all functioned together to make the Program work would be incomplete without a description of its pedagogical features, those unique aspects of the Program, which taken together became the vehicle for the realization of its design.

In order to learn how the various features of the Program operated and how they were related to each other and to the Program as a whole, participants were asked how they felt about the readings, the lectures, the seminars (both with faculty present and without), and the writing they were asked to do: the papers, the journal, and the intellectual autobiography. The common thread running through participants' remarks about these central pedagogical features of the Program was the wide variability of their judgments. Each of these features was thought to be a very important and useful part of the Program by at least some former students; and conversely, almost every one of them, with the exception of the reading list, was thought to be one of the least appealing and useful aspects by somebody else.

THE READINGS

The one educational feature that regularly drew the most favorable comments was the reading list that formed the basis of the curriculum. There were over 35 selections to be read (and reread), discussed and written about over a two-year period, each selection one at one time, and each to be read by everybody, faculty and students alike. Many of the participants talked about the impact individual readings had made on them, although some could remember only a few of them. Three-quarters of the participants judged the readings as a whole to be a good or very good part of the Program. Their comments included: "Fantastic. I think I can probably recall just about all of them"; "some were excellent, [the one on the Peloponnesian War] was some of the greatest writing, the most impressive piece of history I've ever read"; "Thucydides was very compelling reading"; "I really loved the readings, I enjoyed everything we read. I could probably tell you just about the whole syllabus right now"; "One of the things that the Program did give me is this stock of imagery and basic literature like *Paradise Lost*. I can look at something and say, 'Well, hey, that's Miltonian"; "Plato's *Republic* made a big difference but I can't tell you what specifically"; "I loved them. I want to read them all over again . . . I can't think of anything off-hand that was not fascinating"; "The readings I think were valuable . . . this was a whole range of literature that I had just never been exposed to, a whole political spectrum, reading the *Iliad*, Thucydides. I really enjoyed doing that"; "It was a well-selected reading list—I'd love to go back and reread some of the stuff"; "It's a luxury to spend six weeks reading one book"; "I remember doing all the reading, and enjoying talking about the reading. There wasn't a huge amount of reading" (other participants differed on this score). All three participants who would not chose to repeat the Program also had positive things to say about the readings. Even the one who had the most negative reflections on the Program said, "I think the basic readings were brilliant, wonderful . . . it was the great literature."

One man talked about the effect of having read these books on his life today.

> I feel well-educated having read those books, and I know a lot of people have never had the time to do that in undergraduate school. Having read Thomas Hobbes' *Leviathan* from start to finish three times, and Locke the same thing, I feel a sense of authority. I mean to this day if somebody talks about Hobbes or Locke or they say something wrong, whether I contradict them or not I know in my mind whether what they're saying is correct or not, and it's nice. Locke and Hobbes don't come up all the time in a conversation, but when they do, it's nice.

One man explained the importance of the relationship of the readings to the purpose of the Program.

> I liked the readings; I thought they were very thoughtfully and very skillfully chosen. They were important reading to open students' minds up to social thinking, social philosophy. Real questions to try to make students really address the questions of right and wrong... and how does that fit in with social principles, right and wrong. How do you figure out what society really wants to do? I guess there's no final answer, but at least they are serious questions that are worthy of some study and review. And the reading that they selected did raise those questions.... How should individuals act and think in society?
> The readings were well picked to bring focus on those issues of social obligation.... Do we have any social obligation? Well, this is what some of the Greeks thought, this is what it says in the Bible about obligation to other people. This is what some of the English constitutionalists thought about it.... It would be nice if people realized that they shouldn't just obey the laws, but they should have a sense of obligation, of social contract. So the readings did bring that home, and it showed that people have been struggling to define that somehow for a long time.

Other participants reported that while they thought the readings were good or interesting, they did have some difficulty with them. Their comments included: "Most of them I enjoyed very much. Some of them were killers. I do remember particularly reading Marx, the German writers. I mean [they] were just killers to just slog through. But I enjoyed it. I think they were things that I would not have read, ever, on my own. I think I would have gotten too frustrated in the first few chapters"; "There was an awful lot of reading; there was just an awful lot of material to cover"; "I would have liked fewer large works—they really are tough to plow through"; "I'm not sure I remember much about the readings. I remember reading Hobbes and I remember reading the Peloponnesian Wars and thinking this is the longest, most boring book I've ever had to read. I remember thinking this is all great stuff I should be reading. I'm glad somebody's asking me to do it. My impression is that it was a lot, and it was difficult stuff"; "There was an awful lot of reading, an awful lot of material to cover, but I thought it was really interesting. I think it's just a really good basic approach to learning about civilization"; "I felt good about the readings. Some of it was difficult for me. Not readings that I would have picked up on my own. But that doesn't mean that I'm sorry about it"; "Herodotus got a little thick. The Greek plays are a little more fluid than some of the seventeenth-century political philosophy. Hobbes was pretty impenetrable"; "We read some pretty heavy books . . . those are some of the most important books that I've ever read. . . . Plato's *Republic* made a big difference to me, but I can't tell you how specifically it may have affected my thoughts."

Several participants reported having mixed, but still generally favorable feelings about the readings. It was possible not to enjoy all of the readings, but still appreciate the list as a whole.

> I was impressed by the reading list. A lot of it was screamingly dull. The Supreme Court justices are not scintillating writers. *Leviathan* was not fun to read. Milton writes in a style that hasn't been popular for three hundred years. You always have the sensation in the back of your head that Plato's really a senile old fascist and you're reading something you don't want to read. Freud was wonderful. And Malcolm X and some of the other things were just a pleasure to read. In retrospect, I would say it was a great reading list. These are things that everybody needs to read.

Even though the readings did not always seem as valuable to some students as other parts of the Program, they formed a basis for the lectures, seminars, and papers. One participant said,

> Sometimes I think I got more out of the lectures and writing and discussing what I was writing with the professor than I did necessarily from just the readings alone. I don't know that they would stand out as being something that I would find at the top of the list as what I remember as benefiting me from the Program.

And while acknowledging the difficulty of some of the readings, one man nevertheless attests to their usefulness, to the important difference between the readings in the Program and in other parts of the University, and to their value over time.

> They [the Program] got Milton into my head. If I'd been over in the University on a regular course system, I wouldn't have had that helpful metaphor. . . . When you go to English [class] and read Milton, you don't go to English to find out what Milton has to say, you go to English to find

out how Milton fits into the general scheme of Western literature. What kind of meter did he use, where does this fit into the development of the English language, whatever the particular specific aspect that the instructor happens to want to be interested in. It's a professional training. It's [Milton as taught in the English department] not designed to teach you to say, "Milton says this. Is this right, is this wrong, does it make sense? Is this good, is this bad? Tell me about it." You don't ask those questions. Not "what does he have to say to me now?" And that's the fundamental pedagogical difference between the Program [and the rest of the university.]

We actually read Milton. And if I hadn't had to read Milton, I wouldn't. It's awful stuff the first time. As a matter of fact, it's something that's much better to have read than to read . . . it's awful stuff to slog through.

The King James version of the Bible was referred to frequently by participants. One man thought "the history of the Jews as told in the Bible stood out as being a part of the course equal in size to the history of England as we get into the age of the Civil War . . . I enjoyed it very much." Several participants mentioned reading the Bible as literature to be a novel experience. "We read the Bible as literature. That idea had never, ever entered my mind that anybody even did that"; "The Bible was the only one that sticks with me because . . . who would read the Bible in a nonreligious capacity? And I do remember being interested. I'm glad I had that experience because I was not raised in a religious background, and I'm not religious now. But my view of the Bible is quite different from most people's as a result of this." Two participants, from Catholic backgrounds, were also amazed to be reading the Bible as literature; one of them found that "taking the Bible and reading it in the Program was kind of the first step towards seeing the Bible as a piece of literature separate from all of my preconceived notions and all of my attachments that I had had in my childhood." Another said, "It was very interesting for me, having gone to a Catholic high school, and having done a lot of study of the Old Testament and New Testament, it was very interesting to do a reading of the Bible in a whole different sense, and that was fascinating to me. . . . I enjoyed it, that was great."

The subject of the readings elicited a kind of confession from one participant who thought in retrospect that he had "cheated" himself by not taking them as seriously as he should have.

> At the time I didn't complain about them. I don't think they were inappropriate readings, or bad readings, and I didn't think they were too much. I just wish that I had been more diligent and serious about them. . . . I think that [if] that had happened I would have gotten more out of everything. Because I didn't take them as seriously as I should have. They became functional for my writing, and sometimes for discussion, but I wasn't filled up with them and their content when I went into these seminars like I would probably want to do now. . . . [W]e read the Bible in that period, and that was frustrating for me because they wanted us to read the King James version, of course, and that was very difficult because frankly that's not my English. I like the newer translations because you can understand them better. . . . I felt bad about it but I cheated in the sense that I'd get another version to read to find out what it was I supposed to be understanding. . . . I know they wanted me to read it for the language but . . . I [rationalized] "Look, I've got to write a paper on this, and I can't understand what they're saying in some of these parts." There were no Cliff Notes[1] on the Bible.

The numbers of men and women who found the readings good or very good were similar, but men were more likely than women, in both cycles, to be extremely enthusiastic about them. (As noted earlier, more men than women in the study reported that the curriculum appealed to them from the start. The impact of the curriculum as a whole was somewhat different for men and women as we will see later in the chapter dealing with the major impact of the Program.) The reading list remained essentially the same for both cycles, although there may have been some minor additions in the second year of each cycle in response to students' requests. Participants from both cycles reported similar reactions to the readings, including the very clear difference in the way some participants reported their feelings about the readings in the second year of each of the two cycles of the Program as compared with the first year: many reported a kind of let-down in their interest in the second year selection. Several spoke of the enjoy-

---

[1]Commercially published plot summaries and discussions of works of literature designed to make them easier to understand.

ment of reading about the Greeks and about 17th-century England, and how that contrasted with second year readings. Some couldn't remember the second year readings at all. Others found: "the first year's readings were overall more interesting to me. They were a little more varied, until you got to Hobbes, and even that became fun with some of the ideas that were in there. In the second year, reading the Federalist Papers, no one enjoyed that I know of"; "I really enjoyed the first year's readings. The second year's readings don't stick in my mind."

One participant was more specific, and his comments help to explain why the second year's readings were less interesting to many students than the first year's.

> I think as we got into the American period, I became a little confused. I wasn't sure that what I was reading was really that interesting. When I was reading Homer I thought, "Yeah, I'm reading Homer, this is great," and then when I read Lincoln Steffens or Malcom X, I thought, "Well, I'm not that interested in Lincoln Steffens and Malcom X. . . . " We read some of Marx's work and some of Freud, and I somehow felt it was thin. . . . I felt the treatment wasn't quite right. I guess I believed that you could read Homer more or less out of context, or the Bible out of context, or Milton out of context, without secondary sources and historical background, but I didn't really feel you could do that with Marx or Freud. I think to read Freud or to read Marx you do have to become knowledgeable in psychology or in economics, I felt this was sort of wrenched out of context. . . . I felt they were not given their full due in a sense . . . they seemed to be an afterthought, not to be essentially a part of the Program.

Tussman's theme for that second year was American. "America is the living society we now try to understand in the light of fundamental ideas which it embodies and issues which it faces." In contrast to the first year readings about Greece and England that presented general ideas, the second year readings were concerned more directly with context, and "the great books are not as obviously there" (Tussman 1971). But, as with a great many other aspects of the Program, preference for the first year's readings, although more prevalent, was not universal among participants, and at least one of them liked the second year readings even better than the first year because he found them so relevant to the pressing issues of the time.

The reading list was great, I thought. Then the second year became even more interesting because we were reading Supreme Court, we were reading Malcolm X, and Lincoln Stephens of all people, and making connections. Given the political stuff that was going on at the time, the reading list turned out to be fantastically useful and rich, I thought. The Vietnam War business was going on, and all of these questions were coming, what the government does, what it shouldn't do, whether a government should lie, whether it shouldn't, the fight between order and anarchy, and all this stuff was getting played out everyday in the news and in our lives. We have this sort of very slow, conservative tempering, but also some revolutionary stuff, too, and so it became a real dialogue between what we were, and an angry dialogue between what we were reading and what the teachers were standing for and what we were being pushed to do by our youth and what was happening in the Vietnam War. I'm a kid, I want to be part of this stuff, these demonstrations, and you're telling me "no". . . .

We talked about Marx in a very different way than how he'd been used on the barricades or out in Sproul Plaza. . . . There was a real interplay between the readings and the life outside. And it made it hard to be a full-hearted dogmatic revolutionary. I found myself in real trouble with that, I just couldn't do it with quite the abandon that other people did. It just took some of the fun out of it. I just couldn't abandon myself to the bull shit I heard on Sproul Plaza. And I said, "Hmm, sounds suspect, doesn't quite fit in with the long historical process that we've been looking at." But that didn't stop me from being a kid, either.

The Program did succeed in establishing a relationship between the readings and the issues they raised, and the political issues of the day, and that was true of readings from all the periods covered in the Program, not just contemporary ones in the American year. One woman said of the first year readings, "Thucydides was very compelling reading. It came alive a little bit more—I think that was where the Vietnam stuff started to get kicked around." One man observed, "Who would have thought that Hobbes' *Leviathan* would have been the earmark of our discussion . . . about the student protests?"

THE LECTURES

Tussman writes that "While we do not regard lecturing as the chief mode of teaching, it does have a significant place in the program. . . . The lecture program is coordinated with the readings, and its main function is to stimulate and deepen the reading process. . . . We do not lecture about what has not been read; and we do not generally present background or supplementary information. We try, instead, to raise questions, to offer suggestive interpretations, and to sharpen and deepen the issues or problems latent in the reading. . . . " (Tussman 1971). The lectures, unlike the usual undergraduate lecture presented by the course instructor alone with perhaps an occasional guest lecturer, were a varied set of presentations by the six different faculty, sometimes singly or sometimes in panels of two or more, and also occasionally by guest lecturers.

The question about the lectures drew generally but not exclusively favorable responses from participants. About half of them had nothing but positive things to say about the lectures. Their comments included: "I loved them"; "I enjoyed them tremendously"; "extremely stimulating and enjoyable"; "in some ways it'd be like watching 'Firing Line' where you can just listen to the language and be amazed." Several said the lectures were superior to those in the regular lower division program. One gave an example of how the focus of team teaching can shift from the individual faculty "performance" to a collective effort aimed at achieving the goals of a program.

> People would go from lecture to lecture [in the regular university] and [not] absorb the information—there wasn't much reciprocity . . . the lectures in the Program combined with the other aspects seemed different . . . you didn't get the feeling that the professors were trying to assert their point of view in quite the same way as was done in a lot of classes I had taken.

This was another distinctive aspect of the lectures—they were not individual entities in themselves but were an integral part of the whole pedagogical structure and meant to relate to the readings and to the papers students were writing on the one hand and to the discussions in both kinds of seminars on the other. A woman from the first cycle said that although she remembered the lectures least of all the features, "In retrospect, they gave me the background to understand the stuff that I was going to then read. It gave me some context because I did not have, in high school, a very strong historical background."

The way in which material was presented in these lectures also was distinct from the way in which material was presented in the usual undergraduate class lecture in the humanities and the social sciences, where the lectures formed the central part of the educational experience and material from them was meant to be memorized by the student and then repeated on examinations as an indicator of how well the student had learned it. Program students had opportunities to compare lectures there with those in the rest of the university through the one "outside" class they took each quarter or semester, presumably to fill out their lower division requirements, through auditing classes throughout the University as some did, through descriptions of roommates and friends in the regular undergraduate program, and later through their upper division classes. As one woman from the second cycle described the Program,

> There's much less of the game that goes on in most academic things where you have to psych out the professor and figure out where they're coming from and give them what they want to hear. You don't have to do that in the Program, which was great.

One participant, who reported "loving the lectures," in talking about this distinction said they

> weren't like lectures outside [in the regular university] where someone got up and gave you this speech they'd probably given for the last twenty years or something, and they weren't very interested in, and they didn't care if you were interested in it. I never felt that way, I always felt it was different, that this was something that we were very much involved in, even the lectures.

A woman from the second cycle pointed out the relationship of the readings to the lectures.

> I think they tended to lecture very much on issues of integration, that is, "How does this relate to the book we read last week?" It was just very different from what else you would get in an . . . undergraduate setting. And I think that we were certainly getting the fruits of their tremendous stimulation—there was a great deal of collegiality going on there.

Another participant in speaking of the quality of teaching and the involvement of students in the lectures said,

> The grasp of the material by the teachers was excellent. They really knew their stuff . . . they were well prepared and the teachers really were passionate about the material and wanted us to know it and to respond to it. I felt very good about that.

Rather than allowing students to simply passively receive information, the lectures in the Program actively involved the students and not only encouraged but actually required them to make use of what they heard there both in their seminars and in their writing.

Another participant in the first cycle thought the lectures were "more like dialogues than straight lectures," and as we have already pointed out, this aspect of the lectures was perceived by many students to be one of the most exciting parts of the entire Program. We have already quoted the participant from the first cycle who thought "the elegant private biff between [Professors A and B]" to be the highlight of the Program. Others from the first cycle said they "especially liked it when [these two] disagreed with each other. It wasn't always just lecture—there was interchange at times;" and,

> I liked them because at times you would see them honestly disagreeing with each other, honestly challenging each other, and really going at it with each other intellectually . . . you'd have T.A.'s taking on professors, professors taking each other on, and I thought that was really at times fascinating.

In contrast to the many participants who spoke emphatically about how enjoyable and educationally beneficial these faculty debates were, one participant from the first cycle, equally emphatically, found them to be uncomfortable and even frightening:

> I was aware that I felt that every time I was in a seminar and every time I was in a lecture, that it was [Professor A] and [Professor B] arguing with each other, and that somehow in the process of us watching them, we were supposed to be learning something. I was aware of that and I was aware that I was incredibly unhappy about that. . . . [The lecture was] always kind of exciting and it was always kind of frightening. . . . I just

> remember these two men standing up there shouting at each other and they both are huge . . . they didn't like each other very well and they were all cutting each other down terribly . . . the frightening part was these two gorillas at each other's throats and it really grew into great hostility.

It may be significant that this is also the only participant interviewed who expressed sensitivity to the real hostility behind some of the faculty debates during that first cycle, particularly between these two teachers, and who was one of the three choosing not to repeat the Program. Another participant from the second cycle who would also choose not to repeat the Program said of the lectures that they sometimes

> seemed to be more their just arguing back and forth with each other than a presentation of useful material for the students . . . I [was] not too interested in that. I tend to kind of remove myself a little bit from the situation and maybe write letters or have half an ear and sit in the back row and write letters to friends (laughs).

Some former students spoke about not always being totally attentive to the lectures, but found benefits in them nonetheless. One woman said the lectures were

> entertaining and stimulating and interesting on the whole. There was a lot of chemistry between all the professors so that it was really lively. . . . Occasionally I had other things on my mind and wouldn't listen but I'd say, by and large, I found them very stimulating and [they] really got me thinking.

Another woman said she had enjoyed the lectures although "I probably was also spending a fair amount of time at the lectures daydreaming about what else was going on in my life at the time." A couple of other women made references to "teen-age stuff," concern about "who was sitting with whom," as a distraction in the lectures. And one woman remembered the "physicalness of the hall and the smell of the wood."[2]

---

[2] Lectures were held in North Gate Hall. It was designed by John Galen Howard and is another example of the "First Bay Tradition." The wood this woman refers to must be its interior sheathing of Douglas fir (Cerny 1994, 131).

One man from the second cycle who said he remembers the lectures very well even now explains more about how they worked.

> I loved them. I went to every one. I found them very interesting and stimulating. I mean they weren't always great, but it was fun to see these people at work . . . usually one teacher would give the principal lecture and the others would comment and there'd be discussion, and they'd take questions and that was always fascinating to see the interplay between them. They said some things that I remember extremely well, to this day. . . . I knew even . . . as a seventeen or eighteen year old with a reverence for these books and for this culture, that my reverence was probably not the best thing. To hear [these teachers] be somewhat irreverent and take a look askance at the work and see it in a way that a mature person could see it, and that I wasn't able to, that was really helpful to me. And that's what as I recall happened every week in those lectures.

The lectures not only formed an important basis for understanding the readings, they could be linked to the readings through the seminars. Another man from the second cycle, who said that the small seminars, not the lectures, were the high point of the Program for him and the most enjoyable, nonetheless felt that the lectures were

> indispensable to the whole Program because that way different points of debate or different points of view could be brought up to the whole group, argued, presented, and then brought back to the seminar group . . . it provided grist for the mill. You could go in, listen to these pretty smart guys who know what they were talking about—they'd often argue, not always, but often there'd be debate—and somebody could come into the small seminar group and say, "Well, what did you think about what he said?", and that would give a good point of departure for a continuing debate or some more discussion.
>
> So that's why I think that they were important and indispensable, even though there sometimes was a tendency to nod off because somebody's talking at length, you still got the idea of what he said. And it was great because it was like they were doing the work for us, in a sense. They were dissecting whatever it was we were reading, and they said they think this is the main key. Dr. So-and-So would say, "I think this is the main theme." So-and-so, the other guy would say, "Well, that's

important, but I see it differently, and I think something else is the main key." Then you could talk about that later, or write about it later. And they had us work on these journals, so if you heard something in the lecture that you thought really good or really bad, write it up in the journal. And then bring it up and talk about it in the seminars.

These features of the Program were thus integrated: material from the readings was introduced in the lectures; students were asked to write in their journals the thoughts and questions they had about the readings, the lectures, and the seminars; in the seminars, students could then bring up for discussion material from the readings, the lectures, and from their journals. Even if students did not do their journals faithfully, as many did not, the seminars provided a forum for them to discuss questions and points from the lectures and from the readings. The crucial aspects of this system were that each part of this process was intended to be integrated with the others, and that the student was to take an active role in each part, for even though there was not the same degree of discussion in the lectures as there was in the seminars, the lectures were meant to be dealt with in the seminars, journals, and papers, and the tutorials that followed the papers.

Individual lectures often stood out by themselves as well. One man in the second cycle found his memory spurred by the interview.

I'm starting to remember some of the lectures, some of the things that were talked about. There was a fabulous lecture . . . I remember that day being amazed. I don't remember exactly what was said except that [M's] . . . lead-off line was that he was impressed with how much like Dickens *The Autobiography of Malcolm X* was.

This participant also remembered with awe and amusement another professor commenting on *Oedipus Rex*:

If it's been predicted that you'll kill your father and marry your mother, and you're running away to get away from that curse, probably a good rule is "don't kill any old men!"

The lectures drew some criticism from participants for their unevenness. About one quarter of them found the lectures not uniformly good: "I thought occasionally they were brilliant and sometimes they were boring, and sometimes they were thought provoking. I thought they were okay";

"I thought they were great. Some of them were boring as hell, but what else is new." One man from the second cycle found the lectures themselves to be "at times really fascinating and there was a lot going on . . . when the faculty was coming from different points of view." But he also said that

> because they were in such a large group of people there wasn't the open discussion, they tended to be dominated by a few people who were comfortable talking in that situation. . . . I wasn't real comfortable with having my ideas attacked by a huge group of people.

A woman from the second cycle felt "intimidated to ask questions," and said others did as well, following one incident early in the first year in which another student had been criticized by a faculty member for asking a "sophomoric" question. She complained about the unevenness of student discussion.

> We couldn't participate in the discussion very easily. There were some students who would ask perfectly worded, appropriate questions and get answers to them, but it wasn't a dialogue (with students), it wasn't a good, open forum where we could all feel comfortable.

She felt much of the faculty discussion was over the heads of the students but that students' lack of preparation contributed to the lack of discussion.

> Our tendency toward rebellion, and our laziness and all the other things sort of mitigated against comprehending what's going on in the lecture. . . . I think maybe we could have gotten more than we did out of the lectures . . . it was difficult to keep up. . . . We were young and inexperienced and it wasn't easy to enter into . . . it was a hard thing to do [ask a question in the lecture hall] because you didn't have just one professor that you were trying to impress, but you had six, and you had to try to meet their standards. On the other hand, to compensate for that, was the fact that we had this thing called unattended seminars.

Perhaps the best indication of the importance of the lectures to at least some of the students from the first cycle was that some of them continued to attend lectures in the second cycle after they had become students in the upper division.

THE SEMINARS

While the commitment to holding small seminars with a faculty member and a group of students with the purpose of discussing "curricular materials and ideas" was part of the original design of the Program, the implementation of the seminars took some time to work out, even in the second cycle. After attrition eventually brought down the group of students from 150 to around 90, that meant 15 students in each seminar, which Tussman thought too many. And he thought that one seminar a week was not enough. Groups of seven or eight students meeting twice a week, once with and once without the faculty member, seemed more appropriate, he decided, although that number was changed again to 10 or 11. Neither Tussman nor the other faculty were clear from the beginning about either the size of the seminars or just how they would work—that evolved over time. Nonetheless, more than half the participants from both cycles reported favorable impressions of the regular seminars in the charge of a faculty member. Two from the second cycle thought they were the best part of the Program:

> The small group seminars were the top, best thing, because it was such an intimate, just such a close, unpretentious interchange between students and teachers—not artificial, not distant, and easy or casual, comfortable, unstilted.
>
> I think those were the best part because the ideas were really interesting, the format was interesting, the things that the students came up with.

Several others, from both cycles, thought they were good or enjoyable or "really enjoyable." One liked them better than the lectures:

> More chance for interaction among the people and sharing of ideas . . . a better opportunity to find out what really went on behind people's thoughts and ideas and approaches.

Another who felt the lectures a waste of time, thought some of the seminars "were wonderful, I just remember them as being very intense intellectual experiences that taught me a lot." One woman enjoyed the seminars but felt they could have "had more hours. It wasn't a huge commitment in terms of the amount of actual classroom time—I know I would have been happy with more."

A man from the second cycle appreciated the way the seminars focused on the work of the Program.

> I really liked them. I don't know if I talked too much, I probably did. I do recall that among the first readings we did were the Platonic-Socratic dialogues, and I recall trying consciously and conscientiously to be Socratic in my way of participating in the dialogues, really trying to see the point, to see where we were going, to build logically from one step to the next, to go with the digression but then to bring it back and relate it to the main point. . . . I know that I had a good time, discussing things, hearing other people's viewpoints.
>
> What was nice was that there was a sense of immediacy about the work. In other words, you weren't taking a test, and you weren't being graded, and you weren't being judged for your work in the seminar. The point of the seminar, the people meeting at whatever time, in whatever room, was really to discuss the work. . . . I had other seminars in other classes in which . . . you see people trying to shine, to make points with the teacher, to outdo their colleagues in the discussion. There wasn't much of that in the discussion groups that I was in [in the Program]. There was no reward for doing it, except having done it.

One man from the first cycle who remembered the seminars with "real good feelings about them" also remembered feeling very comfortable even though there

> were a few students who were definitely stronger academically than I was, definitely sort of more intellectual types. . . . I remember feeling very intimidated intellectually by the group [but] I don't ever remember feeling afraid to open my mouth.

Other participants from the same cycle who thought the seminars were good, still complained that some people tended to dominate them. One man felt that "it wasn't as valuable to me when people let the students take a little more charge. If there was a little more direction, I found that to be more valuable." One woman thought her satisfaction with the seminars depended on who was leading it and that although she felt pretty confident writing, she didn't feel that confident talking:

> I do remember there were a couple of students who were really very glib and they would sort of take over, and then the T.A. or prof was usually so grateful to have someone with who they could really have a good dialogue. I can certainly appreciate that in retrospect. But then the rest of us would sit there like big dummies.

Apparently the degree of individual satisfaction with the seminars often hinged on whether the student was able to participate freely or not, and on the quality of the participation of other students.

This uneven quality of the seminars persisted in the second cycle. One woman, although she felt the seminars were good, thought

> some of us weren't really as prepared as we could have been both in terms of studying or getting ready before we went to the seminars, or just kind of academically and emotionally ready for it. Sometimes I thought they were just a waste of time because people just were babbling—it wasn't terribly meaningful discussion sometimes.

A man who thought they were good, and enjoyed them because "I thought they were a good way to get into issues and to learn," said the seminars were something that he'd never really experienced before, and that must have been true for most of the students in the Program.

Other participants from both cycles gave the seminars mixed grades, and sometimes dissatisfaction was linked to faculty leadership. Some thought they were "pretty good, depending on who [which professor] you had." Another said, "Depending. In some groups, the professor was the one who really did most of the talking and others of them really wanted to have the students do more of the talking and thinking." One man from the first cycle thought the bridge between the ideas presented in the lectures to the students' daily lives was not successfully made, that "much of the process was strained." Another first-cycle man complained that in the seminars

> we sort of sat around talking about how we all reacted to having read Hobbes' *Leviathan* or *The Iliad* and so forth, rather than working seriously with people who knew the subject on poetic text analysis.

(This man obviously disagreed with the man from the second cycle quoted earlier who appreciated the fact that the Program did not deal with such topics as poetic text analysis, "what meter did he use?" but asked instead "what does Milton have to say to me now?")

Another man from this first cycle compared his feelings about the lectures and the seminars:

> I looked forward to the lectures and looked forward less to the seminars because at the time I didn't know how much I could bring to the discussion. I think I might be able to now if we did the stuff again, and probably would look forward to it more now if I really took it as seriously as I should have.

This suggestion of lingering feelings of guilt over not having participated to the fullest in all aspects of the Program surfaced from time to time during the interviews in relation to almost every one of its features.

Half a dozen participants, all from the second cycle and mainly, but not exclusively women, talked about their feelings of inadequacy in seminar discussions. Some of their comments were:

> I remember being very nervous when no one would say anything . . . for periods in these seminars. I didn't know quite how to handle the dynamics in a seminar group.

> I wish there would have been some way that we could have participated more in them—they were mostly like little lectures as I recall. And the professor was really doing eighty percent of the talking. There were a couple of students who were on a level where they could provide feedback and some interaction [but] I think the rest of us sort of sat there with our mouths open.

> I didn't particularly like the seminars because it's a small group of people and you're more out in the open. I'm sort of a shy person so I found them more difficult.

> I remember feeling a bit put on the spot . . . I don't have a vivid recollection of the seminars other than to say that I was probably fairly reticent in my contribution in the seminars.

> I really did feel it difficult to take part in the seminars and to offer my own opinions and to listen to other people's opinions and be able to

assimilate and share those kinds of things. I did feel the seminars were difficult.

One woman found participation difficult in both seminars, with faculty present and without, although she felt the direction supplied by the faculty member in the regular seminar made it easier for her to have "something to hang on to, and that I could develop."

Clearly, the seminars did not work equally well for each student, and many felt they were not able to take advantage of them because they felt constrained. Since it was rare for entering students to have had previous training in seminar participation, and it seems fair to surmise that faculty had very little if any training in leading seminars as well, they apparently became a hit-and-miss affair, satisfying when they succeeded and disappointing and frustrating when they didn't. Student satisfaction with the seminars in the Program seemed to depend to a large degree on whether or not the student was able to participate freely, and on the quality of participation of other students, and those might have been linked to faculty skills in directing student participation. The great potential of this teaching device, especially when integrated with the lectures and "unattended" seminars, was realized only part of the time in the Program. This points out the benefit for both faculty and students in receiving training in the giving and taking of seminars for this form of teaching and learning to become more uniformly effective.

THE "UNATTENDED" SEMINAR

The "unattended" seminar was the name applied by some participants in the study to the weekly meeting of the same students from the regular seminar, minus the faculty member, intended to shift the educational "burdens and responsibilities" from faculty member to student. These regularly scheduled "unattended" seminars were held in addition to weekly seminars led by a faculty member. No one from the first cycle could remember anything definitive about seminars without faculty present, so it is assumed they were not a regular part of that cycle. All further remarks here about the unattended seminar refer to events taking place during the second cycle.

The unattended seminar drew very mixed responses. At their very best, they represented an unusual opportunity for students to take charge of their own education. One man reported enjoying them so much he attended others than the one assigned to him. Another spoke of the usefulness of the seminars and felt the most important thing about them was

> that you can get yourself out on a limb, explore ideas and not feel uncomfortable about doing that . . . it taught you, in a protected environment, how to argue. It's like putting you in a swimming pool and then going out in the Bay to swim and you can swim in the Bay because they taught you to do it in the swimming pool.

Others mentioned the freedom they experienced in these seminars of not having to impress a professor. Some mentioned the seriousness of the discussions. One said, "I don't think there was ever a bad faith seminar." Another expressed surprise

> at how well they went. You wouldn't really digress into talking about social activities. They did tend to focus on course work [with which] you were involved. It certainly gave a lot of students a chance to come up with their own ideas that perhaps they had not been able to get out in other seminars.

Another felt they were better than the attended seminar and that although they

> sometimes went off on tangents, most of the time they stayed on top of . . . they were usually pretty good and a lot of times very productive and challenging.

One man emphasized the importance to the success of the unattended seminar of keeping up with the journal.

> If you were regularly doing the journal, regularly thinking about what you were reading, you were developing things, and you would get into the habit of discussing them on paper and that made it much easier for you to talk about it. It built a habit of conversation, of civilized discourse, talking seriously about serious subjects, on your own, without anybody there to tell you whether you were doing well or not. . . . In retrospect, I'd say unless people were working regularly on their journals, it didn't work very well.

According to participants, there were sometimes digressions where "people would talk about baseball and all kinds of things that had nothing to do with the seminar, but sometimes they would get back on the topic." One woman thought they were mixed, sometimes good, sometimes not so good, but that even when there were a number of people who didn't say much, "there was always someone who stepped forward." She felt "frustrated when sometimes they didn't work, and fascinated when they did." Another woman remembered that she herself was more active in some than in others, and that

> it took a while for it to be productive, for us to sort of figure out how to handle it, and some groups figured it out faster than others.... I think it was a good experience to have [that] responsibility, but it wasn't always successful.

Criticisms of the unattended seminar focused on two aspects: the tendency for students to digress from the assigned task of discussing issues from the readings and lectures and "attended" seminars and their journals; and the tendency for some students to monopolize the discussions. In contrast to the man quoted earlier who said it was surprising how well it worked, how students took it seriously, one woman said, "You'd be surprised at the number of people who don't really want to just talk about ideas." One man described the unattended seminars as

> sometimes good, but it was often the case that students let them degenerate into a bull session about nothing that had anything to do with the Program.... I can remember several occasions a couple of people would be hobnobbing about what they did at the shopping mall and it would be a real drag on the effort of the students. Students who were trying to really conduct the business of the seminar would have to either ignore these people, or try to tell them to be quiet, or to get involved....
> I was often disappointed with the non-faculty seminar because in my memory they often just wandered off into oblivion ... they often became like cocktail parties ... just gossip.
> There's a logical progression from Thucydides to how many times the cops thumped somebody down in Sproul Hall last night. You can actually branch from the one thing to the other through a whole series of things, but when it would get to that point, people would get emotional about it: "Somebody got hurt last night and we're upset about it," so

they'd talk about that. There was a lot of lost time, and I really feel that our time may have been better spent if we'd had all faculty guided seminars.

Both the attended and unattended seminars were difficult for another woman who reported that it was hard for her to relate to other people in the Program, socially as well as intellectually, and that that made it hard for her to participate in the seminars, particularly the unattended seminar. She was quoted earlier as saying the direction supplied by the faculty member in the regular seminar gave her "something to hang on to" that she could then develop, and that aspect was missing from the unattended seminar. Another woman thought that rather than "leaving the group alone to have their discussion, [it would have been better] if there were a teaching assistant to lead that discussion." However, she hastened to add,

> but still having all the other closer contact with the professors that you don't normally get otherwise—that's what makes it unique—I'd say, keep that, just inject a little teaching assistant element into it.

The hit-and-miss quality of the seminars was described by one woman:

> There wasn't a leader, so if somebody did emerge, sometimes you became a victim of that person. But more often it was a shared kind of thing. It was a big thing to be asking us to do, and yet I remember it as a good thing. If we took it seriously at all, which a lot of people didn't—a lot really conked out on this. But if you really tried to hang in there and figure out how to do it, it was great for skill strengthening. We began to learn how to lead seminars, and how to figure out what kind of issues you did want to grapple with.

One begins to suspect that some amount of satisfaction with the unattended seminars may have had to do with which students did the talking. One man actually said the best of the "leaderless" seminars was a fairly small one in which he was "forcefully talking all the time."

Although he was not necessarily the only one talking in that particular seminar, one woman thought it was not good if one person dominated a seminar.

> One person could just get carried away . . . some kids just aren't ready to take that responsibility, to lead their own discussions without a person watching them.

She also reported having had some seminar training in high school in advanced placement classes in history and English, and that that had been helpful to her in college. It becomes clear, then, that the unattended seminars were sometimes very successful and sometimes not at all, and that the hit-and-miss quality in part was a result of the fact that students in the Program received no training or preparation for them. Their success seemed to depend on the group dynamics of each individual seminar, who participated actively, who monopolized the discussion, who digressed into material not relevant to the Program.

It is interesting to note that while there were no discernible differences between men and women in how they responded to the various features of the Program we have discussed so far, there were more favorable comments from men about the unattended seminar, and more unfavorable comments from women. It is hard to know from these interviews whether woman felt squelched by men "forcefully talking all the time," or that they found it difficult to speak in discussions where they were not led and supported by faculty. In spite of the variability of their success, however, the unattended seminars held great potential for both men and women for an unusual self-directed educational experience. And it is a woman who offers these observations:

> Sometimes we did get into what was happening in our lives. I remember somebody's boyfriend had just been arrested for draft evasion. We spent some time in the seminar talking about that, and I think we tried to relate it, but that was fair enough, I thought. In some ways they were a joke some of the time because we were so kind of bad at it, and wasted a lot of time, and goofed around. But I still think that the idea of it, and the discipline of it . . . was a good exercise in trying to get ourselves to take some responsibility for our own education.
>
> There might have been ways to help us more, to give us some guidelines, or some expectations, or something to have made it a little bit more accountable. But I can still remember some of those conversations. What was set up to be possible for us was to really grapple with some issues that might be important to us. It was an opportunity to take conversation seriously and to be peers to one another.

When they worked, obviously, the unattended seminars could be intensely rewarding, and when they didn't, they were time wasted. They seemed to be subject to the same fault as the "attended" seminars did—the tyranny of the few over the many. But as an educational experience, there may have had to have been room for error in order for learning and development to take place. Perhaps the process of "figuring it out" was as useful educationally to students as the eventually successful end product. As one man put it, "It was an experiment. I don't know how else they would have done it." Yet one wonders if more guidance, some amount of training, some attention by the faculty to just how the groups were operating, some accountability, some direction in terms of allowing for, or perhaps even insistence on, a more even distribution of discussion, and stress on the importance of the journal to the unattended seminar would not have helped these earnest students to more easily and successfully realize this unique opportunity for self-directed learning.

THE PAPERS

Writing was an important part of the Program from the beginning. Tussman says "we expected to assign a paper every two or three weeks . . . the student should be steadily under the necessity of bringing his work to careful expression . . . we thought of it as a useful pedagogic tool, as revealing the student's mind and as providing a basis for helpful analysis and criticism." That goal of students writing papers regularly was not fully achieved during the first cycle when students ended up writing "nine or 10 papers on average, with some writing more. The length varied, some students averaging 4-5 pages, others 10-15 pages. The range in quality was from unusually good to very poor" (Tussman 1971, 83-5). As mentioned earlier, papers and tutorials became more regularized during the second cycle when the goal became about five each quarter. (Examples of some titles include: "The Case Against Satan: The Problem of Knowledge"; "The Individual as the State Writ Small"; "The Iliad and Today: Social Change and Human Stability"; "Leviathan: Conscience and Law.")

According to study participants, the papers were definitely the most successful of the writing assignments that included journals and an intellectual autobiography as well. Half of the participants thought the papers were a good, or important, or even a crucial aspect of the Program.

One man from the second cycle explains exactly how important writing papers was to understanding the readings.

> I liked the papers. The papers really helped me to clarify my thinking, clarify whatever theme it was that seemed important in what we were reading. They would usually give a writing assignment clear enough so that you could focus on some theme or subject. You had to identify as best you could what you thought the reading was saying about that theme, and then what you think about what it says. After writing the paper, I would have a much clearer idea of what it was that I thought it said in the reading, and what I thought about what it said. Without the writing, I wouldn't have had that opportunity. The writing was very, very helpful and really very crucial to getting the most out of the reading because it made me analyze the reading and it made me clarify my own thinking.
>
> If you have to make a statement, you have to think something through, and you have a better understanding of it. You may not understand it thoroughly but at least you've attacked it. Not all my papers were terrific but they all forced me to grapple with it [the reading]. That was the real big key to the whole thing.

Another man saw the usefulness of the papers in the integration of the material presented.

> The papers were the best exercise to try to get the students to think out and digest what had been going on for that week, or that two weeks ... what we were talking about was all pretty theoretical. It wasn't like taking a botany class where you've got genus and species and everything's identified and set out and ordered. It really was a nebulous subject we had—Western Civilization—for God's sake! I mean it's a pretty broad concept and at the time, I thought that I was doing a pretty good job of pulling together a number of elusive concepts.

One woman remembered the papers "made me really have to think"; another that they were "a good exercise in analytical writing." Others spoke about the skills they acquired in the process of writing the papers and going over them with the teachers in the Program:

> One of the best features of the Program was that we had to write all these papers. The writing in this quantity and with the close reading that we

got, that the teachers gave to these papers, I don't think you'd see in almost any other setting in the University except in an English class. It was wonderful. I think it was [Professor N] who worked with me on my style and diction, and said, "Look, this is a bad sentence."

Another man developed writing skills in the Program that served him not only throughout the rest of his education but in the writing that he does now:

In retrospect, they [the papers] were crucial. I realized it was an important exercise and I struggled with it. I did learn a lot of very good writing skills. I thought I knew how to write when I came in here [the Program] just because I knew what a semicolon was. And then they taught me the use and abuse of the semicolon, the virtue of the short phrase. One of the books that was required reading that wasn't on the [formal reading] list was Strunk and White. They made us all get it; it's a wonderful book. It stood me in good stead throughout my education and throughout everything I do, and half of what I do now is write.

Learning grammar through writing papers was important to another participant who wished faculty had been more demanding in this regard. She saw the full value of the writing only later, but that the papers were a

"good exercise . . . some of the professors reviewed them more for content, some would give you the content and then they'd go the extra mile and really get on your grammar and diction and stuff. I wish they would have sat on me more, I really do. I probably wouldn't have said that at the time, but to be honest, I mean you don't realize the value of it when you're doing it—something to do with your age. I wish somebody would have sat on me in terms of content and form in writing.

A man from the first cycle shows how the encouragement of faculty was helpful in doing the writing assignments.

[We] generally got favorable feedback, and I enjoyed having the freedom—we read a book and we could write about any aspect we wanted, and that I really enjoyed. And the fact that the judgments were fairly noncritical—you put forth an idea and there was encouragement in the sense that they responded favorably. So it was easier to write.

Another man from the first cycle also spoke of the freedom Program students enjoyed in writing assignments, and how that freedom encouraged creativity:

> The papers were an opportunity to both be a smart ass and be creative. I have almost all my papers I wrote in the Tussman Program. I've probably written thousands of papers, but I would say, of all the papers I wrote, I probably have almost all the Tussman and very little of anything else. Because I poured myself into them. It was the descent into the self.
>
> I remember my favorites. I did an analysis of the *Odyssey* and the *Iliad* in iambic pentameter. It was about twenty pages long. It was great because [Professor C] read it and said, "This is brilliant but your syntax is off. Let me tell you where your beat is off." And I didn't know what the hell iambic pentameter was—I was doing it as a lark. I remember writing a paper about the Supreme Court justices and their relevance to Rousseau's *Social Contract* variations and similarities. And I know that I made use of what I wrote in the Program to help me in the "free" [outside] class that I took.

A woman from the second cycle stressed the amount of writing required in the Program, and how that effected her writing skills.

> There was a fair amount of creative writing that I learned doing the papers. I enjoy writing in general, and to tell you the truth, when I was looking through these same old groups of papers . . . I didn't recognize them as having been my own. I'm not sure I could write a cohesive statement today. . . . I think if I had not done the Program, I doubt very much that I would have done as much writing as I did in that first two years. Compared to the roommates that I had at the time who were doing general ed courses, [they did] not nearly [that] amount of writing. There would be in English courses, but there wouldn't be in the philosophy course, say. I think doing a lot of writing definitely improves your skills. . . . I think it did improve my writing skills.

Another woman observed that the degree of writing in the Program did presume a certain amount of ability and motivation on the part of students.

> It did require a fair amount of self-motivation, self-starting and self-completing abilities in terms of writing. If it was an agonizing thing

> each time I think it would have been overwhelming . . . I don't know if the Program was set up to handle a situation like that. I did get my papers in. I don't know what happened to people who didn't. Maybe that's what happened to the other seventy-five (who dropped out). . . . I think it would have been very hard for a student who was really struggling with writing to get through.

While the intended purpose of the subject-A requirement was to prevent students from having to take an additional noncredit class along with the other credit course, another unintended consequence might have been to screen out students who might have had real difficulties with the writing assignments.

Students sometimes submitted poetry or plays on the assigned topic, and all were accepted. One man from the first cycle also stressed the importance of this flexibility in the writing assignments and how the relationship between the student and the teacher affected student writing.

> It seemed like the faculty were tolerant of one coming up with any kind of research or writing as long as it was sincere and relevant to the material and I felt that was a good thing. It seemed like it was good for a lot of people. And it was challenging—people worked hard on them. I've always had difficulty writing papers, so I resisted a lot, but I have the memory of one semester's paper having really worked out well for me. I think it was based on rapport with the faculty member.

And another first-cycle man explains the importance of the faculty attention to the papers in evaluating students' work.

> The papers were challenging. The critiques of them were good. The teachers who reviewed them spent some time going through them. It just wasn't a quick review. They looked and tried to evaluate our progress as students as well as the ideas we were expressing. It wasn't just for an academic grade. It was getting in to them, the materials themselves.

Many participants found the papers to be challenging and enjoyable, and some found them challenging and perhaps not so enjoyable. One first-cycle man, who now teaches writing to college students, needed more help in structuring his paper-writing, but did not seek it from his teachers in the program.

> I could have used a little more direction on the papers. As a freshman, I know now that I was not that good at framing a topic. I didn't realize how to do it until I got through school. I appreciate the spirit of freedom they were trying to engender in us but at the time they might have helped some of us with a little more direction. I take some responsibility for that because I could have said, "Well, what should I write about?" I didn't jump up and go in for individual conferences and say, "Help me figure out what I'm going to write about in this paper." The individual conferences were always available to you, though I didn't take advantage of it.

One woman in the second cycle, viewed the papers as necessary even though not enjoyable, and did not give them her best effort:

> I think they were horrible (laughs). I don't think I was one of the best students in the Program because I think that my papers might have been more simplistic than they should have been. I don't know why. I think it was probably because my mind was elsewhere on other things. I didn't particularly like the papers [but] I think they were useful to bring the material together.

A few participants did not remember anything at all about the papers, and a few, all from the first-cycle, were critical. They reflected the absence of regularly scheduled papers and conferences, a serious shortcoming of the first cycle. One first cycle participant, however, thought they were frivolous.

> I didn't think much of them—I thought those papers were kind of fun and games, studying some work of some historical significance and then slopping together something of your personal reactions to it.

Another felt "the assignments were not always well thought out. Perhaps more short papers might have been [better]. Certainly . . . shorter writing assignments might have helped people's writing." One woman said she suffered from the lack of regularly scheduled papers and tutorials in the first cycle, and she, too, did not seek more help from faculty. She expressed

> disappointment with the papers, especially since the teachers supposedly had more time. I didn't mind having only one paper for each semester or quarter, but I felt a lot of the times the teachers really didn't do that much

with the papers.... I remember getting very little help with the writing. ... I'm not good at imposing on people so if I didn't get it right away, then I wouldn't get it.

Since Tussman has said that about five papers were to be assigned each quarter and by extrapolating that figure, probably about seven or eight each semester, this participant definitely was given short shrift in her writing assignments, another indication of the lack of cohesion in the first cycle.

During the second cycle, with regular and frequently assigned papers and tutorials, the papers assumed greater importance and became a more universally effective teaching device. Students actually could feel they had produced a body of work, perhaps a kind of a portfolio, so it is no surprise that many participants mentioned having saved their copies of them all these years. Two of the participants, both men from the second cycle, volunteered to bring me their collected papers to aid in my research. And copies of all the papers students submitted during both cycles of the Program are still on file in Tussman's office, and could one day form the basis of a further inquiry into student intellectual development during this crucial period in their educational careers.

TUTORIALS

The major purpose of the tutorials was for students to discuss their papers with faculty. According to both Tussman and participants in the study, during the first cycle of the Program they were handled in a rather haphazard fashion—not regularly scheduled, and more or less arranged on the demand of either the student or a faculty member, varying, sometimes widely, from professor to professor. By the second semester of the first year of the second cycle, however, a new system was instituted. Students were assigned papers to write regularly every two weeks; they brought two copies of each paper to their scheduled tutorials every two weeks, one for their professors and one for them. The professor and the student then read each paper together.

The following are all comments from participants from the second cycle. A woman remembered tutorials with [Professor M]:

He and I used to take walks up to the pool, and we used to go over the papers that way. I remember sitting down—it was neat to have this professor spending all this individual time with students. I enjoyed that. It was almost a fatherly type of attention. In some ways it was the ideal way of teaching, this one-to-one, going over the papers to improve the writing.

One man reported his tutorials with enthusiasm.

> They were just the greatest times for me. . . . The close reading [of the papers] that we got, I don't think you'd see in almost any other setting in the University except in an English class. It's wonderful. [N] worked with me on my style and diction . . . I think they were really good.

This rare kind of individual attention was not always easy for every student to accept. One woman felt undeserving.

> Sometimes I felt like I was getting such royal treatment for such a (laughs), such a very—I just felt that I didn't deserve this. I felt I was just still stumbling over my thoughts in my writing and to have such great attention—because I never really had that close attention before with my writing. So it made me a little overwhelmed by that attention. And I really appreciated it and benefited a lot by having someone really go over my paper like that and talk it over with them.
> I never had quite that again, really. I mean, I wished I could have had it later on, too (laughs), when I felt my thoughts and abilities had developed a little more. But it was so nice to have that connection with professors. You had to meet them on so many other levels, but to finally have that one-on-one contact with their mind and your mind I thought was really quite unique for an undergraduate. I think I took advantage of it as best I could."

Another woman said that she considered the tutorials only as "useful," but that may have been because of her anxiety.

> I think looking back from now to then, I see that I tended to [put the professor] way up on a pedestal, get through it as quickly as possible and leave, rather than as a participatory—getting in there, really use this person, and take charge of my own education—kind of thing. So I think it was, "little old student and here's the big professor" . . . I never had anything like that before in school, an individual tutorial. I'd always just

get the papers back from the teacher a week later with a grade on it. And this was going over the work, dissecting it. So it was useful.

One man, among others, was aware of the uniqueness of having individual attention from faculty.

> The tutorials varied—they depended on the professor. Useful and important, but not as crucial as the papers or the seminars. But very important because there's no place else to get that kind of feedback and that's one of the things that contributed greatly to the writing.

One man who thought the tutorials were "excellent" at the same time repeated the theme of the unworthiness of the student.

> They were always a little scary . . . I was never really satisfied with my papers . . . I didn't think they were worth really talking about. But I do recall that I thought it was a good thing to have the attention of this teacher to me, for this hour. I learned some things in those discussions. I can't say I enjoyed them—they were a little too scary for a kid to be with the professor for an hour, and to wonder if you're boring this great mind.
> So they weren't anything I ever looked forward to. But they were just fine. I mean I didn't want to get rid of them—I strongly believed that this was part of this kind of program. . . . It was just that I was never very proud of my work and didn't really want to have it analyzed by someone whose mental processes were sharper than mine (laughs).

One man made the distinction between tutorials focused on his "performance" and those focused on the subject matter. Though in general he thought they were fine,

> They weren't really as terrific as they might have been [when] they didn't really deal with the subject matter, they dealt with me. . . . And [when] we actually talked about one or more of the issues of the subject matter of the course, we got into an actual debate about one of the points, one of the philosophical points of our subject, and I thought that was great.

Since he was the only participant to make this difference in emphasis between personal performance and the subject matter, presumably that was the exception rather than the rule.

The tutorials then could be used for broader purposes other than to simply review and criticize students' writing and to track their intellectual progress. One-to-one faculty-student debates on the subject matter were possible in this setting, and sometimes stretched to include other aspects of the Program. As described earlier, one woman used a tutorial to challenge a particular professor's interpretation of the very conduct of the tutorial itself; another woman's tutorial, at the professor's instigation, turned into a debate, an intense "row," about the relationship between political values and political actions. Students could discuss personal matters that they would have been unable to discuss in anything other than a private setting such as this. One woman who lived at home while in the Program reported being able to talk to Professor J and explain how the pull from home, where she still lived, was affecting her work. Tussman says in his first book about the Program (Tussman 1969, 86) that the conference, as he calls it, "inevitable makes the faculty member aware of a frightening range of problems, most of which he is not professionally prepared to face and all of which have a bearing on the student's education." There was no indication, however, from participants in the study that students used these tutorials as personal counseling sessions. On the contrary, some did mention that need and wished there had been a place in the Program to serve it.

Tutorials in the Program helped to break down the common myth of the inaccessible and uninterested professor. One man in the second cycle said he learned through tutorials how to approach professors in the rest of the university:

> Something I hadn't touched on earlier is the tutorial we had here. There are so few freshmen in the university that ever have a chance to sit down with a faculty member and have his undivided attention for an hour—throughout an entire course, much less do this every two weeks—and have to be prepared when you come in with your paper. . . . That had a big value I think, for some students, in terms of realizing who faculty members were. They were people you could talk to. It certainly helped me in terms of my university career in . . . pushing my foot through the door, making myself be known to other professors, other class instructors. It gave me the experience. . . .
>
> Certainly a unique opportunity within the university system to have that much time devoted to a lowly freshman or sophomore. One of the things you learn in a university system is how to fight for faculty time. And to have it presented to you, if you were not either intimidated or

awed by the situation, or just the reverse of that, very belligerent towards it, which there were some people who had that attitude, it could be very rewarding. It certainly made you feel more important, which is a problem students have in the university. That you were given this time and consideration, care, by a full-time professor. Because you learn later on in the university, the people who give you your full time care, if you can get that, are usually your graduate assistants—faculty members rarely.

When the method of scheduling conferences was introduced during the second cycle, another kind of problem then apparently arose for some students: a few participants thought the tutorials were stressful for them. One second-cycle woman says about the tutorials:

> I just remember always being, especially with some faculty members, seeming apprehensive beforehand. And usually feeling pretty relieved and relaxed afterwards. It was never terrifying, but sometimes just stressful. And especially if I didn't feel real good about the paper I was turning in.

Another woman, although finding the tutorials stressful, also found them helpful in gaining confidence in her ability to rise to the challenge they presented:

> The way that writing was evaluated was kind of stressful in the beginning. We used to turn in two [copies of the] papers and meet with our faculty member, a different one each quarter for the six quarters, and we would have to sit down and read a paper aloud to the faculty member. And those were professors, you know—there weren't T.A.s—so they were risky, stressful.
> I never really felt that I was in danger of getting kicked out, but I felt I was really exposing myself and that it was kind of scary to do that at the beginning. It depended a little bit on the professor. Some were easier to do that with than others. I actually have all my papers. I don't know how much difference there was in the papers from the beginning to the end as much as in my confidence, my feelings of self-confidence in being able to go in there and read it [to the professor] and understand what I had written.

That so many of the second- cycle participants remembered the tutorials as being "overwhelming" and "scary" at the same time they thought they were "really good" and "important" may offer possible clues as to why in the first cycle, when they were not regularly scheduled and were often left up to the initiative of the student, fewer took advantage of them. The theme of student "unworthiness" runs throughout these interviews and appeared to be the biggest obstacle many students had to overcome in order to make the most of that opportunity. Scheduling them rather than leaving them up to student initiative succeeded in getting students into the habit of doing them, regardless of their insecurities. "Stressful" or "risky" as they may have been to some, they did provide opportunities to gain confidence in being able to deal with their work in a one-to-one relationship with a faculty member—a kind of an academic "Outward Bound" experience many of them would not have undertaken on their own.

THE JOURNAL

In addition to writing papers every two weeks, students were expected to keep a daily journal. The journal was not to be a personal diary, but was supposed to represent ideas growing out of the reading, discussion, or lecture. According to Tussman (1969, 133), it "should be a page or two which develops some idea raised by the reading or in seminar or lecture. The log is to be available for faculty scrutiny on appropriate occasions"—apparently during tutorials.

Some participants remembered doing the journal faithfully and finding it valuable, some did it sporadically, some didn't do it at all, and some don't remember anything about the journal or whether or not they did it. There seemed to be no sanctions for not doing the journal, and few participants reported any teacher actually asking to see the journal—perhaps the expected "appropriate occasions" were too vague and did not often present themselves. Although it was intended to be an integral part of the Program, an opportunity for students to form the habit of writing down their ideas emanating from the readings, lectures and seminars, it was not routinely attended to by faculty apparently, or by many of the students.

The lack of sanctions for not fulfilling this requirement was evidently not replaced by inner motivation in most cases. One man said that he kept a journal off and on, and only now realizes the value of it.

> Maybe I did 35, 40 percent of the work that was expected of a journal . . . I argued that I would prefer to spend the time talking with someone.

> ... There were periods when I would go for a couple of months writing every day. I'd look back at this, and say this is doing me no good whatsoever. I got less out of this compared to what else I could be doing with my time at this point. I don't think it was ever enforced. There was no one really standing over you making you do this. It was assumed you were doing it.
>
> It was supposed to be part of your daily intellectual life. Sitting down, taking half an hour or an hour and focusing on an idea, trying to really develop it. It was not meant to be filled with poetry or short stories. It was supposed to be something at least evolved from the basic coursework. The idea being that when you finally do evolve your writing style, [you'd have learned] how to take, let's say, two pages worth of journal and form it into a paragraph. Let the journal be the free form flow of these ideas, then sit back, look at it, tighten it up, and finally come up with the idea presented in a more terse and sensible way. . . .
>
> [It was just that] at that point I felt constrained by it. I did not like this. Instead, I'd go down and see my friend [in the Program] and start talking about the ideas that I was trying to write down, and we'd just have an oral journal. Maybe I should have taken a tape recorder along. . . . I can see now the value—Joe wanted us to learn how to write as a discipline. Something you have to do as part of your education. And I certainly feel like I sort of missed the boat on that—not realizing that early on.

When students did use the journal, however, they usually remember finding it useful, sometimes very much so. Participants testified earlier how important the journal could be to the successful operation of the unattended seminar. The journals also could have value in and of themselves. One man who later majored in journalism spoke of the communication skills he acquired in the Program.

> [They were due to Tussman] forcing you to write all the time. It allowed me to think, to articulate my views and think about something and have to write it down on paper. We did a lot more writing than anybody I know [outside the Program] in that two years. And I think that was important. I think that helped me a lot. When you do write, particularly keeping a journal, you had to actually write down your point of view and make it into something comprehensible, rather than it just churning

around in your head, "Yeah, I'm in favor of People's Park[3] because everybody else is." You can't just write that, you really have to sit down and justify it.

Another man spoke of the self-discipline required and described the journal as

tricky. I kind of drifted in and out of it over the two years. When I did it and kept on it, it was very rewarding. I could see the evolution of my thinking over a period of time. On the other hand, I really had a lot of trouble disciplining myself to do it for long periods. It was expected that you would discuss the journal in the tutorials, and every so often that would be the focus of the discussion. But after awhile that kind of got dropped, it fell by the wayside. Occasionally there would be hortatory statements from the faculty: "you will do this; don't forget the journal; we haven't dropped this." But it really wasn't pursued very heavily.

Many participants had only hazy memories of the journal.

I can't say I did it daily. Well, a couple of times a week, I'd try to write something out. I thought those were pretty good. I think the major advantage of that is that it just gets you into the habit of writing stuff down, but I don't think I ever went back over it. I presume I brought those journals along [to the tutorials] and that we'd talk about things.

The journal was useful . . . we probably talked about them during the tutorials.

I do remember trying to write in the journal something that had to do with what we were studying, but I didn't write in it every day like we were supposed to.

I think we had to turn our journals in. Ever so often have them [faculty] look them over. But I don't remember discussing . . . unless they saw something they wanted to talk about.

It appears that the assignment of writing in the journal daily, just as in the case of the unattended seminars, was a potentially very useful part of the

---

[3]See Appendix C, 1969.

Program, but one that needed some amount of preparation, training, and tracking in order for that potential to be reached. One woman said the journal was the

> least emphasized thing. I think there were very few students who really kept it properly. And professors would forget to ask for it. You wrote it all the night before, you know. [They should have taken] it seriously. I think they would have had to work at it. They would have had to give us some tools, some ways to develop that as a discipline, rather than just tell us to do it. And because we had the papers we were writing as the real focus of the tutorials, there wasn't any real reason for using the journal.

One man also complained about the lack of direction from faculty for fulfilling this requirement.

> I did it a little bit, and then fell off. Keeping journals, my God, that's a fantastic tool. I didn't do it, I was too young. It wasn't made clear to me . . . I didn't know why it was so important or why it could be valuable to keep a journal. I did it *pro forma* because occasionally the teacher asked to see it [but] I didn't even [remember] if they did. I think that it felt artificial to me, and I just didn't want to put the time into it.

While most students seemed to have understood clearly the intended role of the journals in the intellectual life of the Program, it is not certain that everyone did. One woman says that while she enjoyed doing the journals, she was

> acutely embarrassed by them when I read them, after the fact. There was almost a stream-of-consciousness kind of stuff about what was going on. I remember I was writing in my journal at the time when Robert Kennedy had been killed. I guess [that] just had to be written down, but it was embarrassing looking back at it, all the feeling, the emotion that was there. I think I was also writing some stuff about my lack of being able to participate in seminars. . . . My recollection is that nobody read the journals. I would have changed what I wrote quite a bit if I'd known that somebody was going to read them.

Perhaps the fact that some students did use the journal for personal, rather than intellectual ruminations might have served to put off faculty from asking to read them, producing a circular effect: when students came to believe that their teachers would not read their journals, some then made such personal entries so unconnected to the Program that faculty would see them as unconnected to the intellectual work of the Program and perhaps also be embarrassed to read them. At the same time, the usefulness of the journals even in this personal way had a meaning to some students apart from their academic intentions. One woman thought the journal "was a really important part of the Program," and that she still keeps a journal as a form of self-expression. Another woman did not remember doing a journal in the Program, but has kept them since, and guesses that may have been because of the Program. One man from the second cycle explains how the idea of doing a journal began in the Program, and how important keeping a journal has become to him since.

> The journal's been real important. Indirectly that was another emotional outlet that had emotional benefits. . . . It was a seed that just . . . that I struggled with like everybody else while I was here [in the Program], and probably got serious about the moment I left. Although I did keep a sporadic journal while I was here.
>
> It saved my life. I really attribute the reflection that I was able to generate to that. It took me through a number of crises of a personal, family nature. [It provided] a reflective space . . . the journal's always been a free space for me to be myself to write and develop what styles and interests that I have where I haven't had to conflict or compete.
>
> I renewed a friendship [by means of] my journal style of writing. My reflective style, my own writing style needed an audience. It was bubbling out. I renewed a friendship with a good friend whom I have known since I was eight years old. I started to write and address issues we had left when we were eighteen or nineteen. Our friendship renewed itself based on the style I developed [from the journal writing in the Program] which became psychological. I've gotten very interested in Jungian psychology, archetypal, mythological stuff, which I attribute to coming right from the Greeks—the way the Program handled the Greek experience. I was able to use that stuff, that was the connection.

The difficulties many students had in keeping their journals may have been connected to the theme of "unworthiness" expressed by some participants in their discussions of the papers and the tutorials. If they felt awed that these respected professors would take time and effort to read their papers, and to talk with them about their papers, they may have felt it to be even more risky to present faculty with such unformed thoughts as may have been recorded in their journals. It certainly seems possible that this feature of the Program could have been more useful to more students if faculty had regularly asked to read them, giving them the same kind of attention they did to student papers.

The one participant quoted earlier who had found keeping a journal in which he developed his thoughts about the readings indispensable to the success of the unattended seminar had certainly made the best use of both of these features. The journal and the unattended seminar were the two features of the Program students carried out without any faculty supervision or even observation. They therefore required a certain amount of motivation on their part that was apparently not universally shared by all Program students. Again, some amount of faculty guidance or coaching from time to time might have helped them learn how use the journals to enable them to develop ideas, as this participant said he did, to discuss them on paper, and then in the seminars to talk "seriously about serious subjects, on [their] own, without anybody there to tell [them] whether [they] were doing well or not."

THE INTELLECTUAL AUTOBIOGRAPHY

This is the most obscure of all the Program's features in the memories of participants. Tussman does not mention it in his writings about the Program—all the information about it comes from the interviews. One aspect of the intellectual autobiography is clear, however: in both cycles it was the last piece of writing required at the end of the two-year Program. It was apparently meant to represent a culmination of student thinking about the curriculum over the two years, but the exact nature of this requirement is unclear. It was remembered, if at all, by more first-cycle participants than second, and it may not have existed at all in the second cycle, or have changed in character. For the few who did remember doing it, the intellectual autobiography varied widely in its perceived value.

Almost all of the comments come from first cycle participants. One man recalled needing prodding to finish his.

> As I remember it was something that should have been done over a period of time and that I really didn't do it. Then I think it was [G] who said,

"Get it to me when you get it done." Then I buckled down and did it and it was fine and I passed.

Other participants were more critical of this requirement. One said, "That one really struck me as ill conceived." Another was somewhat cynical:

> It was a logical, kind of an obvious, unimaginative idea. I got a little bit of the impression at the time that Joe wanted us to write a story about how we had been converted to his philosophy of life. . . . That's what I thought then. I don't know now (laughs).

A woman from the first cycle connected her difficulties with the intellectual autobiography with the general developmental level of second-year students.

> It was a real problem for me . . . maybe that's what's adding this tone of "not really regret," but something of [the tone of] "not quite grasped." Because I think that the sense was that this should sum up your experience in the Program. . . . How you understand your thinking, whenever you started until now. And it was a really tough thing to do. This is not a confessional thing, like "I used to like to roller skate." This was your *intellectual* autobiography.
>
> And I actually think it was—now this is the first time I've thought of this—but I think it was [Professor A's] lack of psychological mindedness that created this mistimed and misplaced assignment. I don't think sophomores at the University of California at Berkeley in 1966, after all the kafluey that was going on in both the culture at large and the community in general, were in the remotest reasonable position to make this kind of assessment. I don't think developmentally you are. But certainly historically we weren't. . . . I'm not sure I would be able to write that paper until I was in my twilight years and the dust had really settled.

Perhaps this woman sensed the very difficulty in assessing an educational experience too close to the time it was experienced that any evaluation of the Program as a whole was subject to. Indeed, it might be useful to find out how Program graduates would deal with this kind of requirement now that the "dust had really settled." Implicit in the difficulties she experienced with the intellectual autobiography, however, was her judgment about how her views fit in with the "message" of the Program, probably what the man quoted earlier meant when he referred to being converted to [Professor A's] "philosophy of life," and the conflict she felt about those views:

> I think [Professor A] was very anxious . . . with the Vietnam stuff . . . It wasn't whether the war was good or bad in Vietnam. It was if you're a citizen, you have a commitment to uphold your duties as a citizen and that everybody can't decide if they like the wars or not. You have to go to war. That's probably being simplistic, but it was not so far off. . . . And I think that people [in the Program] were in great conflict about that in particular . . . I think he asked the wrong thing at the wrong time.

Another man who also found the intellectual autobiography "difficult," also thought he was not ready for such an assignment.

> That intellectual autobiography felt a bit much. It felt premature to be able to—I didn't feel that developed intellectually. It felt like you had to write your dissertation. I could understand writing an autobiography . . . but to put it into an abstract form of, "what are the fruits of these two years in an intellectual sense?," felt kind of foreign to me. I didn't have a way to put it all together . . . so I didn't really like it. It was too big a project. It was [the part] of the Program that I least liked.

Not all comments about the intellectual autobiography were negative. One man compared writing it to writing a resume.

> To me it was more important than doing a resume. I can remember when all the kids were doing resumes, we were doing intellectual biographies, which is nice.

And for one participant in the study, the assignment to do the intellectual autobiography may have been confusing at first, but over time it has come to have more meaning for him.

> Now I can see all this stuff in retrospect. They gave us *The Education of Henry Adams* to read, and that was supposed to [be a] model for us. Now that I think about it, it was an intellectual biography. I read it, but it didn't dawn on me that that's the model. I don't mean we had to

follow it in structure and organization, but I mean, this is the *kind* of thing you do when you write one.

So I just gave them a journey through my thoughts, the ones that were salient in my mind at the time. I didn't feel negatively about it, and after I finished I felt positive [about it because] it gave me a chance to think deeply about—and find out what I really thought—about things that I would not have probably disciplined myself to think about if I had not been forced to. The thoughts would have been there in some amorphous, uncongealed way, and this forced me to congeal these things and figure out exactly what I felt and why. I still have it, and it is interesting to go back to read, because it does give me a point of reference. I say, "How was I feeling then about these things?" I thought it was good self-disclosure if nothing else. I'm glad that we wrote it, but at the time I didn't have strong [negative or positive] feelings about it.

There are some signs that by the time of the second cycle the intellectual autobiography had been dropped as a requirement, or this final requirement had changed in character. Only two participants remembered anything at all about this last assignment. One of them spoke quite positively about other aspects of the Program, but recalled the intellectual autobiography with

> a sense of unease . . . because I wasn't really working on it. I didn't feel inspired to write an intellectual biography. I don't know why. It wasn't coming easily to me, and it wasn't something that I wanted to do. I did it as a rather *pro forma* fulfillment of the requirement. It wasn't a satisfying assignment for me. It was just a chore. I recall another student in the Program wrote quite a long thing, dozens of pages. He'd been working on it for quite a long time, weeks and weeks, and he was pleased with his effort. . . . In the end, I don't think I did it well.

The other one had quite a dramatic response to what he called his "final paper": "It changed my life . . . although I wasn't aware of it at the time." According to him, this requirement was

> "the graduating thesis," and the assignment was to "write a paper about community and why support it. . . . I realized . . . suddenly that what we had been studying over two years were different forms of community. . . . I remember *very* clearly knowing that I had gotten the point of the Tussman Program. . . . This is my definition of "getting it,"

what they had been leading us up to over this two year period was ... at the end of this time to have some idea of what your notion of community was and how a community should work.

(The way this "big lesson" in community affected his life is further described in the chapter on major impacts of the Program.)

It is possible that this "final paper," or "graduating thesis" replaced the intellectual autobiography of the first cycle, or that it was an additional requirement—the exact details of both requirements have become murky over time. No other second-cycle participants could remember anything about that last assignment—even the man just quoted could remember almost nothing about what he wrote in his paper, only the impact it had on him.

Both of these last two writing assignments certainly were of potential pedagogical value, particularly the journal as it connected with the readings and helped the unattended seminar to function more successfully. But participants have also said the final paper, whether an intellectual autobiography or summation on the concept of community, has been helpful to them in "life after the Program." However, both the journal and the intellectual autobiography seemed to require self scrutiny, an internalized sense of discipline and a degree of developmental maturity that was largely beyond the capabilities of most of the students in the Program, judging from those interviewed for this study. In both cases, it is possible that students could have been more successful with these writing assignments if they had had more guidance or training in conceptualizing them and in carrying them out. They had in all probability never before been asked to do either an intellectual journal or an intellectual autobiography, and unlike the papers regularly required and regularly commented on by faculty, the autobiography was a one-time assignment, asked for only at the end of the two years, and the journal, while it was to be a daily task, was apparently not read by faculty, at least on any kind of regular basis.

With each of these assignments, students had virtually no comments of any kind from faculty along the way, unlike the steady flow of comments on their papers. And since they were highly personal in nature, they presumably had no chance to discuss them in any kind of formal way, as they did their thoughts about and reactions to the readings, which could be discussed in seminars and tutorials. Being more personal in nature, they were probably not expected to be discussed informally. One wonders if a tutorial assigned entirely to the intellectual autobiography, as well as questions asked routinely in the regular tutorials about how the journals related to the papers, would have helped "socialize" students' tentative responses to these two requirements and allowed them to test out faculty reaction. Simple outlines, or examples, or one-page summaries might have helped students learn if they were on the right track, before committing themselves to the entire assignment.

THE INTEGRATION OF PEDAGOGICAL FEATURES

Looking at what participants had to say about them, we see how the Program was supported by its various features. The readings, the lectures, seminars both with faculty present and without, the papers, the tutorials, the journal, and to a lesser extent, the intellectual autobiography formed a web of intellectual activity within this special academic community that served to stimulate and to reinforce student learning. The variety of learning opportunities open to students catered to a diversity of learning styles available to a wide spectrum of student interests and abilities.

The fact that all students and faculty alike shared the common curriculum was a crucial starting point. Faculty teaching together in the lectures and dividing up the work of the seminars and tutorials represented an effort at team teaching in the best sense, allowing students to benefit both from the collective presentation of curricular material and from the individual teaching styles and expertise of faculty members. Giving students opportunities to discuss the reading and lecture material in seminars, challenging them to deal with this material on their own in the "unattended" seminars, insisting that they grapple with the material in their papers and their face to face meetings with faculty, and affording them opportunities for informal discussions with faculty and other students at the House led to a more thorough integration of the curricular material than the usual lecture-notes-exam routine. That the whole of the Program could be greater than the sum of its parts—the reading, lectures, seminars, papers, tutorials, the journal—is suggested by this woman who said,

> I just had a good, solid warm feeling about it [the Program]. I was glad that I was in it and I never would have considered not completing it even though there were times when I felt insecure or anxious about the writing and anxious about the seminar or maybe bored with the lecture or

struggling with the material. [But] that was never to the extent that I didn't feel good about being in the Program.

Testimony about the effectiveness or lack of its various features, however, tells only part of the story. An equally important part consists of the judgments of the participants of the effects of the Program on their lives, and the long-range impact of the Program as a whole. They comprise, in a sense, the results of the experiment—what do participants say about whether or not and how it worked. It is that question we turn to next.

THE RESULTS

CHAPTER 6

The Major Impact on the Lives of its Participants

Now that we know about the students, the faculty, the House in which it all took place, and how the Program worked through its various educational features, we can turn our attention to what participants said the Program has meant to them in the course of their lives. In order to look at the long-term effects of the Program, we asked participants if they would repeat the Program again if they had the chance to, and if they had any regrets about having done it in the first place. We also asked them what they believed to be the major impact of the Program on their lives.

"WOULD YOU DO IT AGAIN?"

A tally of the answers to the question, "Would you do it again?," revealed an overwhelming majority, 37 of the 40, answering "yes" in one form or another. That category of positive responses included "Yes! I would love to do it again with the experience I have now," "Yes, if they improved it a little (by offering help in choosing a major)," "You bet!" and "Yes, I would absolutely do it again." Included in the category of positive responses were three people who qualified their answers as "probably."

Three of the 40 people interviewed would not repeat the Program. Two were definite; another said "I don't know, probably not." They were two women and one man; two people were from the first cycle and one from the second. There was no discernible pattern of reasons for not wishing to repeat the Program—in each case there was a different explanation. One thought his participation in the Program had prevented him from taking other courses that would have provided him with a more thorough education. One was the participant who reported the unfortunate encounter with Dr. Z. that was discussed in the chapter on faculty, although that was not given explicitly as a reason not to repeat the Program. Two of the three thought their entire undergraduate experiences at Berkeley had been unsatisfactory and they would have been better off attending small, liberal arts colleges. The only reactions the three had in common were that they were all uncomfortable with faculty arguments, all expressed some degree of dissatisfaction with not having grades—accountability, as some expressed it—and all wished for more structure in the Program. None of them gave these as reasons for not wanting to repeat the Program, but rather as overall criticisms of it.

"DO YOU HAVE ANY REGRETS?"

Even fewer participants had any regrets about having been in the Program. In answer to the question, "Do you have any regrets about having been in the Program?," all 39 participants who were asked answered "no" or "none," including two of the three participants who said they would not do the Program again. The third participant who would not repeat the Program had many regrets about having been in the Program, including complaints about not learning how to read, how to write, how to think critically—in direct contrast with the majority of participants who thought the way the Program taught them these skills was among its greatest strengths. But even this participant saw some good parts to it, and suggested changes for its improvement.[1]

---

[1] The interviews, and particularly the questions about repeating the Program, regrets, and proposed changes, elicited two other kinds of general unsolicited comments. These had to do with the revival of the Program. Several participants said they hoped the Program would be tried again and hoped this study would be a part of that process. Two of them expressed an interest in starting or helping to start an Experimental College Program of their own. Several others said they hoped their own children could participate in such a Program, and some said they hoped the Program would be revived in time. This generative dimension as an outcome of the Program experience was unexpected but should not be surprising

THE MAJOR IMPACT OF THE PROGRAM

While responses to these two questions offer a brief, overall assessment of participants' views of the Program, they by no means give the full story of the impact and effects it had on them. Interviews opened with the question, "What has been the major impact of the Program on your life?" The answers to that question drew the most extensive responses of the interview schedule and usually revealed the participants' predominate views of the Program. Other questions about the gains and benefits of the Program, what they learned and, what changes they experienced—as well as spontaneous comments throughout the open-ended interviews—produced more information about the impact of the Program and are included here.

The reported effects of the Program were are sometimes simple and direct, sometimes subtle and diffuse. They were often mixed with effects of other aspects of their lives and formed part of what one participant called the "tapestry" of his life. Several participants expressed certain aspects of self-selection to the Program that served to minimize its influence on their lives. One woman said: "I came to the Tussman Program with a certain set of political and social values that I think maybe were shaped slightly and intensified." Sometimes they began their answers with a disclaimer—"I don't know about the impact"—but then went on to talk about some pronounced effects.

Sometimes their statements approached eloquence; sometimes they struggled to express ideas not easily put into words. Because I feel it is important for the reader to have a first-hand sense of just how the participants responded to the interview as a whole, to the questions asked, and to the spirit in which the interviews were conducted, the answers to that first question will be presented here preliminary to an analysis of their meanings and implications. Although the interviews were not conducted in any particular order, they will be grouped for presentation here by cycle and by gender, in order to allow for differences between these groups, where they do exist, to emerge. They are quoted here, in their edited form and presented in order of the first cycle first, women first.

---

in view of its mostly positive effects according to participants and is perhaps connected both to its long-range impact and to its developmental intent.

FIRST-CYCLE WOMEN

For one woman who has had an academic career and is now raising young children, the most important aspect of the Program was the role it played in her intellectual awakening. It helped her to define herself in terms of her intellectual orientation and goals, something she did not experience in other parts of the university as an undergraduate. In answer to the question about the greatest impact of the Program on her life, she said:

> I realized that I enjoyed intellectual pursuits. It was something that I got out of it personally. It wasn't just to go to school and get a good grade, but there was something more interesting beyond that. . . . I went to graduate school . . . I think, partly as a result of the Program . . . as opposed to the other classes I took at Berkeley where I kind of floundered, not knowing what to major in and so on . . . but the notion that my thoughts were important, had some validity. . . . And when you wrote something about the *Iliad*, you wrote what you thought, you didn't use secondary sources. . . . There wasn't a right or wrong answer. There were answers that contributed to understanding whatever it was we were studying.

She compared the relative influences of the sorority and of the Program on her life and described how the Program came to be more important to her and helped her to pull her life together.

> I think I had some mixed feelings about being in the sorority and it [the Program] somehow helped me compensate for it a little bit in my own mind—the stereotypical sorority person, not a very serious student, only social. I didn't see myself as only that kind of person. I think it helped me see myself more whole.
>
> I was continually experiencing a culture shock every day of being in the sorority and being in the Tussman Program. In fact, after the Program was over, my sophomore year, I moved out of the sorority. In a sense, my life became more integrated but much more on the Tussman model than the sorority model. It's like if I had had to choose between which world I was going to put my feet into, that's where I put my feet—the Tussman side.

Another woman, a lawyer, also stressed the intellectual impact of the Program on her intellectual life, and how it taught her to think for herself.

Her testimony reveals how Program effects were often realized only after it was over.

> I think it was a terrific advantage that we were taught from primary sources rather than secondary sources. Rather than reading what somebody else thought about Euripides you actually sat down and read it first and thought about it yourself. . . . I think it makes a much better approach to education, to first actually read material, think about it, put it together with other material, before someone who is a scholar says, "Well, what this really means is so and so, and the ways things fit together is here." Because unless you can do some of that fitting together yourself, you're never really going to learn. . . . I think that it is a much better educational base to put the things together yourself, to learn how to put them together yourself and write about them than to just take different classes where they're kind of artificially joined. . . .
>
> I think that it became more apparent to me later on, when I got my degree in political science because then, in the third and fourth year, I was working more in the secondary sources and having somebody tell you what it means and really thinking a lot of the time, "Well, you know, they don't know any better than I do, and they are guessing, and this is based on sort of, their opinion." And I think that it wasn't until much later that I was really appreciative to have spent that time reading certain things. . . . [I would have said I was learning] how to think. I think that's what education is supposed to be, how to think for yourself.

Learning to be an independent thinker was of primary importance to this next woman, a teacher, as well as the responsibility she learned to take for her own education:

> I think for me, it was the realization that things at school weren't going to be nearly as prescribed as they had been in high school, and it was being forced to be independent and be an independent thinker. I look back . . . and that was a real shock to me. The requirements weren't as clear-cut as they had been in high school and we were given a tremendous amount of time to be studying independently. And that was at the time a tremendous adjustment for me, the lack of structure. But looking back on it, I think that probably had the greatest impact, learning how to make choices about how I would spend my time. . . . There wasn't any way of really checking on whether you were going to do the work or not, and realizing that I ultimately had to take charge of my own learning.

The Program had another major impact for her that she did not recognize until she entered the upper division.

> I remember a number of [history] professors [in the upper division] that we had small groups with whom I did establish relationships. Maybe it just took me a while to learn how to do that. Maybe I did figure it out because I do remember participating fully, much more fully than I had in my first two years, and feeling confident. Maybe it was my experience in the Tussman Program that made me feel that way. Because when I look back on the history seminars, with a number of the history professors, I remember feeling very much like, "I can do this. This is no problem."
>
> I've never thought about it before, but I remember myself in the Tussman Program very differently than I remember myself as an upper division history student. I think there must have been [an effect]. If nothing else, then by osmosis I realized somewhere in my unconscious that this is how you're gonna get what's going on, you know, this is how you're going to make the most use of it. And when you had the opportunity . . . I can remember specific history seminars . . . that were really quite similar to the Tussman Program, but I wasn't similar anymore—I had grown.

This carry-over effect of confidence in relating to university professors in the upper division was reported by other participants, both men and women.

A professional woman, a social worker taking time out to raise young children, spoke of gaining confidence in herself in the Program, as well as broadening her perspective educationally. She mentioned of the feeling of security the Program provided beginning freshmen.

> Probably without the Program I never would have looked at some of the areas that the Program covered, some of the fields of knowledge . . . studying the Greeks. I think it gave me a broader perspective than I probably ever would have had, maybe opened up things a lot more for me then, than might have been the case if I'd just taken the regular required courses and looked for a major. So it might have just broadened the way I looked at things. . . .
>
> I think it made the beginning of Berkeley a lot easier than it might have been otherwise, too. Just thinking back on it, I know I was real excited about going to school, but I was anxious, too, because I had an

older sister who hadn't done very well academically, initially, although she went back and finished and did fine. Her freshman year she had trouble and so I assumed, just assumed I would have trouble, too, because I knew she was smarter than I was. I think that I gained a lot more confidence than I might have had otherwise [if I had not been] in the Program. I think that we felt like we were sort of special somehow, and they made us feel that way, which was nice, in that big atmosphere of Berkeley.

In explaining how the Program gave her a good start with her university education, and with the rest of her adult life as well, she said:

> My efforts were encouraged and rewarded and recognized. I think I liked all the other classes I had at Berkeley [but] in some of the larger classes I didn't have much of a sense of how I was doing then with grades and stuff. If what I was thinking and . . . the things I was learning were worth[while]—if I was doing what I was supposed to be doing. [In the Program] I don't think that anybody was put down or anything. I think that we were all given the feeling that what we thought was important and valued and somehow that it was special. We were special.
> It really gave me a feeling of success right early on, which was really helpful. . . . It helped me at Berkeley just to feel that I was doing okay. That I could manage all right; that I wasn't going to fail. It was a good experience. To continue to feel like "I can do this and I can do that." That progressed. I think it would have been a good beginning to the rest of my adult life. To feel that I could succeed and think. . . .
> It gave me an idea of how to learn things really, I guess, more than anything had. By looking at particular areas and how people have done it over—and how the Greeks did it and how they did it in seventeenth century England and what man thought about it and how they looked at problems—the way to look at learning things.

The program helped another woman, who had an older sister with whom she could compare her educational experiences, escape the adjustment problems that her sister had had to deal with at Berkeley.

> I went in to college knowing I'd be a science major, so I suppose there are a lot of things I would have missed without [the Program]. I would have taken sort of the bare requirements and then just gotten into science. And sometimes I'm not sure how I would have adjusted, just going to college, going to a place that was that big and being that anonymous. I'm *sure* it

helped in that sense. My sister had a lot of trouble in adjusting to the University. She ended up quitting after a couple of years. I never felt that . . . lost. And I always thought that it probably made a big difference to me. It gave me more of a sense of belonging; it was somewhere to go. I wasn't just some number in a big lecture hall all the time. So I think that helped.

A sense of belonging to something identifiable, a smaller community within the larger university, helped give this woman the feeling of confidence she felt she needed to successfully complete her undergraduate education following her older sister's failure.

The Program gave her a boost with her choice of majors. Although three others in the study, all women, ended up in professional fields requiring a science background (optometry and psychiatry), and one man majored in math, she was the only participant interviewed who actually started out in math or science. Having made a commitment to major in science before she entered Berkeley and before she signed up for the Program, she took her extra outside course work in science, and went to summer school, in order to keep up with her requirements. She spoke of an attitude of condescension toward nonscientists she found common among scientists, and how the Program worked in her case to prevent her from narrowing her views of nonscientists.

> I know a lot of people in sciences or math or engineering who have that feeling that "that's it." That's where all the smart people are, and all the people who do other things do them because they can't do something else [i.e., science]. And I've always thought that because I had more exposure to it, I didn't come away with that kind of a feeling. There are different fields, but it didn't make somebody better to be in one. I mean, someone who's a doctor isn't smarter than someone who does something in literature or history.
>
> I think there is that bias in sciences. We just tend to think that science people are "smarter", and it's the people who couldn't do it [science] who end up doing other things. And I think it's partly because . . . if you take the bare requirements and nothing else, there's often so little exposure to other fields, that people can come away with that kind of idea in their minds. I mean, they just go through life thinking that.

She talked about another, more subtle effect the Program has had on her life. In describing volunteer work she has been doing in her community, she said,

> I don't think I would have tried it otherwise. I suppose that's one way it's [the Program] influenced me, that I've been more willing to try other things. I don't think I would have tried them otherwise. I think I probably would have said, "Oh, no, I can't do that," and not even have tried. This way, at least I say, "Well, I'll try it."

Participants made many comments about how the Program taught them about learning, even if they did not actively participate in discussions in seminars. Another teacher distinguished the curricular content of the Program from the learning process itself:

> [The Program] created an awareness and a real sensitivity to what I feel learning is about. . . . It was rounded, it was integrated in a lot of ways. There were different aspects of learning that were included. . . . I think that the Program affected me a lot in general—in my life, just the way I think, just the way I look at the world, in terms of what freedom is about. And then my choice of being a teacher. . . .
>
> I think my ideal way of being at a university is what I think of as the Tussman Program. . . . Actually, I didn't ever think of that before, but it's just people discussing things and getting all excited about them, and ideas. I just think that was fantastic. And even though I was very shy and didn't participate, I was very excited by all the discussion, about all the different things that were going on.
>
> I think it was very helpful to have the freedom of not having major exams. That made me take learning more seriously and—I'm not sure about the impact—I just think that that's been a theme in my life, thinking about what learning should be and that that's the impact it had . . . I think that the content, although interesting, was less important.

Another professional woman spoke of the stimulating social and intellectual milieu of the Program,

> and discussions lasting well beyond the Program. [It was] intellectually rich and quite exciting. . . . Some of the people ended up continuing to sit in salons and have intellectual discussions for years after the Program. . . . It spanned many, many years. . . .

And speaking of the value to her of the Program later in life, she said; "I don't know if I can say I applied it directly, but it gives me a little ballast." Describing her professional and personal development, she said the Program helped her to grow in "all sorts of ways, absolutely."

For another woman, whose work combines her artistic and business abilities, the Program gave her self confidence in a somewhat different way. It also helped her achieve independence and establish an identity, even though it was through her artistic creativity rather than intellectual endeavors:

> I really hadn't even thought about the Program at all since the day it was over and I walked into my junior year. I would say the major impact would be that I had a sense of it buying me time, personally. When [Professor A] talked about that in one of his first orientations to the whole group of students, that was one of the things that he stressed, that he felt that the Program was really set up to buy us time out of the usual exercises and whatever that had to be done to be part of university life as an undergraduate. And that really hit a button for me. Unfortunately, I don't really think that I used the time very constructively. That was a time of great political ferment and a lot of drug experimentation. . . .
>
> Looking back, I'm seeing how I've structured my life really through trial and error. I've had the freedom and the self-confidence to try, and I think that experiences like the Program really helped strengthen that self-confidence. . . . In the long view perspective of my life, having been involved in something like that does make me feel sort of special and unique. And I treasure that, I value that. Having been part of something that was an experiment to stretch the boundaries of traditional [education] . . . I'm proud of having been a part of that, having tried that. That's something that means something to me. [I would have said I was learning] just to be myself. To find out who I was. [The Program] helped in that it gave me the freedom to flail around.
>
> The Program, through the way it was set up within the University structure, did teach me that you can survive and prosper, perhaps thrive, or at least survive. Making your own choices and wending your own path. I think that was a pretty valuable lesson. I really like to create something from nothing. And certainly the Program was doing that. . . [Professor A] took an idea and made it happen. That really was an act of creation. . . . That kind of energy has always really appealed to me. And the fact that the Program survived and actually went ahead on a second year, and that people are still interested in what happened there. . . . There

was somehow the confidence that I could make something happen for myself even though it's not sort of a normal or at least conventional pattern....

In her efforts to "find herself" she dropped out of the university, although she eventually returned to finish college. She feels that if she had not been in the Program, she would have dropped out sooner, a claim made by others as well.[2]

For another woman who dropped out of Berkeley to marry and raise a family and who did not complete a degree, the Program did not have the same effect in building her self confidence. If anything, the Program may have had the opposite effect, at least at the time.

> The first thing that comes to my mind when I think back about being in the Program is that I always felt so stupid. There were some students who were in there who were—seemed to be so articulate and so smart, and I was totally overwhelmed. Not totally, but I was really overwhelmed. I was real shy. I just can picture it now, a few of the kids totally blew me away by how smart they seemed to be. I was wondering what I was doing there....
>
> I think as the years went by and I looked back, I realized it was just kind of the way I was at that time, at that age. I think it was just a matter of being shy and sort of inarticulate. Not that I have less skills or was less smart or anything. I guess it was just a certain skill that I felt I lacked at the time, which I think over the years, you naturally get more confident as you get older, usually....
>
> I felt a combination of enthusiasm and frustration. Enthusiasm because it was very exciting to be in college, and frustrating because I felt so inarticulate.... I don't know that I have any quarrel with the Program, what went on, I just wish that I had been different.... I had a lot of growing up to do before I went to college that I hadn't done.
>
> I lived at home, and I think that had a lot to do with the way I felt at school. I had to go home every day, and I wasn't able to hang around down here, and be with other people. I would come down to the House, to study—I used to get away from home sometimes, and I enjoyed that a

---

[2]There is some evidence, at least from the first cycle, that students who completed the Program were in fact less likely to quit school and more likely to graduate from Berkeley than students who had been in the regular undergraduate program from the beginning (see Chapter 7).

> whole lot. I just remember the huge meetings downstairs in the big room. I remember [only] one conference I had with one professor. . . . I remember the lectures were interesting and very good. I can't remember any specifics. . . . I don't remember a lot. I don't actually remember all that much about college in general.

Again this woman reported the kind of hesitance about speaking up in the Program that we have heard from other women. Perhaps regular tutorials, as took place in the second cycle, would have helped her overcome some of her reticence. In this case, she dropped out of college after completing the Program, so perhaps there was no opportunity for the "delayed learning" that others talked about in later university years to take place. Living at home, and coming from a cultural tradition that discouraged assertiveness on the part of women, may have been contributing factors.

Summarizing the comments quoted above, first-cycle women reported educational gains in the form of a better understanding of what education is all about, learning to be independent thinkers, becoming intellectually awakened, and gaining more confidence in dealing with the rest of their undergraduate and graduate education. They talked about the sense of security they found in this small program as beginning students in a large university. They testified to the personal gains in self esteem they felt were a result of their participation, with the exception of one who thought she was not mature enough and confident enough at the time of the Program to profit from it. There was little mention of the curriculum, and one woman said that while the content was interesting to her, it was not as important as the process of learning itself.

Turning to the men from the first cycle, we see these themes repeated, together with some new ones.

FIRST-CYCLE MEN

One of the most enthusiastic of the former Program students was a man, now a highly successful business executive, who found the Program had impacts on his life at several levels.

> I would say that my drive for more education . . . was strongly pushed forward by participation in the Tussman Program. I went on to

get my master's and my doctorate, and I lay a lot of that to the support and the motivators that I had working with me in the Program. . . .

I was learning to challenge more than anything else, challenge ideas, challenge patterns. And the Program gave me a way to challenge. What it showed me is that whether I'm talking about the Minoan period, or classical Greek period, or Roman civilization, or whatever, the same fundamental issues were important in each one of them. The same political issues, organizational issues, social issues, inequality issues.

And in attesting to the long-lasting quality of this effect, he said,

In fact, in a way the Tussman Program was like a global village, it was the pre-Marshall McLuhan global village for me, in terms of ideas. Now, the Program to me is like a net, an intellectual net, and it has just stretched over time.

A member of an underrepresented minority group, he experienced gains of a more personal nature as well.

[During the summers] I did a lot of travel. That's one of the single biggest motivators—the Program really motivated me to want to go see all these spots I was reading about. I wanted to go to Delphi, I wanted to go see Seville, I wanted to go to Hamburg, had to go. I had wanderlust then, I've got wanderlust now, and the Program just fortified my wanderlust.

Specific benefits of the Program for him included the encouragement of his creativity, along with the many facets of his life the Program affected in a positive way.

The ability for close interaction with some heavyweights, in terms of faculty, a definite benefit. The opportunity to be a little creative, and perhaps even non-structured in terms of paper writing, that was great. The opportunity to hear some of the classicists and world-acknowledged leaders in their fields give special lectures. . . .

The Program pretty much defined my life the two years I was in it, in terms of social, organizational, and political relationships. Look at it from a political perspective, an economic perspective, a social perspective, an intimate perspective. I don't think there's any perspective that it didn't touch. . . . I don't know any other ways it [my life] could be different.

Another far-reaching effect that the Program had for him had to do with his decision to become a conscientious objector.

> I ran the risk of going to jail for my ideals, and I drew an awful lot upon what I learned in the Program to get me through it. . . . I don't think I would have had the courage or the stamina . . . to have undertaken that process if it hadn't been for the Program.

For many participants, the impact of the Program has come to be felt mainly after the passage of time, as this man, a lawyer in public service, reported.

> I think the major impact has been that it made me appreciate the value of just a general liberal arts education. I'm a strong advocate of that. It's been real instrumental in my views on education. For one thing, I found it very enjoyable. It was not a chore to come to class. And as I look back on the Program and I see so many people who seem to have gotten rather specialized very early in their careers. . . . I think it has made people who are more specialized, a little flatter personally. I think it's important—even if you're not an academician or involved in teaching, but in whatever you do—it's very helpful to have an understanding of history and of philosophy and of civilization. And a lot of people that I run into these days don't have that. And I think that the Experimental College fostered that, and made me understand that.
>
> Maybe not so much when I was actually in the college—I just found it a very enjoyable intellectual experience [then]. But in looking back on it, I realize that it was . . . really a valuable Program. As an undergrad, when I think back on my college course, that's what I think of, really, is the Experimental College. There are one or two courses I took . . . in upper division that I found really enjoyable as well, but they weren't as—I mean, they were just sort of discrete classes.

The format of the Program and its overall educational benefit was its major impact on a psychologist who was close to completing a Ph. D. at the time of the interview.

> I think it's part of the theme of the sort of educational experience I value. I have been a student for so many years—small group processes that feel intimate, where there is a sense of cohesiveness over time.... The desire for the personal in education, it's a piece of that. I think it [the Program] reinforced that desire for small group process and cohesion of people over time.

In trying to assess how his life would have been different had he not been in the Program, he said:

> That's really hard to identify. It's one piece of the tapestry [of my life.] It's more subtle. It could—it's possible ... that it would have taken a real different course. Either I would have dropped out of college, or ended up in Vietnam, or would have stayed in [professional] school, put up with things I didn't like as much. I see possibilities for my life having taken a more negative course.... I was encouraged by [Professor G] to stay in school.... If I'd been thrust into the regular lower division, I think I would have been less pleased with my experience, less motivated to stay in school.

And it is unlikely he would have become close enough to any single professor in the large lower division classes for any kind of personal discussion to take place about his choice of whether or not to stay in school.

Some participants, who had difficulty pin-pointing the specific impact that Program has had on their lives, nonetheless could remember and describe its benefits. One man, who has combined his artistic abilities with a business was sensitive to Tussman's developmental approach to education.

> I was pretty overwhelmed by Berkeley. And my memory is that the Program was a wonderful—it sort of felt like a family—that house ... I remember feeling very comfortable there.... But in terms of the impact—now I don't know what the impact on my life is. I know that at that time it fit in.... If I had to sum it up, the Tussman Program gave me the freedom to ... think more broadly than I might have if I had been studying English 1a and History 1a and Math 1a....
>
> What I remember is ... an attitude that those guys had: "Think for yourself and you can probably do what you want to with your life." I mean, I get this feeling that a lot of what Joe was thinking about had to do with how students develop. I don't think it was just education [in the

> usual sense], it was sort of a lifestyle. I feel that that place generated that. The informality of the thing. The big group meeting. The first name approach to everybody. I think that was a whole package....
>
> I think I did much better, [at Berkeley] generally, having been in that Program than had I not been in the Program. But of course, it's speculation, because, who knows? I'm not sure that I feel I'm being as articulate as I should or could be about what it really meant to be in that Program. ... There was a quality to it ... it was exciting intellectually, and stimulating. It got you thinking.... It was stimulating and at the same time demanding and I don't think I always met those demands.

Another man, a musician and teacher who lives abroad, responded to the curriculum in ways that, in combination with other factors, have influenced his life in an unusual way.

> I got the impression that the dominant theme among the faculty members was an interest in ... [a] philosophy of state, political philosophy, utopias, and so forth ... I think that what I got out of the Program is the tendency to view the world and the human condition on what oneself is involved in from a viewpoint that corresponds to that orientation.
>
> I wonder if the interest in that aspect of society doesn't have a lot to do with the orientation of the Program, or at least that the Program reinforced that type of interest ... because it was explicit that that would be the type of orientation of what we were gonna do.... The orientation of the Program toward a study of, or at least a comprehension of, philosophy of state, and politics in that sense.... I found after several years in [Europe] and several years back in the United States that I simply felt more comfortable in a European parliamentary system with permanent political parties with rather specific, if constantly evolving, political ideologies.... The fact that I feel politically more comfortable in a European parliamentary system may have something to do with the intellectual orientation of the Program.

The theme of the Program "reinforcing" tendencies already present in the attitudes and outlooks of its students is not uncommon, but rarely are the effects so pronounced as to help to shape the outcome of such an important life decision as which country in which to live.

A lawyer, who thought he probably would not choose to repeat the Program, still reported positive, long-lasting effects.

> When I came out of the Program, I had a much greater respect for the importance of political philosophy, for the study of it, than I did when I went in, as a tool for understanding. . . . The study of the present doesn't always tell you a heck of a lot about the future, and often it's good to go way, way back. . . . I've gone more in that direction [the study of history] than in the social science direction in terms of my own approach to things. I think that's certainly one of the things that I got out of the Program. . . .
>
> I feel that participation in the Program gave me a sense of the value of great literature for its own sake; it gave me a sense of the importance of the recurrence of great ideas. . . . It taught me to some extent not to be so concerned with the ideas of the present as they're expressed by the people of the present.
>
> [I would have said at the time I got out of it] a sense of accomplishing in school for my own benefit rather than for grades. . . . I had the sense that whatever I was doing I was doing because, either out of a sense of personal and moral obligation, or with a genuine love of learning. And I thought that was an important attitude to internalize. . . .
>
> Maybe I listen a little bit better than I would have, maybe I'm willing to admit to the relevance . . . to the correctness of somebody who approaches things completely differently.

Some participants claimed they couldn't answer the question about what had been the major impact of the Program on their lives, and, nonetheless, went on to describe significant effects. This man, a college teacher and Ph. D. candidate, and a member of another underrepresented minority group, spoke of the Program's impact on his educational philosophy.

> I couldn't tell you what the major impact has been; it hasn't been so profound that I can articulate it very quickly and easily.
>
> It made me realize that there is some efficacy to interdisciplinary learning and that essentially it is often difficult to separate learning out into these artificially constructed disciplines. That was one thing that I got to appreciate . . . and wish that more of education could be like that.

He went on to describe the value to him of the integrated approach of the Program, which was in fact nondisciplinary rather than interdisciplinary, a common semantic mistake among participants, and how that became apparent to him only after the Program.

I came away with a fuller sense of a period because we looked at a period in a lot of different areas, unlike your normal course which might have looked at Shakespeare in literature, but then not looked at anything else. And that would have been all you would have had of seventeenth century England. . . . I got the theoretical benefit, that there is a benefit to the integration of knowledge. You understand something better when you understand the relationships of knowledge across disciplines as opposed to in isolation. I'm not sure I would have articulated it that way then, but I'm sure that's a benefit that I got because I think I began to see it better later on and so I'm sure that it had that impact on me.

He also appreciated the opportunity to learn in small groups.

The one long-term effect it had—the [appreciation of the] efficacy of small group work. Unlike my other peers, who had these large lectures and small sections, most of my undergraduate work was done in the context of these small groups, with this individual attention. By individual attention I mean we all knew each other individually . . . and the person teaching you is right there. . . .

My tenure at the University was not one with the kind of impersonality that many people have, because I think the impersonality that students encounter tends to take place more in the freshman and sophomore years, because you have these requirements that can only be met in big lecture courses. And because of the Program, I had a minimum of those.

Explaining how his experiences raised his level of awareness in lasting ways in both personal and political situations, he said:

I'm sure the fact that we had to write this little intellectual biography—autobiography—had something to do with a lot of decisions I made. It was the process of having to think, "What do you really think about these things?" forced me to ask myself these hard questions. So a lot of decisions that I made—important decisions about what to do vocationally, what to do after you get out of here—the Program helped me raise, because it forced me to raise them in writing.

I remember when I was in [the Education Abroad Program in a European country] I became much more aware of the political nature of the world, the political arena, of the variety of politics that goes on in the world, and how people try to resolve political problems. I remember thinking to myself: "Most people really don't have what I would call a moral foundation for solving these problems. . . ." I decided most people had no real general universal or fundamental sense of justice. . . . That most of the time what people thought ought to be done did not grow out of some larger conceptual framework. . . . When you see people taking political positions on both sides, even if it's a political position you might happen to agree with at the time, it's not grounded. The popular opinion that expresses itself on that side isn't grounded in anything other than what happens to be the popular way to look at it at that point.

Echoing the participant quoted above about learning how to entertain different points of view, he said:

The Program certainly didn't hurt me in having an appreciation for listening to people from a variety of areas. We certainly heard a lot of people from a variety of disciplines talking about various things that I'm not sure any of us would have necessarily sought out for ourselves. It did give me this sense of seeking—it did start me—and I'm sure that that sense was cultivated by other experiences I had. I can entertain the idea of going to a bookstore to hear an author talk about his works, and it may not be in an area that I've even read anything in . . . it certainly started that.

The gains of the small size and the intimacy of the Program were apparent to one lawyer.

What I was getting out of it was the sense that I was a person within this large student learning institution, as opposed to a number someplace. The people knew me and recognized me and therefore had some degree of caring, knew your work and could comment directly, speak to you directly. . . . If you were ill or something in the Tussman Program, people knew it; if you didn't show up for a couple of days . . . they would ask, "How are you? Were you ill?"

The curriculum was also important to him, sometimes in a personal way.

[I would have said I was] studying the classics more than anything else. . . . I was learning and trying to get some appreciation for why people had so much respect and awe for some of these people that I had read so much about . . . some of the great authors—Plato's theories of the

Republic—what it all meant to be in a democracy. . . . I got a real appreciation for that which I could not have had in a large class. Just because of the interaction and the exchange of ideas. We were reading about Plato's *Republic* and we were indeed acting like one. . . .

I still have a strong appreciation for not only the idea of the Tussman Program and the academics who put it together . . . [but also] what . . . programs like that can teach you. But I also think I have a better understanding and appreciation for the people we studied, the people we read about, the poets. I must confess, with the exception maybe of Plato, I've never gone back to those books, but I still feel like they were part of my growing up, my history. An important part [of what] I felt, at the time and still now, that these authors were my authors in a way. And I appreciate that. It's kind of a personal thing.

Social aspects of the Program were important to men as well as women. One man, now a fundraiser, says the main effect of the Program was to introduce him to people, fellow students and teaching assistants, who became important to him, with whom he is still in touch, who were "some very strong personalities, [who] influenced a lot of things I did, certainly out of college."

In discussing the way in which the Program influenced his political life and philosophy in lasting ways, he said:

I've always been political. [And for all its] emphasis on citizenship and political theory, the Program was not political. You didn't learn a thing about how to run a government or run a campaign. . . . [But in the area of citizenship] there's probably things, issues that I consider, that maybe other people that I deal with don't consider. . . . I think that's probably something I do out of a different sense of citizenship than a lot of people. That's in there and it won't come out. It [the Program] certainly planted an idea. . . . [It is] always going to be there as part of my thinking . . . how I evaluate candidates for office. [I'd say that was] not overwhelming, but leaning toward significant.

Another participant, a computer software designer, expressed difficulty in judging the impact of the Program on his life, and in sorting out its effects from those of the particular period at Berkeley, and of adolescence in general. Although he saw the value of the Program, he wasn't able to take advantage of all the Program had to offer him, largely because of the pull of the political pressures of the times. His comments are worth quoting at length.

> That's a tough question [what the impact of the Program had been for him]. I've had difficulty assessing that question myself. I've asked it of myself many times and the difficulty for me in answering the question is that, number one, I don't personally have anything to compare it to because I didn't go to college anywhere else. I didn't have the experience of being an undergraduate for two years somewhere else. And secondly, it's been difficult for me because the period of time in question was not only difficult for an individual, being adolescent, or being that young, but also it was just tumultuous times. Here at Berkeley and probably, undoubtedly, at many other campuses as well. And I found the experience of undergraduate education at Cal in the mid-sixties to be personally primarily unsatisfactory. I also felt that the University was not really very well structured for undergraduates.
>
> And yet I was in a very isolated program. I was in a program where I was supposedly given individual attention. As I understood it, that was a lot of the reason for why the Program was set up to begin with. Because universities were considered by some people in higher education to be mass factories where educations were cranked out, and that was part of the whole purpose of having an alternative. But I found that I couldn't really escape that experience. The experience of the factory and the experience of the society, really kind of ripping apart. I couldn't, and didn't want to isolate myself from that. And so I experienced the Program as kind of a paradox in that on the surface it was a very well structured way to take me and 149 others out of the mainstream kind of rat race with the first two years of undergraduate education and give them personal attention and some sort of privacy and dignity.
>
> I don't know if it was the fault of the Program in any way but it was more of the fault of the times. I guess . . . what the Program meant to me was that there was someone or some group of people who were concerned about the quality of mass undergraduate education. Concerned enough to use their knowledge and their experience and authority to set up an alternative program. But I also felt, more given the times than anything else, that it was building a sand castle and facing the tide in some way. I wasn't able to really experience it, I think, the way it was intended.
>
> The Program succeeded in isolating me from, I think . . . the pressures of first year English . . . the mass courses given in large . . . anonymous . . . lecture halls by people who've given them year in and year out . . . I was protected from that. I was isolated from that.

And I was given a program that was, I believe, modeled on a Greek kind of Socratic dialogue model. And yet I would walk out of class and I wouldn't have to walk more than fifty feet before I was confronted with students protesting over things some of which I had very strong sympathies with and others I felt were just incredibly destructive and divisive. And that ended up being much more important to me. It made more sense to me. It was more real to me. . . .

My understanding of the higher education in ancient Greece was really basically something for the privileged few. That was an education of reflection and patience and rationality, or rational evaluation. It was like I was seeing it on T.V. . . . where you can see an orchestra, hear the violins but are very aware that [it is] in a little box. It did not succeed in taking me outside of what was going on on campus which was just explosive. I was simply not a focused enough individual at the time to be able to come here and shut that out and say, well, I'm going to be a doctor or go to law school or something.

I believed in this idea which I thought was worth investigating so much that I obviously volunteered for the Program, willingly, and yet I felt in a sense it didn't have a chance. I don't know what kind of traditional structured, reflective educational activity at that time could have had a chance.

I guess, despite what I've said before, that I do have memories of being able to, [for] periods of a few hours, of being able to reflect on ideas and thoughts and things that I've read. . . . I tended to buy into that, how it was presented to us, and I wanted to believe in that. I wanted to believe that this was a liberal education in an old tradition. . . . The experiment was all about . . . going back to an older way and a more traditional way to a broad, so-called liberal education. That had become increasingly difficult in the modern world. I subscribed to that. I like that idea and I wanted that to happen. I believed in that and I would say that to an extent that happened . . . with reservations . . . that the benefits did accrue.

I think in some ways it affirmed a conviction that I already had which maybe I would have got more out of it if it had been something new. But it affirmed in a kind of a beautiful way the possibilities of higher education. . . . I had always been brought up with the belief that the university education was a very rare opportunity to . . . have a little freedom to step out of the grind of life and make some kind of *a priori* kind of convictions. Develop some kind of a foundation for the rest of one's life. I have felt that I didn't do a very good job of that for myself

personally . . . the Program affirmed my conviction that this is real and a
value and is worth pursuing.

This participant, who dropped out of Berkeley after his junior year and did not graduate, described the intense personal and ideological conflicts some students suffered at the time, and he contrasted the mode and meaning of the Program with a strong sense of political urgency. His statements provide a good example how these strains and conflicts made it difficult for some students to accept the Program and reap all the benefits it offered. Although he admitted to less than full participation in the Program, and had criticisms of it which will be discussed later, he nonetheless said, "I can say without reservation that I have no regrets about having done it and that it was positively valuable."

In looking at what these male participants from the first cycle had to say about the effects of the Program, we see that they spoke, as did the women, of educational gains: the importance of liberal education; of nondisciplinary learning; the efficacy of small group work in the Program. The Program kept many of them interested in school and kept them from dropping out.

Men also spoke of the personal value of the Program to them: the feeling of family and security it created; the tolerance of ideas and of individuality it instilled in students. But men in this first cycle also talked of the moral and political education that the Program was about, the education for political vocation: the moral foundations for solving problems of society; for assessing political candidates; for choosing which type of government under which to live.

SECOND-CYCLE WOMEN

Women from the second cycle as well as the first said the opportunity to work from primary sources was an important benefit of the Program. But some also gave evidence of their receptivity to education for responsible citizenship that the Program intended to instill. One woman, a civil servant involved with the interpretation of state laws, attributed her career choice to the Program.

> I learned how to think, and how to read, and how to go to primary sources for information, which I feel has given me something of the real

McCoy attitude in terms of how I evaluate what is good reading material.

> The other major impact has been it was part of a process in which . . . I learned to value institutions in our society . . . and I don't say that they shouldn't be changed . . . but I think from the Tussman Program I learned to value the contribution that institutions make to the social fabric and I've chosen to work within . . . as a career, to be in State service.

She went on to testify to the ways in which values acquired in the Program interacted with other values she'd held previously.

> I was also very influenced by the Catholic institutions that I attended, Catholic schools. . . . I was very impressed that one of the philosophers that Joseph Tussman had with him was . . . a Catholic priest. . . . I don't think I was very much aware of it at the time, but on reflection I'd say I have held on to that philosophy in my life . . . that religious values are important. He had other philosophies represented, but I thought that was particularly important since there is the selection of philosophical frameworks around which to hang your life experiences, you know, there's Nietzsche, I mean there's a lot to choose from. Anyway, that was influential in my life, and I'm happy with it (laughs). . . . What I'm saying is it guided me, my respect for institutions made me look upon them as a resource in life. I chose a career—it's a vocation to me, to choose an institution to be a part of. It was a good thing.

We find women emphasizing not only learning to think independently and to use primary sources, but the opportunity there for students to assume responsibility for their own education, learning to treat each other, and not just faculty members, as part of their own educational community. One woman, who has an advanced degree in theology and whose work involves teaching and community service found these all to be benefits, some of them lasting ones.

> Writing the papers and doing the tutorials, that discipline. . . . It helped us to think for ourselves, because all of the writing we were doing, all of the papers we were doing, was an integration of material that we were reading and not a lot of research and quoting other people's material, so we were much more relying on our own reaction to materials than really any courses I've taken since. . . . It really forced us, in a way that

most undergraduates are not, to think for ourselves. Even though there was a very strong bias in what we were reading, in one direction, still the discipline was to think for ourselves. And then the way that was followed through was through the papers and the tutorials, and that was a real good way of learning. Very challenging and stimulating. . . . My first inclination [now] is to do my own integrating rather than to find out from somebody else how to choose or synthesize material.

The other thing that's been very valuable—two other things—was the emphasis on writing, which for me was real important . . . and the other thing was in the unattended seminars . . . the idea of it, the discipline of it, was a good exercise in trying to get ourselves to take some responsibility for our own education, for our own conversation . . . it was an opportunity to take conversation seriously . . . and to be peers to one another. . . . There's no question that directions for the future came out of the Program . . . I think it was one of the best decisions I could have made for my education. I think it compensated for the disadvantages of Berkeley, while still giving us the advantages of Berkeley, meeting people from all over the world. . . . I am very grateful.

In attesting to the lasting effects of the Program, she said:

I feel the foundation . . . in law and the nature of government, of society, of man, is all useful. I didn't go along with it in the form that we got it, but the questions are still *the* questions.

A librarian answered the question about the major impact in terms of the emphasis in the Program on reading for ideas rather than to pass tests, and the value to her of the coherence of the curriculum and the integration of teaching methods that became apparent to her only after she finished the Program.

One thing that really sticks with me from the Program which is one of their intentions was to learn to read for ideas rather than to answer questions on a test. And I think they succeeded in that with me. I learned how to integrate my reading and my thinking and my writing and my speaking because so many—so much of school you don't often get to do all those things at once. At the time, I don't know [what I would have said about what I was learning]. I think its hard to get a perspective on what you're doing when you're right in the middle of it. . . . As for what exactly I was learning, I couldn't say, "I'm learning English or I'm learning history" . . . it was all blended together.

There was another way in which the Program's introduction to higher education afforded her advantages throughout her lifetime:

> It's such a big campus and having that closer circumstance really made it a lot easier . . . it really helped ease me into the whole environment and in that respect it had an effect on my college experience which then had a positive effect on me now.

A medical practitioner spoke of the value the Program had for her at a critical time in her development precisely because she did not go on in humanities or social sciences, as well as long-lasting effects on her ability to think critically.

> The content, the great books, the Western civilization content is obviously very important to me. I was exposed to the thinkers . . . in a depth that I certainly haven't looked at before. . . . I feel it enriched my life and my perspective on things . . . the ability to think through a problem in its breadth . . . and [to get across] my point of view more effectively. . . . That's the age when one [develops] I think, in college. . . .
>
> I have to say that I think I'm a little more circumspect and a little more critical about reading things, about interpreting the news, about discussing things with people than I might have been. Than might be if I hadn't had that experience in the Tussman Program. In fact . . . I think I probably am a little more critical in my thinking. I might not jump on bandwagons quite as fast.

She said the Program, while not the only source of social contacts to which beginning students had recourse, nonetheless offered them a kind of haven and focus of identity, as we heard earlier from the woman who belonged to a sorority.

> The goal that I had of having a smaller unit within the University and the sense of community that I felt was a real benefit. It wasn't my only contacts, my only social life on the campus; on the other hand it was real important. I think it gave a sense of security and feeling of belonging and a place to be, socially and personally, psychologically, that was really a benefit.

This theme of the Program providing a kind of educational sanctuary for beginning students within the hurly-burly and confusion of the larger university was repeated many times over. The teacher and community organizer already quoted above said,

> In some ways it was comforting and nurturing. And that was something that I needed as a freshman. I think it's very easy to get lost in a big place like Berkeley. . . . [It was] a utopia of a learning situation.

The owner of a small business talked about how the setting of the Program within the larger university, "the best of both worlds," made it unique and particularly valuable as she realized fully only later when she got to the upper division at Berkeley.

> This was a great model . . . it's important to have some kind of cohesion and some kind of structure for kids as they enter. I think it's a confusing world, the college . . . I guess if anyone pays attention to what this is all about, I think there's a real place for a program like this within a large university. . . .
>
> The major impact was probably not real evident to me until I went into the second two years of college and I started comparing what other people's experience had been with their first two years. I felt like I had the best of both worlds. I had a small college situation within a very large one. So I had all the stimulation of what was going on at Berkeley at a time which was very exciting for me. I came from a high school of 500 kids [in the Bay Area]. It was college prep but it was Catholic, and to come into a place with a lot of foreign students, a lot of excitement, that was great for me. I didn't feel lost in the system. I had a real anchor. . . . It was a very cohesive education which I didn't have anything to compare with and I didn't realize what a good thing was going on until I looked at other people and saw how scattered their first two years were. And a lot of people really got left by the wayside.

Many participants agreed with a woman who felt that the structure she got in the Program not only helped her during the first two years but "made you stronger for the rest of the college years."

A photographer and businesswoman spoke of how the moral and ethical dimension of the curriculum had its impact on her.

> It's had its good impact, it's been the stimulus for my interest in other things that have branched out from that. Like an interest in classical art, Greeks, the Greek myths. . . .
>
> Also I think it had an ethical impact. It . . . gave me a way or stimulated in me a new way of thinking about society and the individual. There are a lot of ideas bouncing around about the meaning of law . . . a kind of higher meaning of law, other than just a statutory point by point kind of small claims court kind of idea. That was really important to me. . . . It was very stimulating. I learned a lot; it was an opportunity to learn, to be really involved in an intense experience . . . [in] a lot of things that have to do with a sense of individual rights—and . . . ethical responsibility . . . a sense of yourself as a civic being. . . . I vote and am really interested in things that are going on . . . some ideals in government that I still believe in.

Another woman made the point that this was a crucial time in their development for students to be hearing this particular message.

> The history and ethics of the world, discussing morality in a context of history. . . . Those are very formative years and you're very idealistic and very open to certain things, and I think it was a real positive force. I think I probably have a lot of the values that came out of there.

Another librarian, for whom much of the Program did not seem to have a great "practical" impact, found that the "message" of political responsibility nonetheless did reach her.

> I think there might be a commitment toward being a part of a community and having a political responsibility that I'm not sure I would have had without going through that program—being part of a community in the sense of being part of a larger whole. All through my life after college I think I've always thought about being part of the community that I was in, not necessarily just voting and being part of the structure of government, but in smaller ways—working in school groups and doing volunteer activities. . . . I think it's something that I've always felt important, and I can't say that it wasn't there before I started the Program, and it didn't come from my family or something. But I think that maybe being in the Program made me more aware that this was an important thing to do, that it is important to look for ways to become involved in that kind of activ-

ity ... there was something that made it more tangible ... But *practically* speaking, I'm not sure it had that much of an impact on me."

She seemed to have perceived the intellectual aspects of the Program as if from afar, perhaps to protect herself from the risk involved in making an intellectual commitment. Despite a feeling of alienation, she was not uninvolved:

> I really did do a lot of thinking during that time, and a lot of that thinking came out of the Program. So I guess I was in a lot of ways alienated from it, but in the same way I think I was stimulated and involved by it. . . . I guess [I] was really involved with the message and was trying to tap it, even though I wasn't totally committed to it . . . sort of the academic ideal, or intellectual commitment to ideas. I would have liked to have been a real part of it. It was just I think [I was] probably never really willing to take the risks to do it, at that point."

It is apparent that even though this woman was not totally involved intellectually in the Program, she still absorbed enough of the importance of the concept of community for it to have affected her in later life.

It would be a mistake to think that the few people who said they would not repeat the Program if they had it to do over again did not gain anything from it. A woman in the second cycle, a teacher, who had not wanted to go to Berkeley in the first place, said that rather than repeating the Program she would not enroll at Berkeley at all but at some small liberal arts college instead. But as in the case of the man from the first cycle who would choose not to repeat the Program, she said the Program had benefited her in some ways. She spoke about the way in which it mitigated some of the negative effects of being in a large university instead of a small liberal arts college, and how it affected her writing skills.

> I learned to write ... because I'm a good writer and we did so much work writing and composing. Between the structured work we had in junior high and high school learning the techniques of writing, and then the practice of it in the Program. . . .
>
> I think the Program provided me with a particular continuity that I might not have had in the first two years at Berkeley had I not been in something like that because the population was so huge at Berkeley the first couple of years. I think I would have been a little more lost, college

wise, if it wasn't for the continuity that I had in the Program.... Being able to read the works that we read, which were valuable, and doing the writing that we did, and being able to experience professors in probably a somewhat closer relationship than I would have if I'd just been in one of those three hundred students in an anthropology class.

Looking at these collective comments from second-cycle women about the major impact of the Program on their lives, we find the same themes of the value of critical and independent thinking and the importance of learning to use primary sources that women from the first cycle reported. As for both women and men from the first cycle, the safety and security of the small community within the large university was important to them, and had effects that lasted throughout their college careers and into their lives beyond college. Second-cycle women spoke of the value of the coherence and integration of the curriculum, and of the Program's influence on their views of law and government, society and its institutions. Several of them emphasized the ethical importance of the Program to them, even when, as one reported, the Program as a whole had had little impact on her life otherwise.

SECOND-CYCLE MEN

The central importance of the concept of community, the values instilled and encouraged in the Program, its long-lasting and cumulative effects have been its major impact for several men in the second cycle. One of them, an owner-operator of a small business, did not recognize its effects until later.

> As I think back on it, I wonder if they were giving us an opportunity to say, this is really how we'd like to live our lives. Maybe this is more than they anticipated, maybe they weren't thinking this loftily, but I'm convinced that a lot of things that I've done, that my caring about community . . . and the environment [comes from the Program]. I know part of that is coming out of the sixties because that's what everybody was involved [in], but I didn't just come out of the sixties, I came out of that Program, and I think it's maybe one of the reasons that I'm [more] interested than some of my friends who have "sold out"....
>
> I maintain there's still some of us out there who are trying to live our lives in a slightly different way and that do care about our world, not only

today, but twenty, fifty, a hundred years from now. It *is* our problem, because it's a world problem, and the fact that what we do effects the world. And I think that has to do with my notion of community, and I think the fact that I have thought about that in my own head and articulated a notion of community, from that Program, initially, has affected, probably, the way I choose to live my life. . . .

I am better able than most of my friends to articulate things. . . . I think of issues in a different way than other people do, and I think of things in terms of society, community, because of my training—I had two years of this. And although I didn't "get it" right away, it was all going in there. I mean I didn't ignore it all. . . . I'm sure part of it was Berkeley, part of it was the sixties. But I'm sure Tussman had an effect on me. I'm sure that it did. . . . Part of a notion of community, I think, is you have to look at the big picture, to do some things that may not make sense or seem popular in a short term period, but that over the course of a long term make a lot of sense.

It is interesting to compare this man's response to that of the woman librarian quoted earlier who didn't realize the impact that the Program had had on her until she was asked about it, and who said it had not had much of a "practical" impact on her. In spite of their varying responses, they both carried away with them its emphasis on community, and each have incorporated that into the way they live their lives now.

The way in which the Program helped some students to clarify their own values, as we learned from the woman who became more committed to Catholicism because of her experience in the Program, is repeated in his experience:

I may have understood what I wanted out of life sooner than a lot of people because I was, in a sense, forced to, or given an opportunity I should say, to think about what was important to me in life, in terms of a living situation or a community. I mean, you say "Tussman Program," and I say "community," instantly. That's *the* thing that came out of that. . . . I also feel very strongly that the Program did instill in me something that I carry with me today, and probably always will. Even if it was just forcing me to think about how I wanted to live my life in a different way than other people did. And [it was] not specifically that I remember the lecture on Plato's Republic that I'm going to carry with me all my life—just that they gave me an opportunity to formulate my thoughts in a different way. . . .

But I think that's a real important thing that I got that a lot of people didn't get. I consider myself very lucky, very fortunate that I was given the opportunity to view the world in a slightly different way than other people. And I really believe that I was given that opportunity by the Program. And I wish more people were given that opportunity.

Describing the process that led to this understanding, he says:

It kind of all came together at the end for me. It's like the two years all coalesced in the last month [of the Program] for me. And suddenly, I started thinking, "Oh!," and you know, "maybe I should have been paying more attention." It was really this sudden rush at the end for me, as opposed to this sort of gradual building up to this thing.

The contrast between the coherent intellectual focus of the Program and the regular lower division "knowledge oriented" classes, as this next participant called them, was a theme repeated with this group of former students, a comparison they could not always make until after completing the Program. An economist said:

I had the experience—I realize it now, after it's over with—the experience to really engage in something intellectual and not just a knowledge enterprise like most of college is an acquisition of knowledge. But [the Program was] an intellectual challenge, of really thinking. I mean, some kind of effort to go after understanding some of the threads in social life and social issues. And I realize, in talking with other people who have gone through a lot of years of school, that they've missed that opportunity to really focus on major social themes.

I realize, twenty years later, that I had a very unique and very privileged opportunity to get a guided tour through an intellectual inquiry, which is what the Program tried to do . . . to look at problems of social living through some of Western history. And to have the close interplay with the teachers, the seminar setting, and the lecture setting. It was a very unique and a very, very privileged kind of environment.

I knew that at the time, but I didn't know it quite as clearly until later on when I got out and took other courses in college and went on and did some graduate work, that everything that I was exposed to afterwards was *knowledge* oriented facts, mastery of subjects, and so forth. And that wasn't the main thrust of the Program. The Experimental College was not an acquisition of knowledge, but an understanding of principles, social principles. . . . I just realized even more *now* just how much of a privilege it was. How fortunate I was to be able just to be there at the right place and the right time to do that.

While he does not use the term "community of scholars," that is what he described:

It lived up to my ideal, or my fantasy—the small group, guided seminars with the professors. I thought those were really a special opportunity, really a privilege to be sitting in there with a group of maybe six or eight or ten students and a senior professor. The setting was just about ideal for my idea of a university level learning, a small group with a professor and everybody intimately involved, engaged in the subject matter, as opposed to a professor standing up in front of a hundred and fifty people, talking about some stuff and watching you try to write it down, [and] maybe you—daydreaming—or missing the class. The intimacy of it, that was the best, the most, that was the closest to meeting my fantasy of what this should be.

[I was learning] about social ethics and intellectual inquiry and different cultural approaches to grapple with the problems of social conflict—the Greeks, the British constitutional, the religious, Bible kind of "what to do about ethics" . . . I learned to think, to take seriously the whole problem of . . . what is ethical behavior for individuals in society. What do we owe to society? That's what they were trying to say, "Well, let's look at how it's been addressed over different snapshots in human history, in Western history." That's what I say we were trying to do, and I think they did a good job of it. . . . It was the high point of my academic career, no question about it.

A lawyer recalled the impact of the Program as subtle, direct, and long-lasting. He described how its unique method of instilling habits of mind, which he distinguished from teaching, led to his finding a sense of direction which he called "the moral compass":

The impacts were subtle. They become apparent more and more as you get older. One of the things that I think it did, probably the most important thing, was to take you from the art of merely being glib, which is what gets most of us through high school, and even through college, to a point where you can pick up material, learn something from it, and use it. It really does what, I guess, you're supposed to get out of school: it

> educated us, taught us how to read things, how to learn for ourselves, how to think about it. Well, I take that back, it didn't teach us how to do it, it got us into the habit of doing it. I mean, everybody, pretty much, comes to the university with some basic skills and what it did is it took us from the bad habits of cramming for exams and feeding people back what they wanted to hear, to actually looking at what's in front of you, seeing what that thing or person has to say, and deciding for yourself whether that's something useful, interesting. I think that's it's [the] major direct impact.
>
> The less subtle impact is that it probably gave us a greater sense of what is involved in a democracy, particularly the American democracy. The sense of culture, sense of place, sense of person, sense of issues.

This man also talked about the overall sense of community he found in the Program.

> I don't have that Marxian sense of alienation that I don't belong in this society, or that I'm abused; I feel like I'm part of the community . . . being able to object to things but to still be able to live in your community. . . . I think the attitude you take from it is that tolerance for other's views, that interest in other things, and that feeling that there's more to what's going on here than just my particular economic status. So I participate in the local governments. I do a whole array of things, and the education that I got here [in the Program] helps me understand those things, helps me deal with the stresses of that, helps me to try to get back to that [moral compass]. You've got that center, you've got a sense of direction that this is the kind of thing that one does because this is what makes a community work.

Another man spoke of the Program's effect on his teaching, which is connected for him with the concept of community, and became a driving force in his choice and practice of a profession.

> With the Program I became aware of foundations, and I realized that I didn't have any (laughs). The Program provided this opportunity to see that there's this long history that I was a part of, but I didn't *feel* a part of. So going into it was like going into elementary education—was in my imagination going back to origins for me. We had all sorts of lingo, but the polis was one, and in my imagination the polis starts in education. In children. We had several metaphors floating through [the Program]. One was the polis, one was the eternal city, or the life of the polis, and

participating and contributing to the enterprise. And that was the language.

And I remember talking to Tussman. I said, "Well, so how does this relate to teaching children? You're covering [the period] after adolescence, and this is a foundation program, but what's the program that comes before the Program?" And he said, "I don't know. (laughs) It's a good question." So that was a question that I decided in Program language to put myself into. So I put myself into the world of elementary education, with the idea of looking for how we create souls to live in the eternal city.

These effects for him were gradual and played themselves out over time, a long-term effect of taking the "long view" as he called it.

The kind of atmosphere the Program created gave me . . . an orientation towards solving problems in terms of a framework which was sort of a philosophical approach. I became a history major after that, having a . . . reverence for history, for the long view, and then applying it to whatever the situation was, and being able to look for and not be surprised by parallels.

This was in my mind when I was 21 or 22. [Not] in the Program, no—it came later. Towards the end of the Program, I got this sense of a tradition that you could join, or become a part of, or participate in. And that was from the Program. That was from the discussion that was going on, and the respect that I was given, and the ears that would listen to what my opinion was about what was going on. It's a real powerful psychological line, and I have great respect for it, because it still guides me now. . . . I would say it [my experience in the Program] was very successful. I mean, it set me up in a way. It was a foundation experience for me. It was really important.

There were other ways in which people testified to the deep and lasting effects the Program had on their thinking and the ways in which they viewed crucial issues in society, regardless of whether or not those issues were connected to their work. This man, now a literary editor, said:

It awakened me to issues that continue to be near and dear to me. I mean, questions of human nature, and political activity; a question of natural law and moral law, and first principles. And what is the relation of person to person, of man to man, man to his fellow citizen, of states to each other. These things kind of occupy me—not in a professional way—I don't deal with these things professionally. But the issues brought up in the Program seem to be still critical and still crucial. Every now and then they'll surface in the popular culture, and there'll be a sort of flurry of activity and people will discuss this and that, and then somehow it dies down again.

I guess I'm thinking of the book by Allan Bloom, *The Closing of the American Mind*, which people loved and hated, that touched on some of the same issues of education—what's our education for, what's it about, is there a content that education should have? Or prior to that, is there a content that human nature has, and that has to be discovered, or brought out in education?

And then the flurry at Stanford about undergraduate studies now. I'll say this: it seems to me that if I hadn't been through the Experimental Program . . . to read about the controversy at Stanford, I'd be interested, and I'd be confused. I wouldn't know what to make of these arguments—I wouldn't be able to understand them in the way that I can understand them now. So I'd say because I've been through the Program—I credit the Program with this—when I read about Allan Bloom's book, and people's reaction to it, or read about the Stanford curriculum, and people's reactions to that, it looks to me like most of the people commenting on it are wrong on both sides. The extremes on both sides are missing the point. And I think because I went through the Experimental Program I'm able to see, I . . . have a better idea than I would have what this kind of education really means.

He explained how the Program shaped his views on education and the Western tradition.

It has a very different look from the inside than from the outside. When you've been dipped into the canon, or into the Western tradition, you realize that, for instance, the members of the Western tradition—let's say, the authors of the great books—aren't quoting themselves, they're not referring themselves to the Western tradition, they're creating it, they're working it out, they're making it as they go. The Western tradition, so called, is not a monolithic thing, to be feared by some, or revered by others. It's an actual living thing, but you can't really know that until you get into it, and you can't get into it until someone puts you into it. I mean, it's a lucky accident if you do get into it, and that's the kind of lucky accident that I had with the Experimental Program.

It is an intriguing notion he puts forth that some of the arguments made for and against the place of the teaching of western civilization courses in our colleges and universities today may be carried on by people not as familiar as they should be with the actual meaning and content of this tradition.

He went on to give more of his thoughts about education engendered by his experience in the Program and about the long term effects it had on his life:

> I can't tell you if it would have helped or hindered a given career track, but for the uses to which I put my mind and soul, it was great. I can't think of anything better. It was really my education, I think. The place where I really got down in the muck and sort of chomped around in, (laughs) in the really stewy and fermented parts of . . . the human mind and soul. That's where I really . . . did my work, you know. I mean, I really found out things there. . . . It furnished me with intellectual material on which to work for the rest of my life.

Another lawyer attested to the Program's repeated theme of education for citizenship, and the long-term effect that it had on him.

> Well, there are lots of major impacts. But the most major was having an idea that an education was something wholly different than I had ever imagined it could be. And also, being exposed to these great books, although I was pretty slovenly and didn't read everything, nonetheless I got a chance to be really exposed to this idea of what it means to be a citizen, what it means to be part of, and a real member of the democratic process. That was really powerful and has lasted.

He cited other ways in which the effects of the Program are realized only after some time has passed, and they have a cumulative effect:

> As I've grown older, the impact sort of accumulated in a weird way. I remember somebody— [Professor N]—said in 1967 or 1968 that, "You won't know," he said to the students, "about the truth of what we're saying, you're just *children* now." And of course, we were. But what's happened for me is that the longer I've lived with these books and with the clear strains that go through these great mature thinkers, the longer I've lived with them, the more I see that it's true personally in my life, and also in terms of my overview of history and culture and the present.

> As you get older, you just know more, and you live more, and you have suffered more losses, and you have more sense of the complexity of the world and then you start to see. . . . You read a poem of Yeats when you're fifteen or sixteen or seventeen, and you read a poem of Yeats now and it's—you can have it now. You couldn't have it then. And so these books have really always been there [for me]. . . . So it's managed to . . . inform the way I think even now. And so that's the big impact.

He noted the achievement of the Program's goal in what he was learning:

> I would say I was learning about—(pause)—what these great thinkers in Western civilization thought about the big problems of responsibility and freedom and order and anarchy and the dualities and polarities that are standard in culture and in the human mind, as Tussman thought. And getting some kind of historical sweep so that I wouldn't just be operating on the present. I think the message was clear then, and I think I have very different responses to the same problems, but I think even now I see . . . what was being done, and that in some ways we were being educated to be citizens, and to take part in a democracy in an intelligent way. And I think in many ways those goals were achieved.

For some former students, the structure of the Program and the educational process itself assumed primary importance. The major impact of the Program for a documentary film maker was its capacity to teach him to focus his attention on one topic at a time, which in turn effected his later education and his work.

> The fact that there was the opportunity to concentrate on one subject at a time, for a period of a couple of years . . . interestingly, it sort of continued in [a European country in Berkeley's Education Abroad program] because [that country's educational system] is a kind of similar set-up, although very, very different, but in fact took one subject at a time, and focused on that . . . [we] studied just that one subject intensively. It really gave me a taste of doing things that way [and made it] my preferred mode of working, rather than having fifteen things going on at once, I prefer to focus on one thing at a time.
> It also gave me an opportunity for the first time to really study certain things in depth. I'm interested in a lot of different things but it's rare that you really get the opportunity to focus, and I think that was the thing that

it taught me, if you can focus your attention on a topic, even if you're bringing in a lot of different aspects to think about, it's really the ideal way to conduct your education.

As to the intellectual content, and to the way the content was interwoven with pedagogical method, he said:

I always thought of it as more than anything else a kind of political philosophy course. It was almost like an intellectual orientation to Western civilization . . . written in very broad strokes obviously, but still studying how to read critically and how to write.

The close relationship between the structure of the Program and its intellectual content was illustrated by another man, the owner of a small business, who said the part of it that had the greatest impact was:

The idea of a community of scholars, of being associated with the same faculty members, the same students primarily over two years with a physical location identified with this house here. The chance to grow up with a group of people experiencing the same things that you were. Not being caught in just your own little independent world in the regular University. That was probably the primary value.

I think that the whole environment is what then helped the rest of the Program go. The development of your mind. This . . . learning how to look at issues, seeing how things we're looking at today can be viewed as what was going on in the *Iliad* thousands of years ago. That there is some sort of continuity to human experience no matter how different the things may seem today. And the basic foundation of our Western thought is as valid now as it was thousands of years ago. But I think what really needs to come before all of this is the overall physical set-up of having the same students, faculty discussing the same course work for that length of time, and the individual attention you received as part of it.

The preparation and training for taking part in a democratic community, was also important to him.

I would say what we tried to do is lay a basic foundation for philosophical . . . development of Western civilization, political civilization . . . The basic formation of democracy here, the thought processes that went behind forming our constitution; and then looking at challenges to it, does this system work. The overall point being trying to produce people, voters who can think. And the only way you can think and make an educated choice as a voter, as a member of a democracy, is to understand how this whole system has been put together. What the roots of it are . . . the roots of American democracy.

It certainly underscored the value of a sense of community, of belonging, of not just being an individual in this chaotic scene, but being part of a group, no matter how small a group. It's something that makes sense in this chaos.

He gave an illustration of how what he learned in the Program more than 20 years ago has given him the basis for making decisions today of a philosophical as well as of a more personal nature:

> It always comes up, ideas that were talked about in the Program. I always find myself sort of touching back to things. Just recently I got involved in a discussion about something having to do with compromises and I just said to the person I was talking with, "Well, this brings up a point I learned in my early years in college. That compromise is probably the worst form of government or decision-making process to have." And that referred back to a very heated argument that went on within the Program over compromises in which the obvious point being—was it King Solomon who decided to divide the baby in half and give one half to each mother as a symbol of compromise to find out who the real mother was?
>
> Well, things like that came up. They do constantly touch on things in my life today. . . . It has given me a background in which to think about [how] to make decisions, whether these are actual day-to-day life decisions, or just philosophical ones. It's provided a base of knowledge, a system of looking at philosophy, political philosophy, and having something to refer back to, to make sense of it—it's organized [my] thoughts in a way. That would be, probably, the lasting value.

He separated the structure of the Program from its contents:

There are certainly some lessons I learned through this about what is a better form of education. Regardless of what you're teaching people, the important thing is just the structure itself. . . . [I would say] I was learning how to think. How to look at problems, and how also to develop a background on which to look at these and make decisions.

But he conceded the difficulty of assessing all the effects of the Program even after 20 years:

> It certainly has had a probably profound influence I still don't fully understand or appreciate. Or maybe I was going to become the person I am today anyway, and it was just an experience of becoming this way. I really—I don't know. It will vary from . . . how I feel about myself right now. So it's a hard question [about how the Program had a bearing on how he made important decisions]. Probably the answer to that will always change, or be in a state of flux.

Another lawyer spoke of the usefulness of the Program in his life today, as well as during his college days:

> It got me through that first couple of years of college and a little older, that was the immediate pay-off. In the long term pay-off, I think I've got what you call a "good, general, liberal arts" kind of background, as far as Western civilization goes. I mean, our roots, intellectual roots. And it seems like I use it all the time. I've no idea what would have happened to me if I hadn't gone into the Program, so I can't tell you what difference it made in that sense, but it seems like the Program gave you a way of looking at the balancing forces that you're confronted with every day, or week, or month, just in the world, or in your own life, or anything. And that kind of process was good. Being able to recognize and identify pressures in society, culture, and civilization, and how you can work out ways to get these to balance each other out, hopefully with a minimum of bloodshed and violence.

How he uses this process now to help him understand how problems of ethnic conflict might be solved today is illustrated in the examples he gave:

> Right now I'm looking at the Muslims in Iran and that sort of thing, [how] things are going over there in China and I'm wondering—I just got this terrible urge to find a book on Cromwell and find out what happened in the English Reformation, how we got through that. That seemed to be a sort of parallel situation. It was not a period we covered in the Program or anything. I don't know anything about the Reformation or what happened there, but I know that there were some pretty radical shifts in the way English culture was set up, and I'd like to check it out as soon as I get a chance.

This man said he took great pains during the interview not to "parrot back Meiklejohn's or Tussman's theories. I digested it and to a large extent adopted a lot of their thoughts, their conclusions and their thought processes, but this is me talking." He mentioned the importance of the passage of time in assessing the effects of the Program: "It's easier now, it's easier now that things have focused a little better than they were ten years ago. This would have been—more difficult to do ten years ago." Assessing the long-term effects of the Program on his life, he said: "It contributed to all facets of my existence, but it wasn't the cause of anything."

A few participants were hesitant about answering the question concerning the major impact of the Program on their lives, perhaps because of the difficulty of sorting out influences from different sources, or perhaps because the effects are simply still not always that clear. This man, a lawyer, said:

> I don't know the impact on my life because I haven't lived a life not having taken the Program. So [I see no way you can compare. You would have to]—live one life one way, and then live one life having taken the Program, and then see the difference. Not being afforded that luxury, I don't know the answer to the question. It's really hard for me to say whether it's the Program that's had an effect on me. I mean, certainly, I enjoyed the Program, and I had a good time there, and I thought it was useful, and I worked hard, and I got a lot out of it at the time. It helped me, maybe, to write well, and how to organize my thoughts clearly. . . .
>
> I've always regarded the Tussman Program as something that was a lot of fun to go through and very different than . . . most people have experienced. . . . Certainly it was part of my life, and it was an important part of my life. I remember it with fondness and certain aspects of it very distinctly, but I don't know that I could point to the Program and say that was the reason I've done anything.

Although there were clear signs of the intellectual impact of the Program in the other groups, in this set of interviews from men in the second cycle we see the strongest evidence of it. The language many of them use to describe the long-term impact of the Program certainly reflects its goals. Some of them mentioned still being in contact with some of their fellow Program students; some said they had been part of the group that "took over" the House: both indications of their deep involvement in the

Program's learning community. Other explanations of the Program's particularly strong impact on this group will be considered in the next section.

SUMMARY OF MAJOR IMPACTS AND GENDER AND CYCLE DIFFERENCES

What has been presented here is the central theme of each participant's statements about the major impact (or impacts, as some participants mentioned more than one) that the Program has had on their lives. To have summarized these various replies in a few pages would have omitted the richness and diversity of their reactions, recollections, and opinions of how they were affected by this special and complex program that occupied the first two years of their undergraduate education. The quotations give the reader a feeling for what was uppermost in their recollections and judgments of the meaningfulness of the Program. They provide a sense of the range of responses, as well as their depth. They clearly reveal the types of effects and impacts, long lasting as well as immediate, and the fact that many were realized by participants only after the passage of time.

No quantification of any kind can substitute for their own words in describing the impact that the Program has had on the lives of those who experienced it. However, in order to pull together some of this information in a more wieldy manner and compare the responses of first- and second-cycle participants, and of men and women, these responses to questions about the impact of the Program, its gains and benefits, the influence of the Program on life decisions, and spontaneous comments about the effects of the Program made throughout the interviews can be classified into three very broad categories:

(1) Content—those comments dealing with the impact of the content of the curriculum: with the educational and moral purpose of the Program itself, the political philosophy behind its design; the recurrence of great ideas; values and ethical considerations put forth by the Program; the concepts of citizenship, community; and the ways in which some of the world's classical literature dealing with moral crises instills the sense of tradition through the centuries;

(2) Educational Structure—those responses concerning the effects of educational structure of the Program separate from the curriculum, that is: the encapsulated two-year program; the substitution of lectures, seminars,

and tutorials for the ordinary classes; the absence of grades and exams; the training for independent thinking that the Program fostered; the transdisciplinary nature of the curriculum; the use of primary rather than secondary sources; increased educational awareness resulting from the Program; learning how to think, how to write, how to speak, and how to integrate these skills; the continuity of books, ideas, faculty, students, and setting; the focus of the curriculum on one book at a time; the cohesion of the whole program and the intimacy of the learning community it fostered; and

(3) Personal—those benefits of a more personal nature: the sense of belonging the Program created, the ease, comfort, and protection it offered entering students; the enjoyment in learning they found there versus what they might have experienced in regular classes; the confidence they gained in themselves through their experiences there and how that carried over to the upper division in the regular university and beyond; the interest it engendered in other parts of the world; the validation of creative rather than routine approaches to problems; and apart from all of the above, the incentive and motivation to remain in school when they might have otherwise dropped out.

Looking at these responses collectively, by group, these major findings emerge:

(1) Responses in the second two categories look much the same for all groups. All four groups of male and female, first- and second-cycle participants put roughly equal emphasis on the educational and personal gains from the Program. There were no major differences among any of these four groups, except that women showed a tendency to mention personal gains more often than men.

(2) All four groups differ in the emphasis they put on the curricular content. Twice as many participants from the second cycle (12) as first cycle (6) said the major impact of the Program had come from the content. Twice as many men (12) as women (6) from both cycles said the content had had a major impact.

While it is true that the total number of cases in this table is not large, making the subgroups even smaller, and the group as a whole may not be a representative sample, they do collectively represent roughly one-fifth of the students who completed the Program during its two-cycle, four year existence, and are suggestive of the entire group. There are some differences among some of the groups that emerge here and that deserve attention.

It is the first category of curricular content that appears to be most crucial to understanding of the differences in effects between the two cycles of the Program. As already mentioned, the first cycle could be thought of as the maiden voyage of the Program: the Program "director" and the faculty recruited to the Program were often not in agreement about the goals and means of achieving them; there was a 50 percent turnover of staff from the first to the second year; they did not meet together regularly; conferences with students were held on a haphazardly basis. From all accounts, the second year of the first cycle may have been even less unified than the first.

We know that during the second cycle of the Program faculty remained constant throughout the two years and were largely in agreement about goals and ways to achieve them. Staff met as a group each week; conferences with students were held on a regular and more frequent basis. The second-cycle faculty were much more cohesive as a group, and apparently got the purpose of the curriculum across more effectively to more students. Although there were some of the same problems with the reading list during the second year as there had been in the first cycle, the strength of the curriculum did not appear to dissipate during the second year of the second cycle, and a few participants reported that "it all came together" for them close to the end of the second year. It seems fair to conclude from the responses of this group of participants that while some of them from the first cycle demonstrated the potential benefits of the Program for its students, many more participants from the second cycle were able to realize more fully the meaning of the curriculum.

In spite of those differences in response to the content of the Program among first- and second-cycle participants and between men and women, the educational and personal effects of the entire Program remained approximately the same for all four groups of these participants. That is, the Program offered its students educational and personal benefits even when the impact of the intellectual and moral content was not as strong as it might have been.

The fact that women as a whole had fewer things to say about the impact of the content of the Program than did men is open to interpretation, and there might be a variety of explanations for that discrepancy. It may be that this group of women participants placed more value on the educational and personal effects of the Program than they did on the content. (Women also talked less about the Program in general during the interviews. The longer interviews tended to be with participants, both men and women, who did talk about the curriculum.) Perhaps the way the Program gave women confidence in their academic abilities, awakened awareness of intellectual interests, and eased their way into the upper division at Berkeley overshadowed the significance to them of the more abstract intellectual/ethical content. Although they mentioned community involvement in their present day lives about as often as men, they may not have isolated that as coming from the content of the Program. But there may be another explanation for this gender difference based on the way women students related to faculty in the Program.

Half of the women in the first cycle remembered wishing for more and closer faulty contacts, as did some in the second cycle, indicating the possibility that women, especially in the first cycle where student-faculty tutorials were not regularly scheduled, were shyer about initiating that contact, and needed to be drawn out. This difference might also reflect a major change in educational expectations that many women must undergo when leaving traditional high schools, where test scores and grades and completed assignments have earned them rewards, and where they have been taught mostly by women, to college classrooms where courses are normally taught mostly by men, and where original thinking and effectual discussion in group situations earn recognition, as was certainly true in the Program. (At the time of the Program, in the middle and late sixties, the Women's Liberation Movement had barely begun to have an effect on the campus, and only three percent of faculty teaching at Berkeley were women in 1969.[3])

But the differences may also be a reflection of the crucial importance of close faculty-student relationships: in order for the content of the Program to have any substantial impact on students, their relationship had to be close in the academic sense, allowing for argument, debate, and the intellectual give and take reported by some of the participants, both men and women, in the study. When students were too shy or hesitant to engage faculty, or allow faculty to engage them, in the intellectual substance of the

---

[3]D. Lyn Hunter, "Berkeley Women at Century's End," *Berkeleyan*, Vol. 26, No. 13 (November 5-11, 1997).

The Major Impact on the Lives of its Participants

Program, perhaps that substance was less likely to have had an impact on them. (Other differences between men and women in their responses to the Program will be discussed in Chapter 13.)

This section on the impact of the Program on participants has dealt only with what they perceived to be the major impact, what they picked out as the foremost effect on their lives as they viewed it some 20 years later. There were many other important effects of the Program as well, particularly in the area of education, which will be discussed next.

CHAPTER 7

The Educational Effects

While the primary purpose of the Program was to educate its students for responsible citizenship through the use of the pedagogic structure and techniques I've described, it had a secondary effect on their educational experiences that could be seen as separate from that goal. For instance, one of the most commonly expressed effects of the Program was to increase awareness of educational issues and concerns, heightening its students' appreciation of the value of a liberal education. In what may have been unintended consequences, it often enhanced their feelings of academic self-esteem and led some to believe they were part of an educational elite. It helped them to acquire specific academic skills—in reading, writing, discussion, and critical thinking—and in the ability to integrate all four. And although it was to be "subdisciplinary"—a moratorium on the major—it helped some students channel their interests into upper division majors, while only a few others thought they might have been short-changed by not being able to sample more of the university's intellectual offerings in the lower division.

EDUCATIONAL AWARENESS

One of the most prominent aspects of the interviews was the way in which participants talked about educational issues. Their experiences in the Program seemed to set up many of them as experts in their own education in particular, and thoughtful observers of higher education generally.

Sometimes the interview came to be almost a kind of educational forum for some of them, a place to discuss their beliefs and attitudes toward education. Much of what they had to say on educational matters is included in the following sections dealing with other more specific educational benefits of the Program, but some general comments deserve to be quoted here under the heading of educational awareness.

In the previous section on the major impact of the Program on its participants, we quoted a woman who said it was the awareness of and sensitivity to learning that the Program created in her. She went on to describe how the Program set up a lifetime pattern of concern about education and learning.

> I was thinking about what learning and education should be like, what freedom was, and those are things that the Program really helped me think about because everybody was talking about them, and discussing them in reference to the material we were studying, and without reference to that as well. It influenced me all my life, I believe, because I've . . . thought about education and learning my whole life—about what it should be like, when I was in school, and since I've been out of school. And now that I have an eight year old son, I've been thinking about it a lot in relation to his schooling. . . . What I've been interested in a lot is alternative education, ways of going about learning without the other baggage that goes along with it, a lot of the unnecessary kind of competition. . . . We were really allowed to go our own way [in the Program] in a lot of ways within a certain structure. We were allowed to have our own interests and . . . I thought that was really good. . . .
>
> [The Program] made us think about what we wanted from our education . . . more than going through the regular university where you had to worry about a lot of other things. . . . It's not just the content of what you're learning, although that is important, but it's . . . what your feelings are about the learning that [is] very important as well. . . . That there should be an understanding of the reasons why you're doing this, a larger view of what you're doing, and I think that that was what the Program did.

That long-term appreciation for the special educational benefits of the Program not available to students in ordinary undergraduate classes is reflected in another woman's comments, together with her feelings about the dangers of early specialization:

> I'm increasingly grateful for having had something else than what's generally offered ... that's not available to most people and seems real important. I think society is fairly bankrupt educationally. I think that this is one place where it could easily be remedied really, and isn't, and instead it's being notoriously neglected—that education is more and more at the graduate level. It's more and more specialized, it's less and less general, and that's a real loss. I see our culture stack up very poorly against other cultures educationally, academically—that we're historically illiterate, literally illiterate, we're just illiterate in so many ways. And it's devastating to our culture, as we live in a global world, and we don't know it. ... General education is a way of getting people to be aware of disciplines and attitudes and perspectives beyond their specialized interests and fields. I just want to say that (laughs).

One man spoke of realizing the value of this kind of general education only with the passage of time.

> What I would have said [I was learning] at the time is different from what I would say now. What I learned at the time was a good deal about several areas that we studied, the Greek area, and something about how they thought and how they viewed the world. And similarly with seventeenth-century England, with the American Revolutionary period. [And now] what I learned I think is ... that there's great value to having a broad cultural education and not becoming too specialized too quickly in life. You have the rest of your life after college to do that.

Another man said the Program gave him a rare opportunity, perhaps his only opportunity, to think about issues of western civilization.

> I was learning. I was becoming a more conscious person. I was learning about the kinds of questions that people in Western civilization have asked and will continue to ask, and some attempts at answering some of those questions. And thinking about a lot of these issues for the first time, maybe the only time.

One man noted the experimental aspect of educational reform at the heart of the Program.

> The Program was a beautiful hiatus. It's like, "Time out from the way the rest of the educational systems are going in this country ... We don't

think it's really working. So let's get at least one minuscule group of people somewhere that have this classic grounding. And then we'll come back and check them out later on." It's almost like a science fiction story . . . that there's a seed planted generations in advance to create leaders, experts.

Program participants were not only critics of higher education, but became critics of the critics of higher education, as did the man we quoted in the last chapter who felt that his experience in the Program showed him how both Alan Bloom's supporters and his critics often missed the point. We have no data on how Program graduates would compare on this dimension with graduates of the regular lower division program at Berkeley, or with other special programs, but we do have some data from the comparative questionnaire on attitudes toward education reported in Appendix F. In answering the question, "Would you agree that undergraduate education would be improved if there were less emphasis on specialized training and more on broad liberal education?," 86 percent of respondents who had completed the Program answered in the affirmative, as compared with 67 percent of the respondents who had applied but not been admitted to the Program. Since we can assume both groups were probably similarly disposed toward values of liberal education from the beginning, experience in the Program appears to have strengthened these attitudes independent of participants' earlier sentiments and leanings.

ELITISM

The idea that the Program created or developed in students special qualities, or that they were chosen to be in the Program because of some special qualification, was mentioned by many participants both spontaneously and in response to the question, "Did you ever feel you were part of any kind of intellectual elite?" Participants were divided over this question—about half said they did feel they were part of an elite group while in the Program; about half said they didn't. Among those who did, some reported feeling a sense of snobbery and exclusiveness. Even participants who did know that they had been selected randomly from those who had applied to the Program, nonetheless developed a feeling of being special, partly, as one said, out of a need to identify with a group. The notion of eliteness took hold even within the Program. One first-cycle participant said that some of his peers looked down on the second-cycle students, feeling that they "didn't have it as good" as first-cycle students; a few second-cycle participants said they thought the second cycle was much better than the first.

Several participants are still convinced they were either selected to receive invitational letters to apply, or selected for entrance on some criteria that made them part of an elite group. One thought that she had been selected because she had graduated with honors from high school; another because applicants had to have B averages, or that they were "of a little better cut than just the average freshman group." Some said they had been told by the faculty that they were special. One attributed the feeling of elitism to a set of factors:

> There were just a few of us in that Program, and it was a selected group, and we got all this individual attention, and we were pampered by these professors. And the people in there tended to be fairly intellectual.

As mentioned earlier, the requirement of passing the Subject A exam possibly contributed to a feeling of having been specially selected.

Some participants thought their feelings of eliteness arose in response to the opinions of other Berkeley students: "Some other people treated us that way . . . because they didn't know quite what the Experimental College was all about." Others saw that they were not an elite group to begin with but were "developing into that" because,

> I felt I was doing something special, I felt I was a member of certainly almost an elite group of students . . . I felt I did more work than the average student did, compared to my roommates, for example, in the dormitories.

That notion that the Program students were not an elite group to begin with but became one by virtue of either what they did in the Program, or how they came to view themselves, is probably the most accurate assessment of what actually did happen, in light of the fact that they were really a randomly chosen number from a self-selected group of applicants.

Not necessarily feeling that they were part of an elite group as some participants did, other participants suggested they felt special in different ways. The idea of privilege was an important aspect of this feeling of specialness. Many said they felt being in the Program made them appreciative, made them feel "lucky." "I guess I viewed myself as sort of privileged to be able to participate in this thing, and a lot of us felt we were lucky to be doing this." One participant thought it was "just a privilege to be accepted at Berkeley, an honor, and on top of that, even more of a privilege to be in this Program."

One participant rejected the elitist feeling in favor of a sense of responsibility, as if he was part of a "chosen" rather than an elite group. "I somehow feel that because we were in the Program, those of us who were so fortunate should be better than others—but I don't know how." Others rejected the label of elite on grounds of egalitarian principle alone. One man said the elitist attitude was not "useful" to him afterwards, that it contributed to his feelings of "grandiosity," and that he had to overcome the "snob factor" in order to figure out what he wanted to do in life, to get "grounded" and get a job "in the world."

Some participants recognized that the Program was not selective, not an honors program but an alternative, and "if you felt you were in an intellectual elite, you must have just—you had to conjure that [up] on your own." Another man felt he was part of an intellectual elite only at the beginning.

> As I got through the Program, I began to figure out that I wasn't as smart as I could tell myself I was. It was mostly [being] glib. And somewhere during the Program it dawned on me that this wasn't an intellectually elite exercise at all. They were looking for a way to train the ordinary folks out there and I was probably about as ordinary as they came.

That recognition that the Program was for "ordinary folks" rather than the elite did not in any way detract from the meaningfulness or value of it for him—he was enthusiastic about what the Program had meant to him at the time and later in his life as well.

Another view of the source of the idea that Program students were part of an elite came from one participant who thought that students came to feel that way largely by virtue of their self-selection:

> Well, I think that people who selected the Program—maybe I'm just projecting—but my sense was that the people who selected the Program were like me, kind of willing to take a risk, something of a risk on a

basically untested Program, but yet [were] people who were attracted by the notion of it being unconventional. I mean, that was part of its attractiveness. And, those people just tended to be among the brighter folks at the University.

The Program was certainly "unconventional" and "alternative" and "untested." And there is some evidence that it did attract an academically better prepared and more confident group of freshmen. (See Appendix F.) However, the notion of risk-taking in the Program was rarely expressed by participants, as discussed in Chapter 2. Asked, "Did you see entering the Program as taking a kind of risk?," a large majority said no. (A few said that since the Program was experimental they remembered hoping it would last long enough for them to finish.)

Not only did most others not see the Program as a risk, many thought that being in the Program was a "safer" way to matriculate to the university in view of its size and impersonality. They saw the Program as small and encapsulated, requiring no decisions about what courses to take, no long registration lines to stand in, fewer risks in the pass-nonpass grading scheme, and more attention from faculty. It must have appeared to them a kinder, gentler introduction to university life, a sort of half-way house between high school and the large university. For many, that is just what it came to be.

In spite of the fact that invitational letters were sent to all entering freshmen, and that entrants were chosen at random, students in the Program *were* a special group by virtue of their self-selection to an alternative program, the only one of its kind on the campus at that time, although others soon followed. And this program would have been thought of as a very special program anywhere, let alone in the large public research university where it was located. As participants noted, if they were not an elite to begin with they did become a special group simply by virtue of the special education they received there. That very few of them viewed it as a risk perhaps reflected their initial academic self-confidence at entrance. The risk for them may very well have been enrolling at UC Berkeley in the mid-sixties, and the Program became a way of mitigating the undesirable effects of the size and impersonality and social/political chaos they might expect to find—and did find there.

There was certainly a kind of Hawthorne effect to the Program that both faculty and some students were aware of. That is to say, simply due to the special attention alone they received and the special circumstances under which they operated that were very different from regular lower division students (no grades, a house all to themselves, specially selected faculty who could be considered an academically elite group, and so forth), their morale was undoubtedly raised. While the positive effect of the special attention they received could be thought of as obscuring the pure effects of the experiment—that is, the students were bound to do well and think the Program a success simply because it was an experiment—that would not negate those positive effects. The experiment actually intended to produce such a Hawthorne effect on students, and students were told by faculty in the Program that they were special. A lower faculty-student ratio, easier access to faculty, and greater faculty attention to students' papers were undoubtedly a large part of the attraction for applicants, as discussed in the section on the appeal of the Program to its applicants: they probably came to the Program already feeling special.

In summary, whatever degree of disagreement there might have been among participants about whether they felt part of an elite, about whether they were taking a risk by applying to the Program, about whether they were a kind of academic "chosen people," should not in any way obscure the fact that the Program generated a sense of identity with a special group of students within the larger university and sometimes even an identity with a certain way of life. The sorority woman quoted earlier illustrated this by choosing to identify with the Program rather than with her sorority. That was a powerful condition the Program created, one that allowed its other effects to be so pervasive.

ACADEMIC SELF-ESTEEM

Related to but separate from the feeling of elitism and privilege is the concept of academic self-esteem. The heightened awareness of educational issues and the feeling of being part of a special educational experiment may have had some effect on the way students felt about themselves academically, both while in the Program and later in the upper division where they joined regular students who had not been Program participants. One could imagine participation in the Program either enhancing academic self-esteem through association with the classic curriculum and an educationally high-minded approach to learning, or diminishing it if students felt inadequate in meeting its intellectual challenge, and there is evidence that some students reacted in both ways. These possibilities led to a set of questions in the interview schedule about what changes in their own assessment of their academic abilities resulted from participation in the Program.

Most participants reported they had thought their academic abilities were high upon graduation from high school. This suggests that high school graduates with low estimates of their academic abilities might not have been interested in the Program, or might have dropped out of the Program when they found themselves in the company of other more academically confident students. One man reported a feeling of ambivalence about his academic ability and how that changed in the Program:

> I thought I was pretty smart, alternating with thinking that I was not worth a damn. More brilliant than anybody else, but also a dog. I was somewhere in the middle.

But once in the Program, he found out that he could

> synthesize like nobody's business, and that was very helpful. I'd never had a chance really to let myself get extremely creative. And I got a chance to do that, and got rewarded for it . . . and I got some confidence that way.

He went on to describe the way he had previously felt in high school, that he had to hide his creative impulses, but with the encouragement of one Program faculty member in particular, he was able to risk displaying his "poetic" gift. And later in comparing Program students with others in the upper division he said,

> We just had a great view of the world, and those other people just didn't have what we had, and didn't know how to think about these big subjects. They were just scattered, they didn't have a picture. They didn't have a sense of how the great themes of Western life get played out over the millennia. . . . We had at least the three or four thousand year sweep, and I thought it was a wonderful thing. It was just the cat's pajamas.

One man who had reported having a low opinion of his academic abilities not only in high school but throughout his academic career including professional school, nonetheless felt he had been part of an intellectual elite while in the Program. "I was at the bottom of a very high class. You know, I was right at the bottom of the cream that rises to the top." He spoke of the sense of adventure he had in the Program and the pride he felt knowing that it was not the common approach to a college education. He appreciated the enthusiasm for the "process" that Program professors displayed and the feeling that students were getting a "pretty special deal." Whatever the source of his lower academic self-esteem, it did not interfere with his appreciation of the Program, of his feeling special and elite by virtue of participating in it, and his ability to use what the Program gave him in the way of an understanding of his "intellectual roots" which he uses today "all the time . . . every day, every week."

For other students who came to the Program feeling confident of their academic abilities, their experience there only confirmed that feeling. But for the majority of this group of participants, comparing themselves with other freshmen at Berkeley and in the Program led them to reassess their original estimates. Several said they had been "big fish in little ponds" and found the reverse to be true at Berkeley. Being at Berkeley, and in the Program, required them to "recalibrate your competencies" as one put it and therefore to make some kind of readjustment in academic self-assessment.

This sense of deflated self-esteem some students experienced initially in the Program was not necessarily permanent. One man described his academic abilities as a high school graduate as, "Unlimited. I could do anything." Then participation in the Program "taught me that there were people that could do more than I could." His earlier feelings of confidence returned, however, in the upper division where he observed that in the university as a whole,

> The sharpest people I met were in the Program. . . . For example, I didn't meet anybody in the honors program in history who had the same intellectual capacity that some of the people in the Program did. It may have been who was attracted to the Program, it may have been just my own bias having been through it. I felt I could compete with anyone. Not only felt that I could, but did.

For others, the reassessment of academic abilities took other forms. One participant who had attended an exclusive private high school and who had thought of herself as "smart," said:

> [I] wasn't afraid of the meeting, or wasn't intimidated by the papers . . . nevertheless [I] ended up feeling less of a bigwig intellectual . . . my heart just didn't get into it in a certain way that I felt from [Professor A] and [Professor B] and some of the other kids. . . . There were some people who I thought were smarter and who seemed to have more intensity with this material than I did. . . .
>
> [It may be] somewhat distorted and grandiose, but it seemed to me that our group—and I wasn't even in the center of the group—was really the life of the class. I mean it was sort of a core group . . . so I would compare myself against maybe the five or six people who were sort of better read and more aggressive intellectually.

This rather severe kind of self-scrutiny was repeated in the experiences of other participants. One woman said she had felt pretty confident of her academic abilities in high school, but that in the Program, "I didn't feel like such hot stuff," and her academic self-esteem was "put in its place."

Another woman talked about the difficulty of judging her own performance in the Program, and this was probably one of the biggest differences between high school, as well as the regular university, and the Program. She said she "knew how to do high school real well," but in the Program:

> We never got any grades, and I think that was the way you judged yourself, in high school. You got these grades, and they told you if you were doing good or not, and we never got any grades out of the stuff in here [the Program]. So you had to sort of make other terms of figuring out whether you were doing well or not doing well, and I really felt pretty inadequate a lot of the time, just in my response to a lot of what was going on. . . . I probably didn't feel as confident about my own intellectual abilities after that or during the Program.

Unlike the woman quoted earlier who gained confidence in her abilities to participate in later upper division history seminars while in the Program, this woman never was able to "become part of the small group discussions," although she nonetheless "could still put stuff down on paper and get As and Bs out of it [in the regular university]." She accepted this as a permanent condition:

> I still feel that split in me and maybe I just have to come to terms with the idea that I'm not a person who does well in seminars or in small groups

of people who are throwing ideas around, that I really am going to be mostly an observer in those situations, and that if I make a contribution, it has to be after the fact and in writing.

It is interesting that some students were able to overcome their difficulties in discussions and put to use what they learned in the Program, while this one was not. Whatever the underlying reasons, these examples point to the need for the training of both faculty and students to be able to take part in seminars rather than leaving seminar performance up to whatever abilities each of them happen to bring to the seminar group.

Another woman, who finished the Program but dropped out of Berkeley before graduating, told of her frustration in not being able to participate in discussions.

> It's the kind of thing where I'd think of something and I'd think, "That's just stupid," and then somebody else would say it, and everyone would go, "Oh, yeah".... I was just too scared.

She attributed this fear to cultural conditioning:

> [I was] just never encouraged to speak out or say anything controversial at home or say anything that would make anybody uncomfortable. It sort of gets ingrained in you, and so it's real hard to do that in a class.

But she did eventually gain more confidence in herself over time, as was reported in her statement about the major impact of the Program, the last one quoted of the first-cycle women. In time she realized her reticence wasn't due to being "not as smart as the others" but simply to a certain skill she "lacked at the time."

Another woman's background in a selective all girls' high school seemed at first to put her at a disadvantage in a co-educational college, although she had felt competent academically in high school.

> During the Program I really felt like there was something wrong with me. I was very shy so I wouldn't talk very much and I thought that was important. I . . . didn't give myself a chance. I had some memory problems at the time and I was feeling unsure of myself. I felt kind of intimidated by the whole thing.

And then I saw lots of men being mostly the talkers, the people who debated the questions. And although it was very interesting to me to listen to other people's ideas, it just felt bad that . . . coming from a girls' school where everybody was a woman and so the brightest kids were women . . . it didn't feel like I was really up to par somehow, even though I did okay in the University and I actually really think that I was competent but I just didn't think I was . . . I don't think the brightest ones were men, necessarily, but the most verbal ones were.

This particular woman, after realizing that in the Program the most verbal men were not necessarily the brightest students, gained self-confidence after college when she joined a women's literature group and was able to hold her own in "complex discussions about things from different points of view." This lack of confidence in herself in the Program did not interfere with her benefiting from it—she was the participant quoted earlier whose concepts about education and freedom have "stayed with me all my life."

Other women handled the reassessment problem in different ways. One said she had been a "fairly big fish in a fairly small pond" in high school and realized when she got to college that there were "a lot of real smart people out there." And although "I certainly did not feel that I was the most brilliant participant in the Program, I'll tell you that I definitely felt like I belonged." Her reassessment of her intellectual abilities did not erode her academic self esteem because she was able to identify with the Program as a whole.

Even entering freshmen who had not been "big fish" in their high school ponds did not need to feel discredited in the Program. One man who said he did not feel "particularly confident in myself in academic matters," at the same time said,

> one of the good things about the Program was that it was fairly open ended about one's academic . . . identification, and someone who perhaps didn't have a certain grounding in how they felt about themselves academically could go to the Program and feel unintimidated.

The ability to identify with the Program as a whole seemed to serve as a kind of safety net for the inevitable erosion of academic self-esteem that resulted from rubbing shoulders in the Program with what some considered to be the *"creme de la creme."* One woman talked about characteristics of some of the people who left the Program.

> I did feel some insecurity . . . that there were others that were more incisive, better able to concentrate on their subject. . . . I think there were some really good people in that Program, and the ones that weren't as good—weren't proud [about being in the Program] or didn't feel good about being there—were gone probably by the beginning of the second year. So the ones that stayed were I think pretty good.

The absence of grades must have lessened any sense of competition the less able students might have otherwise felt when comparing themselves to others. Even though this same woman saw that other people in the Program were "pretty smart," she

> did not feel like I was competing with them *per se,* because I didn't get a sense that I was being externally compared to them, but I was internally comparing myself to them.

Her ability to identify with the group left her feeling

> proud of being in the Program. I didn't necessarily feel that I was making any intellectual leaps personally but I felt that I was part of a group. . . . It made me [what], I guess, you would call elite, intellectual and elite.

The idea that participation in the Program could actually help people through this readjustment in the estimate of their abilities that many go through on entering college was also expressed by this woman who said her academic self-esteem became

> a whole new thing . . . it changed my views because I just always thought I would be at the top . . . [I realized] I wasn't going to be the "A" student in every single class in every single subject. . . . The Program helped me through that—what must be a real difficult period for most people who run into that situation.
>
> And I think that's probably why you get the high freshman drop-out rate. I think that a lot of people hit that and just give up. They don't want to cope with it. The Program helped me through that—it didn't mean that I couldn't be there, and it didn't mean I couldn't learn. . . . At the same time, you discovered that you weren't going to be at the top of this group,

the way you were in high school—you also had a cushion there, something that made you feel it didn't matter that much. . . .

I guess that had been part of my whole identity until then, you know—the top student. And then suddenly you feel like, "I don't even know what these people [in the Program] are talking about. . . ." And I think if you take that away with nothing [to replace it], that it's very difficult to make that kind of adjustment. I found it hard at first because I'd always had grades—grades were "it," you know. And so to give that up was, in some ways, very hard. And yet at the same time, I think, it taught me that you didn't always have to do everything for the grade, you weren't just in there learning for the grade. You weren't learning *the* one thing that the teacher wanted you to learn and write back on the test. So [the Program] was a better way of learning, like learning to *learn* instead of trying to remember.

At the same time that the Program took away the yardstick that grades had provided and required many students to reassess their estimates of their intellectual and academic abilities downward, it gave them a new way of looking at an education focused on learning rather than on grades. It replaced the sense of individual academic competition which had enabled many of them to do so well in high school with an identification with a group of faculty and students engaged in an intellectually serious academic endeavor. Perhaps this helps to explain the higher retention rate and more favorable academic performance by first-cycle Program participants in their upper division years compared to other students as reported in a study done by Professor Samuel Schaaf, who had taught in the Program in the first cycle. He found a higher percentage of Program students earning B.A. degrees by the end of their fourth year (58 percent) compared to percentages in the high forties for three comparison groups: (1) former Program students who transferred to the regular lower division, (2) applicants not accepted to the Program but enrolled instead in the regular lower division, and (3) other lower division students who had not applied to the Program. First-cycle Program graduates also earned a higher grade point average (3.08) compared to the other groups of students who achieved g.p.a.'s from between 2.91 to 2.99 (Suczek 1972, 113).[1]

---

[1]The numbers on which these percentages are based are not included in this table, but earlier in his book Suczek reports that the study used 145 Program

The sense of belonging engendered by the Program that some women reported was also experienced by men. One who "didn't judge myself as all that bright" said, "the fact that the group felt easy made me feel more confident." Another who began questioning his academic abilities shortly after arriving, and was concerned at first about whether or not he could make the grade, was "put more and more at ease while in the Program.... By the time I got to the third year, I was feeling that I did belong, [that] I could make this," and all the while his grades in his outside language course were improving. While he didn't describe himself as shy, he did recall "not being a volunteerer of information." He learned a lot "just by listening," as did some of the women mentioned earlier. But by the end of the Program he

> became more and more accustomed to speaking and voicing my own opinion and recognizing that, yeah, it did have some validity . . . [there was] a sense of growth that probably would have been stymied in the larger program [the lower division]. It might have taken me longer to get to that point.

After reassessing his abilities, another man became less intimidated by others during the course of the Program.

> I guess I felt that I was not as creative in thinking about various concepts, or looking at what I was reading . . . I didn't come up with a lot of real interesting arguments or viewpoints on what we were studying. [But as time went by] I developed a somewhat different view. I wasn't as intimidated by the other students as I was initially. I realized that not everything that was said was a real pearl of wisdom. I became more discriminating.

He was elected to Phi Beta Kappa and felt "pretty good" about his academic abilities by the time he graduated.

The Program attracted bright, verbal students and insisted on discussion in small groups, both with and without faculty present, where everyone

---

students, 135 students who had applied to the Program but had not been admitted, and 209 freshmen who had indicated they were not interested in the Program but who had satisfied the Subject A requirement (Suczek, 12-13).

The Educational Effects

could be heard, repeatedly and at length. In the absence of grades, and with the privacy of the one-to-one tutorial, the only basis of comparison students really had of each other's ability and performance must have been based largely on these discussions. It is quite possible the more competitive of them strove to excel in the discussions, setting forth a model that other, less verbally aggressive students could emulate. Over time, the sense of identification with the Program as a learning community could then replace the individual competition among students and create a better learning situation.

The actual intellectual content of the Program played a role for some men in focusing their attention away from their own shortcomings. One man, who thought he was "very capable and smart and intelligent and wonderful" in high school, found the Program, while

> not overwhelming . . . a little bit intimidating at the beginning because the ideas and the method in which we were tackling these ideas was fairly intimidating, and [Professor A] can be a kind of intimidating guy.

He accepted the challenge and "participated in everything . . . I know I enjoyed it, and I think I benefited by it," and had no subsequent academic problems in the upper division.

Another man who had felt confident, even "cocky," about his academic abilities found the Program only increased his self-confidence. It

> amplified [my self-esteem] because I felt then that I was really, honest to God, getting an intellectual challenge in the Program and meeting it. . . . I felt that now I was actually grappling with concepts, understanding intellectual struggle, debate, and I was handling it. . . . It also left me a little less secure because they did take away the yardstick of grades. . . . That takes away your security blanket. Especially if you're a person who is used to getting A's. . . . That didn't bother me . . . I was studying at a much more serious, intellectual level that is not measured by A's, B's, and C's. It's measured by how serious you are. . . . And I felt that was more important than [grades]. It was rewarding to be in a serious program where they don't measure you by grades.

This new ability to relinquish the rewards of grades in favor of the rewards of serious intellectual enterprise was available as well to people who were not as confident academically. One man who had a modest estimate of his intellectual abilities in high school but was "very good at what he was interested in," didn't remember how he felt about himself academically, just that he knew at the end that he'd "gotten it" and "then I knew that what I had done was worthwhile. I don't remember thinking that I was a great student because of it. I just remember thinking I was lucky I had 'gotten it,' that it all made sense."

For students who stayed to complete the Program, it had the remarkable effect of refocusing their attention from grades, and from external competition to a large extent, to what they were learning and what they were gaining from the Program. This led them to the kind of mature attitudes toward their own education one expects from graduate students, not freshmen and sophomores. For the absence of grades they were able to substitute a feeling of specialness, if not elitism, that they gained from "spending all this time and immersing yourself [in] these wonderful books and ideas," from being "pampered by all these professors," and from being in a small, special, experimental college within a large, very prestigious research university. Those who did not realize their full academic potential in the Program could observe how to participate in seminar discussions and put that into practice later in their academic careers.

Asked how they compared themselves to students who had not been in the Program once they got to the upper division, students said the question of comparison simply did not come up for most of them—they had no way of comparing themselves. The exceptions were the ones who compared themselves favorably to other non-Program students: "I was pleased with [my experiences in the Program], and the more I compared it, the better a deal that I think I got."

We have been describing feeling of educational awareness and academic self-esteem and identification with a serious learning community that participants got from the Program. But were there specific academic skills students gained as well? What were the effects of the Program on subsequent academic life?

THE ACQUISITION OF SPECIFIC ACADEMIC SKILLS

A series of three questions was asked of participants, about how their participation in the Program effected their ability to write, to argue effectively, and to reason critically. Since the question about writing did not distinguish between the technical aspects of writing—grammar, syntax, punctuation and the like, and expressive writing—and writing to express the meaning of what they'd read and heard, participants sometimes interpreted it both ways.

It is fairly clear from the answers to that question that for the most part the Program offered not much help in the area of technical writing. Even though they had all passed the Subject A examination and were therefore, according to University standards, technically proficient in writing, many students still felt the need for more help:

> [They were] the right kind of projects, and I think that thinking about the point of the papers was important, but I felt that they could have spent more time teaching us how to write. Although, maybe that wasn't their job. I really am not sure where you go in the University to actually learn how to write.

One woman thought that the Program may have been short on writing skills and techniques, that it would be better if students had had that training first, or at the same time. Her high school writing experience worked well with the practice in writing she received in the Program. A couple of participants wished they had been forced to write more because they lacked that self-discipline; another said she didn't "recall getting much discipline. I probably could have used a much, much better writing course than the Program was.... They could have scrutinized our prose a little more."

Some participants claimed, however, that even though the Program might have seemed deficient in teaching writing skills, it did as well or better than regular classes in the University.

> It certainly gave me as much writing skills as I ever got out of college. I wished it had been more.... You ask me what I think of as a weak spot in the Program and I think that's it. But I can't tell you how they should have done it other than what they did do.... I'm certainly not criticizing their approach. I don't know if it's their responsibility to make me learn or if it was just their responsibility to give me the opportunity and let me do my best.

Yet for others, the writing experience in the Program was useful. One participant says of a friend from the Program: "He writes fairly well now because he had been made to do it in the Program."

One participant viewed the writing in the Program as creative rather than scholarly writing. A man from the first cycle said, "We wrote papers that had a tendency to assume the characteristics of a course in creative writing . . . it was simply not scholarly, not professional."

But others of his peers enjoyed the creative part:

> I think I probably did some of my most creative and some of my most heartfelt writing in the Program, and afterwards a lot of it was just pale in comparison. . . . I would say that in terms of the structured approach that was expected by the teachers in the other classes, that the Program spoiled me, and I had to get back into a more constrained mode of writing.

Another man from the second cycle found the gains in writing prose made up for writing deficiencies in high school.

> It pushed me along, and gave me prose. I hadn't had much experience in my high school writing prose, and so for me it was really the first time I got to really expand, really write, and really try to put stuff together, and deal with the material, and so it was very useful for me, very useful.

No matter how well writing was taught in the Program, it was the integration of reading, thinking, and writing that made it unique and that some students found to be most valuable. One woman now teaches writing in a public school.

> That's what I teach at school. It forced me to be much more serious and original in my thinking, and in translating that into writing. It forced me to use writing as a way to explore thinking, which was something I had never done before . . . it definitely improved my work as a writer.

In describing how writing and thinking were related in the Program, one man said,

> [The Program had] a very helpful, very, very informative, very constructive influence on my ability to write, my appreciation for the usefulness of writing and thinking, and they are almost the same thing . . . organizing, analyzing. . . . So, it was a profound help in my writing ability, and in my appreciating the value of writing.

> The Program was nice because it forced me to use a synthesis kind of approach towards writing, drawing from different readings, drawing from different viewpoints, trying to bring them together and balance them, compare them, and that sort of thing.

Several participants mentioned that the amount of writing required in the Program was significantly more than was expected of other students in their lower division courses. And that led some of them to conclude that the Program was of real value in helping them learn to put their thoughts on paper, the expressive part of learning to write. One man says,

> I wasn't aware of it at the time . . . but I'm more and more convinced as I think about it that . . . the communication skills that Tussman gave you by making you, forcing you, to write all the time allowed me to articulate my views and think about something and have to write it down on paper. . . . We did a lot of writing. And I think that was important, you know, I think that helped a lot. And I think when you do write, particularly either keeping a journal, although you're writing about the subject, you're having to think about what you are about.

A lawyer talks about how the help he got in writing in the tutorials was useful to him in teaching others.

> I've taught writing to graduate students from what I learned from the tutorials. And these people all claim they write well now, and they get good grades, and they've done well in their law firms because they learned writing from me, and all I'm doing is teaching them the basic . . . skills that I learned [in the Program].

He also makes the connection between writing and reasoning in the Program:

> I think it's difficult to separate your ability to write without having critical reasoning skills, apart from creative writing. And you can't really write very well unless you do develop good critical reasoning skills. And I think the Program did a very good job in inculcating those skills to anybody who was willing to work in good faith.

In one clearly unintended consequence of the writing experience, one man admitted, somewhat sheepishly, that he got so good at writing there that after the Program he was able to become a sort of ghost-writer for his friends who needed help in writing their papers in the upper division. He attributed the acquisition of his writing skills to the fact that "you couldn't fake a paper in the Program," because, although you didn't get graded, you weren't done with it until it had been discussed in seminars and tutorials, and "graded by this little group of people."

The fact that papers were discussed was also a factor in this woman's assessment:

> Just the amount of writing that we did was important. I think, also, discussing the papers and having comments on the papers was very worthwhile to me. It did teach me how to put thoughts more clearly on paper. And I've never had a hard time writing, but I think that . . . probably knowing that [the paper] would be up for discussion definitely made me try to put a little more concise thinking into it.

For some people there was a carry-over of these abilities learned in the Program all the way through to graduate school. One woman says about the Program's effect on writing, critical reasoning skills, and effective arguing: "I never would have made it through graduate school [without it]."

The integration of thinking, writing, and discussion in the Program was mentioned by many participants. One said that effective arguing was "definitely one of the things that they encouraged . . . that's the process—thinking, arguing, talking, and writing it down." Another man, who had considered becoming a lawyer as many others actually did, stressed the interactive aspect of the Program:

> The Program was a dialogue. If I had to use a single word to describe the Program, it was a dialogue. It wasn't the didactic, unilateral lecture flow approach. And in a dialogue you've always got to be prepared, you've got to weigh all the possible alternative responses. You've got to anticipate. The Program I think would have prepared me eminently to become an attorney, if I'd chosen that path. I didn't do it, but I almost did.

In describing the way in which writing and reasoning skills were related, another man said:

The Educational Effects

> I'm sure it helped . . . [develop] analytical skills, because you had to express them through writing. . . . You had to think of these topics [for the papers] because nobody gave you, force-fed you the topic, so I'm sure it helped us in that regard, too. Even though I can't pinpoint these things, I'm sure there was a cumulative effect that helps me be able to define topics and do some of the things that I know that I can do now.

As with other aspects of the Program, some women indicated that while not participating directly in discussions, they nonetheless learned from what was going on around them: "listening to everybody else and absorbing all this." Another said that it helped her "tremendously" to learn to argue effectively:

> If you can learn from listening to other people argue, which I think you probably can—I don't know how much arguing I did, but certainly there was a lot of arguing going on, good, interesting arguing. I remember listening to that in seminars a lot and questioning. . . . It was always questioning—you know, the real Socratic stuff.

One woman spoke of the special value of discussion in the Program at a time when students were exploring the relationship of freedom to authority, and how these discussions, even though she didn't participate directly in them, were important to her:

> We were really in such an exciting time and we were all having questions about what authority was, what freedom was and what the balance of power in the culture was. Then we related that to what we were reading and they were real exciting discussions. It made me think a lot, even though I didn't participate in the discussions very much. I actually learned a lot from watching other people do that.

Another woman speaks of how her critical reasoning skills were helped by observing others:

> I think it really challenged me to think a lot about what I was reading and what it meant and seeing other people who had done it a lot and had real strong ideas about how to reason things out. It was a good model. I think that was probably one of the real strengths of the Program.

And while she did not take part in the discussions directly, the close contact with faculty encouraged her to gain experience arguing in the Program:

> It certainly stimulated me. I remember arguing with [Professor A] and remember being comfortable doing that. I had a chance to do that and it was a safe environment to do that. It must have helped. I do think that I argued more in graduate school [because of this experience in the Program].

Men also found models in the Program that they could absorb for later use. In speaking of his critical reasoning skills, one man said:

> I think it gave me a good model, something to keep in the back of my mind as to how the process worked. I don't think I got any practical application of it until quite awhile later.

Another said: "I modeled my writing on [Professor J's] prose and [Professor K's] speaking voice. It didn't work all the time for me, so I later had to work on my style, but those were good models." That method worked in improving his skills in arguing as well.

> Because I could model the way I thought about things on the way I saw these guys talking. I could see how things got put together, and how they sustained their arguments. So I'd argue, almost in a way of mimicking what the teachers were doing. But it helped. You got to see people talk about big issues, and take a position, and stick to it.

Instead of a single lecturer presenting material from only one point of view, students benefited from observing at first hand the dialogue among faculty. But for two men in the first cycle, where there was some bitterness among faculty, arguing took on a different meaning. One said, "There may have been so many argumentatively opinionated people that actually, it made it harder to formulate and carry out an argument." Another felt the arguing was compulsive.

> [It was] obsessive. [Professor A] would try to get you into a position where you would either have to subscribe to his point of view or rebut it .... There was an obsessive kind of extreme to the argument that I found

impossible to agree with . . . not on the basis of the content but on the need for that kind of compulsive argumentativeness.

A couple of participants found practice in arguing not within the Program but outside it while defending it to other students.

In looking over what these former students have said about the acquisition of academic skills in the Program, a picture emerges of a kind of training suitable for graduate or professional school through the writing they were required to do for the papers, the training they received in defending their papers before others, and the process of integrating reading, writing, thinking, and discussing. In the absence of practice in the Program of specific skills useful in regular classes—note-taking, exam-taking—one might wonder how these students were to fare in the upper division of the regular university. Would they suffer because they had missed two years of preparation in regular classrooms along with their contemporaries with whom they would now compete for grades? Would the Program stand them in good stead in any way as they left its elite, intimate setting and found themselves immersed in large classes in the more impersonal setting of the university without the support of the faculty and students in their special learning community?

TRANSITION TO THE REGULAR UNIVERSITY PROGRAM

Several questions were included in the interview about the transition from the Program to the upper division at Berkeley. In answer to this set of questions, the great majority of participants said they had no real problems of any kind switching over to the regular college program. Most said the transition was not difficult, although some said "taking classes for grades was a little different."

Some anticipated the change with pleasure. One said, "I think by the time that the Program was up, I was waiting to do something different. I missed it, that closeness and stuff, but I was eager to be doing something else, too, so I don't remember really having any major problems with transition." Another said, "I don't remember being all that bothered by [the transition]. I was looking forward to taking some of the other courses that were in the catalog, being able to do some shopping around."

Many participants talked about how their participation in the Program helped in their upper division years. One woman talked about what it gave her in the way of an intellectual direction and the freedom from concern about choosing courses.

> I really didn't have any academic or intellectual goals when I came from high school to college. That was one of the reasons why the Program was attractive because it seemed to offer, at least for two years—you don't have to worry about . . . this is what you're doing. It probably gave me some intellectual curiosity and helped me to create some goals for myself.

Others pointed to specific benefits of the Program for their upper division years. One man reported the effect in his philosophy classes.

> [I took] quite a few philosophy classes [in upper division], and I did well. It was certainly a helpful background . . . logic oriented, traditional, thinking about a problem. . . . Generally the better the class was, probably the more the Program helped me.

A woman said, "[the transition] was different, but I think I learned a lot about getting deeply involved in the subject . . . I just think I felt more prepared. I know I did real well once I got out. I just don't think I would have done as well [not having been in the Program.]"

Some found the upper division work easier.

> There was more expected of us in the Tussman Program, because you're expected to do papers and read, but we were also expected to think and to discuss things. Up in the University you weren't expected to think and discuss things a whole lot, you were just expected to do the work. So it was easier in a way. Not as interesting anymore, generally.

Others said the fact that students had been required to take one outside course each quarter or semester (some audited courses as well) helped in their adjustment. "The fact that I took an outside course each quarter let me know what I was going to be doing. It wasn't like it was a different world completely." Another repeated that theme.

> I went to a very small program [a preprofessional program] after the other Program . . . so I had no problem adjusting. And you also had to take one outside class, so you were exposed to the big class, the "big Berkeley," as well. You know, [the Program] was not totally isolating for anybody.

While others said they had no real problems as such switching from the Program to the regular university, several mentioned adjustments they needed to make. "I don't recall them being real problems, but it was less leisurely and more complex." Another thought experience in the Program offered trade-offs in entering the upper division:

> It was a lot harder . . . to be in the University. Maybe all those other kids that had been dealing with it before were a little better prepared for it, in some respects, than I was. But I guess there is a certain amount of confidence that you know how to—you feel as if you know how to read and think. But just in terms of orientation to the steps you have to go through to get through a course, if you're not used to doing it that way, it's a bit of an adjustment when you have to prepare for quizzes and mid-terms and that sort of thing. But in terms of writing papers, it was a lot easier. . . . Yeah, I'd say it probably evened out.

Some participants, in comparing the two programs, found the upper division disappointing. It suffered by comparison to the Experimental College Program in different ways. One said, "Upper division curriculum was a little bite here and a little bite there and there's nothing at all to tie together except for whatever I learned here in the Experimental College."

Another described the more passive approach to education he found in the upper division. The transition for him was a let-down.

> It was like going from technicolor to black and white . . . it wasn't a great problem for me. It wasn't very exciting . . . I felt like a spectator versus more of a participant which is the way I felt in the Program. So there was a spectator approach in the other classes I took as an upper division student as opposed to this much more intense and familial, involved way of being, in the Program.

One woman thought that some upper division classes hampered her self-expression. The transition was

> "rough" (laughs). I felt like no one really wanted to engage in anything like that. It was just kind of, report to class, week after week . . . there were classes that I really enjoyed a lot afterwards, and others that I didn't really feel that they allowed me to express myself all that much. . . . I

think it probably made me less able to deal with the graded kind of academic scene than ever.

One man described the change of pace and size as not enjoyable.

> Once I got back into the regular University after a quarter of it, I didn't enjoy it . . . the traffic jam sense. Here you are in the new country roads of the Program and then you get flung into the rush hour traffic. I took one course which had 1,200 people in it.

Even the smaller seminars in the upper division were not as satisfying as the Program to some of its former participants.

> I don't recall any of the feeling of disturbance or whatever going from the Program to the greater University. One thing I do recall is that the seminars, such as they were, in other classes, in history or English, were often thin and somewhat disappointing. People didn't have the same vocabulary, didn't have the same intellectual furniture, so to speak. There were few common reference points in a given discussion of students. I found that discussion groups in these classes were often disappointing compared to what we had in the Experimental Program just because we built up sort of a community and a background in the Program which we didn't have in the broader University.

While some participants reported having to make adjustments from the Program to the regular university, they found those changes were not difficult, and the experience in the Program then left them better prepared for the upper division. One man says he went through an initial adjustment period but then felt farther ahead.

> [I felt] paranoid for a while, because the whole idea of specialization was kind of alien. You'd gotten away from that idea of having to fit all of this nice book you were reading here, with all of these great ideas, into this box so that it matched up and tied to these five points and "don't bother with the rest of it because you don't have time to learn it." But those skills came back fairly quickly, and when matched with what you had in the Program, you were far and away better equipped to deal with anything that required reaction, thought, anything other than straight memorization.

One woman from the second cycle found the transition more difficult because most faculty left the university at the end of the two years.

> ... [the transition] was hard mostly because the professors didn't stay around [so that they could become advisors in the upper division.] But not as hard as it could have been. I mean ... I think most of what was required of us [were] things that I think we were prepared for, so in that sense the transition wasn't bad. ... I think there was also just a straight transition from this integrated curriculum to a course system which was rigid and limiting. I compensated for that a little bit by having an individual major and doing the integration myself. But in some ways that also made it less integrated because it was an inter-departmental thing [and] I had to provide the glue in between. ... I took a lot of responsibility for my own education.

After making a false start because he wasn't quite sure where to start, one man was then able to duplicate some aspects of the Program.

> Then [I] discovered the seminars, which I really enjoyed, so what I did was recreate the Program for myself through those courses ... so there was no real adjustment problem between lower and upper division.

While these adjustments students had to make to the upper division were for the most part not really difficult to accomplish, they were accompanied by feelings of loss in many instances. One woman from the first cycle was discouraged by the contrast in educational styles:

> I missed having kind of a small protective community, even though I hadn't made the most of it. I remember being dismayed and discouraged at huge lecture classes and the inaccessibility of the professors. ... It was just an adjustment. By then I had easily adjusted to campus life and just the in's and out's of how to register and all of that. ... But I remember one particular—I think it must have been the first lecture class I took—it was world history of some sort, and the professor wasn't very inspiring, and it was in a big lecture hall ... and it was just god-awful boring, and seemed so irrelevant, just mostly memorizing stuff. I remember the contrast was just startling. There was no question-answer—there was nothing except—he gave the lecture, you read the history books, you regurgitated it all on a test.

> And I remember, even at the time, thinking, "This is not what learning is all about." [The educational style] didn't seem very meaningful and didn't again become more meaningful until I was in some of the small seminars that upper division students get to take . . . my senior year.

Not all lecture classes in the upper division, however, were as disappointing to her as the first, and the difference was attributable to the style of the lecturer which was similar to teachers in the Program.

> I took an English lit or world lit class from a professor, I'm sure it was as a junior, in a large lecture hall, but he was so caring about his students and very accessible and really made everything come alive. And I guess it was so much more similar to what we had done in the Tussman Program, and that contrasted with . . . taking physics and all this other nonsense.

So the mere size of the class was not the crucial factor for her, but rather the attitude of the faculty member towards his students.

Another woman spoke of the splintering effect of her upper division classes that led to a feeling of confusion.

> It became apparent to me that my education was not being very cohesive . . . it was pretty piecemeal . . . there wasn't a real structure that it followed. One piece didn't relate to the next. Even within the sociology courses . . . I can't remember all of the courses. That's how much they related to each other. It was just a contrast. And I think that it was confusing, somewhat. And it . . . just didn't make as much sense, that's all.

As will be discussed again in the next section, several participants felt the Program was good training for the law profession. But one found the educational contrast between the Program and law school to be too great, as others had talked about the contrast between the Program and upper division.

> My idea [was that maybe I would like] law school because we read great constitutional [law in the Program]—but law school was a whole different experience. It's like going from really great philosophical issues, to nuts and bolts and this total dullness. And so, [the Program] didn't prepare me at all well for law school [in] that way.

Law school stacked up so poorly in contrast to the Program he dropped out and took up another profession. But in the transition to upper division, the Program was of use "in terms of personal growth, the way the Program affected . . . probably through the friendships it provided . . . it probably provided a certain amount of the security that probably helped me." He kept a connection with faculty from the Program by taking a course from a teacher formerly in the Program and by majoring in the same department, which offered him some experiences not unlike those he had found [in the Program]. "[It was] a small major that involved writing papers mostly. . . . I . . . found a niche that didn't seem all that different from the Program. So it was just less of a shock."

Several participants reported feeling sad and let down after the Program. One first-cycle man felt "overprepared" for the academic work in the upper division, and that had a negative effect emotionally.

> It was not a tough transition, it was sad . . . it was the detumescence of my intellectual budding at Berkeley. Everything else was downhill after the Program. . . . I remember specifically seeking out classes that were taught by either [Program] professors or TA's outside the Program because I wanted to continue the climate of the Program as much as possible.

(That option was for the most part available only to first-cycle participants, however, as second-cycle faculty, with one exception, returned after the end of that Program cycle to other colleges and universities.)

Others testified to feeling somewhat dejected after leaving the Program. One man said,

> In terms of just the mechanics of doing it [the transition] or being intimidated by the system, no [there were no problems]. It was really—it wasn't a problem at all. It was a little depressing.

A woman felt let down by the change in teaching approach and the absence of discussion.

> When I went to the other classes [in the upper division] it wasn't quite the same, it really was very "questions and answers" oriented. So it was a little let-down afterwards to go from one to the other. . . . I missed it.

Another woman felt a need to come to terms with the fact that there was an ending, a termination, when the Program was over.

> I was sad when the group ended. We had been together for two years and there was a feeling of security—and closing one chapter of university life and going on to something else. I don't think I had a particularly difficult time adjusting to the upper division. I think my patterns of study were pretty much the same.

One woman admitted to having a difficult transition.

> Yes. I mean, in a sense, what happened was because I liked the intellectual rapport and all the stuff that was going on in the Program, it almost did a flip-flop for me in the sense that these other classes started seeming very irrelevant, and what was the purpose of them? Because I didn't know what my purpose was, where was I going to be going with whatever I was accumulating. I didn't have a goal or direction. . . . I felt lost, intellectually.

After a year and a half in the upper division at Berkeley, she transferred to a small liberal arts college which was for her,

> coming back to a Tussman thing, in a way, because the classes were very small. There was a lot of interaction with the faculty. I did special projects with two particular faculty members and it [her intellectual self-esteem] kind of got restored again.

She felt students could have been helped in this transition. "I'd like to feel that there would be some help in making the transition [to the upper division]. We were sort of like little fish thrown out into the ocean"—an adjustment a few found difficult. From big fish in a little pond in the Program to minnows in the ocean. This particular woman did adjust, and went on eventually to get a Ph.D. from another prestigious research university.

There were two people from the first cycle who did not have an easy time getting used to the upper division. In both cases their difficulties seemed not specific to the Program itself but due to other factors that they brought with them at entrance. Interestingly, both were Berkeley residents and neither had wanted to come to college at Berkeley, but did so either because they were not accepted elsewhere or because of the wishes of their family. Neither appeared to have fully come to grips with their being at a place in which they did not want to be, and there might have been some reflection of that in their difficulties in discovering a course of study leading to either future educational or professional goals.

Whether or not going to university in the same town in which they had grown up and in which their families still lived had a decelerating effect on the separation and individuation process underlying their successful transition to adult independence can only be speculated upon here, but it does seem quite possible that played a part. Being somewhat hampered in their natural development toward independence perhaps left them with unresolved feelings that may have led to their "floundering about" more than other participants in their upper division years, although both eventually became successful professionally, if not, in their own views, educationally.

Both of these students dropped out of Berkeley in the upper division, although one returned later to graduate. It seems likely from their histories that both of them would have had difficulties completing their education in the university at the time, whether they were in the Program or in the regular lower division program. It is possible that the Program helped them to finish at least two years, although that is only speculation.

In spite of whatever difficulties some Program students had in the upper division, Professor Schaaf's data show us that students who completed the Program in the first cycle graduated at higher rates than both the group of regular lower division students not interested in the Program and the group of students in his study who had applied to the Program but had not been accepted. (See the previous section on academic self-esteem.) It is impossible to make judgments at this point, however, about how these two particular students would have fared in the regular lower division, whether for better or worse. And it should be borne in mind that in Schaaf's study, while students who completed the first cycle of the Program had significantly higher retention rates than the two comparison groups, close to one-third had still not graduated by December 1969, a full four academic years and one quarter after entering Berkeley. (All three participants in this study who reported dropping out of Berkeley after the Program were from the first cycle; all second-cycle participants in the study remained to graduate, some in less than four years. Second-cycle students were not included in the Schaaf study, and there is no way of determining the percentage of them staying to graduate from Berkeley.)

It might be expected that most students would, as some of the ones quoted above, be eager to get on with their upper division years at Berkeley after their experiences in the Program. Somewhat surprisingly, there was a group of four participants who did not go straight on to the upper division, but chose instead the Education Abroad Program, the "junior year abroad" at Berkeley. There is no way of knowing now just how many Program graduates did likewise, but we do have these four on record, two from the first cycle and two from the second, one woman and three men. Three went to Continental countries, one to Great Britain. Two of them, both in the same European country but at different times, experienced no real problems in transition even though they were required to learn the language of the country to which they went—to read, understand lectures, and take exams in that new language. The fact that in this country classes were not large and that only one subject was studied at a time may have made their adjustment easier.

One woman did not experience any particular difficulties in taking up a new program in another country, and did find a supportive professor, but she expressed deep dissatisfaction with her entire undergraduate education at Berkeley. As with the two Berkeley residents discussed above, the problems she had finding any kind of educational goals during the Program persisted in her upper division years. She eventually did succeed, however, after graduation, in establishing professional goals, completing graduate school and becoming successful professionally.

One man ended up in his junior year abroad in a country under a Fascist regime at that time with a particularly authoritarian kind of educational system. It was necessary for him to accommodate to huge lecture classes, great professors as "god figures," who demanded rote memorization from their students. His was not an easy transition.

> It was not appreciated if you asked any challenging questions. Of course, the whole Program was based on making us ask challenging questions. . . . I did not do well. I got very poor grades. I failed a number of the classes I took, largely because I couldn't stand them. I just felt alienated, frustrated, and extremely disappointed—bitter—that the classes that I was taking over there were just so dumb compared to what I was doing here. I mean, I had been involved in an intellectual pursuit here,

and then I was thrown into this Mickey Mouse thing over there. . . . My last year was an anti-climax because the first two years were super, the third year was an absolute crusher, and then the fourth year was just simply a matter of patching—of repair work.

In his adjustment to his junior year abroad, his choice of countries in which to study presented him with the greatest possible contrast to the Program. In spite of his difficulties his third year, he managed to graduate ahead of schedule, earn an advanced degree, and teach for a time at the college level.

One important aspect of the transition to upper division was the necessity for Program students to choose a major. That choice was for them perhaps a more abrupt one than for students in the regular lower division, for although they may have been considering their choices of majors, they had not had the opportunity to explore very many classes presented from a disciplinary standpoint. Were there problems then for Program participants in choosing upper division, and if so, what were the nature of those problems?

THE PROGRAM'S EFFECT ON CHOICE OF MAJORS

By design, the Program afforded its participants a kind of moratorium on the whole idea of the major; the Program was, in spirit and in practice, "submajor" as it was "subdisciplinary." Rather than considering their curriculum in terms of disciplines, students were involved instead in a global, adisciplinary or transdisciplinary approach to their subject matter. They were not forced to choose one separate disciplinary path—history, anthropology, political science, philosophy, literature—to the exclusion of the others, although parts of the Program curriculum might be thought of as fitting into each of these areas of scholarship. It seems likely that the question of upper division majors was not discussed formally in the Program.

The university accepted completion of the Program as having satisfied the reading and composition, social science and humanities, and American history and institutions requirements. The outside course permitted students to satisfy the language requirement and either the science requirement or some prerequisites for the upper division major (Tussman 1969, 109).

Choosing a major for Program participants was perhaps made more difficult for some students by the fact that they had not had the freedom in their lower division years to "shop around," to try out different classes in different disciplines, to sample their wares, to try on disciplinary identities the way some participants believed lower division students in the regular program had been allowed to do. One participant experienced an abrupt change.

> I felt then that as a junior I had to do something [major in something but] ... I didn't have—I felt like I was just starting the University, as a junior.

Another had trouble learning how to drop classes in which he was not interested.

> I took too many courses when I was a junior and senior that I probably should never have stayed in. I [wasn't] sophisticated about it. You walk into a lecture and you just realize that this guy's not for you, he's not going to hold your interest ... and you just have to be able to make those decisions. I think I stayed in a couple of classes that I probably should not have done. And maybe if I had had the experience before ... when I was a freshman and sophomore of making those decisions, that maybe I'd had more practice dropping out, moving around.

Because he had always been interested in a variety of fields, one man felt he had lost something by not being exposed to more choices in his lower division years.

> [I felt] a little bit limited in what I could be doing. I found my first two years I was really just looking at philosophy. I felt a little bit of loss there, of not being able to try all these different menus that the University offers and see which one I would follow. ... You can see the value in being thrown into the chaos of the University and having to really establish yourself then. Just going off on all sorts of tangents, but maybe at that stage in your life, you shouldn't be so limited in two years. You should be able to experience more of the intellectual world of the University, other courses.

In contrast, another man felt that through his attendance at outside courses while in the Program, he was seeing more of the University than just the Experimental Program at the time and nothing that I saw told me that I was missing out, that there was something better that I could be doing.

The advantage of "shopping around" in the regular lower division may have been more imagined than real, as some participants came to believe. One woman said,

> The only time we had to take other courses we had to use up on language and science requirements. So the opportunity to sort of relate to the University at large or do a little course shopping really wasn't there. I think we lost something in terms of just getting exposed and shopping around.

But when asked what the consequences of the loss was, she replied: "It's hard to tell. In the long run I don't think it's been a big problem. I think it was just a frustration at the time." In comparing her experience with that of other students in the regular lower division, another woman said, "You know, really, after two years they didn't have any better idea where they wanted to go than when they started."

In describing the struggle to settle on a major, one woman said the Program had no effect on that process.

> I think if I'd not gone through Tussman I think I would have gone through the same thing. I think that was more a reflection of me than the Program.

Another woman saw no disadvantage in having been in the Program.

> There may have been some advantage to having taken that smorgasbord of classes in different departments because I didn't really have a good sense of what else was available . . . I ended up majoring in psychology. . . . I'm not sure that I really would have done anything different looking back on it so I'm not sure how [big] a disadvantage it was because I think the advantage of having been in the Program was great.

And the moratorium served a useful purpose for her:

> It's good that we got to wait two years . . . I was pretty young to decide at that time what I thought I wanted.

Another woman would have preferred to stay in the Program another year. "I really wanted the Program to last for three years. I had to shop around when I went to the regular University, but that was really okay." And one man said,

> I didn't get to take a lot of individual courses that some of my peers [in the regular lower division] did, but I don't call that a disadvantage. I didn't suffer from it . . . it just made things different.

Another participant said, "I didn't feel as though I was prevented from taking whatever other classes I wanted to take." Others reported being able to shop around in upper division courses, even in the Education Abroad Program. One man found a major in an outside class he had taken while in the Program.

In spite of this testimony from those who completed the Program about the general lack of negative effects of not being able to sample more regular lower division courses that the university had to offer, we may be hearing from only those students who whom this wasn't a significant problem. Perhaps some students found this a serious enough drawback to the Program to justify their dropping out, while there may have been others who never applied because they realized being in the Program for their first two undergraduate years would inhibit them in this way and for whom that factor was important.

Since their lower division social science and humanities requirements had already been fulfilled by the Program, several students chose a major from those fields. In that way, the Program may have limited them to some extent, funneling them into majors in these fields rather than exposing them to a wider variety of disciplines. Instead of shopping around for a major, there is some evidence some students instead took the easiest way out. One participant said,

> There were a couple of fields you could glide into easily . . . I think history and English were the other departments [besides anthropology] that were easy to step [to] from the Program into the regular University, and not be way behind.

One woman from the first cycle who had been an academically self-confident high school student yet whose participation in the Program was "marginal," said that she did not feel she could go from the Program to a regular academic major in the upper division. "Sitting around on cushions on the floor and just talking somehow made me feel that I wasn't really qualified to go into a junior or senior academic class." She majored in art history, something that

> gave me pleasure . . . because it was something I did know how to do . . . I felt quite confident being able to do that. There were a lot of other subjects or areas that I just didn't feel very confident [about], and part of it I think is because I had missed the exposure as a freshman and sophomore. For example, I never took a poli sci course. Now I guess in some ways you could say the entirety of the Program was a poli sci course but I didn't know that, you see. And I actually did want to [take a] poli sci course, but I was afraid.

Her comments perhaps reflect the disorganization of the first cycle. She recognized that while she was

> not living up to my potential, no one ever did anything about it . . . I was not called to task for it. I was not asked to leave the Program . . . and I learned that I could fake it.

A Berkeley resident, she had wanted to go East to college and not to Berkeley as her parents insisted. Instead, she found that participating in the Program was in a sense "running the other way," a means of escape. A gifted high school student, she found the Program was not in line with her view of what a traditional college education should be, the kind of education she might have gotten in an eastern liberal arts college that she would have preferred to attend. She felt that since the results of her academic work would not be seen in the form of thick papers and reports (and probably grades), no one would know how she was progressing educationally, leaving her free to pursue personal rather than academic goals. Coming to Berkeley by default in order to please her parents, and into the Program by default in a spirit of defiance, her case was unusual among the 40 participants interviewed for the study.

The effect of the Program on choice of major was idiosyncratic, and there was no set pattern. Some participants said that they had been thinking about various majors even before joining the Program. History, political science, anthropology were some examples of majors already chosen by these students when they entered Berkeley. Some said being in the Program had no effect on their choice of majors. Others reported no problems choosing majors while in the Program. Some said their experience in the Program was a contributing factor:

> I think it probably did make a contribution to my choice of history because I think it opened up reading so much about these periods. I think I became more interested in learning more about what was actually happening, getting a larger overview.

Another was also drawn to history.

> It was during those first two years that I'm pretty sure I came to the conclusion that I wanted to major in history, and I think it has something to do with the kinds of things we were reading, the kind of things we were thinking about, historical thoughts, the history of ideas coming up through there. I think that maybe it gave me that goal to major in history, or let me define that goal.

A few participants talked about the role faculty members from the Program played in their choice of majors. One remembered

> talking to [Professor A] a number of times. And I think he had a big influence on my decision to major in [anthropology] (although A taught in another department). I think [the faculty were] very, very influential in determining—helping to determine what I wanted to do educationally.

One man from the first cycle sought out classes in the upper division taught by one Program faculty member and then majored in that subject.

A factor complicating the procedure of choosing a major for all Berkeley students was the chaos and confusion resulting from the demand for educational reform accompanying the Free Speech Movement. Students were allowed to create individual majors of their own, with what appears to have been minimal guidance from faculty in some cases. One participant said, "My major was . . . just for the bureaucracy really, because I had taken lots of different kinds of classes." They may have welcomed the freedom to do that at the time, but in the end, it is not clear they were all well-served by that freedom. Several of the participants bemoaned the state of education in the upper division at Berkeley in the sixties, a condition not confined at the time to Berkeley alone, of course.

Some students felt that choosing to participate in the Program meant they had to forsake future careers in the sciences—medicine, engineering, and the like—primarily because they could not fulfill the heavy science requirements with only one outside course allowed each quarter or semester.

For the most part, they reported not being unhappy with this choice, and were fully accepting of this consequence. One said, "It reinforced a basic tendency of mine not to really emphasize a heavy science kind of major." For the most part, these students who realized they were choosing *not* to pursue academic and vocational careers in science as they entered the Program were men. Participating in the Program did not preclude majoring in science, however, as one woman from the first cycle testified. She had come to Berkeley and the Program having decided when she was very young to become a biologist. Having made that decision early, with total commitment, she simply took her science requirements during summers and during the Program as her outside classes. She graduated on time, reported no strains in doing both the Program and a science major, and pursued an advanced degree in her field, later teaching at the graduate level. She was the one quoted earlier who felt that her experiences in the Program strengthened her in her scientific career, and that it was important to her to have had those experiences when she did, early in her education before taking up her major. Rather than using her two undergraduate years exclusively to fulfill science requirements, she did some exploring, if not shopping around, in the humanities and social sciences through the Program.

Three other women reported taking pre-med after completion of the Program; two immediately after the Program and one some time later. All three are now practicing in branches of medicine. One said being in the Program had not stood in the way of her taking science courses:

> I don't consider . . . that I would have done that the first time around if I hadn't been in the Tussman Program. I probably would have gone the social science, humanities route anyway. I was not going to start in the sciences as an undergraduate anyway.

She also felt that spending her first two years in the Program was not only not a hindrance in her eventual pursuit of an advanced degree in medical science, it was actually of help. It was necessary for her to attend a junior college and summer school at Berkeley to make up for the science courses she had missed as an undergraduate, but she was able to do that fairly quickly in under two years, partly because of the Program.

> I think the study habits and the direction that I had from working in the Tussman Program really made a difference in my ability to do what I did. It was much easier going back and taking these courses and taking them when I did than . . . if I had been a freshman taking them I'm sure. . . . Looking back in retrospect, I was more mature, I was goal-oriented at that time. I had a lot more confidence in myself as a student, and I'm sure that the Tussman Program had something to do with that.

(It is interesting that these four women were open to choosing science careers after the Program, while about the same number of men had felt they had been precluded from choosing careers in science by choosing the Program—perhaps an indicator of more career flexibility on the part of women.)

There is some evidence here that the Program may have influenced, or at least reinforced attitudes students had previously held about choosing a major, and the meaning of a major—that majors were less important and therefore less restricting to them because of their participation in the Program. One man in the first cycle decided that since no undergraduate major would lead directly to a job anyway, he would choose a major according to the classes he would have to take to fulfill the major requirements, classes that would be most interesting and "least burdensome" to him, and chose sociology on that basis. He described the role the Program had played in this process:

> The experience in the Program did make me realize that you really [should] take what you want to take to the extent that you can in undergraduate school . . . I realized that if I wanted to maximize my education I should take as much of what you want to take, not what somebody else wants you to take.

This man went on to take a graduate degree and to teach in the humanities rather than sociology.

Another man thought the Program taught him something about how to make educational and vocational choices and influenced his decision to leave law school.

> Had I not been in the Tussman Program, I don't know how I would have been, but I think it may have impacted my decision not to be a lawyer, and to maybe follow more the dictates of what I would want for myself, to make up my own mind about what would please me, partly because I'd had an educational experience that I really valued, and I knew what that was like.

He also mentions the influence of the rather special, private high school he attended so that "the Tussman Program just seems a piece of many experiences." But he does go on to say,

> I'm sure I would have found my education to be a lot less pleasurable, or more alienated . . . being in the Program helped me pick an area where I wouldn't feel alienated.

One highly successful businessman who went first from the Program to study and work in public service, attested to the way in which the Program influenced the way he thought about his economic future.

> [The Program] had propelled me into a very broad humanities based set of majors [as an undergraduate and graduate student] . . . I think it affected my economic horizon because I was busy pursuing very broad horizons and not putting a marker in the ground. . . . . Instead of coming out of the Program thinking, "I've got to make $18,000 year one and $22,000 year three and $30,000 year five, my thought was, Okay, what's going to be over that next set of mountains over there?"

Participants' experiences in the Program did, however, give many of them an orientation they found useful, a framework for choosing majors, and choosing future careers. One man, now a lawyer, said,

I had become oriented toward the type of subjects about which the Program revolved, so I threw together an individual major about political theory.

A teacher talked about how the Program shaped his interests.

> I appreciate the Program because . . . it's so practical (laughs), you don't think of it as practical [but] it gave me an attitude and a framework within which to apply whatever interests would come up. I just did not know what I was interested in, so I don't think the lower division sampling would have done that, I wouldn't have had an orientation.

He said that the Program had helped him "lose my capacity to study what I wasn't interested in." And his choice of major (history) was influenced by the Program because

> out of this emerged a pattern of liking to read books that other people are reading and talking about, and the history department had a lot of seminars. . . . I became interested in a couple of fields, and I sort of pursued those. With no real ambition to become an historian . . . I got to so enjoying the small group mode that I sought that in the University. . . . I think it [the Program] set up a mode for me that I wanted to complete, I wanted to stay with, and it related to some interior development, it did not relate to "making it" in the world.

So for these men, career choices, professionalism, money making, were all pushed into the background by experiences in the Program. They actually did delay their career choices until after graduation, and since all pursued advanced degrees and are now satisfied and successful in their current careers, their experiences can be seen to justify the principle of the avoidance of premature specialization upon which the Program was built (Tussman 1969, 74).

For some women, the choice of major was also influenced by experiences in the Program. A civil servant, who had majored in French, said,

> I loved literature, I'd always loved reading books . . . I really liked the word, the written word . . . and a lot of what we read in the Program was that sort of thing, as opposed to people in science or math backgrounds. . . . I really liked the stories, the Greek tragedies and the comedies.

There were other ways in which the Program influenced the choice of majors. One woman said that designing an individual major in ethnic studies was surely "related to the concepts of the Program in some ways. Not being able to settle on any one discipline, and not being comfortable just with anthropology or just with sociology." Two Program faculty members were helpful to her in formulating this "comprehensive" approach to her upper division studies.

Another man, now a lawyer, also designed an individual major with the title "American Legislative Process." The role of the Program in the development of this major came about because

> we were into democracy, and the lobbying just sort of grew out of the sense that you don't want to be a revolutionary, you want to be a worker for change within the system.

Lobbying in the state capitol was part of this major, and "clearly the Program was the impulse for that."

The Program, then, influenced its students in their choice of classes and majors in the upper division in a variety of ways: the curriculum stimulated some to pursue history further; the concentration of reading books one at a time intensively was a method others wanted to continue; the education for democracy at the heart of the Program was further pursued by some. Looking at subject matter from a variety of viewpoints and not a single, narrow disciplinary outlook was an experience some wanted to continue. Others wanted a humanities background even though they later pursued studies and careers in science.

History was the major chosen most often by participants in the study. Taken together with art history, one quarter of the group who were interviewed, 10 altogether, chose that area for further study. Anthropology and political science followed with five majors each, and the rest were scattered among French, rhetoric, ethnic studies, biology, journalism, psychology, art, math, sociology, social science, and a variety of original, self-designed majors.

More important than whether more Program participants majored in history or French or biology is that many of them came to see the choosing of the major as not the main focus of their educational planning. Instead, they chose majors and careers because of their inherent interest in them. They did not look at the major as a preprofessional requirement; many took graduate work in fields either completely unrelated to their undergraduate majors, or only tangentially related. These attitudes of "learning for the sake of learning" and the lessening in importance of money and social status when considering future careers were reinforced, of course, by the prevalent values of the times on college campuses. It is possible that in other times of greater concern for jobs and careers and the importance of "success," the Program would not have attracted as many students in the first place.

And while they may have de-emphasized occupations and careers as undergraduates, three quarters of these participants in the study did go on to take some graduate work with 65 percent of the total earning advanced degrees and one third of the total earning a Ph.D., M.D., or J.D. If the Program, as some said, did not lead directly to an upper division major or to a career, it did apparently lead to further education. These figures suggest that in spite of holding rather loose attitudes towards careers as undergraduates, Program graduates were still capable of eventually formulating and pursuing career goals.

Chapter 8

The Vocational Effects

It was never the stated intention of Meiklejohn and Tussman nor any of its faculty to in any way influence the eventual occupations, careers or even the further education of its students. Tussman sees the lower division not only as a moratorium on the major, but also a time when "commitment to a vocational path is generally being deferred" (Tussman 1969, 74). The "Athens to America moral curriculum" could hardly be thought of as preprofessional training, except perhaps for future teachers of the classics. Yet, in spite of the focus of the Program away from occupational concerns, interviews with participants did reveal effects of the Program on subsequent occupations and careers of many of them, in surprisingly varied fields. It is not surprising that the Program influenced the attitudes of many of them regarding the place of work and careers in their lives.

The effects of the Program on the occupations, careers, and attitudes toward work of its graduates differ as widely as the occupations they hold. At the time of the interviews, some 20 years after having completed the Program, the participants in this study were employed in a variety of occupations ranging from college teaching to stock-brokering to butterfly-raising. The largest number of them in one profession were lawyers, eight in all, one of them a woman. Four people listed teaching as their occupation, including one college teacher. Six others say they taught in the past, or did part-time teaching in addition to their main occupation. These part-time teachers all taught or have taught in the past at the college or graduate school level, making a total of 10 who taught or who have taught part time. There were an equal number (10) in business occupations—shop owners of various kinds, a wine merchant, a designer/manufacturer, a bookkeeper, a computer/software designer, a director of computer/communications for a large, multinational company. Half a dozen of these owned or were co-owners of their businesses. Four participants were psychotherapists—practicing either psychiatry, psychology, or social work. One was a minister. Several were in the arts or related fields—musicians, photographers, a documentary producer, designers, a calligrapher. Three women, all from the first cycle, gave their occupation as full-time mothers or homemakers. Two women were librarians. Other occupations included fundraiser, community organizer, economic analyst, court clerk, speech therapist, workers compensation consultant. While not necessarily representative of Program graduates as a whole, this list of occupations does illustrate the variety of jobs and careers Program graduates pursued.

Some of the same attitudes toward majors and upper division studies fostered by experience in the Program also appeared when participants were questioned about whether or not, and how the Program had influenced their work. Several felt there had been no influence or very negligible influence. A few others said it combined with other influences: "It's a piece of a lot of experiences . . . a piece of a tapestry. I don't see it as being an outstanding piece of that tapestry."

For a few others, all men, the Program provided a kind of intellectual zenith that was hard to match in what was to follow, academically or professionally. It is hard to say whether the Program actually had a negative effect on their careers, but it seems they have not been able to connect their positive experiences in the Program with any kind of career or occupation. One man told of having chosen a career in the theater in high school, but abandoning it after entering the Program. "That kind of intellectual rapture . . . drew me away from what my previous really strong interests had been." Another man had difficulties finding himself academically and professionally after the Program.

> I had much, much higher expectations of what I was going to be doing [after the Program] . . . the negative thing was feeling this thing of being special and yet being a complete failure at the same time. . . . [The Program] was [an] ivory tower, completely removed from the realities of

> . . . your future career . . . my first two years were wasted in terms of career development, in terms of increasing my worth in the marketplace.

He had, however, reported many benefits from the Program. Working as a postman shortly after graduation, following abortive attempts at graduate school, he said "I thought back on the Program—I thought at least I'm educated, at least I've got a mind that is doing this work. I'm not detached from it—I enjoy it in some ways."

In contrast, of the half a dozen participants whose jobs were in the field of business, two, including the man just quoted, felt their experiences in the Program had not prepared them for their future careers. Two other businessmen and women felt the emphasis on community in the Program was important to them in their adult lives, and one traced his enjoyment in being in a small business to that concept of community he found to be the Program's main message.

> I'm a community oriented business, a small business . . . probably the way I choose to live my life is partly due to the Program and the idea that I do think about my life in terms of a community. . . . I think the Program gave me some of this, or made me think about it. I think it's important to contribute to your community . . . I've volunteered in certain organizations. . . . And I think the Program, again, made me think about my world and my life in terms of community, as opposed to in terms of myself.

Another businessman said that while the Program did not prepare him for the business world, it did prepare him to become a leader. "It showed me what the characteristics of leadership are." He now works in the area of international information technology, and holds two advanced degrees. His first career he described as that of an "intellectual missionary" in adult education, work that "seemed like a natural extension of . . . implementing the philosophy and the orientation of the Program." He also taught at the graduate level and tried "to use a lot of the same techniques and some of the style that the professors in the Program had." He said the Program had affected all three areas of his work since he graduated.

While one would not expect the education that participants received in the Program to be of much immediate value in the field of business, and in a few cases participants felt it did not, the training for leadership and attitudes toward the community fostered in the Program have been important to others in their business pursuits. Two self-described merchants write newsletters for their clients, and trace their skills to the training in writing they received in the Program.

The emphasis on writing in the Program has been of use to its other graduates in other fields. One man who writes scripts and produces public information films said that although he had been interested in writing before, the opportunity to write in the Program kept his interest alive. One woman found "the ease that I have in writing that resulted from the Tussman Program" to be of use in her medical practice. A lawyer said writing skills learned in the Program helped in writing briefs.

Effects of the Program on participants' work have been amazingly varied. One teacher reads Greek myths to kindergarten students as a result of his exposure to them in the Program. A social worker, working in "a hospital setting with an interdisciplinary team of doctors, nurses, psychologists and people from all different kinds of theoretical backgrounds who never agree on anything," found that "learning in the Program to respect other people's opinions and values is very useful when it comes to people who have different orientations." A librarian said "being a librarian is what being in the Tussman Program really probably prepared me for, which is a little bit of everything—very broad, liberal education background." One lawyer finds it useful to list the Experimental College Program in his resume; another submitted papers written in the Program in his application to law school.

The group of lawyers who had been in the Program had other things to say about its importance to them. One lawyer said:

> the Program or the professors and instructors had an influence on not only my upper division work, but also, to some extent [on my] going into law. . . . I think it had some influence on my analytical development and critical thinking.

Another said that as he

> was already somewhat predisposed to law, the Program was interesting from a career building respect. Just the chance to speak in front of a large group of people and respond to questions and be prepared for interruptions. It was a good opportunity to learn how to think on your feet—something which I thought lawyers went through.

The Vocational Effects

One man attributes his decision to go into law to the Program:

> I'm sure it [the Program] did [have an influence] because of the argument and the balancing, and the respect for the process of how you come to a solution is a big thing in the law business. One of the books we had on our list was this little thing that Tussman had put together, just a collection of Supreme Court decisions on church and state problems. I liked that because it was [a] major philosophical discussion focused on a very concrete issue, instead of a major philosophical discussion just blasting into the universe, like Kant and Hegel.

Another lawyer cited Tussman's "pamphlet on Supreme Court decisions" among the influences on his career.

> [It was] really a very powerful thing. We had no idea what the Supreme Court did, and Tussman had that very interesting book where he took the Supreme Court decisions and edited them, and then gave them to you as Greek drama, and how the democracy works this stuff out.[1] Now, I have all kinds of fights with that, but it was great . . . why I went into law school has another whole series of reasons that don't have to do with the Program, but that was real important for me, reading those decisions, that was part of my idealism about the law. . . .
>
> I wrote very well, owing again, I think, to the Program . . . Public service [his first job after law school in the State Attorney General's Office] was a natural kind of thing to do, actually, out of the Program. It felt like a very good way of being a lawyer. . . . I think the Program, if not just the general milieu of the sixties, but the Program I think specifically gave me a sense of the value . . . of having a public life as an active citizen, in some way contributing to the common good.

In explaining the numbers of Program graduates who became lawyers, another of them says,

> [I]t probably gave us a greater sense of what is involved in a democracy, particularly the American democracy. A sense of the culture, sense of place, sense of person, sense of issues. It may have made a bunch of us lawyers because most of the people I'm still in touch with

---

[1] Joseph Tussman, ed., *The Supreme Court on Church and State* (New York: The Oxford University Press, 1962).

from the Program all turned out to be lawyers. There must be about twenty others that I've heard of who turned up as lawyers and I think we all sort of fell into it.

Maybe that is because the Program teaches you the basic habits of thought that are useful in the practice of law, or at least law school. I think what it really does is gives you more of a grasp of the basic tension in the American Constitutional scheme between obligations and what you want to do. And the internal compass, that tension between the internal compass and the requirements of all of the society . . . [O]ne of the things that the Program focused on was resolution of conflicts, with reasoned discourse, tolerance of differences and coming up with adjustments, and that's really, when you get down to it, if you're serious about practicing law, that's what you do. . . .

Instead of trying to find out what you've got to say to pass the next exam, you're looking for the basic core of "what's going on here?" and then you find a way to explain it to other people. You don't have to be a lawyer to do that [but] we've institutionalized it. That's the essence of the political obligation, being a representative, and ultimately a lawyer is a representative. I guess that's way I meant earlier when I said that's the basic skill they taught us . . . that's what I felt I took away from it.

We spent a fairly large chunk of time dealing with constitutional analysis by the Supreme Court, mostly on the issues of church and state, but when you get that kind of [immersion] you get a real, solid, genuine feel for the kind of constitutional analysis that the Supreme Court goes through. And I tell you when I took constitutional law in law school, I knew more than the professor did about the analysis and he'd been practicing for forty years. . . . Lawyering is perhaps the one institution in the society where people regularly explain their thought processes in making rules and decisions. . . . It's the same process we were going through in the Program. . . .

That fundamental grounding in the principles . . . I keep coming back to this, that long-term aspect of the Program, where they ground you in your culture and the principles and get you looking at that history that you've dealt with in school but never really came to grips with, [not the] dates but the meaning, the importance of it. . . . Training in law doesn't get you there, that's just technical, that's just like taking training in engineering. You may develop a set of technical skills; that doesn't mean you've got any ability to use them. . . .

[If] you come in with no compass to guide you in the use of these skills, or no way of getting one, you wind up kind of splaying yourself across the landscape, making deals as they seem convenient, and winding up lost. . . . I think they [the Program] helped you find it [the compass]. They didn't give it to you, but they made you go through the process, the sorts of things you have to go through in order to develop one . . . you're presented with that kind of opportunity or that kind of education. . . . I think the Program really started me on that—maybe gave me more than I knew.

Several lawyers spoke in similar ways about the foundation for law that they received in the Program, although there is no evidence from the interviews that students were guided in any way by faculty in the Program to enter that, or any other field. Some of those interviewed had wanted to be lawyers before entering the Program. However, the curriculum certainly did give people who were interested in the theory and practice of law an experience in legal analysis that serves them to this day.

Program graduates other than lawyers also felt they had been given foundations for their professions. One teacher, the director of a preschool/kindergarten said:

I actually applied what the Program was about by going into education. . . . I could see it as a place . . . where one could find one's calling . . . calling in the highest sense, of a purpose within the framework. . . . It was the one place I could earn money (laughs) at working at the foundations of the community. I mean, that's what a teacher is, that's what education represents.

A woman who works for the state as a workers' compensation consultant and deals regularly with lawyers has also been able to apply principles and skills learned in the Program to her work.

What I got out of the Program was that it's important to go to primary sources whenever possible. . . . So I learned sort of a time-honored, traditional, intellectual approach to things. I learned about a careful reading of the text. I learned that was important, because I learned that even two very distinguished scholars could read the same text and come up with entirely different points of view. That's what we were witnessing all the time in the lectures. That prepared me for this job, because I see the same thing here, two very well-trained attorneys can read the same medical report, or the same legal document and argue opposite ends of the spectrum.

> [I learned] to go to primary sources for information, and to read thoughtfully, and to read carefully. I cannot tell you how much I use that skill in my present job. I have to match wits—I don't want to overstate my importance—I do not have a big, high-powered job or anything, but I have to, on occasion, match wits with *magna cum laudes* from Stanford Law School and U.C. Boalt, attorneys who do not read, and are not prepared (laughs), and I am. There's a little craft to what I do. I have to listen very carefully to questions that are asked me on the stand because they're leading, and they're trying to trip me up. An "and" or an "or" could make a difference of several thousands of dollars, so I have to have an acute sense of hearing, and language, and thought, and be able to really concentrate on what literally the judge has said here, keeping close to the text.
>
> A lot of it, the structure . . . I also attribute to my exposure to Latin that I didn't get in Tussman's Program. But what I'm saying is that being able to read fragments of sentences and then to stand back and look at the whole meaning—this is an exercise that we did in the Program. In some of the seminars, you were asked to read parts, and then discuss the meaning. . . .
>
> I think the best training I've had is being part of a system of justice. . . . [From the Program I got] the reverence for the state as an institution, and for the system of justice. . . . I was prepared to take my work seriously and to do a good job because of the [materials on] church versus state that we read in the Tussman Program. I don't think my *skills* were really honed in the Tussman Program; I thought it was becoming acquainted with sort of the larger principles of Western civilization, the Judeo-Christian values, that really operate a lot in our society.

This is another illustration of how the Program provided not specific skills, but an intellectual and moral foundation that participants found later served as an underpinning and support for a profession. There were effects of a more immediate nature as well. An optometrist found the Program provided a background for her in the way she conducts her practice. In diagnosing underlying problems with eyesight, she takes a problem-solving approach that involves looking at a patient's entire situation.

> Often I get to know people and meet their whole family . . . their parents and their grandparents and their grandchildren. And I feel like . . . I have a different approach to the world as a result of my background and the Tussman Program is a part of it. . . . I don't worry too much about philosophy while I'm examining eyes, but in the Old World global sense

of what I do, and how I provide care to people [the Program has been helpful].

ATTITUDES AND OUTLOOKS

Some participants said that the attitudes and outlooks that came from the Program directly or indirectly affect their work. Another lawyer cited one effect of the Program:

> I guess I'm always looking to longer term solutions to problems than most people are . . . a calmer and more long term view to a lot of problems [where] I might otherwise get sucked into some kind of short term solution to things.

In a similar vein, an economist working as a staff analyst says,

> I think that I can cope with problems, off-the-wall problems, when somebody has a problem or an assignment that I completely don't understand, don't have an idea about, I think I might be able to grapple with it in a little better [way], come at it from new angles, try to chip away at it a little bit better because of the mental training I got in the Program than I might have without the Program.
>
> Certainly, what we learned in the Program doesn't have a direct bearing on anything I'm doing at work. But maybe in the ability to be flexible enough to take a fresh look, or alternate approach, maybe take a backdoor way of getting at the answer to a problem, I think maybe the Program helped to give me a broader view, a more flexible mind, in general. I think that going through the Program helped me think up new ways of looking at problems and maybe to be a little more imaginative.

The Program affected how people viewed the role of work in their lives, and the value of money and status. A musician said that while the Program did not cause him to have certain values, it did reinforce them.

> I think this is more a question of the Program having reinforced tendencies rather than caused something . . . I made an unconscious decision that what work I chose would always have a kind of a low priority, that it had become relatively unimportant to me to have a job that had some social status involved . . . what was more important on the other hand was to get that taken care of and then these other aspects of life that youth are always

concerned with ... moving away from our parents, discovering sexuality, being involved in student political activities, *et cetera* ... were more important, and the rest of life would revolve around them, and any kind of status pertaining to a career was of somewhat less significant. And I think the Program reinforced that in some way.

Since the philosophy, curriculum, and intent of the Program were to be "subdisciplinary" according to Tussman, it was also subprofessional, and subvocational, and this fed into the rejection of materialistic values that was particularly prevalent among college students during the sixties and seventies. Students could find in the Program a justification for these beliefs and a philosophical basis for them. It could also offer them something to take the place of career-oriented values. One lawyer says,

> I mean the whole thing was pretty idealistic, going to school and learning the great books. It doesn't teach you how to make a cabinet or earn a living, [but] it's good stuff to know. Maybe helps you figure out your place in life. But that's not practical. That was an age when students weren't concerned with dollars and making a living. You were concerned with what's right and what's important, and money was not important ... that sort of education, that liberal education may not have been useful in the direct practical sense of helping you earn a living but it would be useful, maybe assist you in figuring out your place in life ... you make some inroad into the classical questions of life—does life have a meaning, what's the purpose of [it]. . . . I'm not saying I got some answered in the Program, but I started asking questions.

Another lawyer said the Program gave him a view of life beyond whatever his career might be.

> I'd started to buy into this Tussman view that there's a larger world out there, and there's more to it than just being here in the University. . . . It changed the perspective, ultimately, from being really concerned about having just a career to being able to look up from the trenches and see that there's more there.

While the Program's agenda was in line with the attitudes among college students of the sixties who were subordinating money and status to moral and ethical concerns, it certainly swam against the tide of the counterculture emerging at the time in respect to authority and responsibility—"do your own thing" was not the message sent to Program students. The developmental needs of these late adolescent students to achieve independence from authority figures must have roused tensions between the values many participants expressed about connecting with the larger world, as the Program urged, and seductive invitations from the counter culture to "tune in, turn on, and drop out." It is no wonder that many of them actually did drop out.

When they did, for whatever reasons, it did not necessarily mean the end of their education. Three participants who dropped out of Berkeley after the Program, all from the first cycle, are now occupied in professional careers. One came back to Berkeley to graduate two years later with a 3.5 grade point average. One former Program participant who was interviewed but not included in the study because she dropped out of the Program before the last quarter, then dropped out of Berkeley; she did return eventually and go on to earn a Ph.D.

While Tussman could argue persuasively about the educational needs of lower division students, his answer to those needs was based on the assumption that students shared similar developmental needs. The Program did take into account certain needs of developing adolescence, particularly in the areas of moral and cognitive development. But some students had needs in other areas—in professional and vocational preparation, for instance—that the Program could not meet. The way the Program met developmental needs for some students, and not for others, is the subject of the next section.

STUDENT DEVELOPMENT

CHAPTER 9

The Role of Development

With the knowledge we have gained in previous chapters about the students and faculty who conducted the Program, the purpose of the Program and its curricular content, its structure and features, and what participants in the study had to say about its impact and its effects on them, we can now hope to arrive at a deeper understanding of the ways in which the Program operated.

Information former students offered in the interviews reveals the way the Program achieved its effects in three major areas of growth and change: (1) moral/political—how the Program contributed to students' understanding and acceptance of the moral and political basis of the democratic tradition—what could be called the content of the Program; (2) educational/cognitive—how participation in the Program led students to advance their thinking and writing, and (3) personal—the role the Program played in helping students to deal with the stress of late adolescence and the adjustments necessary for adaptation to the demands of college life. These categories correspond to categories of the major impact of the Program discussed in Chapter 6, and reflect the three major areas of the Program's influence on its students.

The interviews also reveal how two major aspects of the Program aided growth in these areas: one, through the creation of a community in the intellectual, the social and the personal sense; and two, through the pedagogical methods inherent in the structure of the Program and the way teachers employed them to help lead students toward their goal of education for democracy.

Looking at the operation of the Program through the prism of student development is indispensable to a full understanding both of its effectiveness for some students and its inappropriateness for others. Students who were entering the Program, usually aged 17 or 18 (although sometimes 16 and almost 19), might differ in the degree to which they had achieved social and intellectual maturity, but they still shared some general developmental needs and propensities—learning to deal with the physical, cognitive, and emotional changes accompanying adolescence, developing significant personal relationships apart from their families, and starting down the path to becoming self-supporting, financially as well as socially and emotionally.

Adolescents face some fundamental tasks in their transition to adulthood: the adjustment to physical changes of puberty and later adolescence and the flood of new feelings brought on by sexual maturity; the development of independence from parents or other caretakers; the establishment of effective social and working relationships with the same and opposite-sex peers; and preparation for a meaningful vocation (Mussen, Conger, and Kagan 1984) Some theorists would add identity to this list, that is, discovering and understanding the self as an individual.[1] While the Program was not intended to help its students perform any of these tasks, it nonetheless played a role for many of them as they struggled with the changes involved in this stage of their development.

With such a program as this, requiring no exams and giving no grades, student progress cannot be judged by simple statistics such as the numbers achieving a passing grade. Examining the climate the Program established conducive to student development and the degree to which its participants could take advantage of this opportunity for growth is one way of assessing outcome. This next section will deal with the ways in which the Program might have depended for its effectiveness on students reaching certain levels of development; and how developmental changes that Program students, as late adolescents, were undergoing—personal, social, cognitive,

---

[1] Julie Elmen, and Daniel Offer, "Normality, Turmoil and Adolescence," in *Handbook of Clinical Research and Practice with Adolescents,* ed. Patrick H. Tolan and Bertram J. Cohler (New York: John Wiley and Sons, 1993).

and moral—might have been influenced by their experiences in the Program.

THE ADOLESCENT TRANSITION

Developmental changes young people deal with at this age, particularly physical ones, may seem to have nothing to do with their studies, and yet taken together can have a bearing on their ability to do college work and to complete their college education. While the students in the Program were roughly the same age, we can assume they were not at the same place in their progress towards adulthood. All but one had entered the Program directly after high school—that one had graduated from high school the January before—and none had taken time off between high school and college. Several from the Bay Area were still living at home at the time they entered the Program, although most of those moved to other living quarters during or after the first year in the Program. What they all had in common was the dramatic changes their lives were undergoing just by entering college. Several participants talked about what life was like for them when they entered college, and the Program. One man said,

> Everything was new. I had my first love affair, I had my first really deep intellectual experience in the Program, I had my own apartment for the first time, my first real contact with people of different religions, different economic backgrounds, and so on. My world was turned upside down . . . everything was new, everything was for the first time, everything was thrilling . . . I'm surprised I got any reading done at all, there was so much else to do. That's one of the disadvantages of (laughs) being eighteen.

Another man said,

> I don't think much about the usefulness of late adolescence, when you get out of high school and you're seventeen and pimples on your face and you're still bumping into things, trying to figure out what you're doing. And all the entertainments of being away from home, living in Berkeley, in wild times, floating around trying to get on top of sex and drugs and your social life and trying to keep your finances together. And reading Blake and Hobbes and the Bible all at the same time. You have to fit things into whatever your priorities are. I often tell people that the major

thing I got out of college was being twenty-two instead of being seventeen which is, you know, a blessing.

Several women talked about beginning to be rebellious toward their parents and one said, "I think that was probably more significant in the kind of changes I went through than anything at school." Several participants mentioned widening their social horizons to include people they had not come into contact with before. Meeting people from different ethnic and religious backgrounds was "a real eye-opener" for some women participants. One minority participant dated Anglo women for the first time in the Program; another man's relatives were worried he was associating with Communists and Jewish radicals at Berkeley—just the very people he in fact welcomed to help him expand his own conservative Catholic background.

It is natural for students, having recently left their own families, to seek out substitute or surrogate families in college. Fraternities and sororities, co-ops, athletic teams, music and drama clubs, and the like, can fill the gap and help to play a part in students' progress toward independence. As well as being based on the cooperation of fellow students, most of these voluntary groups involve some kind of adult presence in the way of coaching, supervision, or sponsorship. But there can be dangers involved in these shifting allegiances: in an unhealthy way, political or religious cults may offer a substitute authority structure for young people just leaving home that allows them to transfer dependence from family to cult authorities rather than to develop their own independence. And the sixties and seventies were the age of the guru, another kind of authority substitute who could have detrimental effects when fostering dependence rather than autonomy.

While the *Sturm und Drang* theory of the transition from adolescence to adulthood has been losing favor with developmental theorists,[2] the Program did encompass a time of major social upheavals, particularly in the lives of college students: the Civil Rights and anti-Vietnam War movements; the drug and sexual revolutions; the beginnings of the feminist movement, and to some extent, the drive to reform undergraduate education—each one bearing on issues of authority and identity important

---

[2]*Ibid.*

in the adolescent transition whether stormy or tranquil in itself. Students enrolled in the Program and their contemporaries in the regular university would have been affected by these dramatic societal changes, but the Program may have had an influence on young people trying to cope with the late adolescent experience that was different from the experience students usually have in the regular university.

For some, the Program apparently represented a kind of half-way house, a bridge from dependence on the family to full adult independence. One man observed:

> The fact that it was somewhat protective probably helped me feel more securely independent. . . . It was sort of an anchor . . . there's one house to go to, there's an ongoing group of students to relate to, a faculty to relate to.

One woman spoke of the ways the Program was helpful in her adolescent transition; by structuring the first two years of her academic life, it left her freer to concentrate on other changes.

> There were a lot of new experiences that I was having, and to have that basic structure of the Program was very helpful to me, very helpful. It gave me a real anchor. I took an outside class all the quarters that I was there, but that was kind of like sporadic education, shall we say. It was comfortable knowing what I was going to do for two years. And it all enabled me to comfortably go through a lot of other changes that were happening in my life. Social changes, just being responsible for yourself, that's a big change, coming from a family and learning that you are the only one that knows if you don't get home at midnight or one o'clock. I would say those were the big benefits for me.

Another woman told how the Program helped her through this period, although she didn't recognize the advantages until later in college:

> It was basically a very cohesive couple of undergraduate years. And those were an adjustment. I think just being on your own and living on your own, having to study yourself and learning to come in before midnight and that sort of thing. There were a lot of things going on and I think having not quite as much stress with those two undergraduate years was terrific. It was a more cohesive environment in which to learn and it wasn't as stressful as having every quarter to come up with a whole

new program . . . I think I just totally took it for granted the first couple of years and I didn't realize it until those last two years [in the upper division] what a good experience I had, what a good thing we had going, basically.

One man also found social aspects of the Program helped in his adolescent transition by providing a forum for development of all kinds.

> When I was in the Program I was eighteen and nineteen, and there were three or four important sides of life that were going on for me. I also noticed they were going on for other students at the time. I was breaking away from my parents, as everyone must, I was studying in this Program, I was beginning to be actively interested in women and sex, and the Vietnam War was going on, and finally my interest in Scandinavian history and culture had germinated.
> I think that as it turned out, of all of these categories of personal development, the academic content of the Program may have been the least important. But the Program itself in its other aspects constituted a kind of forum in which those other areas of intellectual or emotional commitment could develop. The Program and it's social structure probably constituted a rather more tranquil environment for a young person to go through all these things, all these various problems of youth than an ordinary American university education would have.

There was evidence that the Program community was instrumental in helping some students deal with adolescent changes. One woman found discussions with other students in the Program to be particularly useful:

> I remember sitting around talking about, arguing about things—I think that was pretty important, looking at the issues of life that were going on at the same time and being away from home and growing up, finding your way on your own. I don't remember talking with people in other classes much at all. The other bigger classes I was in were much more isolated so that I experienced more give and take about what you're reading and what it meant there [in the Program] than later, until graduate school, probably.

One man noted developmental growth in several areas related to the Program.

> I was doing some growing in the Program, personally, and in the relationships that I developed in the Program, with the teachers, and with the material. The two years' work gave me a lot, I think, intellectually, at least. I got some sense of myself, and politically I changed from being completely naive to something else. It was such an engaging thing, the Program, that those two years of my life were really centered there, and I just got a lot of stuff. Even on two cylinders, which is how I was operating, and even with anger and even with this withdrawal [in relationship to one faculty member]. It was a real rich environment.

Perhaps because the Program held constant the academic side of students' lives, the personal, cognitive, or social changes they were going through became more apparent to them than to ordinary undergraduates who had to deal with many different unrelated classes, lecturers and fellow students.

"DRUGS, SEX, AND . . . "

The other students in the Program, and the House itself, figured in some accounts of new experiences with drugs and with sex. Although the House was intended to be a place for informal meetings for students and faculty primarily focused on curricular material, some students took to using it for other, unintended purposes. One woman said the major change in her life during that period was becoming sexually active, and that she had carried on a relationship with a man from the Program, often in the lounge of the House itself, which to her was "just like my parents' living room." This was a time of liberation for her.

> Just the pursuit of an adult life as defined by sexual activity and living space of your own, some kind of transport of your own and an ability to make your own choices in terms of where you are going to go during the day. Not to have to answer to anybody. And even the drug use, although I never took really bad, nasty, heavy drugs.

It is natural for these late adolescents, now out from under the direct control of parental authority, to experiment with various forms of freedoms allowed adults. (Experimentation with new identities is also a part of the adolescent transition, and that will be discussed in Chapter 11 on community in the Program.) While trying out of new roles, new freedoms and new responsibilities goes on with college students whether or not they are enrolled in any kind of programs like these, the Tussman Program happened to offer something else to students who were going through these sometimes troubling changes that the regular program did not.

One first-cycle man described how the Program structure helped students cope with new experiences, unintended and extracurricular. He said that 90 percent of his sexual encounters were "defined by the Program." (He was the only participant in the study who later married another student from the Program.) Drugs played a moderate part in the social life of the Program and some of the Program students were dealing drugs, although he thought that the Program functioned to reduce drug use among its students.

> There was probably a lot more of that stuff going on in the regular academic environment. The Program in a way required a lot of self-discipline. You couldn't really come to school screwed up and expect to be an effective participant . . . and you've got a safety net, some basic tenets, you've got a value—a moral, intellectual structure you can fall back on.

The Program apparently provided a moral/intellectual centering function for some students, and although never intended to serve as any kind of *in loco parentis*, could be used to set standards for personal behavior.

The Program proved useful in different ways to different students in their moves toward sexual maturation. A second-cycle man said that learning to cope with sex and drugs were his "major hurdles getting out of high school and getting into your early twenties," but his relationships with women in the Program were not sexual.

> [They were] sort of brother and sisterly because you couldn't be too casual with the opposite sex 'cause you were going to be living together for quite a while. So there may have been a little extra degree of responsibility in the way we interacted.

He did become involved in drug dealing.

> I got side tracked to some extent that way for about six or eight months. [But] I got out of it, too. I guess it was part of the growing up process, part of getting from high school into adulthood.

Not only did students have to contend with the sexual and political revolutions of the sixties, they had to face the drug "revolution." According to participants, drug taking was so widespread it effected many students even if they were not taking drugs themselves. One woman from the second cycle said that a number of people dropped out of the Program, and some out of Berkeley, because of drugs, but that she learned from their experiences.

> It was a real transitional time. . . . There were a number of unfortunate problems with people who were in the Program, and that was real upsetting to me. That whole drug world was a new thing to me. It was probably something I would have considered trying, [but] I saw what a negative experience it had on a number of people, and that sticks in my mind a lot. It was a learning experience.
>
> The three people who were having drug problems in that first year did end up dropping out of school in general, and one guy ended up in a mental hospital. There were some pretty serious things. And another fellow called me up and was threatening suicide. That was very troubling. And it probably kept me out of a lot of trouble because I looked at this and I thought, "This doesn't look like as much fun as it's supposed to be." So I would say it kept me out of any particular drug involvement.

She remembered that for some who were experiencing drug problems, the Program also provided help.

> There were a lot of people from a lot of different backgrounds and a lot of people had a hard time going to college, even within that [Experimental] College. I think that they were given a lot more encouragement and a lot more opportunity to succeed than they would have been if they were just in the general college because [there] I don't think anybody follows up on you if you're floundering. They were given a lot of opportunities to work things out [in the Program]. If they missed seminars or they were not turning in papers, the different professors really tried to work with them to work things out, to make that successful for them.
>
> And that was important, that kind of support group. I think when people get into trouble, everybody knows it. They're not showing up—we knew it in that small of a group. In the larger University, in general . . . if you're in a lecture class with six hundred, nobody knows if

you show up or not. You can dig yourself into a deep hole before anybody knows what's happened. So I would say even for the people who had unfortunate experiences, they were given a lot more support than they would have otherwise.

Indeed, faculty as well as peer support undoubtedly was one of the factors in lowering the drop out rate of Program students compared to other U.C. students. According to Suczek, only 22.7 percent of the Program students withdrew from school compared to 34.1 percent for those students who had applied but not been accepted to the Program and 34 percent who had not applied. He concluded that "these withdrawal rates again seem clearly related to participation in the program" (Suczek 1972, 114).

The prominence of drugs on campuses during the sixties and seventies is legendary. Psychedelic drugs became commonplace and easily available and added to the confusion and distractions students faced as they adjusted to college life away from their families. Even some faculty, at Berkeley and elsewhere, in addition to the well-known Professors Leary and Alpert at Harvard, were also experimenting with, promoting, or condoning drug use at the time. One former student provided insights into the meaning of drugs for students at Berkeley then, and explained how some students related drugs to ideas brought up by readings and studies. This student described how the "drug-related and politically-related discussions, the rich and heady ideas of the sixties," in the "salons," played a part of campus life and life in the Program.

> I wasn't a heavy duty druggie. I was pretty scared. But there were some people who went crazy and I think some people never quite came out of it. But that's part of the whole thing of Berkeley in 1965. I smoked my first hashish, and I took my first acid trip. . . .There were some that were very sort of macho about it—these huge dosages, and wild, flamboyant tripping out on mountain tops and such—and I was not quite in that league. I was more conservative, but I certainly smelled all the flowers and with no regrets. . . . We'd sit around and get high and we'd *talk* about *books* and politics and stuff. It was sort of phenomenological inquiry . . . it's all sort of mixed up now . . . it was like an intellectual frontier . . . I found it wonderfully adventuresome. . . .
>
> We were very blessed and cursed in the sixties here. We genuinely felt something [that] had never been done before. So the elders didn't have a lot to say to us. It was the traditional adolescent stuff. The times

really fed it, and there was a real sense of great power in the streets and amongst us. . . . I had friends back at Harvard and they felt out of it. It was happening here in 'sixty-five and we knew it, so between the psychedelics, which no one we knew had taken, we were the first people to do them . . . plus the kind of riots . . . that turned out to be quite empty revolutionary activity, but it took me a while to understand that. . . .

There was a sense of an enormous unknown, that it was not going to be like anyone else's future. And that included we were never going to get old. I don't think we really thought very seriously about having to work. And I think there was a sense that we could sort of—not break the rules—I mean there were strong anarchistic elements in this—but just not make rules. But we could make it any way we wanted to and we wouldn't make the same mistakes, we wouldn't face the same terrible ordinary human unhappiness—we just weren't going to be saddled with that. I don't think it lasted that long, but certainly during the Tussman program, that *huge*—call it grandiosity. . . . But it was also a kind of innocence. It was a kind of headiness. It was just a very powerful component. It just made us feel privy to something. Certainly it was alienating. It made us feel that someone like Joe Tussman—I'm sure he knew people were using drugs and I'm sure he disapproved, but it wasn't something that could be talked about. It became a little bit of a source of a kind of schism of generations, I guess. It emboldened us to think that we didn't have to be as deferential. . . .

The trip was something in and to itself in that certain things were discussed and talked about and certainly when you're smoking hashish and were talking about, you know, Noam Chomsky, it's a different kind of discussion than if you weren't smoking hashish. . . . But there was no embracing of the kind of goofy-like fraternity parties, with people getting high. If you couldn't keep your thoughts together, if you couldn't finish your sentence right, if you couldn't make a good point, then you were screwed up. So it wasn't like you'd get high and everyone would just babble and rave and it would be nonsense. People were pretty disciplined, they were pretty smart. I think a few people got a little lost in terms of what the drug itself meant, and what it did to their personalities. But for me I don't think that that was what was happening. I don't think for most people that was that.

There was one bad drug thing that happened in our group. I'm trying to remember . . . somebody jumped off the roof here [in the House]. (In another account, this party did not occur in the House, but was attended by some of the Program's TAs.) It was icky. I think (another Program student), who was a wonderful, wonderful guy, got a little bit lost and went a little crazy, which was a terrible thing. . . .

You were bold enough to take something which nobody else could tell you about, or could guarantee. There's something sort of really dangerous about it . . . but no one was like an acid head. It wasn't like the acid or the mescaline had become a thing in itself and they were just sort of lost to it. It was part of the spice of life. . . . It was an intellectually challenging experience, is what it was seen as, more than "ooh, the rocks are melting." More analyzed than just the experience.

This student's memories of drug use in those days is not perfectly clear, although people in the Program are remembered as "pretty disciplined" and there seemed to be an effort to keep from being "screwed up." Trying to keep thoughts together in order to take part in coherent discussions and to be able to "make a good point" apparently kept drug use under some sort of control for most students in the Program, so that it became only "part of the spice of life," rather than a central feature. Feeling a need to be on their toes intellectually, even while taking drugs, was perhaps a deterrent to overindulgence for many Program students.

There is no evidence in the interviews to suggest that students used faculty in the Program as personal counselors in drug-related or other personally troubling matters, although that may have happened. But the interviews do tell us that students' work was carefully monitored by Program professors, particularly in the second cycle, and if a student's work was becoming slack, faculty were usually quick to pick that up and to offer help, support, and encouragement and thus to provide a stabilizing influence. While that was clearly not enough for every student to help overcome whatever it was that was interfering with their ability to do their work, it apparently worked for many.

In their responses to the College Attitude Questionnaire, Program participants were almost twice as likely to feel there were professors they could turn to for advice on personal matters during the lower division than in the upper division (38 percent vs. 20 percent), whether they did so or not.[3] But even more of them were likely to have found professors who took

---

[3]The assumption is made here that "lower division professors" referred to Program faculty, although no distinction was made on the questionnaire between Program faculty and lower division faculty in the other "outside" courses students

a special interest in their academic progress in the lower division than in the upper division (53 percent vs. 34 percent), and somewhat more likely to do so than people who had applied to the Program but not been accepted (38 percent vs. 32 percent) (See Appendix F). It may be that for the large percentage of participants who found professors to be interested in their academic progress while in the Program, that was of equal or greater importance to them in establishing "a safety net . . . a moral, intellectual structure you can fall back on," as one put it, than in being able to turn to professors for personal advice. The Program may have served *in loco parentis* after all, not in the form of rules about hours and so forth imposed from the outside, but rather as a set of expectations about the formation of and adherence to values and to academic standards set from within, a kind of super ego in Freudian terms. Program students seemed to feel they had been treated in many ways as if they were adults, but at the same time were supported by both an academic and social structure and by the close attention of the adults in charge.

STUDENTS AND FAMILIES

Most American students usually begin college at ages 17 and 18 and while more and more older students are enrolling in colleges and universities today, that was much less common in the sixties. European students are generally somewhat older, usually at least 19, when they begin university. A year or two can make a significant difference in emotional maturity at this age, and because of that, American college students are perhaps more in need of some kind of parental-like support structure than students in European institutions. In Europe this need has for some kind of structured support has been recognized for a long time, and been met in the form of centuries-old student societies such as the *Nations* in Sweden, the *Burschenschaft* in Germany, and the colleges that combine living and learning in Cambridge and Oxford. In the past in the United States the functions of *in loco parentis* were traditionally carried out in living units on campus: fraternities, sororities, and dormitories had house mothers and/or junior faculty and older students living together with young students and exercising various degrees of control and guidance. After the influx of

---

might have taken.

large numbers of older students, veterans of World War II attending school on the G.I. Bill, on American college campuses in the late forties and early fifties, the *in loco parentis* function of colleges and universities came to be viewed as superfluous and difficult to enforce and has largely disappeared. Yet the need for some sort of familial setting for beginning college students may still exist, particularly in large universities such as Berkeley, as suggested by the testimony of many of the participants about the way in which the Program met such needs.

One man from the second cycle spoke of the transitional aspects of the Program in relationship to the family.

> For me, the Program was this pre-period before I really got involved with the world. It's that last bit of being within my own family and its orientation, and then being exposed to the Program.

Because of troubles within his family that were very difficult for him to deal with,

> it's amazing that the Program stuck at all. Because I really count that time as a real change for me. I was looking to get involved with a family that was very different than my own. I just had totally out of hand rejected everything that it had [been]. So I think it's a tribute to the Program that it made such an impact on me in a time before I had faced a lot of things in the world that I had yet to face, that were independent of Program issues.

Another second-cycle man said,

> The Program offered almost a family life, with the friends made there, the way it was set up to remove you somewhat from the cruel world of the regular university. If anything, it helped soften any negative impact of the university in general.

Another participant spoke of changes in her relationships to "parent figures" and described the way in which authority was exercised in the Program as a "good kind of authority . . . the people that were chosen were really good people to interact with young people." Several other participants likened the Program to a family, its faculty to parents or fathers, and its students to their children. Erik Erikson,[4] discussing adolescent development, quotes Peter Blos's phrase "regression in the service of development," which seems an apt description of the use to which many students put the familial attributes they attached to the Program, its faculty, and their fellow students.

In addition to its function as sanctuary from the large, impersonal university, it is possible that Program faculty offered their students an opportunity to focus some of their changing dependency-independency needs on them instead of on their parents. One second-cycle man said about a Program professor, "I wanted a good father, not a mean one." While he reported an unsatisfactory "enmeshed" relationship with this teacher, he found others with whom he did get along, and one in particular who he thought "saw and appreciated the kind of mind that I have." His relationships with faculty were evidently important to him, and he was one of a handful of participants who reported any kind of relationships with any of the faculty lasting beyond the Program. It seems then that even if he found one "bad father" there, he also found several other "good fathers" as well. But the notion of the faculty member as father was so intense for this man that he became upset when there were serious public disagreements among faculty, even though they were fewer in the second cycle. Referring to the deep division between Professors J and L discussed earlier in Chapter 3 on second-cycle faculty he said,

> It was like seeing your parents fight, and there was no real coming back together after that fight. It's like watching through the door, your parents have this terrible fight, and there's no reconciliation. And how does anger get worked out? Here's a case where it doesn't. Here's where you're supposed to have this intellectual debate, but what's really happening is that human beings are treating each other terrible, and they're not working it out. I think that frightened people. It frightened me to see that . . . I don't know how many kids dropped out because of that. And I don't know what effect this fight had on other students there. It just wasn't talked about very much. . . .
> It was dangerous. . . . It was very disturbing to see the parents not dealing with this stuff well. . . . It was a kind of reenactment for I imagine everyone there of some unfinished and weird stuff in their family, and it

---

[4]Eric Erikson, *Identity, Youth and Crisis* (New York: W. W. Norton, 1968).

was getting acted out, and it was very uncomfortable for people.... I wasn't drawn into the Program as deeply as I could have been had there been more attention paid by these top people to their own process ... to encouraging difference, allowing for and dealing with anger healthily.

His reaction to this "parental" dispute was very similar to the participant from the first cycle who had also been frightened by public fights among faculty. While a few other participants from both cycles reported feeling uncomfortable with faculty fractiousness, these two seemed particularly sensitive to them. The two viewed the overall effects of the Program, however, in startlingly different ways: the first-cycle participant, for several reasons, viewed the Program as having a deleterious effect on her subsequent academic life and would not repeat the Program; the second participant had no regrets about being in the Program, was enthusiastic about its positive effects both then and with the passage of time, and would do it again. The one man from the first cycle who would choose not to repeat the Program also objected to fights, not only between faculty members, but between faculty and other students.

There were scenes that I remember in lecture halls where there was just these ... verbal brawls between [A] and one of the other professors and some of the students, and I just thought it was asinine, I thought it was inappropriate, I thought that's not the way schools should be.... You might disagree with them, but you don't get so dramatic about it. I just thought that wasn't right. I didn't like that.

Just how students reacted to dissension in the Program was apparently idiosyncratic and depended probably on other, undefined factors as the second-cycle participant suggests, including "unfinished ... stuff" from their own families. For example, from what they said, none of these three seemed to feel free to express their feelings openly to faculty themselves about their conflicts, and that may have had to do with the state of their own particular relationships with authority. Tussman's memoir testifies to the real animosity underlying some of these fights with particular faculty in both cycles. Presumably faculty tried to prevent students from seeing just how personally bitter they could be, but some students for reasons of their own were perhaps more aware than others of their grievous basis and more sensitive to their implications of deep discord.

Obviously the pleasure that some students took in challenging authority in the Program, and in witnessing faculty challenging each other, was not shared by all. It is possible that some Program students found arguing or "fighting" in the Program, between faculty members or between faculty and students, to be so upsetting that they dropped out because of it. Since the expectation of close faculty-student relations was a major factor leading many applicants to apply to the Program, it might have been especially important to them that faculty hold up their end of the bargain by behaving in ways students thought appropriate, including conducting congenial relationships with each other. Stanton and Schwartz (1954) have demonstrated how lack of agreement and harmony among staff members of mental hospitals can be reflected in more exaggerated symptomatic behavior among their patients, and we know how children can be affected by serious dissension between parents. It seems logical, therefore, that some students could also be affected by how well the faculty leaders of this special, small, encapsulated community appeared to get along. It is quite possible that [students were led develo]pmentally to view authority, as [seemi]ng less than unified.

[As with the Adul]ts House, its parental and sibling [figures affected ho]w students should seem in some [respects rebellious. B]ut there were important differ[ences. As with the auth]ority figures, that authority could [be—and as will] be discussed in Chapter 13 on [rebellion, seve]ral participants did report using [the Program to play] with and testing out defiance of [authority and agreeme]nt. No student was reported by [any faculty at th]e House for talking back to their [parents, for wearing thei]r hair long, or for going barefoot! [This may be a clue] to some who still needed more [overt signs of] rebelliousness.

"THE ODYSSEY EXPERIENCE"

[Developmental events] are one of several important [types of experience]. Smelser calls the "Odyssey experience,"[5] an out-of-the-ordinary event for young people that "make people who do it special . . . challenges offering students an opportunity for mastery . . . a moratorium when no other decisions are being made at the time . . . a disruption from expectations . . . a sense of community with close, ongoing personal relations with other participants . . . [with] the affect always running along, side by side, with the cognitive . . . [sometimes] a romantic voyage," not only in the physical sense, but also intellectually.

Smelser's own major Odyssey experience was his attendance while a Harvard undergraduate, at the Salzburg Seminar in American studies where students engaged in the "broader European picture." He sees characteristics of the Odyssey experience in the Rhodes Scholarship program at Oxford, in the Education Abroad programs for undergraduates, and in the Tussman Program. While the Experimental College Program did not take place abroad, it certainly engaged students in some historically important aspects of democracy going back to older European and American times, and its curricular emphasis on Greece and England did inspire some of its students to travel. The man who said the Program "fortified my wanderlust," who traveled abroad during the summers to "see all these spots I was reading about" has already been quoted. One of the three participants who would not repeat the Program did enjoy that aspect of the Program that dealt with Greece and England:

> I loved Greece, I thought it was wonderful. I loved learning about that and I ended up going to Greece and staying there for six months. And I ended up in England [in the University Abroad Program] so it's obviously had some effect in that sense.

Another participant quoted earlier thought his decision to eventually come to live under a European parliamentary system was tied in with his exposure to the Program's "intellectual orientation toward a philosophy of state."[6]

---

[5]Neil J. Smelser, "The Odyssey Experience," unpublished manuscript.

[6]There were some other suggestions in the interviews of the importance to college students of breaking with the past at this point in their development: while close to half of the participants in the study had gone to high school in the greater San Francisco Bay Area, two of the three who had gone to high school in Berkeley

Smelser sees the Odyssey programs "conducted under relationships with authority very different from what [students] have experienced previously." He found at Salzburg "not a single faculty member but a family of faculty members . . . a family of mentors," and that even if a student has negative feelings toward a faculty member, the development of different relationships with different faculty permits students to "put it together" in their own terms. He argues that the multiple relationships with the "whole family" of mentors is potentially healthier than an intense relationship with one professor where students become "clones" of that particular professor and overly dependent on only one faculty member. The family of mentors in the Program did not encourage dependency on one particular guru-like figure (although in the first cycle there was at least one professor who, according to Tussman's essay, apparently tried to promote such relationships with students)—it was a team teaching effort designed to expose students to all the faculty—and its aim was to get students to think for themselves. Yet the challenge to Program students to "put together for themselves" a new set of relationships with multiple teachers or mentors under new conditions of authority may have been too daunting a developmental task for some of these beginning college undergraduates in cases where there were personal conflicts between these authority figures as described earlier in this chapter.

Sometimes a feeling of guilt accompanies the feeling of being special, of having been selected over others for this special opportunity, and can lead to a kind of feeling of let-down or mild depression. A few participants did express some degree of guilt at having been chosen for the Program, even though they knew that had been at random. One participant said,

> I was trying to remember how I was lucky enough to be in it. If I recall correctly, it was simply a random selection. I thought I was real fortunate for that alone . . . I didn't even earn this, you know. I was lucky.

---

said that they regretted that they had not gone away from their home town to college and thought their college experiences would have been much enhanced if they had. Perhaps even the Program, set as it was in Berkeley, was not enough of a physical and intellectual "disruption from expectations" to counteract the familiarity of their home town.

Others expressed guilt at staying up too late playing cards while in the Program, several for not doing all the reading, several for not working as hard as they now feel they should have. It is quite possible some felt separation anxiety over having left family members, friends and friends and abandoned previous loyalties to join an elitist group at an elitist university.

Smelser also identifies the "danger of regression" many students face when adapting to these special programs where "academic authority isn't what you expect it to be"—in the case of the Program, more individualized and flexible and less punitive, especially in the absence of grades. Although he says "the regressive element might be especially important as an early phase of adjustment," it could have been overwhelming and caused some students to drop out of the Program and back into the regular university. To be invited by faculty, who exercised none of the familiar sanctions and offered students none of the usual symbols of approval, to come up with original interpretations of material they were all reading together might have been too threatening to some who needed both personal distance from faculty and validation in the form of good grades from educational authorities. In the light of these possibilities, one begins to wonder if all of the political differences with faculty that led many students to drop out, as described in Chapter 12 on politics in the Program, were always simply that, or whether some could have been a screen for difficulties some Program students experienced with this more challenging and perhaps uncomfortable relationship with authority.

The Program, as an example of an armchair type of Odyssey learning experience, aided student learning in several ways. In terms of cognitive development, it required its students to put together for themselves material from original sources. In contrast to the usual large lecture classes freshmen and sophomores attend where they are ordinarily required to learn, in some cases only memorize, material in accordance with their professor's prearranged scheme and particular interpretation, Program students were asked to perform "mental operations," in Piaget's term, on their own, to act on the material rather than receive it passively. In Piaget's scheme of successive stages of cognitive development there is a period of "disequilibrium," of cognitive disruption followed by "assimilation and accommodation," incorporating new facts into an existing framework and changing the framework accordingly (Piaget 1950). A parallel might be drawn here since Program students were expected to reorganize their customary intellectual orientations to come up with original responses to

The Role of Development

curricular material without the usual system of accountability based on examinations and grades. This may, for some, have led to a climate of uncertainly but for most to relief from the anxiety of competition. To succeed in these intellectual tasks leads to a sense of mastery, and, in turn, to increased self-confidence and enhanced self-esteem—feelings many participants reported when they completed the Program and entered the upper division. Meaningful achievement is one of the three basic conditions fostering ego development, according to Weathersby (1981). The Program could be seen to satisfy the other two as well—varied experiences and roles and relative freedom from anxiety and pressure—thus offering its students an environment more conducive to growth than could be counted on in the regular university.

As already discussed, the Program provided its students a family of mentors from which to choose, an opportunity to put together for themselves the beneficial aspects of those relationships. It represented a kind of initiation into an egalitarian community of scholars. Under the aegis of this learning community, individual interactions with authority could be more deliberate—the views of some Program faculty could be accepted and others rejected. And when faculty argued their positions publicly, students found at least tacit approval for them to publicly disagree with them and with each other—in the spirit of their common intellectual enterprise.

The Odyssey experience shared common themes with the Program: a state of moratorium where no other decisions were being made; a disruption of ordinary expectations;[7] relations with a variety of faculty-mentors, and a different kind of relationship with authority; a community of peers involved in the same intellectual material and going through the same kinds of developmental changes; an involvement in a broader international picture; perhaps an element of romance; and the challenge to the student to reassemble the disrupted pieces, to "put it all together," for her or himself.

While the Program was different in several obvious respects from the Salzburg Seminar—it did not select only the best and brightest students (although many did come to believe they were part of an elite), it did not take place in a castle in a romantic part of Europe, and was not staffed by leading international figures in the students' chosen major fields of

---

[7] Asked if the Program had met their expectations, most participants replied that they had no clearly defined expectations of the Program beforehand.

study—it did share these other aspects already mentioned and could give students a sense of academic competence and self-assurance. To be especially selected to travel to Europe as an undergraduate for an intensive six-week seminar with world-famous intellectual leaders, or to be randomly chosen to spend two years in an intensive series of lectures, seminars, and tutorials dealing with classical literature about periods of world crises throughout history led by distinguished university professors, were both experiences designed to lift students out of their ordinary lives and challenge them to mastery of new and different ways of perceiving man's relationship to society.

The interpersonal and cognitive demands on students in these programs, conducted in climates of uncertainty and disruption of customary learning experiences—to act intellectually on the material presented rather than to passively accept it, and to construct their own benefits from the faculty relationships offered to them—provided opportunities for personal and intellectual growth and an integration of the two. A closer look at just how the various features of the educational structure of the Program fit into and took advantage of cognitive developmental patterns of late adolescence is the subject of the next chapter.

CHAPTER 10

Teaching and Learning

The Experimental College Program rested on two broad educational pillars. One was its content, that is, its curriculum—what it was that it was proposing to teach—shaped by its purpose of educating students for their role as citizens in a democracy. The other was its educational design and pedagogical methods—how it was structured to teach its curriculum and the methods it employed to advance student development. This chapter is devoted to an examination of the latter, to the Program's pedagogical structure and features and their effects on the learning process according to participants in the study, and how these were keyed in the Program to the intellectual development of its students.

The educational impact of the Program was achieved through several means: through the overall formal structure of the Program such as the lectures, seminars, tutorials, etc., and the ways in which they were interrelated; through the role students played in their own and each other's education; and through the role of faculty in teaching the curriculum and implementing the Program's coherent, two-year design. The way in which the Program functioned as a learning community is further described in the next chapter on community, but its significant components included

- the concurrent reading by all members of the community, faculty and students alike, of the literature comprising its curriculum
- the closeness of faculty and students produced partly by the informal setting of the House and by the assignment of papers and individual tutorials in which faculty and students discussed the students' work

- the large lectures in which all faculty participated
- the smaller seminars in which students were expected to ask questions and discuss the curriculum
- the encouragement of student discussions of the material both more formally in the seminars with faculty and in those without faculty present in which students took charge, and more informally in the places made available in the House for student discussions as well as other activities, and in tutorials.

In terms of sheer logistics, the amount of contact faculty members had with students in the Program was much greater than in the regular lower division and helped faculty achieve a significant impact. With six professors (or at least five) each working to realize the Program's intent, especially in the second cycle when faculty were much more unified, there were many opportunities for reinforcement of learning from a variety of teaching styles and formats.

Participants from the second cycle describe the impact of the educational environment created in the Program. One man talked about the feeling of intimacy that he got from the way the Program was structured.

> The closeness to the professors, and they were very approachable and they weren't distant figures. In a sense, they were kind of distant when we had the lectures. We had two lectures a week, I think it was, and then they were up in front, and they would have a panel, or maybe one of them would give a two-hour presentation, or they'd have a panel discussion, or whatever it would be. And that was more or less your typical kind of lecture scene.
>
> But that's fine because it's good for them to present some material, and then we think about it, or read about it, or whatever you want to do. But that didn't put me off because we had this close, intimate seminar setting which was really a phenomenal kind of experience. I think back on that. I just think how unique and how different that was from the education that I had seen before or after. Because it was a tutorial kind of setting . . . and with a small group. And then we even had individual meetings on a regular basis with teachers for reviews and that kind of thing.

Teaching and Learning

He apparently did not find, even in the upper division seminars, the closeness and regular individual contact with faculty that he valued in the Program.[1]

It was the interplay between the various teaching and learning opportunities there that also struck another man as special.

> [The seminars], they were wonderful. I think the idea of breaking into small groups and then going into more depths and having the teacher there be the kind of leader of that small group. *Fabulous* idea for how it goes between the large group and into the small group and then into the individual tutorials and back into the small group and back into the lecture . . . really a fabulous way to work the teaching process.

The impact of the various pedagogical features of the Program have been reported earlier as they appeared to participants individually. But it was their interrelatedness that was of special significance and allowed them to have an effect greater than the sum of their parts.

OVERALL STRUCTURE, GRADES, AND ACCOUNTABILITY

Several participants from the first cycle had comments to make about the overall structure of the Program, some of them critical. Faculty-student tutorials were not required during the first cycle, and that must have had some effect on how regularly students turned in papers, a very important factor in view of the fact that the Program depended on students completing their writing assignments. Since faculty were not as unified here as in the second cycle, communication among them about student progress could not have been as regular or as effective. Instead of team teaching, they probably presented to the students more of a teaching collective, each interpreting their teaching responsibilities in the Program somewhat differently. The effects of this lack of coordination among the first-cycle faculty were evident in the impact of the curriculum on the students. For

---

[1] As well as classes they took in the upper division, Program students had opportunities to compare it with the regular undergraduate program as they participated in "outside" classes along with the Program. They were also encouraged to audit other undergraduate courses, and some of the participants said they did that.

example, one woman from the first cycle was ambivalent about the amount of criticism she received on her papers:

> We were just allowed to sit around and think and read and write. But sometimes I just thought it was a little too loose. I mean, just not structured enough, not disciplined enough, not critical enough. You'd write a paper, and it's not written very well, and then they didn't really . . . I just felt that in ways, I did slide a little bit. Not gross—they didn't let me get away with gross underperformance—but I just don't remember feeling scrutinized in a certain way, maybe in a careful enough way . . . especially in the writing. I think it would have been very hard. We all were so fragile, we were little young buddies, and maybe we couldn't have stood it. So maybe it was nice just to fan the embers of thought, and not worry if there's a little brush fire here and there.

Another participant from the first cycle, one who would choose not to repeat the Program, was less forgiving.

> In my opinion it was a failure because you didn't *have* to have the book read by the end of the week. You didn't *have* to have the paper written. You didn't *have* to study for the test. You didn't *have* to participate in the seminars. You didn't get graded on it. They didn't *have* to do anything. [And the consequence] is that they don't do anything.

Another participant from the first cycle who would not repeat the Program said he would have liked more structure, more accountability, and a more traditional educational approach.

> I objected to the fact that there was as little structure as there was. There appeared to be several different approaches . . . I didn't feel that they demanded enough work. You could do as much as you wanted. . . . It was to some extent a soft touch. There just weren't that many books we were required to read, and given an opportunity, I think the average eighteen to twenty year old, myself certainly included, will not work hard. You've got to demand it. . . .
> I want to give them high marks for having extremely good intentions, for staying with it, but—and maybe this is inevitable with any new experimental college—it was not rigorous in the sense that . . . the Program kept changing. First we were to meet twice a week, then it was once a week, because they couldn't get it together, or there was fighting,

or whatever. The lectures, to my view, became increasingly disjointed....

I believe people should be tested. I think there should be accountability in education. I expected a more rigorous program, both in terms of the organization of the material and its presentation. I expected it to be more in the nature of my understanding of the academic tradition where people who are learned in a particular field tell you what they know. I thought there was a little too much—not bull shit, but a little too much—"Let's sit down and see what we all think." I don't think that is the best educational approach. I think some of that's good, you get some fresh approaches, but I think there has to be a point at which you cut that off and say, "Listen, this is what the scholars in the field say." I believe in professionalism....

I didn't do enough. I didn't feel that I worked as hard as I did in high school ... or law school.... Maybe I should have been more self-motivated, but I think if they had just demanded more, I would have learned more. The more you read the more you learn, and we weren't expected to read that much. I think a little more accountability—maybe I'm saying more about myself than I am about the Program ... looking back, I just wished I read more when I had the chance to do it.

Not every participant reacted the same way to the absence of carrots and sticks. Some saw benefits both personal and intellectual in not having a traditional structure. But for some students the transition was not easy or immediate. One woman said that while she did learn to take more responsibility, it took time.

I suppose at the beginning I felt like I had *too* much freedom. I mean, it wasn't, "You'll do this by next Tuesday, or this by the following Tuesday." And I suppose it taught me more responsibility because there wasn't someone doing it for me. There wasn't somebody standing over me saying, "I want you to read these eighty pages by such and such a day." You had to get it done, but there wasn't anyone there everyday checking on you to see what you'd done, and if you'd done what you were supposed to do last night. And in the end you have to take on more responsibility for yourself. I think if I'd come to it later or there'd been a second program for upper division that I would have made better use of the whole thing.... If I'd come in there with a better background and having had more freedom in terms of assignments then I wouldn't have had to spend so much time learning *how* to do it.

For others in the first cycle, such as this man, the looser structure was ideal.

> The Program was a good structure for me. While there were assignments and deadlines, my memory is they were certainly looser and the boundaries were looser than in the regular University with classes and assignments. I'm not saying that the Program didn't have a schedule because it did—you had to be at a certain place at a certain time—but my memory is that the whole thing was less structured and that was good for me.

That kind of freedom and encouragement to develop and play with ideas can be instrumental in getting students involved in the curriculum and helps to foster in them a responsibility for their own education.

Getting work in on time was important in the Program, and the faculty made it clear it was expected, but sanctions for noncompliance appeared to have been missing, or at least weak, during the first cycle. The assigned reading and writing were crucial keys to learning in the Program, and if students were lax in those ways they were compromising their ability to learn in that setting. If students were unsure about their understanding of the material, the lack of strict deadlines and sanctions might have encouraged them to procrastinate. They were expected to assume responsibility for their own work themselves, but were apparently not being guided by faculty or taught how to achieve this new degree of responsibility. By the second cycle, faculty, aided by the regularized one-to-one tutorials, seemed to have paid much closer attention to how students were progressing with both the reading and writing, and there were no complaints from second-cycle participants about loose requirements. There were, however, reactions from participants in both cycles about the absence of a regular grading system.

(It should be noted here that while students received only pass grades, if they were thought to be failing by Program faculty and asked to leave, they still received passing credit for work they had done. And it was possible to receive letter grades when the situation demanded them. One participant had to receive a letter grade in order to get off academic probation; another to get into his upper division major. Another participant lost a scholarship because he didn't get a grade in the Program, but had he asked, he would have received one.)

When participants said they appreciated the absence of grades in the Program, it was often in terms of relief from the pressure of grades. But comments went beyond that feeling of relief to the real advantage of having the freedom to concentrate on the curriculum. One woman said,

> The one thing I can . . . think back on is remembering just how lucky I was that I wasn't going through all the pressures that all the other undergraduates around me in my dorm were going through. Sometimes I think we all took advantage of that and just were lazy. I have to grant that. There's a certain amount of laziness that comes with knowing you don't have a test or you're not going to have a grade. But I remember feeling really lucky that I didn't have that pressure, kind of like I was in another era and I was able to just sit back and read and think. I felt like it was a luxury.

That sense of luxury another man interpreted as elitism:

> It gave me sort of an elitist feeling. We were in this special program, looking at things in a different way. It turned out to be a liberal arts program taught in a conservative manner, within frameworks. But the whole no-grades thing, that was all very attractive, and there was a kind of elitist view, a philosophers view. . . . Part of my [previous] training was to try to please. It was hard [in the Program] to find someone to please. You couldn't just get a good grade, you had to come up with an idea and talk about it. That was a big change, that people were listening to ideas, and not just watching performance.

The "big change" for this student, as for others in the Program, was the transition from the importance of grades to the importance of ideas, and away from external authority toward internal discipline. One woman, while granting the usefulness of traditional education, still thought that the Program offered an advantage over traditional classes. "It's not in getting grades or meeting standards so much as in preparing ourselves, giving ourselves the background that we need about what's gone before." Grades and standards came to mean less to her than the kind of knowledge and perspective the Program provided her, certainly representing a shift in her values and a developmental progression.

The absence of grades could be helpful to students who came to the university not as well prepared as others academically. One participant, a minority student, clearly intelligent and capable but from a background that she said had not prepared her well for college, could compare her experiences at Berkeley with those of her sister. Both she and her older sister had been top students in high school but found the scholastic competition much greater at Berkeley. While her sister who had attended Berkeley before her had "a lot of trouble" in the regular program, the experience of this woman was markedly different because of her participation in the Program.

> I never had that feeling that I was just out of it, that I was lost somewhere. It wasn't like we had tests with grades posted . . . where you saw that you were here as opposed to other people being somewhere else. So I never really had that feeling that I was down at the bottom . . . that . . . I might have [had] in a regular class. Coming from a place where we always were at the top and then suddenly finding that maybe you were in the middle or towards the bottom would be real hard to cope with. . . . And I think it helped ease that pressure, that I could go ahead and learn and do what I could do without worrying all the time about, "Is it too late? I've already failed anyway." And . . . that helped a lot because I think you can get real caught up in that, just worrying about, "Is this the right answer? Or am I doing the right thing?" I didn't feel the pressure to do that.

The focus in the Program on the exploration of ideas rather than on the accumulation of facts required a different kind of basis for judgments of students' progress. In the place of grades, verbal comments on each paper during the individual tutorial provided students with evaluations of their work. Rather than letter grades on mid-terms and finals, and perhaps a paper or two each quarter or semester, students received faculty attention not only to their regularly submitted written work, but to ongoing oral presentations, in seminars as well as in informal discussions. This regular attention to their intellectual development was also beneficial to students who did not feel particularly academically vulnerable as did the woman quoted above. A man from the second cycle spoke of the evaluative process in the Program in contrast to the rest of the university.

> I liked continuously turning out work that was being discussed and evaluated. I liked that constant feedback and interaction, versus just being a sponge, absorbing it all and than regurgitating it at the end.

No doubt there were many students in the Program who had been top students in high school and who, had they been in the regular lower division, would have been earning high grades there, too. For them, not having grades may have felt like something of a loss. One woman said, "Getting grades is a feedback, so you weren't getting that *cum laude* experience out of the Program." Particularly bright students were not handicapped in the Program of course and were appreciated by faculty and admired by other students, but academic brilliance was not necessary for success. One man observed:

> There were those whose mastery of things had been quick, and who were quick studies. Who had gotten through school and through life that way, being quick studies. And the Program did call a halt to that kind of thing. I mean, it was fine if you were a quick study, but you went over and over this stuff so much that it was the intellectual endurance more than quickness that mattered.

And since the Program was designed to include ordinary students, and not necessarily honor students, a participant who said, "I didn't do well with classes, and I didn't do well with structure, and I never did well with grades," could still succeed there and feel that he had profited from it.

If, as mentioned earlier, the Program provided a moratorium for students on having to make choices about courses and to prepare for majors in the upper division, it also provided a moratorium on competition for grades. Students were competing essentially with themselves and not with other students; they were shielded in the lower division from the temptation to concentrate on academic subjects in which they achieved the highest grades, excluding other areas that might interest them but in which they felt they did not excel. That tendency can lead to premature specialization that does not leave much room for a liberal education such as the Program offered.

The absence of grades proved to be more than simply a relief from the pressures of studying for grades; without grades and exams, students were freed to concentrate on the curriculum, a process that served to unify them as members of a learning community, rather than divide them as competitors for the limited commodity of high grades. With faculty removed from their customary roles as judges of student's rankings in relationship to each other, they were free to concentrate on guiding students in their intellectual development wherever they might be in that process. By relieving faculty of their role as formal arbiters, faculty were freer to join with them in their common intellectual work, and rather than concentrating on pleasing faculty, students were given more responsibility for their own learning.

In spite of these advantages of not having grades so many participants spoke of, a few said they would have liked to have grades in the Program. In the report on the Harvard Assessment Seminars, Richard Light points out the difficulties Harvard students today have with not knowing where they stand: "The big point—it comes up over and over as crucial—is the importance of quick and detailed (and later he adds 'frequent') feedback . . . on homework, quizzes, and even in-class exams . . . especially [in] math, sciences, and languages."[2]

While this need for frequent evaluation is understandable in course work involving the mastery and memorization of detail, and in a competitive classroom situation such as Harvard (and perhaps betrays students' anxiety over competition), it was apparently felt by some Berkeley students enrolled in the Program as well. One second-cycle man thought that if someone had been "picking up on my writing and actually giving me bad grades and telling me why, I might have paid more attention to it." All three of the participants who would not repeat the Program mentioned the lack of grades and what they thought of as the lack of accountability as criticisms. Two of them have been quoted above. The third, from the second cycle said,

> Maybe I wanted grades and tests and things, so that I knew I was covering "X" content. Because I think as an eighteen year old—thirteen years of school changed into this environment where there were no grades and there were no tests. How did that measure what you were learning? Perhaps what I'm talking about is more grades and more tests so that you had a sense of what you were accomplishing exactly. And where you could improve. . . . So that every six months or every four months you were called to task or you were called to be accountable for what you had learned or hadn't learned.
>
> I'm the kind of person if given a challenge will rise to it, but I also can be a real sloth, just kind of get by with the minimum. I can remember

---

[2]Richard Light, *The Harvard Assessment Seminars: First Report.* (Cambridge, Massachusetts: Harvard University, 1990), 31-33.

writing a lot of letters during lab, during lectures. It wasn't just those lectures [in the Program]. It was any large lecture where I knew I only had to lend half an ear and that was all the participation I had to do, to take notes. I'd write letters or just read. 'Cause nobody knew what I was doing. And always I got excellent grades all through college. And I graduated in three and a half years. I was a slip-by student and still would do really, really well.

All three of the "nonrepeaters" blamed the Program for not insisting, by way of tests and grades, that they work harder. It seems their habit of relying on grades to measure what they were learning was too ingrained to give up—in contrast to the Program student who thought doing a paper every other week and going over it with a faculty member provided him "constant feedback."

LEARNING FROM OTHER STUDENTS

In view of the lack of competitiveness in the Program, the voluntary study groups some participants mentioned could not have been aimed at passing exams and getting good grades, but must have been a group effort to understand the curricular material, another indication of the establishment of a learning community among students. Some participants had nothing or little to say about the role of other students in their education in the Program. One first-cycle man said, "I have no memory of that. Which must mean it wasn't very important." But for others it could be significant. One second-cycle man said of his education in the Program:

> I'd say about a quarter of the intellectual effort was spent with other students. Most of it was internal, digesting the learning experience, and through the reading and writing part. The lectures and the faculty and the seminars were probably worth about a quarter of it. And then the other students worth about a quarter of it. There was a sort of active study group or seminar group, a bunch of people that spent a fair amount of time with a concentrated effort to going over the materials, an independent seminar kind of situation, [although] I really was not part of that myself.

Habits of Mind

Other participants placed even more emphasis on the importance to their learning of their fellow students. Another second-cycle man said other students

> sure as hell were important to my life. I remember feeling this tremendous bond with a lot of people there. I was a really unformed person and I think I got a lot out of it with them. And the seminars were great, a lot of talk, a lot of discussion . . . not once did that happen anywhere else in the upper division.

A first-cycle man said about discussions with other students:

That was good, because they all in the main had at least as high if not a higher degree of intellectual curiosity than students on the outside in regular school. I remember some wonderful discussions with [other students].

Another man from the first cycle expressed awe at

being able to interact with so many bright people at the same time. I really enjoyed that part of it. Not only the professors who obviously were bright or they wouldn't be there, but students who I also realized were bright or they wouldn't be there. But they offered different things and they were from all over the country. They were just bright people and it was like having a study group of a hundred and fifty people, which I never had again.

You were not with the same ten or fifteen people all the time. You moved within the one hundred and fifty or so for different parts of your [seminars] so you got to know, at least recognize most people by face and name after a while in the Program. You got to listen and speak with all of them. I had a very, very positive experience with this University as a whole and that certainly enhanced it. Probably much more so in an earlier stage than if I had been in the regular program with all the other freshmen.

A woman from the second cycle talked of the importance of learning with the same group of people over a period of time.

> I guess that's important to my education. I don't think it matters who they are, I think it matters that we have that kind of time together over a period of years. It wasn't because so and so was there, a particular person, that

we had these great discussions. It was because of the set-up and the continuity. We had this body of reading in common, which is fairly rare in life.

That common body of readings, a crucial feature of the Program, accumulated over time, forming the basis what many participants seemed to feel was a kind of two-year study group, where discussions were not dependent on a faculty or student leader to be successful.

Two second-cycle men described the effect other students had on their participation in seminars. One said,

> I found it challenging because of the intellectual level of the students, primarily. You were forced to think. You didn't just sit there and parrot back who did what. You were forced to think about it, analyze it. That was the challenge, that was what I wanted.

Another spoke about how other students as well as faculty forced him to develop rational positions.

> You have to sit down and justify [an opinion], turn it into something comprehensible. I'm sure in the tutorials and the seminars that if you didn't justify it, you probably got called on it. I'm sure that students would say, "Hey, why are you saying that? Defend that position!" . . . That was part of the dynamic.

One second-cycle man was able to actually observe the education of one of his close friends in the Program, an opportunity unique to an ordinary undergraduate in the regular lower division classes at Berkeley.

> He was very different from me. I mean he came in with a very different set of assumptions, and attitudes, and education. I watched his education take place at that age, and I've watched it since. We're forty years old now, and I'm still watching his education take place, and we're still talking. But to watch him go through this education while I was going through it, and to see that these things that were natural to me were shocking to him, and that things that I took for granted he found sometimes delightful, sometimes upsetting, but in any case, big news. . . .

He went on to describe the importance of other students to his education in the Program.

> There were also these Friday night dinners from time to time that we had in the House. Topics that were current were sort of percolating through our minds at all times, and we were talking about them. And the seminars were very, very interesting, too. Now and then some student would come out with some memorable saying that would stick with me for a long time. I'd say the students were an extremely important mix. I remember some very vividly, and I heard surprising things from them, very often in our discussion, in our lecturer's question period, when you questioned the teachers about the material. There was always good stuff coming up. It was great.

Another second-cycle man, who also believed that other students were very important to his education, learned in the Program to use that kind of interaction to his advantage in other educational situations long after the Program ended.

> [Other students] were very important, I'd say as important as the professors were. And the kinds of relationships that I got involved in, which tended to focus on Program stuff, too. We talked, and our relationships were part of the Program as well as what was going on, so the other students were very important. And that's something that's come out of that. It's always been a saving grace in whatever educational space that I've been in. . . . I think that that's a Program gift, and that it encouraged that kind of interaction that I've always been able to use, in the driest of educational situations. Learning from and being with and interacting with fellow students, and appreciating that interaction regardless of what the professor was doing.

LEARNING FROM FACULTY

Establishing the kind of educational climate where students could learn from each other was one of the distinctive features of the Program. Another was the kind of educational relationships established between teachers and students. The availability of faculty has been noted by several participants, particularly from the second cycle. Besides contact between them in lectures, seminars, and tutorials, faculty "lingered" in the house, not "darting off" immediately after their formal teaching duties were finished, creating the impression that they welcomed informal discussion with students. It should not be assumed, however, that the close faculty-student relations on which the Program was based were meant to include, or did necessarily include relationships outside the educational sphere. Faculty were never intended to form social relations with their students, and from what these participants had to say, they did not. Except in a very few instances, participants reported they maintained completely professional relationships with students which, warm and friendly as they might have been, did not stray into the social arena. One second-cycle man reported that Professor O had invited him to play tennis once or twice, another man that L had hired him to be a research assistant one quarter; one man said that he once took M to lunch at his co-op, and another that J once took him and his girl friend, also in the Program, to lunch. These were the only references from the 40 participants to extrascholastic activity among faculty and students while they were in the Program.

And no participant expressed a wish for more social contact with faculty. As it was, some students had some degree of difficulty in dealing with faculty on such an informal basis. One second-cycle man found the informality of faculty uncomfortable.

> I got the feeling that maybe the faculty wanted things to be a little more informal and they wanted to be friendlier. But I was unable to do that. I mean, we didn't go to faculty members' houses or have lunch together or anything like that. . . . It was difficult for me to be real friendly and real informal. I couldn't discard the role of student/teacher.

There might have been other reasons for students preferring more distance from professors. Another second-cycle man said that questions of adult authority effected relations with faculty.

> [They] were occasionally adversarial. Some of the professors were people you would admire and some of them were people you would like. But it was like being little kids and dealing with the big kids. I guess their function was to be adults and there was the general suspicion at the time of adults being from a different world, different values and all that sort of thing. So it generally wasn't very close. I sort of got to be friends with [M], or [M] sort of made a point of being friends with us. Having been a Jesuit priest and a youth director, I guess he had the skills. And [L] wanted to be on our side, whatever that was,

referring to the renegade professor in that cycle who tried to side with students in their struggles with authority.

Even though faculty-student relations were essentially not social, faculty as a whole had a substantial impact on Program students through a basically educational relationship. To begin with, faculty must have been genuinely interested in and committed to aiding the intellectual development of their students in the Program; it is difficult to imagine them joining the Program without this commitment. As we know through participants' testimony, they were available to students informally, apart from their assigned duties in lectures, seminars, and tutorials, so that the amount of time they spent with students was considerable, frequent, and varied, particularly when compared to the average lower division lecturer whose contact with students outside class is mostly confined to the occasional voluntary attendance at office hours. Besides participating in lectures and panel discussions with the whole group, Program faculty led small seminars—the teaching job in the regular lower division that is usually left to teaching assistants in section meetings with students. And being available in the House led to informal one-to-one discussions or small groups. But their most sustained and focused effort with individual students came in the tutorials based on the papers students had written, and when students did them, their journals.

There was a variety in teaching styles in tutorials as well, and some were given higher marks by participants than others. One second-cycle man who felt somewhat intimidated by faculty in tutorials at first, had to learn how to overcome that handicap.

> Some of the faculty were more encouraging about it, kind of prodded you when you disagreed or would play devil's advocate and say, "Okay, if you think this, what if I said that, how would you react to that?" And that opened up the discussion. After while you'd go, "Okay, it's okay to talk if I disagree and express a different point of view." I think that was important because when you are eighteen or nineteen years old and dealing with faculty in their forties and fifties, it's not an equal relationship. It needs some guidance there to make that happen. It wasn't something that was talked about a lot. It could have been talked about a little bit more openly by the faculty, so that it happened more quickly. Some of them felt more comfortable with talking one-on-one with nineteen year olds than others did, about intellectual things (laughs).

Apparently, some faculty and some students needed help in conducting the tutorials as well as help with seminars as discussed earlier.

Women from the second cycle had appreciative comments about their interaction with faculty. One woman compared the relationship to faculty in the tutorials to that available in the rest of the lower division:

> It was so nice to have that connection with professors. You had to meet them on so many other levels, but to finally have that one-on-one contact with their mind and your mind, I thought was really quite unique for an undergraduate. . . . In the usual lower division . . . all you see is the professor way in the distance and then you mostly just communicate with the TA.

Another woman also saw a contrast:

> I think the upper division years and the course system in general is just much more chaotic. I had some great professors [there] who, I think, took momentary interest, but their priorities were in getting published or giving speeches, so that you might have them for a minute, and they'd be gone.

To have this relationship not just for a quarter or semester or even a year but for the entire two years was indeed an unusual opportunity. A woman who had described some less than satisfactory experiences with faculty in the regular university valued the continuity with Program faculty:

> I think that we within the Program didn't realize the advantage of having people track your progress . . . and knowing your same professors for two years. That was a real experience. I don't think in the rest of my time I ever had a class from the same person twice. You didn't have the same people in groups, you didn't really have people develop ideas back and forth. So it's one of those things you don't know what you have until you compare it to something else.

Engaging in discussions with first- and second-year college students required skills not necessary for teaching the ordinary undergraduate lecture class. One second-cycle man pointed out the difference.

Not only do these people know a lot, they were smart. They could figure things out. They could understand things. They could listen to you and your ramblings as you tried to fumble [for] an idea, exactly what it was that you were saying, lead you to it and give you pros and cons. And while they were doing it, think about it. That was fabulous to see that done. Gave you a role model.

Role modeling was useful for another man quoted earlier:

I modeled my writing on [J's] prose and [K's] speaking voice. . . . I could model the way I thought about things on the way I saw these other guys talking. I could see how things got put together and how they sustained their arguments. And so I'd argue almost in a way of mimicking what the teachers were doing. You got to see people talk about big issues, and take a position, and stick to it.

While role modeling of faculty styles of writing and speaking was certainly available in the regular lower division classroom, opportunities to observe faculty sustaining arguments, taking positions, and sticking to them was rare.

How the faculty went about involving students in curricular material is described by a man from the first cycle.

The way Tussman set it up, while there were sort of minimum requirements . . . you could take more of the Program if you wanted it. They would hang these intellectual carrots out, like [A] would [with] his enthusiasm for Hobbes say, would be out there and you could take it or leave it. I took it. [C] would get you involved . . . no matter what he was talking about . . . they enticed you, as it were. It's there for you to take or not. And I always did better when I felt I had the choice. . . . It's the process that they were after, that's my guess, the process of exchange, sort of throwing intellectual ideas back and forth. The fact was [that] in the big group meetings and particularly in the seminars and then in the individual tutorials, it was all about them listening to me as much as me listening to them . . . but developing the ability to say what you're thinking, to be able to respond to something.

I don't want to accuse the rest of the University, but I remember lectures with 500 people in them where you'd sit in a movie theater [probably Wheeler Hall]. And that clearly is just the antithesis of what Tussman was thinking that education was all about. Because even when the whole [Tussman] college was together you could open your mouth and say something. And certainly the other professors would be able to chime in with their two cents worth. That [was] a process of developing ideas and tossing them back and forth and just thinking with imagination. . . .

You asked what the process is. There's something about it that I can't define—but there's also something about it that makes it a two-way street, an interaction, as part of the process. Hearing what the students had to say was just as important, I suspect, in terms of Tussman's theory of this thing. I mean, that encourages you to think . . . and that was a challenge too. I remember the sense that you couldn't just sneak into the room and sit there and walk away, whereas in all the other regular classes, you could pretty much get away with that. They might call on you sometimes in the smaller [university] classes, but you didn't have to be there, and in the Program you had to be there.

I remember [D] calling on me when we were reading the Peloponnesian Wars. I remember him drawing the battle square and getting his chalk and his cigarette mixed up. They engaged you. They made you be on top of it, which was good . . . they weren't up there to drag you over the coals and that was good. They weren't there to prove how smart they were and ask you questions you couldn't answer. They were there to get you excited about the stuff, and I think they were successful at that. I think we were learning some process of clear thinking. You had to think logically and clearly and analyze whatever was the subject, being very analytical and orderly with your thinking.

Teaching in the Program then meant more than having a lot of contact with students in smaller groups; it meant engaging them in a serious dialogue, establishing a process of interaction, the two-way street that got them on top of it. It was guiding and encouraging their intellectual development so that they became active participants in their own educational growth, rather than passive recipients of imparted knowledge. The importance to students of having faculty listen to them, to their ideas and their arguments about the readings they did in common, must have led to a validation of their efforts, promoting a sense of efficaciousness for students. One first-cycle man talked about the intellectual support he received from this kind of interaction with faculty.

> They seemed to actually care about the ideas that were put forth. They didn't cut me down. And that was real helpful. There was a sense they were all sympathetic and on my side.

A second-cycle man who thought that the respect shown by faculty in the Program was one of its most significant features.

> I got *that* kind of respect at *that* age, just stepping out away from the family. I got *recognition* with other students—I was being spoken to directly about good words, great books.

Another of his peers spoke with pleasure of the egalitarian approach of faculty to students.

> Here's another thing I really liked about all the faculty, that they were not condescending toward students. They seemed to treat students much as intellectual equals, even though we weren't. I appreciated [that].

Treating students with intellectual respect changed their relationships to authority discussed in the previous chapter. Establishing an atmosphere of intellectual respect for students and interest in their ideas aided faculty in their relations with students. Participants responded, sometimes intensely, to faculty opinion of their work. When comments were encouraging, students felt particularly rewarded. Within the educational structure of the Program, students were allowed room for creativity in their thinking and writing, another sign of acceptance. A first-cycle man talked of a paper he had written in one seminar:

> It took kind of a creative turn towards the end and [D] really supported that. He read it and really appreciated it, and I was very surprised and very pleased.

Another student of D's was inspired to write an analysis of the *Odyssey* and the *Iliad* in iambic pentameter that D thought "brilliant"—this participant said he had poured himself into his papers and felt his efforts were justly rewarded.

THE "QUASI-THERAPEUTIC ART OF TEACHING"

The treatment given to student work in the Program was not typical of the rest of the university, or large research universities in general, and reflected the interest in students' intellectual development that was built into the Program. In a series of interviews with me, Tussman described what he calls the "quasi-therapeutic art of teaching" in contrast to the "performing art of teaching."[3] Rather than "putting on a show" by entertaining students in lectures, teachers in the Program "treated" or, perhaps more accurately, "coached" them on how to improve their intellectual performance. They first identified ineffectual intellectual habits and then worked with students to help them substitute better ones. The papers students wrote therefore became a diagnostic tool, a kind of "fever chart," except, as Tussman stressed, students were in no way ill, but rather in need of acquiring, developing, and strengthening healthy intellectual habits. The use of diagnosis in learning situations is not new—it is frequently used in elementary and secondary education. But it is not customarily used in higher education where the burden lies more with the student to learn than it does with the lecturer to teach.

Tussman's examples of students' habits needing to be "cured," included the tendency to evasion and confusion, using "grandiose or fluffy language," repeating too much of what they had read, and their need to learn to use short words and sentences in their writing and speaking. He cited the case of one very bright student who kept just missing the point, using figures of speech or metaphors that were just a "little bit off, just enough so that he didn't have to face the real problem." By asking him to give another figure of speech, or another way of saying what he was trying to say, he would lead the student to more clarity. But in order to do that, Tussman said he could not just say, "be clearer"; instead, he would point out that the figure of speech chosen by the student was "good enough to be close but not clear enough, and he needed another one, thus curing him of a habit of settling for vague resemblance when what he needed was to put his finger more accurately on what he wanted." To simply tell this student his writing was unclear and must be clearer, Tussman argues, would not be

---

[3]Interviews with Joseph Tussman, Spring 1990. All of Tussman's quotes in this chapter are taken from these interviews.

effective. By asking him to "substitute something better" over and over again in each of his papers, "at some point, he will get it."

What is implicit in this process is the degree of courage sometimes necessary for the students to "get it," to "face the real problem," in Tussman's words. In his studies of cognitive and moral development in college students, Perry (1970, 1981) outlines the changes in students' thinking that mark the transition from a belief that knowledge is absolute, and answers clearly right or wrong, to an increasingly complex understanding of the contextual relativity of both truth and choice that might parallel the changes in students' development in the Program. His developmental scheme

> concerns precisely a person's "moral" development, in the sense of his assumptions about values and responsibility. . . . [S]ince each step in the development presents a challenge to a person's previous assumptions and requires that he redefine and extend his responsibilities in the midst of increased complexity and uncertainty, his growth does indeed involve courage (Perry 1970, 44).

In discussing the instructor's encouragement of risk, he describes the good teacher as one "who supports in his students a more sustained groping, exploration, and synthesis" (Perry 1970, 211-12), certainly an apt description of the teaching approach in the Program.

It seems Tussman (and other Program faculty) exemplified Perry's definition of the "good teacher" in the way in which he dealt with students' difficulties in finding the courage to make the leap to the next stage in their thinking. In an example of what he called one of his greatest triumphs, Tussman described how he got a student to break his habit of using very "long sentences with commas all over the place, so long that in the second half of the sentence he would take back what he said in the first, avoiding the risk of completing a thought. To tell him to 'be more coherent' would not help him break this habit of equivocation, of self-protection, of failure to make a commitment, of failure to think." Rather than telling him "not to contradict himself," Tussman simply told him to rewrite the page without using a comma. The student had great difficulty breaking this habit, knowing that to use a period instead of a comma risked completing a thought, and hence making a commitment. He grappled with it for days, and finally succeeded late one night. Early the next morning he called

Teaching and Learning

Tussman at home to tell him of his achievement, of which they were both understandably proud—an illustration of the rewards of this kind of partnership in the educational process.

Tussman finds students' writings reveal:

> the surface of a habit. That's why I thought of this as a fever chart, as symptoms, and you've got to learn to read them so that you can see what is the activity of the mind. Here's a very good mind and it's always defeating itself, it's always falling short, it's always failing to commit . . . not in a moral sense,[4] but failing to commit in a way that saves him the labor of thinking to the decision point that he's got to make . . .
>
> The fascinating thing about teaching in the Program was . . . they would come in with their [papers] and it's like a doctor walking through a ward, and I don't mean the image of sickness. It isn't that they're all doing something wrong because I start with the assumption that they're doing pretty well. This is almost . . . an advanced class . . . [they are] doing things well to get to college.
>
> And yet, it turns out that there are all these things that you discover for the first time when you ask them to write a paper on a topic that you've picked, and not one that lets them ride their old hobby horse in a way that takes you a long time to see through them. You give them a task and you see how they perform it. . . . And at that point—"C, A, B"—all of it is so irrelevant. [What is really involved] is, "What is this mind doing? And how can you get it to exercise more power and clarity as an instrument for himself?" And [that's] grappling with the problem.

Tussman contends that what the Program had to offer students in this way came to override the common suspicion among students that faculty were trying to impose their political point of view on students through the Program.

> Once they see that, I think students don't fight that anymore because you not trying to say, "and so you see that the government is right," or something like that. That never enters into it . . . I'm sure they thought at some point that we've got some message we're trying to sell them. The whole world is assaulting them with things they want to do, and we've got

---

[4]Perry might have disagreed here.

> our thing. And [they thought this was] probably [a] conservative, or reactionary establishment thing . . . especially in the sixties: "What are you guys up to? What are you doing this for? . . . What are you trying to sell?" . . . We would get arguments . . . about, "We want you to write a paper and bring it in." "Well, who are you? . . . Who are you to tell me how to write? I'm going to write my way," as if we were trying to kill their originality.
>
> However, that kind of objection never survived . . . because the issues are so utterly clear. We were giving them, when we succeeded . . . valuable individual advice that was priceless. . . . For them to get professional intellectual attention to their own intellectual operations on a one-to-one basis in a continuing situation is a really exceptional situation. And what pleased me was to be able to prove that you could do it on a relatively cheap basis.

As we have seen from their testimony, many participants in the study realized at the time the unusual benefits of having this personal professional attention. None of the participants in this study complained of having their originality stifled in the Program—quite to the contrary, some said the Program encouraged it. While they may not have been aware of the specific techniques faculty used to get them to substitute new habits of thinking for old, ineffective ones, it is clear that they did appreciate the way their thinking and writing developed under faculty tutelage and many did say they were learning to think critically, to write more clearly, to argue more effectively, and to integrate all three.

But in attributing the ability of students to relinquish their suspicions of faculty motives to the clarity of the issues, Tussman may not have given the Program all the credit it was due. It is quite possible, in view of theories of cognitive and moral development, that Program students were able to overcome the objections Tussman describes because they were able to arrive at a different developmental level where suspicions of authority could be overcome. And that was aided in part by the kind of "benign" authority exercised by faculty and even shared with students, which allowed student to define differently their relationship to authority. (See Chapters 12, "Politics and the Program," and 13, "Authority in the Program.")

A student's moral and intellectual development cannot be assumed to follow a regular and orderly pattern. In the course of moving through some of the nine developmental positions Perry outlines in his model, students often display "conditions of delay, deflection, and regression" by temporizing, exploring the implications of a position or simply hesitating to take the next step; by denying responsibility through alienation; and by retreating to an earlier stage (Perry 1970, 10). He concluded that what appeared to be personality differences or differing degrees of ability in the students he studied were actually characteristics of different stages in the developmental process. The defenses he describes bear a resemblance to what Smelser describes as regression in the Odyssey experience and what Tussman says was a student's "failure to make a commitment . . . failure to think." With the individual, intimate attention given to student writing in the Program, those sticking points in the developmental process could be addressed directly and students encouraged to relinquish old, safe habits in favor of new ways of perceiving and tackling difficult issues. It seems quite possible that Program students having difficulty taking this risk might easily make a convenient "political" retreat to the less demanding lecture classes in the regular university, claiming that the Program and its faculty were too conservative. While this could have been a legitimately held political judgment, it could at the same time reflect the anxiety associated with leaving one developmental stage to progress to another, less certain one.

Understanding student intellectual growth in developmental terms helps to explain why the Program could be beneficial to some students and not for others. Not only can entering students arrive at college in different levels of personal maturity, they can be at different levels cognitively. In reporting on his developmental study of undergraduate students at Harvard and Radcliffe in the fifties and sixties, Perry observed that within this

> relatively homogeneous group in intelligence and academic ability, our study reveals the wide range, in any one college year, of the ways in which they construed the nature of knowledge, the origin of values, the intentions of instructors, and their own responsibilities (Perry 1970).

Cowan noted that there are individual differences in the rate of cognitive development, and that "we should expect to see the characteristics of the 'adolescent personality' emerging at different ages in different people" (Cowan 1978, 294). He cited studies done in the early seventies, and concluded that only between 56 percent and 67 percent of college students reach Piaget's stages of formal reasoning and formal operations (Cowan, 273). Discrepancies in students' levels of cognitive and moral development rather than in inherent intellectual ability may have led some of them to perceive the Program to be beyond their intellectual capacities, or at any rate, their intellectual energies. In view of the facts that the Program demanded of its students a kind of serious attention to reasoning, and that their thinking was continually exposed publicly in seminars, papers, and tutorials, as well as for all the other reasons suggested above, it appears quite possible that some of those students who dropped out may have found the intellectual commitment and intellectual/moral self-examination required more than they were prepared to make no matter how intellectually capable they might have been.

By the second cycle, a system of weekly or biweekly tutorials came into place, although the small seminars had already been established in the first cycle. The small seminars of 10 or 15 students taught by faculty formed the basis for assigning tutorials—the faculty member who taught the seminar met with each seminar student for tutorials. These assignments changed each semester or quarter, when students would be reshuffled with new faculty. The purpose was to allow each student one seminar and accompanying set of tutorials with each of the six faculty over each two-year period. A folder was kept by faculty for each student in the Program that held copies of each paper turned in by the student together with comments from faculty about their progress, in their work and in the seminars.[5] The folder was passed on each semester to the newly assigned faculty member so that he had the benefit of the views of previous teachers as well as the "portfolio" of the student's work to date.

The way in which this system worked meant that over the two-year period each student (at least in the second cycle) had the chance to learn from each of the six professors in the small seminar each quarter that was accompanied by weekly or biweekly individual tutorials with that same professor. (Because two faculty and the teaching assistants left after the first year and were replaced by new faculty the second year, every student

---

[5]Student folders are still in Tussman's files. A review revealed some discouraging comments on the progress of a few former students interviewed for the study who have since become appreciative, and some enthusiastic, about what they had learned there. Faculty assessments of students' understanding and appreciation of what they learned in the Program were not always accurate predictors of students' own assessments of the value of the Program to them over time.

did not get equal exposure to every faculty member over the two-year period.) In light of the diverse backgrounds and teaching styles of all these teachers, even in the second cycle where they were nearly all philosophers, students in the Program interacted with a diverse group of teachers who all got to know them and the quality and progress of their intellectual growth to a degree unimaginable in an ordinary lower division lecture course.

TEACHING BRIGHT AND AVERAGE STUDENTS THROUGH "MEDIATED LEARNING"

With an individualized program such as this, it was possible to educate students from a wide variety of educational backgrounds and abilities. One of the common myths about the Program was that it was elitist, that it was a program only for top ranking students. In fact, it was never the intention to restrict the Experimental College Program to such students. Tussman's commitment was to the "ordinary student"—he did not distinguish between the intellectually gifted and those with average ability. To have been admitted to the University of California, Berkeley, (and perhaps to have passed the university's Subject A exam as pointed out in Chapter 2) was in his mind evidence enough that students could handle the intellectual material in the Program. According to Tussman, the Program was built

> on the notion that every citizen ought to be initiated into thinking about these fundamental problems of freedom and authority . . . we didn't think of it as a program for stars. . . . I don't remember any faculty member saying, "If only we would get rid of the dumber students and just have an honor's program, it'd be much more fun" . . . I think our problem was indiscipline rather than inadequacy of mind. I haven't the impression . . . of slower students. What I do have is the impression of the different degrees of recalcitrance, rebelliousness, nonperformance. I don't think of . . . anything like a "slow student." I think of a student with a block or disorder, somehow . . . beginning to get over that a little bit. . . . The whole point of this program is to show that the ordinary student would perform, or would be turned on, or would wake up. That this could reach anybody who was admitted.

For Program faculty to have that kind of commitment to teaching "ordinary" Berkeley lower division students and to have as a goal their intellectual development is to undertake a degree of responsibility for the education of these undergraduate students that is rare in American research universities. Under the usual lecture-exam system, the bright students do well, often teaching themselves, while the slower students, or as Tussman more accurately describes them, students with learning blocks based on bad habits or inadequate preparation, often fall by the wayside, and are assumed by their teachers to be incapable of handling the academic material. In the way in which it was structured educationally, the Program produced a more level playing field for all students, whether they were especially gifted or not. And it did not accomplish this by "dumbing down" its curriculum; it did so by "smartening up its students"—through an individualized teaching approach that worked for all its students, whether they were "average" *or* "bright." It was in some ways a self-paced two-year program where as several participants from the study noted, "You got out of the Program what you put into it." Rather than viewing students in terms of possessing varying degrees of innate intelligence so that if they "got it" it was because they were smarter and if they didn't, it was because they were less capable, faculty considered each and every student in the Program capable of "getting" the Program curriculum. When there was evidence of problems with understanding the material or with expressing thoughts in writing, those problems were tackled by the faculty as problems in learning development rather than deficiencies in innate intelligence.

This faculty commitment to teaching average students along with the intellectually gifted, to leading them all through the chosen material whatever their difficulties and hang-ups might be and to attack those difficulties themselves with a firm belief that overcoming them is possible, offered them, whatever their intellectual abilities, a kind of education that went beyond simply passing tests.[6] And this way of teaching is not without

---

[6]The use of this step-by-step teaching method where learning is approached sequentially and teachers take it as their responsibility to help students correct deficiencies in learning habits has been given the name "mediated learning" by Reuven Feuerstein (1988). Feuerstein's methods have also been adopted by several school districts as a method of teaching critical thinking to all students, whatever their level of academic ability. His methods emphasize cooperation and dialogue rather than competition and isolation, and are based on learning critical thinking skills and enhancing self-esteem. (See also Judi Hirsch, "A study of a program based on Feuerstein's theories intended to teach high-level cognitive skills to African-American and Mexican-American junior-high school students identified

its own rewards for the teacher. Tussman says you can tell when a student with difficulties makes a break-through: "They stand differently; they walk taller." The satisfaction of being able to play an important part in students' intellectual growth is not often found in the ordinary lecture class.

In getting students to substitute an inadequate intellectual habit for another, better one, Tussman says he became "very Deweyian." But Deweyian, or even Rogerian in his efforts to free curiosity in the student and to "unleash a sense of inquiry" (Marton, Hounsel, Entwhistle, 1984), Tussman was certainly not permissive in his approach, nor could he be called "student oriented." He remained passionately committed to his goal of education for democracy by way of the moral curriculum. His intensive individualized teaching methods were based on the progressive nature of cognitive development—when students weren't thinking clearly it wasn't because they were dumb and couldn't get it, it was because there was a snag somewhere in the course of their intellectual development that needed to be and could be overcome. Examples of Deweyian pedagogical principles applied with effect in teaching younger children, even those from under-

---

to African-American and Mexican-American junior-high school students identified as learning disabled." *Dissertation Abstracts International*, Vol. 49, No. 8 [1989].) Using methods of accountability not through grades but through oral presentations and writing extensive research papers, Deborah Meier, founder of Central Park East Secondary School in East Harlem in New York City, has helped minority students from lower-income families to become critical thinkers. Students are encouraged not to memorize facts, but to question, challenge, understand, and communicate. The building of a democratic community and education for full citizenship are important principles of the school whose success has brought Meier's teaching program into national attention and critical acclaim. (*The Antiochian*. Yellow Springs, Ohio: Antioch College. Fall, 1990; "Islands of Change Create Friction: New York's Alternative Schools," *The New York Times*, May 25, 1995.) The characteristics of these learning programs that work so well for elementary and secondary students—the belief that any student can learn regardless of questionable ability or backgrounds, the substitution of cooperation for competition, accountability through oral and written work, community, the emphasis on questioning and critical thinking, and education for citizenship—can be recognized as characteristics of the Program and were instrumental in its success as well.

privileged backgrounds, are not uncommon; Tussman gives an example of the eminent teachability of the "ordinary" university undergraduate.[7]

The advantages the Program offered its students lay not only in the special features of its educational structure and the intensive, individualized teaching methods employed by faculty.[8] The special community it fostered was as important to the development of its students as the way the Program advanced cognitive development and fit into other aspects of late adolescent development, particularly changing relations with authority (discussed in the previous chapter and again in Chapters 12 and 13). The Program was a unique community to which faculty and students both contributed, and which provided the framework that held together these various components,

---

[7] Another example of the way in which the proper teaching methods can bring forth unsuspected abilities in students, although in this case much younger, comes from the autobiography of a famous English writer. In his primary school in Southeast London in the early 1900s, his teacher was allowed the freedom to introduce the tutorial system into his class of 50 or so working and lower middle class students. They worked in small groups of two, three, and four; they consulted with each other freely in the classroom, in contrast with traditional ways of strict discipline and no talking, with children lined up in rows behind desks. Instead of textbooks, students read and discussed contemporary writers. They kept journals of the thoughts they had about what they were reading, and produced a magazine and a newspaper. "Children who seemed stupid were suddenly able to detect a fine image or line and disentangle it from the ordinary." Because of the influence of this teacher, who "woke up my imagination . . . changed my views of great men in history" and "introduced me to the pleasures of the craft of writing," V. S. Pritchett decided then, at the age of 11, to become a writer (V. S. Pritchett, A Cab at the Door (Harmondsworth, Middlesex, England: Penguin Books, 1970).

[8] It should be made clear here that all uses of the term "individualized teaching" in the Program refer to the kind of one-on-one faculty-student contact that occurred during tutorials, seminars, informal contact, etc., which allowed faculty to "customize" their teaching to include diagnosing particular learning difficulties, paying careful attention to developmental hang-ups, and taking the appropriate measures to encourage development. It does not refer to the more technical use of that term to denote a more formal learning plan which might include a "learning contract" focused on the goal of independent learning, although the two share the overall goal of helping students take more responsibility for their own learning. (See, Thomas F. Clark, "Individualized Teaching," in *The Modern American College*, ed. Arthur W. Chickering and Associates.)

strengthening the effectiveness of each. Because of its importance educationally and developmentally, and because it had more than one meaning to students in the Program, community in the Program deserves its own consideration in the following chapter.

CHAPTER 11

Community

THREE MEANINGS OF COMMUNITY

One of the most distinctive features that set the Program apart from the rest of the university was the creation of a community surrounding its curriculum. It was a community in the intellectual sense as well as in the social sense: it offered faculty and students a forum to discuss ideas generated by the curriculum, gave students an identification with an intellectual enterprise, and provided collegial fellowship for faculty and students. It was a "home away from home" for students, offering new allegiances to replace or add to old ties with family, school, and other home town institutions. Although fraternities and sororities, interest and activity clubs, sports, informal social groups, and the like in the larger university also offered choices for developing identities, the Program was special in that it linked intellectual with social aspects of its community.

In answering a question about finding a sense of community in the Program that left it undefined, students used the term community in three ways. The first was the abstract concept of community as a social and political entity to which its citizens owed a certain allegiance and responsibility, and which some took to be the central theme of the Program. This meaning of community has been discussed in the sections of the book on the impact of the Program and its features. The other two meanings of community are in the social sense including friendships and general socialization, and in the academic sense, the learning community, the sharing of ideas and intellectual interests. It is community in these latter two meanings that is the subject of this chapter.

THE PROGRAM AS A SOCIAL COMMUNITY

Participants, with a few exceptions, found some degree of community in the Program in the first, predominantly social meaning, but there was a wide variation in the degree to which it was experienced. Even the small group of former students who said they might have made fewer friends than others in the Program, most nonetheless found a general spirit of camaraderie, a bonding with other students they did not usually find in other parts of the university. There were no differences between men and women or between participants from either of the two cycles—similar numbers found their social needs met in the Program.

Three women from the first cycle lived at home when they started the Program, and that clearly affected the way they related to other students. One said, "I lived at home, and I think that had a lot to do with the way I felt at school. I had to come home every day, and I wasn't able to hang around down here and be with other people." Even so, she thought the Program gave her a sense of community.

> Being part of the Program was nicer than being out on a big campus. Most of the time I spent with people not in class was with students from the Program.

Commuting also took its toll on her collegiate life in the way it conflicted with her growth in college.

> I'm sure there were things that I missed because I was always leaving. . . . I always felt sort of alienated from college altogether because I commuted. It was like I was living two different lives. In some ways . . . if I'd actually lived in a college . . . things would have been different. I might have made adjustments quicker because I wouldn't have had that sort of home environment to go back to, to reinforce all those things I'd always done.

One woman who lived at home, and worked, found it very difficult to make friends. She said she did not experience much sense of community either in the Program or anywhere else in the university. Another woman did not make many friends there because she had a group of friends from high school, friends in the dorm, and friends in her boyfriend's fraternity, all competing for her time and her intellectual attention.

> I didn't form any lasting relationships [in the Program], which is too bad because it was certainly the perfect opportunity, at a big university where it's difficult to make friends. Ninety percent of my social involvement had to do with a whole other group of people. I think that was hard for me because I was sort of torn. If I hadn't had this whole other group of kids, young adults I was socializing with, I would have spent more time at the House and been more involved. [Her boyfriend] and his fraternity and all the other young women that were going out with his fraternity brothers—it was just a whole different world from the Tussman Program. It wasn't your typical university fraternity. It was a very intellectual, serious group of young men. It was a Jewish fraternity, and the guys were all really top high school students and were all very serious.

Nonetheless, she did find some community in the Program that she did not find elsewhere in the university.

> There was a real spirit once I walked across campus and got to school there. . . . My recollection is that there were plenty of times during the day when people sat around just socializing and chatting informally in the afternoons . . . in the room set aside for the library.

One woman who definitely felt a sense of community in the Program in spite of the fact that her friends were from groups outside of it, had lived in Berkeley and so "had a very broad base of friends to begin with and I was also living in the student co-op, and there were some wonderful people in the student co-ops." She found community in smaller groups within the university.

> But not in the University as a whole because this was a time of great fragmentation . . . to me the University was just sort of like a city that encompassed a lot of little small villages. I could see that there were other communities that I just wasn't a part of. Like all of the kids in the R.O.T.C., or sports, or whatever. For me, I was very involved with the political side.

Another woman found it easier to talk to people in the Program. She felt closer to the people in the Program because you had this in common, even if you didn't have other things in common. I talked to people there that I never would have talked to elsewhere. And once I'd left there, I was in a real small department so there weren't a lot of people that I really did have contact with.

Another woman found the Program expanded her social network much more than her upper division major did.

I made several good friends in the Program, and they were real important relationships. . . . If I hadn't been in the Program I think I would have only gotten to know well the people that I lived around and nobody else. . . . I was a psych major, and I never really got to know much about the psych department or any of the people in it. . . . It was nothing like being in the Program where you knew the secretary and all the staff, and all the people who came in, you at least had some acquaintance with. I didn't experience anything like that anywhere else but there. I lived in the dorms for my second two years and we were always pretty good friends. But [the Program] was where the main community came from. I didn't experience any in the rest of the academic setting at Berkeley.

First-cycle men had varying degrees of social ties to people in the Program. For some they were very important and satisfying. One man experienced a "real strong" sense of community in the Program and "absolutely did not" anywhere else in the university.

The Program probably defined, I don't know, eighty percent of my interpersonal relationships during that period of time. My best friend who I went to high school with was one of the participants . . . my future first wife was a member of the Program, so that was pretty significant. Most of the guys I went to go partying with, and marched with [in demonstrations] were members of the Program.

The Program also formed the most important part of another man's social life.

We tended to very rapidly build good constellations of friendship . . . I got to be best buddies with [another student] and there were several people that I spent a lot of time with, went on camping trips, bummed around town. Mostly, my circles of friends tended to be all people in the

Program . . . we tended to build circles of friends that lasted, friends that I had all through the University.

Other first-cycle men made fewer close ties in the Program, although some wished for more. One of the few participants who remembered the retreats thought there should have been more of them.

I always wished that we'd gotten to know each other better, even though there was some community over the course of two years. Not really as much as you would expect. I know Tussman always used to say he wished that people would hang around, be at the house there, develop more sense of community than we did. We went on a couple of retreats towards the end of the two years, and wished we'd done them earlier. I think some of us discussed that within the Program . . . it's too bad, it was like a wasted opportunity that we hadn't met each other that way earlier.

Still, he found more community there than in the rest of the University.

I think that I had a richer social life within the Program because even though there wasn't a lot of community, I developed more friendships than I would have if I'd just been in the . . . [regular university]. . . . I think it would have felt a lot more impersonal. I think it would have been lonelier. I appreciated the sense of community, and I wish we had developed more of it.

The social aspects of community in the Program were often mixed with the intellectual. Mussen et al (Mussen, Conger, Kagan 1984, 462) have noted the importance of the clique in adolescence that can serve as a "testing ground for a young person's developing social and personal beliefs and values," lending usefulness and some significance to the commonplace collegiate "bull" and "rap" sessions. One woman from the first cycle called her group of friends within the Program a salon, a group devoted to the exploration of ideas that lasted into later years well beyond the Program, but which got its start there and was very important to her:

The main thing [about the Program] was my peers, and the social milieu . . . which was also very intellectually rich and also quite exciting . . . there was my little crowd . . . a bunch of people who were into . . . sort of farther out types of intellectual stuff. Chomsky and . . . and Jung a little bit.

The opportunity to socialize ideas arising in the Program was a powerful educational tool, rarely found in the regular undergraduate program, and one of the reasons some participants likened the Program to the intellectual climate they found in graduate school. One woman compares the two:

> I just hadn't had in high school as much intellectual discussion with friends and in writing papers. [In the Program] we all had the same assignments and we talked about that. . . . I remember talking about things, feeling in terms of intellectual growth, I think, stimulated to talk about things in a way that if I had been operating on my own, I wouldn't have gained as much. I definitely think there was benefit.
>
> As an upper division history major we had giant classes, and big lectures, so I can't say I remember as much stimulation in that upper division undergraduate program as I do later in graduate school or as in the Tussman Program, too.

In the chapter on faculty I noted that it was not necessary (or desirable) for faculty to socialize with students in order to be effective teachers. Some participants in the Program said they did not require socializing as a basis for establishing a sense of community, either. One man described his feeling of community in the Program even in the absence of close friendships.

> I didn't feel I had any great relationships in the Program—that certainly mitigates against the full sense of community that a person can feel. But I did think we had a sense of community in . . . that we all kind of knew who each other were, and some people more so than others because they did have bonds between them, among them, that I didn't participate in . . . even if you didn't speak to somebody you kind of had a feeling of knowing who they were . . . you have a sense of belonging. I guess the common activities we had gave you a sense of togetherness, but beyond that . . . I think I just felt I was a part of the group as a whole and felt that kind of bond, and I think that is a bond that I didn't feel in larger classes.

One man identified with other students in the Program whether or not he had made friends with them. Even though he had "no use for some of the people," he still made a couple of close friends with Program participants, some of whom he's still in touch with. In spite of the fact that he "didn't become *really* close friends with any of the other people in the Program," he still felt he was part of a community. "When I saw somebody on campus who was from the Tussman Program, either during it or after, I felt a sense of comradeship."

As evidence of the self-selectivity that characterized people who applied to the Program, one man compared his fellow students there with other students outside the Program.

> I was pretty tight with one group in the Program but also had these circles of friends outside the Program . . . guys in the dorm were harder to deal with than the kids in the Program. They were culturally different. They were definitely not cosmopolitan. A lot of them were really having a hard time adjusting.

The fact that the Program was experimental was a defining element to one man.

> I felt the sense of community that we were truly doing something different, doing something that the other undergraduates were not doing, and it was serious, it was sincere, it was truly experimental in the best sense of the word. And we were sharing that all together.

There were other men in the first cycle who did not have a full social life in the Program, did not make any or many friends there, but still thought it constituted a community. One was both commuting and working.

> I simply wasn't able to enjoy what I thought part of the Program was, to give you more time to enjoy some of the finer classics and readings and more interaction with the faculty members. But I have fond memories of it—the ease of reading with faculty, students interacting, exchanging ideas—it was much more preferable compared with the larger classes. . . . I did feel a sense of community but again I felt I wasn't particularly one of the real participants in that. I felt the other students, particularly some of them and the faculty interrelated very well.

In comparing the Program and the rest of the university, he did find some sense of community in the R.O.T.C. program with other students who were there to "avoid the draft," but "nowhere as much as in the Program."

Another man, who belonged to a fraternity, experienced community in the Program in a purely ideological way. He did not socialize with students in the Program because he found many of them to be

> sort of affected... I wasn't particularly used to it, nor did I particularly care for it. So that was the one real negative aspect of the Program from my standpoint... I enjoyed it despite that, basically. I got out of it what I wanted to put into it, but I didn't rely on the other students for that. It could have been a better experience if I didn't feel this way. It probably diminished, somewhat, the value of the Program, which I still feel was extremely valuable. I made friends outside of the Program. I had a separate existence... I felt we [in the Program] were a unique group. Self-selected, sort of pioneers in a way. But I really didn't get close to the students, so I guess any community I felt was sort of the concept or the idea behind the Program rather than the people so much.

And the community some students found in the Program could be entirely confined to the time they spent there, without extending beyond it in any way, and without being connected to any other part of their lives. According to one man,

> I make it sound like it's this wonderful—I felt very comfortable there on the one hand, and while I was there it was a community, but I don't really remember lots of activities that the group did or that I did with lots of people there. I had my little group of friends that I spent my time with. While we were there we were all part of a community, but then everybody kind of went your own way at the end of the school day.

Another man found it difficult to form personal relationships within the Program.

> The relationships I made were pretty much outside of the group... friends from high school.... One thing that occurred to me that I didn't realize maybe for many years later was that the courses in the Experimental Program were so broad and the subject matter was so broad, despite the fact that you might be reading a specific book, that the issues that were brought up, that we were supposed to think about and write about, were so broad that I found it more difficult to make a connection with some of the people in the group because I never really found out who they were.

Community

> If I had been in a class, say in German, with them, and we had to write a one page paper in German on something that interested us . . . I would learn about the person. But in the Experimental Program we were always talking about either the material of some famous book or about how the faculty wanted us to construe it. Tussman really seemed to want to talk about the relationship between the individual and society. And that didn't give me a context to make a personal relationship with the other people.

Socialization had not come easy to one second-cycle man, but it became easier over time.

> The first year I was too scared, because there were all these new people and they all seemed smarter than I was. But the second year, I used the House at night. I remember coming in and playing guitar, and dancing . . . it became a center, gradually.

Participants who had lived at home and commuted to the campus frequently mentioned having difficulties in establishing relationships with other Program students. Some women who lived at home had a hard time making friends in the Program, despite its emphasis on community.

> I didn't make any lasting friendships there, as opposed to all my other school experiences. I was living at home and even though the Tussman Program was very conducive to connecting with people, I didn't feel completely connected.

She experienced "a little sense of community" in the Program through a poetry newsletter put out by students there. Another woman who described herself as a "loner" did not find a big sense of community in the Program, except for the House. The House did become an important source of community for some commuters. One commuter thought she experienced a sense of community in the Program, and the House was a "community center," but she was distant from other people in many ways. Another woman who had one special friend inside the Program and others outside also thought the House was "wonderful" and the Program "beneficial," but still did not feel as much a part of that community as she has felt elsewhere: "it had nothing to do necessarily with the Program—it just happens to do with my personality."

Second-cycle women experienced varying degrees of community in the Program. Several had ties in other parts of the University; others had connections off-campus that drew them away from the Program as a centering institution. For instance, in contrast to the first-year women who found more community in the Program than in their sororities, one second-cycle woman found some sense of community there but more in the sorority to which she belonged. While many participants did not think that a lack of closer relationships with other Program students detracted from the beneficial effects of the Program, others did. One of the three participants who said she would not repeat the Program held as many as three jobs at one time while she was in the Program. While not living at home, she returned there frequently since it was near by and maintained friendships from home. She had one special friend from her high school who had enrolled with her in the Program, and they "didn't make any other really close friends in the Program." . . . I had some, but not too much sense of community" in the Program. She would have preferred to have more scheduled conferences with faculty and

> have more scheduled things where relationships were deliberately built . . . have a stronger social program where it's not just academic but there was more deliberateness to the way the kids participated . . . there wasn't much of that, it was more casual. . . . If I had it to do over again, I'd go to a small college where there was a stronger sense of community.

The close friendship she had with a friend in the Program from high school may have served as a social buffer between her and other students there. She apparently need more structured social events that encouraged her to mix with other students, as well as more structured interactions with faculty. In fact, she might have needed a small, liberal arts college to better meet her needs.

Another woman made the distinction between community in the social and the abstract political sense. She lived at home her first year and felt "fairly isolated," she "was never really close with either the faculty or the other students, sort of an outsider." When she moved into a living group on the campus, she began to feel a sense of community there, "but I never really got it out of the Program." However, she did pick up from the Program the idea of political responsibility, having a responsibility to the community. I think the expectations as a member of the Program was really to be a participant, which I didn't fulfill totally, in being an active participant.

Nonetheless, she thought the Program was beneficial to her.

> [I]n the end . . . it was good for me to be exposed to all of that, although it wasn't particularly easy at the time. I'm not sure that going around taking other courses would have been better. And given the options of coming to Berkeley and either being in the Program, even as the limited participant that I was, or going to University and taking courses, I don't think I regret being in the Program.

While these women reported feeling little sense of community in the social sense in the Program, perhaps primarily because of personality factors, or friends or living arrangements elsewhere, others did find a social community there. One woman who worked, and who came from a town close to the Berkeley campus and could go home frequently, still found community in the Program.

> Learning how to relate to people socially, people who had different backgrounds than mine, that was important, and it was a nice framework to do that within. Most of the people I dated were within the Program, and they were of quite diverse backgrounds. It was a comfortable attitude—group to do that within.

She contrasts this with her upper division major.

> If you asked me about the sociology part of my college education, it was not very cohesive to me at all. I didn't really have the experience in my sociology classes of feeling any kind of a sense of community. They were big classes. You kind of went from one to another. They were fascinating and stimulating, but you didn't see the same group of people particularly.

Other participants made the distinction in their responses between using the concept of community in a political sense and community in the social sense. The man quoted earlier who said the major impact of the Program for him had been the realization of the importance of community also said,

"I think there was no question that there was a spirit of camaraderie there that I very definitely remember enjoying a great deal," although he still felt the purely social sense of community much stronger in the dorms. "I don't remember having good friends in the Tussman Program. The friends that I remember were in the dorms, probably because I spent more time there." Another man connected community in his adult life to his obligations to society:

> The sense of community I'm talking about is being able to balance between having your own internal compass, on the one hand, and still being able to deal with the obligations of being in a society of people, having neighbors, friends, relatives, associates.

THE PROGRAM AS A LEARNING COMMUNITY

It is clear from the previous testimony that the purely social aspects of the Program were beneficial to some participants but irrelevant to others. It is when we look at the Program as an academic community, a learning community, that we find its particular effectiveness.

Learning communities have been defined as "generally . . . offerings of large blocks of academic credit in which a single cohort (or "community") of students enroll; they last one or more quarters; and they are taught by two, three, or four faculty members around an overarching question or theme" (MacGregor 1987). While Gabelnick et al. (1990) identify Meiklejohn as "a father to the learning community movement," they also borrow from Tussman, whose "ideas took deep root in the state of Washington in 1970, where a group of 17 planning faculty were designing a new, state-supported 'alternative college,' The Evergreen State College." That institution created The Washington Center for Improving the Quality of Undergraduate Education, a statewide consortium emphasizing both faculty and curriculum development, and has inspired the creation of other learning communities in Washington state, other parts of the U.S., and Canada.[1]

---

[1] F. Gabelnick, J. MacGregor, R. S. Matthews, and B. L. Smith, "Learning Communities: Creating Connections Among Students, Faculty, and Disciplines," *New Directions for Teaching and Learning,* No. 41 (San Francisco: Jossey-Bass, 1990).

Tussman's Experimental College Program, as one prototype, shared many characteristics of these later learning communities—a large block of academic credit, a single cohort of students, a curriculum built around an overarching theme, and collaborative teaching. The Program, however, was a special kind of learning community because of its timing, occupying virtually the entire first two years of students' academic time and credit, rather than a single quarter or more; its holistic academic community where students and faculty read assigned readings together; its emphasis on individualized teaching through tutorials, seminars, and informal discussions and the integration of these with each other and with the lecture; its "moral" theme of education for democracy that related to issues of deep current student concern; and the house it had all to itself in a corner of the campus. All of these factors together led to the creation of a particularly intense kind of learning community, making it hard to compare with others that do not share all of these characteristics.

Still, the evidence of student development gains in recent studies of various kinds of learning communities is present in the testimony of the Program's former students. Moore and Kerlin found students' intellectual capacities for critical thinking and engagement of complex ideas strengthened in learning communities (Moore and Kerlin, n.d.). MacGregor, using Perry's scheme of intellectual development, reports students in learning communities in the Washington Center study "significantly more advanced developmentally than their counterparts in control groups." Other studies in other learning communities show students had higher grades and increased retention rates (MacGregor 1987). Tinto's studies of students in learning communities compared with traditional classes showed them bridging the academic-social divide, their students benefiting from the variety of perspectives beyond that of one faculty member, more socially and academically involved in college life, and seeing themselves as having made greater intellectual gains than students in regular classes. He found these effects to be "as prevalent among 'remedial' students as 'non-remedial,'" and concludes that "learning communities work for many types of students, including those . . . [with] deficient academic preparation" (Tinto 1993).

These researchers generally do not separate social from academic aspects of learning communities, but with the abundant testimony presented here from the Program, it is possible to view the two separately and explore their relationship. Women from the second-cycle appreciated the presence of an academic community in the Program that transcended sociability, and it is in the testimony of participants from the second cycle that the importance of a distinct learning community begins to emerge. One woman spoke of the advantages of the Program's "built-in" community.

> I don't think you can ever substitute community in any form. It is built into the Program, and that was a tremendous advantage. Everything goes from having opportunities to get down with people, talk to people, know people, wrestle with issues, in a safe environment, in a place where it's set up for dialogue and set up for wrestling with the great issues. There's no substitute for it. And there's no built-in forum for it on campus. You can join a club, or something, but already the club would be very departmentalized. It would be by department or it would be by issue, or something like this.

There were men in the second cycle for whom the unique academic community in the Program, sometimes together with the social aspects and sometime not, held particular appeal. It was from these second-cycle participants that the strongest evidence of the success of the learning community arises. In a discussion of the kind of intellectual collegiality he found there, one man spoke of its rarity in the university, and explained in detail how it worked and what it meant to him.

> It was certainly an intellectual community. That was the main thing that I felt, that we really were striving together to deal with intellectual questions, to read together and think together. . . . The sense of community that I felt was not that we all agreed. For instance, I don't think that we could have published a position paper on issue X, whatever. . . . I don't have the sense that we as a group had an opinion, had a position, that we could have expressed. But our community was, in my view, a community of those who met every week to discuss these issues, these books and these ideas, and to me that was plenty, that was sufficient.
>
> I know we had a retreat, I think, in the end of the first year. It's funny because in my memory that didn't add anything to the Program. I don't feel I got to know any of the students or any of the teachers better as a result of that. I'm not saying it wasn't fun, but I think in my experience you could have removed that whole thing and I would have had exactly the same experience that I had. So I guess in my view the community was really an intellectual one. The Friday night dinners were

good,[2] but those were to my view also an intellectual thing, kind of an extension of the intellectual community. I don't think we ever went out and went bowling together or any of these kind of things. I mean, we didn't have dances.

I appreciated the angry people, the people who were arguing. I wasn't one of those who argued about the issues that were coming up. . . . I had been brought up to believe that obedience is the price of membership in a society, and when, from the beginning, we were reading *Antigone* or whatever it was we were reading, and people got hot about this, I was glad to have them there. When the angry people would show up every week and argue, that I felt was intellectual community, and I appreciated that, and I wanted them to be there every week because they were doing me good, I thought. I was hearing something I wouldn't think of on my own. They were arguing against what I was willing to accept, and I wanted to hear that, I wanted that kind of exchange.

That's what I thought intellectual life was, really debating the issues, and with vigor. [L, the dissident faculty member], too, from the beginning was a bit of an outlaw in the Program. I appreciated him coming every week and doing it, and when he started to fade, and to not come, then I felt that he had broken the intellectual community. I felt that he should be there, angry or not, and should be giving what he could give. I felt the same about the angry people, I was glad when they came, and when one of them would drop out of the Program, and I think some did in the second year, I was disappointed. I really wanted as much ferocity as I could get. And to me that was part of the community, a dedication to thrashing these things out together. . . . It wasn't as if someone else were showing me something, were converting me to some view that I hadn't held before, but I wanted to hear all the arguments against my own point of view, my own upbringing, and I still want that.

That's a feature of the Program that was very important to me, and it seemed to me that it came about because there was no reward for being in the Program, except the good talk. In the University outside the Program, basically, people were trying to outdo each other. People were trying to shine, and it was as if there were no intellectual community, the book or idea being discussed was a pie, and everybody was trying to get

---

[2]Other participants have referred to a Sunday night dinner regularly held at the House. Whether they were the same group, or different groups, they were small and informal and composed of students who spent a lot of time at the House during the second cycle.

> as big a piece of the pie as he could. And to those who got the biggest piece of the pie would be rewarded with a pat on the back by the professor in charge. That's a very broad brush sort of picture of it, but in the Program I think people really sort of got down to business and discussed for the sake of discussing, because they wanted to know. And if they didn't want to know, and they didn't care, they probably dropped out. . . .
>
> My intellectual bent was such that I would have been reading, say Plato, or Homer anyway. I would have just bought it at the bookstore and read it, or taken a course in it, in the University. But I really, at all times, I think, felt grateful that I had five or six mature minds—professors—and all these other people working on the same stuff with me. I thought it was just great for me. I felt I was getting lots and lots of benefit out of it, that I was reading the book with colleagues, and not just on my own.

This man's account of the way the learning community functioned in the Program highlights the importance of the members of that community all reading the same things, and "working on the same stuff." The egalitarian spirit and dynamic quality of that way of learning stands out in contrast to what is usually available to undergraduate students, and perhaps could only be fully appreciated later in life.

> I found in later years that to find someone who knows, who has the same sort of intellectual content that you have, who's read the same thing, is such a rare treat. And here we had a group of people everyday, or every week, doing this thing. It was good to have colleagues in your intellectual search. By the second year, you could mention Homer and people knew what you were talking about, knew what issues were likely to come up, and also had some idea of the beauty or grandeur or wretchedness of certain things in the poem. You didn't have to continually explain yourself to people. I work with people who are educated, but who haven't read the same things I've read, and you can't share your reading—your thoughts exactly because you have to explain yourself.

The intense spirit of intellectual community this man found in the Program was not to the exclusion of community in the social sense. He related to professors and fellow students in very personal ways, and he is still in touch with some former Program faculty and students.

Community

I came away with deeper relationships with the people in the Program. I had a very deep love affair in the Program, and one very deep friendship, and other shared experiences that I didn't find elsewhere.

Another man spoke of the importance of this intellectual community, how it compared with his other classes at Berkeley, and how it offered him an opportunity to trace his own cognitive and personal development over the span of the two years.

One major theme, talking about the Program compared to regular education, was the sense of a community of scholars, which you don't get in the regular University. Just independent little classes, where you have no continuity from let's say, Spanish I to Spanish II. You may have a completely new set of people, a new instructor, so there's no continuity there. In the Tussman Program, there was the same faculty, same faces. You might change the people within your small seminars, from quarter to quarter, but they were people you were getting to know. And the same ideas and the same way of looking at things, approaching new topics over time that slowly built on that, which you don't get at all in the regular University. You have these brief little spurts of class course work, and after ten weeks you're done with it. Whereas the Program was something that built up to at the end of two years, you had something to really look back on, on how your own thinking had evolved. You're looking at some of the same basic questions confronting an individual in his role in society over two years. And the same people you had been discussing this with. You can sort of temper this with your own personal growth at this time, the growth of your classmates.

I had a hard-core group of friends in the Program. We lived here [spent a great deal of time in the House]. We would have Sunday dinners here, and I'm sure anybody from the outside would have thought, "What a curious group of people!" We always talked with these same metaphors, really a typical college sophomore sort of behavior, in an intellectual way. These little intellectual games you play within the same context. But having this context was the thing that the Program offered. We would sit around here, downstairs, having dead silence, everyone reading. You'd sit there for maybe an hour, an hour and a half. Then we would suddenly just start talking about what we had been reading, ideas we were working on. . . . It was almost this sort of study cell that evolved out of this . . . primarily during the second year.

This particular "study cell" continues today, and the context from the Program has become a lasting one. There are periodic reunions and former students still talk about concepts used in the Program:

> It's funny. All I need to do is sit down somewhere with one of the other people from the Program, and we can immediately begin spewing forth.

Comparing his experience in the Program with his upper division major, he explained how competition in the upper division prevented any sense of community from arising there.

> I may have tried to make my experience in my major field, anthropology, lean towards more of a community feeling. It was just not there, though. There's too much competition for grades, for time, for attention, basically, in the regular University that defeats all that. [In the Program] I was getting the chance to apply what energy, what interest I had into academics, but not having the pressure to perform in the University sense of taking exams, not feeling the pressure of competing. Eliminating that was a great thing. I guess that at that point in my life that may have been one of the most important things. Also just the long-term association with other students as opposed to things being all cut up by the quarter system, having the same people you saw week after week, for the first two years.

While the Program did not depend on its students making close friends with each other or with faculty in order to achieve a successful educational impact, it did allow for close relationships to develop among students, and for repeated personal interaction based on the subject matter to continue over a prolonged period. But whether they were close friends or not, the more students discussed the curriculum with each other, the more they argued and debated, the more opportunities there were for increasing and strengthening the impact of the curriculum—for reinforcement, perhaps, in educational terms. The opportunities for uniting the cognitive and the affective aspects of the Program were plentiful, especially in the way it allowed for and encouraged frequent contact. It was an intellectual fraternity in a sense, initiating and drawing its members into continuous discussion of its academic themes and moral aims.

The elimination of tests and grades, and of much of the incentive for competition, was important in allowing the sense of an intellectually egalitarian learning community to develop among students. While the

Program offered this to its students, it could not force them to be actively involved—that was voluntary. But even if a student did not actively participate in the learning community by arguing and exchanging ideas publicly in seminars and the like, it did not necessarily mean no learning was taking place. One man talked with fellow students about the readings, seminars, and issues

> all the time. That was the whole value of the Program. That's leading into the sense of community, a community of scholars, and I was one of the students who chose to become part of that and not do it on my own. One of my friends through the Program was very quiet, was not really into the Program as a community, overall. I used to have long discussions with him in the dorm room and we'd sit there for hours on end, talking about things, the assignment for a paper, or something. I remember his roommates always being a little bit amused at this—here were these two philosophers who would get together and trade ideas back and forth. It was funny that he was never really seen as being part of the Program, I think, even by faculty members. It was just someone who was going through the exercises, was doing a competent bit of work, but was not putting his whole heart into it . . . but they just didn't know, or understand him. He was somewhat of a private, shy person, and he was as actively interested and involved in the ideas in the Program, if not so much the structure and the way the ideas were exchanged.

In spite of his reluctance to participate in discussions within groups, this quiet student the participant describes was touched by the community in the Program if not able to actively participate in it.

The man quoted in Chapter Six on the major impact of the Program is worth quoting again here, because he also felt he was part of a "learning community" or a "community of scholars," although he does not use these terms.

> It lived up to my ideal, or my fantasy, the small group, guided seminars with the professors. I thought those were really a special opportunity, really a privilege to be sitting in there with a group of maybe six or eight or ten students and a senior professor. The setting was just about ideal for a university level learning—a small group with a professor and everybody intimately involved, engaged in the subject matter, as opposed to a professor standing up in front of a hundred and fifty people, talking about some stuff and watching you try to write it down, [and] maybe you

daydreaming, or you missing the class. The intimacy of it—that was the best, the most, that was the closest to meeting my fantasy of what this should be.

But that did not necessarily mean he either found or wanted to find community in the social sense in the Program.

> I never really worked closely outside of the formal groups with anybody, like sitting down and working on papers or comparing notes. . . . I didn't spend a lot of time socializing with people from the Program. We did have at least one little retreat type thing, maybe two. I guess we had a retreat each year towards the spring. We got to know each other pretty well. Those were nice. I went on those and I didn't really get real close to the people in the Program because I'm not that kind of a person. I enjoy living alone, and I guess it didn't bother me then not to be surrounded by a lot of people.

The intellectual intimacy of the small academic setting with a small number of students and a professor involved together in the subject matter was of supreme importance to him; the social aspects of the Program, such as the retreat, while they might have been enjoyable to him, were not important at all. The trust engendered through intimacy and the absence of competition was more important in general to students than the social part of the community; although close personal associations could and did develop, they did not obscure its primarily academic nature and goals.

COMMUNITY AND IDENTITY

Community in the largest sense had another specific role to play in student development. Eric Erikson maintains that community contributes in an important way to ego development: "fidelity is that virtue and quality of adolescent ego strength which . . . can only arise in the interplay of a life state with the individuals and the social forces of a true community" (Erikson 1968, 235). One woman illustrated the connection between community and ego development and the formation of her intellectual identity:

> A sense of community is really important because it helped me to be more comfortable in the academic environment. It was easier for me to

establish my sense of self-worth in the academic community knowing what other people that were in the same classes were thinking and feeling and how they were doing. Where [by contrast] in the bigger classes I didn't feel I had much of a sense of myself compared to other people. Given a test grade or score on a paper wasn't always a very good measure for me. Having the sense of personal interaction we had in the Program was really valuable.

Perry emphasizes the role of community in the developmental process. He found in the students whom he studied that for the majority of them,

> their most important support . . . seemed to derive from a special realization of community. This was the realization that in the very risks, separateness and individuality of working out their commitments, they were in the same boat not only with each other but with their instructors as well. . . . The individual may himself derive a sense of community by observing that others are like himself in that their cares and quandaries are like his own. His sense of membership is enormously strengthened, however, if in addition he experiences himself as seen by others in the same way" (Perry 1970, 212).

Another woman described the struggle for identity she experienced between the Program and the sorority she belonged to at the same time.

> I lived in two different worlds at Berkeley, which I really enjoyed. I felt like I got a little taste of both . . . half of my friends would be in the sorority and half were from the Tussman Program. . . . It was the largest Jewish sorority on campus and intellectual pursuits were important there. We were always number one in the sororities of pledge class grades and all that kind of stuff. So it was very stressed and important there. There was another woman from the sorority in the Program, and we would walk down Piedmont Avenue, and it was like going from one world to another. I got something from each one, [but] I basically outgrew the sorority part of it. . . . As time went on [the sorority and fraternity life] became less and less part of my world and by the time I moved out of the sorority, that wasn't part of my world at all anymore. It was much more, I guess what I would call, Tussman-like people, even though they weren't necessarily in the Tussman Program.

Through her friendship with the other sorority woman in the Program, her social life and her identity evolved away from the sorority towards "the intellectually curious" sort of student typical of the Program. She was allowed freedom to explore different identities there without having to choose one or another, although she eventually did.

The way that the Program blended the social and the academic was important to the intellectual development of other participants. One woman, who had a social life outside the Program, said that one of the major impacts of the Program was for her, as reported earlier in that section,

> that whole sense of community, the relationships that I've developed with the people that were in there, even though I haven't stayed in contact with them. There was a feeling I had being on the campus in that group that was very different than if I hadn't been in the Program. One of my closest friends was in the Program at Cal and we actually drifted apart later, after the Program was over. But the friendship that we formed in the Program, and we lived together at the time, and we had several friends that were in the Program, that really had an impact on the way I started college and the way I approached the University. . . . The sense of community that I experienced in the first two years was different than the autonomous feeling that I had in the second two years.

She found in the Program a diverse group of students, including both

> free spirits and clean cuts . . . there was a wide range. I had no trouble fitting in. I didn't have a problem finding a niche for myself . . . having a smaller unit within the University and the sense of community that I felt was a real benefit. And it wasn't my only social life on the campus. On the other hand it was real important. It gave me a sense of security and feeling of belonging and a place to be socially and personally—psychologically—that was really a benefit.

The evidence from this quotation and from others throughout the book indicate that while students might identify primarily (or secondarily) with one or more collegiate subcultures, such as fraternities and sororities, R.O.T.C., political interest groups, and so on, they still could come together in the Program in their affiliation with a preprofessional intellectual or academic culture, whether it was their dominate identification or not.[3] Smelser (1993) notes the opportunities for personal identification various subcultures present for students as a means of "transition from the family-community to later lines of commitment." The Program offered them another kind of identification in addition to these various subcultures—an academic identification that did not necessarily conflict with identification with other subcultures—and that may have been one important factor in appealing to and holding their interests and allegiances.

THE LEARNING COMMUNITY AS IT RELATED TO OTHER ASPECTS OF COMMUNITY

Looking back at what participants had to say about community in the Program, all three aspects—political, social, intellectual—came up in the interviews, even though we have concentrated in this chapter on the social and intellectual contexts. Sometimes participants referred to all three meanings; sometimes two; sometimes only one. Sometimes they were connected; sometimes not. The man for whom the intellectual concept of community had the biggest impact, who said that it had "changed his life," found little or no sense of community in the social sense in the Program whereas he did in the dorm in which he lived. That absence of community in the social sense did not interfere with his appreciation of the concept of community in the political sense, nor did it with the woman who felt an outsider in the Program yet learned there the idea of political responsibility to the community.

Most of the participants who experienced community in the third meaning, in the intellectual or academic sense, also experienced the second, social aspect and said they had close friendships with other students in the Program. But not everyone did. One man called himself a loner, and did not work with other students in study groups, yet still found the seminar with a faculty member and a small group of students all intimately engaged in the same subject matter to live up to his ideal of a university learning environment.

---

[3]See M. Trow, "Student Subcultures and Administrative Action," in *Personality Factors on the College Campus*, ed. R. L. Sutherland et al. (Austin, Texas: Hogg Foundation for Mental Health, 1962).

Although there is evidence of the learning community in the first cycle—students forming study groups, for instance—it is from interviews with second-cycle participants that the picture of the Program as a learning community becomes most clear. Even students who did not make close friends in the Program still found a satisfying learning community there. And at least some second-cycle men in the study in a way are still engaged in that learning community, discussing ideas that arose in the Program as they convene from time to time more than 25 years after they finished the Program.

We know there were important differences between the first and the second cycles that may have aided the fuller realization of the learning community—the faculty in the second cycle were a much more cohesive and unified group for reasons already mentioned. Faculty were left free to present the curricular aims of the Program as an almost unanimously unified group, a vastly different situation from the first cycle where faculty warred publicly over the very concepts of the curriculum. We also know that faculty conferences became regularized and frequent during the second cycle, so that interaction with faculty on a one-to-one basis was now the rule rather than being left more or less to happenstance as it apparently had been. This change alone would have allowed faculty to have a greater impact on student intellectual development. The evidence suggests that personal and intellectual conflicts among the Program faculty in the first cycle compromised the establishment of the kind of community we have seen in the second cycle. Controversy was central to the Program, but only when civil and insulated from acrimony and personal conflict.

There was another important change in the second cycle that undoubtedly had an impact on the realization of the learning community, and that was the establishment of the seminar with faculty not present, the "unattended" seminar. This pedagogical device not only invited but actually made it necessary for students to take charge of their education in a most direct way. While some of these seminars were apparently more successful than others, the message to students was clear in all cases: they were to take an active part in their own teaching and learning and were not to be dependent solely on faculty for direction.

In all these ways, the Program in both cycles taught an important lesson to its students: their thoughts about the curriculum were of significance to the whole Program community—students were attended to, taken seriously and respected. It was not only acceptable, but appropriate and expected of them to ask questions of faculty, to argue with them—and each other—and, in the second cycle, to direct their own learning in their own seminars. This treatment on the part of faculty must have led to a certain feeling of efficacy for students in the Program: what they thought, what they wrote, what they said was important and made a difference to the collective intellectual life of the Program. This was not a completely hierarchical learning enterprise—students were full members of the learning community along with faculty. This joint membership in their common educational community made it possible for faculty, through their openness in displaying "a visibility in their own thinking, groping, doubts and styles of commitment," in Perry's terms, (Perry, 213-15) "to instruct, to recognize, to confirm" and to encourage students as they took the risks of each forward movement in the developmental process.

The central elements of the learning community in the Program—the commonality of reading and discussion by faculty and students; the student self-expression encouraged and supported through writings and discussions; the opportunities for the socialization of ideas within this community; the demonstration by faculty, in the second cycle particularly, of how healthy argument can promote thinking—were all important to the education of its students. Sometimes the various kinds of social life different students found there helped this process; sometimes it was irrelevant. And it is this seriousness of purpose directed toward learning that characterized the testimony of participants as a whole as they talked about what they had gained from their participation in the Program.

The community that was established in the Program was valuable to its students as it provided the framework within which academic identities could be fostered and within which changes in cognitive and moral development could occur. It was the in the context of community that students found encouragement and support for these changes, as we will see in the next two chapters.

CHAPTER 12

Politics and the Program

Politics was especially pertinent to the implementation of the Program from several standpoints: one, the timing of the Program during the height of political activity on the campus, and how that affected the Program; two, the political implications of the curriculum and moral purpose of the Program, "education for democracy"; and three, the way in which the Program fit into the developmental aspects of students' growth, particularly in their relationship to authority. In this chapter, we will consider these three; the question of authority in all its aspects in relationship to the Program will be the focus of the following chapter.

Berkeley in the Sixties

The years of the Program's existence, 1965 to 1969, were as we know highly unusual times at Berkeley. Appendix C lists some of the major events occurring during the period just preceding and during the Program. A simple listing of events, however, gives no real indication of the intense, ever present politically charged atmosphere on and around the Berkeley campus (and indeed on many other college and university campuses throughout the country and in Europe) during the sixties and early seventies. Rallies, marches, protest tables and placards, demonstrations, sit-ins, building takeovers, loudspeakers, helicopters spraying tear gas, fires, bomb attempts, the continuous presence of campus police, Berkeley and Oakland police, mass arrests of students, the National Guard, the nightly national news programs featuring the Berkeley campus—all became commonplace.[1] Even to those who were not active participants in any of these activities, they were impossible to ignore.

Several participants in the study said they had not taken part in any sort of political activity while at Berkeley, but some of them found they could not avoid being affected nonetheless. Even a second-cycle woman who described herself as "as apolitical as you could get" had a brief encounter with the police.

> I think the biggest thing I did was stare with big round eyes at People's Park. I was a spectator, absolutely aghast, and just didn't really know what it was all about, why they were doing all this stuff. I remember walking up around Bancroft near Boalt Hall with my head in a book, reading as I'm walking along, and got a bump on the rear end from some policeman or campus [cop]. I was completely minding my own business and way off the main [protest area] (laughs). I remember Jesse Unruh [a leading state politician] with wet brown paper towels over his face because they were tear-gassing people, and I was just sort of an onlooker. I was absolutely not involved in any of the issues.

For many participants, tear gas became a kind of symbol of the permeating effect of the political tension surrounding the campus during those years. Another second-cycle woman said her political involvement was minimal, even though she was sympathetic to the antiwar movement.

> There was nobody who didn't sympathize with [the Vietnam issue]. I remember getting tear-gassed, and I remember People's Park. I think I was always more of an observer, though. I don't think I ever was politically particularly active.

Another woman described the intense, continuous political activity of the times even for the politically inactive:

> It was very much a part of our consciousness of the dorms that I was in for one whole semester. We were circled with helicopters *daily*. I was tear-gassed twice. I can't say that I was making any big political state-

---

[1]For an account of the Free Speech Movement and events leading up to it, see Max Heirich, *The Spiral of Conflict: Berkeley, 1964* (New York: Columbia University Press, 1971).

ment when I was—I was just trying to get home and I got caught in the middle of it—so I can't say that I'd take any medals for that.

And a second-cycle man made the distinction between observer and activist.

I was sort of on the sidelines watching this stuff happen. I wasn't involved actively in politics. I mean, my heart is basically on this side of the First Amendment, and basically against the war and that sort of thing. As far as actually getting out there and doing something really meaningful like lighting a trash can on fire or something (laughs), I never got quite that involved.[2] And this [had nothing to do with the Program]—it has been a lifetime approach to things.

A vivid reminder of just how politicized the Berkeley campus became during that time is this statement from a second-cycle man, which is in itself a telling comment on the quantity and quality of education available to students in the regular programs at Berkeley at the time:

I went to college with people who didn't go to school for two years, who sat in, who marched, who demonstrated. I remember sitting there about 1971 talking with some girl [not in the Program] and she said, "You know, I actually haven't been to class for a couple of years." (laughs) She had a major, and she was on her way to a degree and so on, but there hadn't been any classes. First they'd had to go on strike about Ethnic Studies, and then on strike about the Cambodian invasion, and than on strike about God knows what else. There was more happening in the streets than happening in the classrooms. There was a lot of politics, a lot of activity, and some time when the school [the University, not the Program which was never shut down by a strike] was virtually closed down.

---

[2]Several of the participants spoke in this rather wistful, almost guilty way about not having played an active role in politics then. One man, who was not part of this study but who was interviewed later by one of the participants in the study about his memories of the Program, said that the only thing he regretted about having been in the Program was that he will have to tell his grandchildren that he "missed the revolution." A woman quoted later in this chapter refers to political activism as "risk-taking." These statements seem to imply that to be politically inactive was to take the easy way out and the real heroes of the day were the student warriors doing battle with the enemy—the administration.

There were times when you didn't go to class, or when you went to class to discuss politics.

In spite of the physical location of the Program—on the Northside at the opposite end of the campus and far away from where most of the political activity went on, around Sproul Hall and the Telegraph Avenue entrance to the campus—and in spite of the lack of political involvement of many of its students, the Program nevertheless was certainly affected by the political scene. And the Program in turn affected the political response of many of its students in varying ways.

Comparative Political Attitudes and Identification

Participants in the study were asked to assess the effects of the Program on their participation in political activities on and off the campus. In addition, in order to explore the effects of experience in the Program on political attitudes of its participants, a series of questions was asked about their attitudes toward authority, on the "givenness" of the Program's requirements (referring to the fact that the curriculum was fixed by the faculty and was not to be modified by students' interests), and on their understanding of the concepts of freedom and responsibility. To add to this, some data on political identification is available from the questionnaire given to both the group of former Program students who were interviewed and to the group of former students who were not interviewed but who mailed in the questionnaire, as well as to the group of former UC students who had applied to the Program but had not been admitted (Appendix F).

Results of that questionnaire showed that 44 percent of the total of both groups of former Program students described themselves as left at the time they were in the Program. When the categories left and liberal are combined, 90 percent of all former Program students described themselves as either of the two while at Berkeley. That figure compares with 84 percent of the third group, questionnaire respondents who had applied to the Program, had not been accepted, and who described themselves as left or liberal. Almost twice as many (44 percent) Program participants described themselves as left as did those who were not accepted in the Program (26 percent). Now twice as many, 29 percent of the total group of former Program students, say they are still left as compared to only 14 percent of the non-Program group.

The Effect of the Program on Political Attitudes and Behavior

There may be evidence here to suggest that although the Program could be described as having a politically conservative theme, and its faculty, especially in the second cycle, expressed more conservative views than many of the students held, it did not necessarily follow that the Program functioned to convert its students from ideological leftists or liberals into conservatives. There is certainly evidence from the interviews that for many it added new dimensions to their thinking about politics and political activity. There is some suggestion as well that it might have affected the behavior of some of its students in one important respect: while most of them reported being interested, if not actively involved in the political scene at Berkeley, and had attended rallies and protests, and almost every one who was interviewed volunteered the information that they had been against the war in Vietnam, none of them reported engaging in any kind of physically destructive political activity. One second-year man described the difference in this way:

> Both during the Program and afterwards [as] I thought back on it, it seemed that the Program somehow tended to make you want to be more conservative, more respectful of the laws, more respectful of society, more respectful and appreciative of the way things are. Don't just rebel for the sake of rebellion because here we're studying the Greek philosophy, and they put this Western civilization together, and they had reasons for it. Now let's not just tear it all down. And that was a thrust that came though the whole Program, the whole two years of the Program. So I was influenced by it. And so I wasn't as involved or active in the antiwar protest as I might have been. And I think it's partly because of the Program. I think the Program had a moderating effect of my political attitudes. I probably was less radical *behaving*, anyway. The funny thing, the ironic thing is that after going through the Program and finishing and getting a degree at Berkeley, I know for a fact, though, that I'm much more left wing, [much more] socialist thinking than I would have been if I'd not gone to Berkeley.

He described the conflict he experienced between what he was learning in the Program, what he felt about the war in Vietnam, and the moderating influence of the Program.

The effect of the Program was to kind of pull me to the right—in other words, to make a normal guy out of me, law abiding, respectful, a guy who likes society, a guy who doesn't want to bust things up. But what was happening on campus and around the whole country at that time was that a lot of students and people of college age were raising hell because of the Vietnam War, and they were tearing things down. They were occupying and burning buildings and bombing. . . . I took the readings and the whole thing very seriously, and I do think that I have a respect for social conventions. I mean, society has to exist, it has to protect itself, it has to have laws, and I think I understand that more because of the Program than I might have understood otherwise. I think I understand the theory behind it, that society has to exist because it protects people, and society is bigger than the individuals. It can't allow people to just go completely wild, burn things down, not just because it's against the law, but because there's a social interest in protecting universities and businesses and streets.

But because I was here at Berkeley, I heard the protests across the street. Everyday I was down on the campus somebody was lecturing, somebody was haranguing. . . . There'd be soldiers who came back from Vietnam and they'd tell what they saw over there. And what our country was doing in Vietnam was so obviously a betrayal of the concepts that we were supposed to be learning. What is the government for? What about the social contract we're reading about here? Well, it's to protect people. Well, what the hell's our government doing over in Vietnam? It's just whipping the shit out of them over there. And there was this tremendous pull, this conflict between—I believed what we were studying here, but I also believed what I heard, and I was still very much opposed to the war in Vietnam. . . . I was getting a strong pull in two different directions at the same time. That was a real political turmoil for me. . . .

I was very sympathetic with the whole antiwar movement and yet I took very seriously what I was studying in the Program. And I think that taking seriously what I was studying gave me more reason to resent what our government was doing because I felt, and still feel, that in many respects our government's betraying the whole concept of a government which serves people, which really has an obligation to it's own society. . . . I saw that there was a reason for those people to be angry about what the U.S. government was doing in Vietnam and at the same time I saw there was a reason not to tear down the institutions. It's still not all that clear, but there was this powerful struggle between what I was experiencing over here [in the Program] and what I was experiencing over there [on the campus].

> It had a profound effect on me. I guess what it did was make me into more of what you might call, in a glib sense, a kind of thinking socialist, or an intellectual socialist . . . versus a rock thrower. . . . I guess I could almost say that it was partly because of the Program that I am what you might call a socialist because I do think that society has responsibilities to itself. . . . What I was reading here, even though it tended to make me tone down, [make me] less radical, less inclined to go throw rocks—I never was inclined to throw rocks. But in being here I was very much less tempted to ever think about throwing rocks. . . .

"Throwing rocks" was a metaphor for the kind of political activity many participants talked about avoiding whatever their negative political feelings might have been about American involvement in Vietnam. Even though they had felt some ambivalence about their actions at the time, two second-cycle students set up a picket line near the corner of the campus close to, but not including, the Program House. After the Program they became lobbyists for a religious organization that supported liberal causes. One of them described the motivation behind their picketing, and how it was connected to the Program.

> I think we did that directly as a result of the sort of political sense of the Program here, as wanting us to be participants in a democracy, and doing it in a way that was not sort of sitting around throwing rocks. . . . There was a real interplay between the reading and the life outside, and it made it hard to be a full-hearted dogmatic revolutionary . . . I just couldn't do it quite with the abandon that other people did. I got cynical too young, maybe. I had lots of questions. I said, "Hmmm, sounds suspect, doesn't quite fit in with the long historical process that we've been looking at."

That effect has persisted.

> I'm a Democratic Party type, tending toward the liberal, but since the Program, it's been very hard for me to deal with the rhetoric anymore. I can't accept any of it, from any side, so it really has given me a hard eye toward political bull shit.

A second-cycle woman spoke of the conservatism of the Program, not in the form of political indoctrination but rather in the form of political responsibility. Instead of changing her political views, the Program apparently helped her to channel her political feelings and beliefs into productive political and professional activity.

> I think the Program was quite conservative. I don't think we were getting a political [line] at all. I just think that the concept of civic responsibility was there, and that was significant. I've been quite involved in the last few years in civil disobedience, for instance, which would be a no-no in the Program line.

Professor M suggested a "nonviolent response" to her concerns about bills being introduced in the state legislature punishing students who had taken part in riots: that she go to Sacramento to talk with legislators directly. She and another Program student formed a delegation to the Capitol with other students where she said they were able to stop every bill before the legislature that was punitive toward students who had been involved in demonstrations on the campus.

> That changed my life. It was a way of responding in some ways to the issues that were being raised [in the Program]. What was our responsibility as citizens.

That experience, initiated by a faculty member in the Program, was indeed a formative one for her—she later became a professional lobbyist for liberal causes in Sacramento.

Another man from the second cycle said that although he held radical views, he was able to understand other points of view and he too was "not a rock thrower."

> I don't remember the Program, specifically, having much to do with my "radicalization," if you will. I stayed away from a lot of it. I felt very strongly, and being in journalism, I got involved that way, but I never got involved with the crowds, and had no sympathy for friends of mine that went and got tear-gassed.

As to the lasting effects of the Program, he said,

> I think the fact that I do have social convictions, and that I vote in every election—that isn't just, obviously, just the Tussman Program, but I think

it's definitely a part that I feel a responsibility to contribute to the community.

Other men from the second cycle spoke of the generalized rather than the specific effects of the Program on political attitudes. One said, "That's where the Program's effect has been more subtle. It moved me more away from polarization...." Another spoke about what he learned about politics in the Program.

> I don't think the Program changed my politics... I went to the rallies and the demonstrations and marched against the War, and listened to what was going on, and debated with the people handing out the pamphlets, and was attacked by the police [just for] trying to get to my apartment, and so on. I certainly was one of the community.... [But the Program] did sharpen my sense of the whole notion of what political life is, what the life of the polis is, as we studied it in the Program. I guess I learned something about political community, the body politic, as opposed to, you know, power politics. There are lots of teachers of power politics around, and perhaps very few who teach about the body politic, and I think the Program is one of those teachers. So whether this can be attributed to the Program or not I don't know, but I tend to look for sort of bigger solutions.

He mentioned several lobbying organization for liberal causes to which he now belongs, and added,

> I believe our chances of [achieving our goals] through understanding and education are much greater than our chances of effecting any sort of [changes] through revolution. From my observation of revolutions of the last couple of centuries, it's been tried and violent revolution seems to bring the worst to the top, to push down the poor even further.... I don't do that kind of politics. Whether I would have not done that if I hadn't been in the Program, I really can't say.

A man from the first cycle spoke of how the Program helped to intensify his political responses.

> I don't think the Program encouraged it, but I think my *participation* in the Program encouraged it, motivated it. When you're into a questioning mood, when you're questioning authority, when you're challenging,

it's only natural to carry that over into the non-Program elements. . . . In terms of political consciousness, I had moderate political consciousness, was a great Kennedy supporter, *et cetera*, and I think the Program did an awful lot to radicalize me to where I was one of those twenty thousand people that signed the petition to get the Peace and Freedom Party going. So in terms of politicization of myself, the Program was a very strong influence. And politicization doesn't mean right, left, center, it just means politicization.

Political Tensions

There is no evidence here that faculty in the Program in any way stifled expressions of political views that were in opposition to their own. According to one second-cycle man, students in the Program identified themselves with a variety of different groups there, apparently rather loosely organized around different themes: a newsletter/poetry journal for one, a group "very into drugs," for another. According to another participant, there was

> a group of radical people who were participating a lot in the marches and stuff. But you see, the Program allowed it. If they were coming and reading and talking, or even just talking, they were still part of the Program.

One second-cycle man remembered different groupings in the Program—a group who got together to discuss the readings, and a more socially orientated group, but thought that the political tension dominated everything in the House. (He was one of a handful of participants who remembered going on a Program retreat and thought that "it kind of reduced the tension and I think it boosted morale for a good six weeks afterwards.")

> But a lot of the time there was so much friction going on politically within the Program that really the topic of discussion if you were around the house was (laughs) "who was still in the Program, who's leaving, what's going on here?"; I stayed close to several people who left the Program, and for me it was always—I always felt a little sheepish about it because I felt I had to justify why I was staying. Because in some ways it was a political statement to leave the Program, and if you were staying, it wasn't quite politically correct in some ways . . . There were lots of discussions about leaving or staying, what was the right thing to do.

> But I'm glad I stuck it out. I felt I continued to get value out of the Program while I went through it . . . intellectual stimulation. . . . I did feel badly about it but I think any reasons I might have given them for staying at the time [for instance, the Program was fulfilling virtually all his lower division requirements] probably were not the real reasons. I think the real reasons I stayed was because it was challenging and stimulating.

He went on to describe the role of the tutorials in creating closeness between faculty and student, and how politics could effect those relationships.

> By the second year the people who were radically split off were either kicked out of the Program or left of their own accord, for one reason or another, and not usually academic, but just because of political differences with the faculty that led them to say, "This is bull shit, I don't want to deal with this anymore, let me outta here." Or vice versa, where one or another of the faculty would say, "Hey, this kid's a pain in the neck, get him off my back." It was such a close situation because of that tutorial. I think it really made for some very close relationships, but also some very fractious ones between the faculty and the students.

(In his own case, he said later on in the interview that he really didn't get close to faculty partly because he didn't "feel good about where they were coming from.")

The fractiousness that he described went back to the very beginning of the second cycle following one defining incident.

> After about two or three weeks [from the start of school] there was the Stop the Draft Week demonstrations in Oakland, and there was a real big discussion right after that because we'd skipped the larger group seminar and went off to the demonstration. Particularly [Professor J] and [Professor O] were both saying, "You can't do this." It immediately polarized the situation and from that point on there became a radical distinction within the group—you're on the out's or you're on the in's—and it never really resolved itself other than a great number of people were gone after six months. . . . Students were probably divided in more than two [groups]. There was a very extreme group, then kind of a middle group that was swaying either way—I would probably characterize myself as one of those—and then another group which was solemnly

under the tamp of the more conservative of the faculty who had been in the Program. . . .

Tussman was such a strong figure, he just really did polarize . . . an intellectually very powerful guy, very powerful reasoning ability and set of beliefs; and he just would go for it straight down the line, saying "This is how it is, this is how I'm gonna conduct this thing, this is my vision for what it is," and you were either with him or against him. He is not a vindictive person at all, but he was just definitely very clear about "this is how it's going to be" and really brook[ed] no opposition.

People from both sides got pushed out. People from the side that sided with him tended to leave for one academic reason or another, [because the Program] didn't fit their style. The ones that got pushed out, I'd say for the most part, either stopped doing their work because they felt so torn by the political struggle that was going on within the Program or they actually were doing the work, but they were felt by the faculty to be divisive and were asked to leave. . . . It was very demoralizing a lot of the time because a lot of the most vocal and capable students within the group got pushed out. It really made the Program kind of dull in the second year in a lot of ways because some of the people who would speak up most in seminars, speak up most in the larger group sessions [the lectures] were no longer in it. . . .

It was not a big deal to get pushed out. I mean it wasn't like you were gonna get kicked out of the university if you left the Program. At a certain point you would say, "I'm just not interested in dealing with this." I mean, first of all they felt like politically they just didn't agree with what was going on, felt like they weren't comfortable there anyway. I don't think anybody who got pushed out really fought very hard. . . . There wasn't that much rancor about people leaving the Program in certain cases because they understood the issue and they accepted it, the consequences of it . . . really the consequences of it when you look at it weren't that terrible because you were still—it wasn't like you were kicked out of the University. It was kind of a bogus issue in some ways because they weren't really pushed up against the wall saying, "Okay, either you stay, come to these lectures, or you're out of an education. . . ."

It appears that the way in which this participant changed and modulated his use of the terms "pushed out" and "kicked out" that he did not mean precisely that. There is no evidence in the descriptions of other participants in the Program and from Professor Tussman that any student was ever actually forced to leave the Program by faculty because of their political views. Rather it appears more likely that students who found the more conservative political positions of the faculty objectionable or intolerable, either quit the Program outright or stopped doing their work and then were asked to leave because they were not working. Not completing the assignments and not attending seminars and lectures and tutorials were grounds for the faculty to suggest to students they might be happier in the regular University, and as far as I could ascertain, the only grounds for such action. And it is quite possible that some students were attracted to the Program with the belief that it was part of the "revolution," and then became disillusioned when they discovered it was not a political revolution but an educational one they had joined. Certainly political activists would have difficulty adjusting to the Program's sober and thoughtful approach to educational revolution.

But not all students who disagreed with faculty on political grounds left the Program. Some of the participants in the study described themselves as "rebellious." And Tussman has said that rather than dropping out, "the rebels stayed to fight," a plausible situation since some of the self-described "rebellious" participants said they had found a forum for their rebellion in the Program. According to one second-cycle man,

> There was always a debate. But if you were a detractor, in a debate, you're a supporter. I mean, if you were chewing on it to get angry at Tussman, then you were *involved*.[3]

The participant quoted above, who told of skipping a Program lecture to attend the Stop the Draft Week demonstration, felt that the events occurring during those early weeks of the Program forced him into a kind of permanent political stance while in the Program.

> I was somewhat politicized in high school by just general beliefs at the time, in reaction to what was going on in this country. But because it was made an issue [in the Program]—if you skip class to do some political activity you are undermining the Program in some way—that was the message we were getting and that tended to politicize me more. I could have separated out the abstract political discussion that was going on . . .

---

[3] A study of drop-outs from the Program would provide their views of the politics of the Program as well as their reasons for leaving, information not available from this study.

> about what was going on in the larger society—it wasn't like I was gonna go off every seminar or every session and go demonstrate or participate in some political activity other than the course—but because it was made such an issue at the time that we did not show up [during Stop the Draft week in early October] I think it forced the whole thing to become political . . . I mean it was a polarized time. It may have been unavoidable but I felt it was—it still feels to me like it was an overreaction on the part of the conservative members of the faculty. I understood where they were coming from but I think it was just made too much of an issue.

This former student channeled his political interests and concerns into academic and professional lines.

> Because of the way the Program was organized it was the first time I saw political struggle within an organization. That's actually when I started getting involved in film making, and [took a course] in the Comp Lit Department. Actually, because of that course, I ended up majoring in that topic—politics and film. That was my independent major.

Filmmaking is now his profession.

According to him, the faculty's openly taking the position that attendance at political demonstrations was not, in their view, an excuse for not attending the Program's lectures and seminars became to some students a call to arms. They apparently not only felt "polarized"—that they had to take a stand against this position—but that polarization lasted the whole two years of their participation in the Program. But what can not be determined from his description of these events, is whether or not the faculty's public denouncement of student absences during the Stop the Draft week deterred students from further absences related to political demonstrations after that incident.

One second-cycle woman, who was involved in politics on the campus only after her time in the Program, found it hard to say to what extent the Program influenced her because there were other factors in her background—her parents' politics, for instance—which had helped shape her views on issues such as social justice before coming to the Program. But she did have something to add about how students might have modified their political behavior in relationship to faculty in the Program, and how the political climate of the campus affected the Program.

In the second year especially, I think, I remember somewhat of a feeling of students against faculty, when [a] kind of an adversarial relationship developed with the students and I remember feeling kind of a part of that scene. The professors were handling things in a more autocratic way than students liked and they wanted more say in the subject matters in the lectures, I guess. But it was so connected with the time at Berkeley—student protest movements—and students kind of gained steam from that . . . I understood where the students were coming from and I felt somewhat sympathetic. I also felt a little uncomfortable and defensive for faculty.

I think that a lot of that tension . . . between the faculty and the students in the second year had to do with . . . the political tensions that were revolving around the campus at the time. The professors were very conservative at times . . . more of a feeling of a need to extract some sense of control and concern about what was going on. And once the Program was over, whatever tension there was between students versus the faculty didn't exist any more. I guess that would be the way the Program had an effect—to broaden my perspective on my thinking. . . .

The whole issue of a students' strike and not going to classes and things like that would have been much more difficult for me to deal with as a member of the Experimental College group because there was this closeness to the faculty. It would just have seemed like it would have been much more [of a] personal statement to a faculty member [in the Program] than it was to a [faculty member in a] big lecture class not to go to lecture. Therefore I really didn't do too much politically while I was in the Tussman Program. Whatever activity I was involved with, any kind of risk-taking, was more after the Program was over.

I did feel a kind of closeness to the faculty even though I had some problems with the way things were run and I understood the student [position]. The attitude that I remember, and this is very simplified, was that you had to be very rational, very historical in one's thinking about the problems that were going on, and the students were being very emotional, showing a lack of circumspection and flying off the handle. . . . Even though politically we might have felt inclined to agree with some of the causes, [we] certainly weren't going to act on them in any kind of irrational way. I guess I have to say that after the Program was over I felt more comfortable maybe being a little less rational and a little more emotional. That's 'cause times changed a little bit. There [were] the Cambodia events, and Kent State, and things got heavy at that time. That rational element got out of perspective a little bit for a while.

From her statement, it seems fair to conclude that the Program had a moderating rather than a squelching effect on her political actions, but not necessarily her political views. The "closeness to the faculty" that prevented her from making a "personal statement" to a faculty member by not attending a lecture or seminar is in direct contrast to students who left the Program in order to make political statements, presumably to faculty as well as to other students, but also perhaps to themselves, helping them to define their own political stances in relationship to authority. (See Chapter 13.)

In a vivid example of how students could draw a line between their participation in the Program and their political activity, a second-cycle man explained how the Program was immune from campuswide strikes. During his time in the Program he said he was only marginally involved in political activity, which was not carried over to the Program.

> I'd go to rallies. I'd listen to what was going on. I did—during the Eldridge Cleaver controversy [over whether or not he should be allowed to teach on the campus]—go into classrooms and announce why there was a strike going on, which was all so hypocritical. There was no strike in the Tussman Program. We were removed from it. But I would go out and encourage people taking regular undergraduate courses to go out on strike, yet I was not on strike myself. We were not part of the regular University. We can strike in the regular University, but the Program is removed from that, the Program does not have to worry about academic freedom which was the big issue then.
>
> I was involved in *some* of the campus politics. For some reason, we in the Tussman Program were either aloof from this or we were immune to it. It's hard to really explain the attitude. I felt very deeply about it. The only time I think we came close to a strike was when [two students] walked out of a lecture that [K] was giving because of [an issue] concerning racism.... And if you believe the theory that student unrest is directly correlated with approaching finals, it would give people in the Program a little less motivation to be out there on the lines because we didn't have that sort of pressure to relieve through [political activity].

Besides the reasons he gives, the loyalty to faculty described by the woman in the previous quote and the statements by faculty after the Stop the Draft Week episode might have served to deter students from striking in the Program. It is possible that the argument and discussion, the wrestling with the issues that was encouraged in the Program were more appealing and valuable to students than anonymous demonstrations in picket lines would have been. Program teachers provided some students (the "rebels who stayed to fight") with more convenient personal objects upon which they could vent their anger.

The relative physical remoteness of the Program from the part of the campus where political action took place as well as its emphasis on historical events helped create the sense of distance from campus events for some students, and perhaps allowed for more abstract attitudes toward campus politics to develop, and at the same time allowed them to see connections between current and historical times. One woman learned to treat the Vietnam War as she did the historical events dealt with in the Program.

> I think it probably let me know that there were a lot of opinions out there. I was probably looking at the war issue like I would have different things that we did in the Program where there were a lot of different points of view.

One woman faulted the Program for not allowing students to bring campus protest issues directly into their discussions, but "relatedness" was apparently in the eye of the beholder. Participants quoted in Chapter 5 said both Hobbes and Thucydides related to discussions on the war in Vietnam. One man spoke of how he connected the content of the Program to the campus political scene:

> We were on this little island just off the campus [on the Northside], with everything that was happening generally [happened in the] Southside Student Union area. And a lot of the people [students] were in touch with that, and very radical, and showing up here [in the Program]. So against this great trauma, we had a classical background. We were reading the Trojan war at the same time all this stuff was happening over here. And it related. You couldn't help but have those basic metaphors to start talking with.
>
> One great example which I'll always remember is [another student] and I, when they took over Moses Hall (laughs) on the campus. They had overturned trash cans and set bonfires around the Campanile. Well, [another student and I] went out with a tape recorder and we hid it, and we [talked to each other], as if we were sort of journalists reporting what we saw just to each other. And it became for us the metaphor. We had been reading Milton and *Paradise Lost*, and this was Hell. It was Milton's Hell, where people were having philosophical debates around fires,

and the different levels of what was going on. It was in the middle of the night with the old Berkeley buildings reflecting fire light, and this odd smell. Oooh! [The relating] was in the seminars because the radical elements [students] were bringing up all these issues, especially around things like Hobbes, this authoritarian, so there was a constant challenging, and debate, and there were different opinions. . . .

This man spoke of the tempering effect of the Program on his political participation.

At the time, it made me cool to the hot goings on (laughs), except from that observational point of view. I think by the nature of it that stuff scared me anyway.

But he thought the Program influenced his union activities later in his professional life when he did find the courage to act on his beliefs in the interest of a community.

[The Program] got me into a lot of trouble. I became a real union advocate and became an organizer and was involved in collective bargaining. I was really in the middle of the movement to get a good contract. . . .

And in tracing the influence of the Program on his union activities, he said,

The basic work I did was on a legal level, which would have lasting consequences. . . . It was a conscious choice and decision to be able to stand up in front of a group of people and say, "This is right, and this is what we need to do." I had to have some confidence, and it was based on the background, on the Program providing a framework, a fundamental framework, within which people can act as a community.

Developmental Aspects of Political Identity

The issue of politics and the Program is a complicated one along several lines. The political atmosphere on the campus, just like the tear gas used by police to break up riots and sit-ins, permeated every activity on the campus, including courses, classes, and the Program. (Indeed, it permeated life in the larger off-campus community as well, where petitions supporting political causes addressed to state and national governments were commonly circulated on the streets, outside super-markets, in churches, and high schools, elementary schools, even preschools, as well as other Bay Area college campuses.) There was a strong pull for students to take sides against authority, and to express their solidarity with the protesters through demonstrations, petitions, teach-ins, and acts of civil (and uncivil) disobedience.

Beginning students in the Program were just leaving home, some actually still at home at least for the first semester or two, and beginning to form their own political identities, whether they were in line with their parents' positions or were radically different or were some mixture of the two, as these participants testified. The developmental course for young people this age requires individuation from their parents (Blos 1969); faculty in close contact with them in the Program provided handy parental substitutes to rebel against as well as handy new and different role models to emulate. Erik Erikson (1968) tells us that adolescents look

> fervently for men and ideas to have faith in . . . in whose service it would seem worthwhile to prove oneself trustworthy . . . [and search] for some inspiring unification of tradition or . . . ideas and ideals. . . . At the same time, the adolescent fears a foolish, all too trusting commitment. . . . If not sure of his identity [he or she] shies away from interpersonal intimacy. . . . Should a young person feel that the environment tries to deprive him too radically of all the forms of expression which permit him to develop and integrate the next step [in development], he may resist with . . . wild strength. . . .

Mussen et al. (1984) observe that "once adolescents become capable of examining the consistency of their beliefs, they begin to question the validity of many attitudes and values held earlier and begin to search for new sets of values and premises upon which to base a philosophy . . . [developing an] awareness of the discrepancy between the actual and the possible helps to make the adolescent a rebel. He is always comparing the possible with the actual and discovering that the actual is frequently wanting." Cowan (1978) speaks of the intellectual changes that adolescents are going through that enables them to "meet adults in their world as cognitive equals . . . for the first time." Using Piagetian analysis, he explains that adolescents are using their "intellectual resources in attempts to change their world" as they are "building theories about political and social environments—about how could it be to how should it be. . . . "

These theories help to explain why the Program appealed to some students at Berkeley in the sixties and why other students rejected it. It certainly offered them a unification of tradition, and ideas about how political and social environments could and should be, as participants in the study have testified. The closeness with faculty who presented themselves more nearly as intellectual equals than ordinary classroom lecturers since they welcomed student thought, comment, and debate, could have been satisfying to some, and at the same time, suspect to others wary of an "all too trusting commitment." And the freedom of expression Erikson says is so important to adolescents could be seen by some as a component of the Program and by others as lacking, a matter of personal interpretation.

It was an intensely emotional time at Berkeley, with political organizations of all sorts vying for student allegiance and urging them to defy authority. (One student political leader encouraged students to steal a book from a local bookstore in order to prove solidarity with the Movement.) The Program and the Movement offered students ways to achieve independence from authority, but in very different ways and pulled students in different directions. While the Movement viewed all authority as dangerous and untrustworthy, Program students defined authority as unthreatening enough to be shared, as one participant has observed. It is understandable if students were confused and conflicted, and some participants' memories of the political aspect of their time on the campus are cloudier than about other aspects.

Summing up participants' accounts thus far, we can detect some of the influences of the Program in regard to campus political activity. Some felt quite removed from the entire political scene, some even frightened by it. That might have been to some extent a result of the self-selection process, since closeness to faculty was a frequently mentioned reason for choosing to apply to the Program, and some applicants might have felt the Program to be a safer place than the regular university, as several participants have said it turned out to be. A sense of security may have been an effect of the Program, located as it was at the corner of the campus where political activity least often occurred, and drawing students back intellectually in time to the Peloponnesian Wars, seventeenth-century England, and Federalist America. For some students, the Program served to broaden their perspectives, to the point of treating the Vietnam War crisis even then as another moral crisis in history. For others, the Program apparently helped to intensify whatever their political views were at the time, forcing them to think through their political views, as well as to their consequences, so that they felt eventually more confident and certain of those views and more willing to act on them through legal means.

Some participants from the second cycle said they felt a "pull to the right," a "conservative" influence from the faculty that they say affected their behavior more than their views—that enabled them to more easily resist the call to "rock throwing" and other acts destructive of the very institutions in society that they were studying. There is no doubt the Program exerted a sobering influence. But for all the resistance some put up to that influence, it may have been welcomed at some level for the respite it brought from the political pressure everywhere else, since one of the chief aims of the Program was to get students to think for themselves. At the very least, it provided a forum for students to work through their feelings on these deeply troubling issues, and sometimes helped to channel them academically and professionally without basically changing them.

Attitudes Toward Authority and the "Givenness" of The Program's Requirements

Confrontation with authority was a major theme during the time of campus unrest at Berkeley. The Movement, the student revolution on the Berkeley campus in the late fifties and early sixties, was first focused on civil rights and free speech issues; by the time the Program began in the fall of 1965 the free speech movement had embraced the antiwar movement. According to Verne Stadtman (1970, 473-74) in his history of the university,

> Because it was so spectacular and so diligently covered by Bay Area press, radio, and television, the Berkeley rebellion had national impact. . . . Berkeley became synonymous with dissent, bohemianism, and organized confrontation of authority. The new image appealed to adventurous, intellectually active people and did not seriously impair faculty or student recruiting (although there was a short-lived dip in Freshman enrollments in 1965).

The complaints of students about the educational system at the University of California, and Berkeley in particular, included

> assertions that preoccupation with undergraduate instruction and research had left faculty members little time or energy for undergraduate teaching; that the undergraduate curriculum was too rigid, had too little relation to the concerns of their generation, and [was] geared to outmoded concepts of what educated men needed to be or to know; that emphasis on grades spoiled the natural excitement of discovery and learning; that too many of their classes were taught by teaching assistants; that there was too much distance between students and teachers; and that counseling and advising systems were perfunctory and unsatisfactory.

Tussman conceived the Experimental College Program long before the first sit-in of the Free Speech Movement and Mario Savio's call to students to make the university stop unless they became "free." Tussman began discussing his proposal based on Meiklejohn's plan of the 1920s with administrators in the spring of 1964. So although the Experimental College Program was not planned in response to the demands of the Movement, and owed its inspiration to a plan conceived decades before, when it opened its doors in the fall of 1965 it went some distance toward meeting many of the educational demands of the angry students of the sixties. Closeness of faculty and students, the absence of exams and grades, the focus of faculty away from research and toward undergraduate teaching were hallmarks of the Program—no wonder it appealed to revolutionary-minded students. Only its curriculum and purpose were not in line with the educational changes demanded by the Movement: in direct contrast to a *laissez-faire* approach that allowed students to follow their own interests, the Program curriculum was based largely on works written centuries before, did not include many women or minority writers, and was firmly fixed by faculty (even though there were some rumblings about student-sponsored additions during the second year in each of the two cycles). The purpose underlying the Program, to lead its students to a commitment to a democratic community, stood in direct opposition to the "do-your-own-thing" motto of the Movement. It was no wonder some dropped out as they realized the Program was not made to their revolutionary order.

Of the students who completed the Program and were interviewed for this study, about half said they were hostile to authority at the time, or did not accept it, or did not respect it, or were suspicious of it. There were no differences between men and women on this issue; somewhat greater numbers of participants from the first cycle than the second reported negative views on authority. Equal numbers of men and women, about half of the participants, reported having no trouble accepting authority, a few more of them in the second than the first cycle.

In spite of what their views on authority might have been, very few participants from either cycle reported any objections to the givenness of the requirements. For some participants who said they had no trouble accepting authority, it apparently followed that they had no problem with the fixed nature of the requirements. One woman said,

> I would have been absolutely shocked if there hadn't been any [requirements]. I respected the teacher—I still do. I have the same attitude about tenured professors.

Another said she had no problem with the set nature of the requirements.

> It was hard, stressful sometimes under the conditions of what was going on on campus. But I guess I really bought the line that this had been carefully formulated and the people that were doing it I trusted, in particular [J]. He is considered very autocratic. And even though he had kind of an autocratic way of operating, I really did trust him.

Several who said they were questioning authority nevertheless did not object to the requirements. A first-cycle man said,

> Authority doesn't necessarily mean that it's the right thing. Maybe I got to thinking about that somewhere in the Experimental College. Not just taking as a given, the truthfulness, or the correctness of whatever authority was handing out.

But rather than objecting to the givenness of the Program's requirements, he said instead

> I liked it. As a matter of fact, I don't think that all courses should be electives.... I don't know, maybe kids are more mature these days, but I don't know that that's the case. And I think that you need some guidance. If you were born wise, you wouldn't need to go to school, and you

wouldn't need to learn things. So I liked it [the givenness]. I didn't find that confining.

Another man who said he learned to challenge authority in the Program did not object to the requirements because "[Freedoms in the Program] were still much broader than one could obtain across the street [in the university]." Another who was "somewhat rebellious, although intimidated as well," and distrusted at first what he saw as an "authoritarian streak" in the ideas behind the Program, nevertheless did not object to the requirements.

> [I felt] really very freed up about that [the requirements] . . . I remember pretty vividly now, I think it came up in the second year: "Students really aren't in a position to choose from the smorgasbord of courses and put together their own curriculum. They don't know enough to do that. It should really be put together in a coherent way and fed to them, not by their choice." Even so . . . I felt it was fairly flexible and fairly free. I mean, the fact that we could write about whatever we wanted on a given book was part of it.

And by the second year he changed in his attitude toward authority.

> [I felt] a bit more trusting [of authority] overall because of having that closeness with various authority figures, substantially more than I would have had in the University.

It may have been that the appeal of the readings, at least in the first year, was strong enough to overshadow the fact that they were required. One man from the second cycle said

> . . . there were times when I think I objected less than other people. I felt that the requirements, the reading list, were for the most part interesting and challenging, even though after a while they seemed to be all coming from a certain political or philosophical point of view, which wasn't my view. It was interesting enough to talk about them, and you could always bring up the counter argument, too, and express it. But there were times when you felt like expanding the curriculum beyond some of the things that were going on, bringing in other kinds of thinking, other kinds of subject areas. And that did become more of an issue, I think, in the second year.

One man from the first cycle who had conflicting feelings about authority did not object to the givenness of the requirements

> for the most part. I assessed them as being pretty fine material with the exception of Hobbes. I thought I'd rather be a janitor than read Hobbes. Frankly I didn't read some of them—I read a bit of them and they seemed real academic to me and I just didn't want to read them, so I didn't. But some of them—there were just some real classics imbedded in there, like Shakespeare and Homer—that was great. I remember there were little squeaks from people now and then about how racially imbalanced the subject matter was, but I have to admit that didn't really concern me. I felt this was first rate material so I didn't have a problem with it.

Perhaps the absence of exams and grades allowed students in the Program to feel they could read just what they wanted, as this man apparently did, and therefore the "givenness" of the reading requirements was more negotiable than if students were to be examined on the readings.

A woman from the first cycle who described herself as "pretty rebellious" did not object to the givenness of the first year's readings and was not happy that the second year's readings were not as fixed. She, too, was not in favor of letting students choose the curriculum.

> The second year wasn't as set when the Program started as the first year, so there was a lot of disagreement among us students and some among the faculty of what we should cover in the second year. I seem to remember we had a lot of arguments about that. But I feel much more affected by what happened in the first year . . . I think the objections came up more when the curriculum wasn't as set . . . I guess the third unit was the American Revolution, the Federalist Period, that was fun. That was good. I remember those three periods real well. It's seventeenth century England, and the Greek period . . . I thought that there was ample time to explore things around those areas, that the required reading wasn't so overwhelming that you couldn't do a lot of other reading.
>
> I don't think that it probably would make a lot of sense to let students just choose which areas they wanted. I think there's a lot of advantage to everybody doing the same thing. Just looking back at it all I remember that part of it wasn't set and that the disagreement was that there were some differences of opinion on the part of the student body on what they would have liked to have seen in the last two quarters. I remember that a lot of people had objections. I'm not sure I even knew what I wanted

to, what area I wanted to study . . . Looking back on it, the areas that we covered that I got a lot out of were very well defined, and I don't remember what we did the other times. It would have been nice to have more well-defined areas so maybe if they had been better defined there would have been less controversy.

The Issue of Relevancy

It seems then that only when the Program reached a state where the curriculum was not clearly defined did room for controversy open up, controversy very much related to the times. A second-cycle woman with a "rebel streak" is unsure now about the value of including "relevant" material in the Program. She had objected at the time to the givenness of the requirements.

> Oh, sure, oh gosh, we all did. This was the time when there was all the big protest on campus about black studies, and any kind of studies, or whatever. I think that a lot of us really wanted to see things that related to our daily lives more. I think that [is] still a valid argument. [But] I think that perhaps that wasn't the right arena for the undergrad years, perhaps, for those subjects to be included. I don't know. I have mixed feelings about that. We could have digressed into everything that was happening now and not learned anything about anything that had happened before.
> And I did feel the worth of—what is the quotation about those people who don't learn history are doomed to repeat it? I do feel that that's worthwhile, you just can't cross off the last two thousand years of history, and not pay any attention to it. I do believe the argument of having education relate to the students who are participating is an important argument. I'm not sure how to juxtapose those two issues, basically. Those discussions did come up a lot in the Program. I mean, if I'd been more aware of women's things, I would have brought that subject up.

In view of the beliefs of the former student quoted earlier who found metaphors in the Program directly relating to current campus political events, the concept of relevance obviously had different applications for different students.

The cry for relevance did become a major tenant of the student revolution; it was the driving idea behind the attempts of the Third World Liberation Front to establish an Afro-American Studies department, leading to the

Third World Strike in the spring of 1969. Don Davis, of the Afro-American Student Union, said about the impetus behind the proposal for a Black Studies Program in the spring of 1968:

> We discovered our degrees meant nothing in terms of our abilities to create and bring about change in the black community. We started to think in terms of changing the university so that it would be of value in the black community . . . this led to our concept of a program of Black Studies—which would develop persons with various kinds of expertise to be able to go back and deal with the problems of the black community.[4]

Relevance became a moral as well as an educational imperative for many students, an extension actually of their commitment to the civil rights movement to which many of them had been attracted while in high school. The Black Studies program was proposed in the spring of 1968; the Third World strike took place in the spring of 1969, during the second year of the second cycle, when the curriculum was not as firmly set as it had been the first year, and when there was some indecision about what the readings should be. It is not surprising, then, that some students in the Program should want to agitate for more short-term relevance of the Program to what they perceived, and which had been defined for them by their campus political milieu, to be one of society's most urgent needs. And the Program's theme of civic responsibility combined with the heightened idealism typical of that stage in the psychological development of young people, fed directly into these beliefs.[5] "How it could be and how it should be" was obviously on the minds of many Program students.

The woman in the second cycle quoted earlier (who had been "one of the rebellious ones") had problems at the time with the way she thought the Program did not relate, or did not directly relate to what she saw as her civic

---

[4]Dexter Waugh and Larry Spears, "Ethnic Studies and the Strike," in the *California Monthly* (April-May, 1969).

[5]Stadtman (p. 439) quotes Katherine Towle, Dean of Women from 1961 to 1965, who characterized students of that period as "articulate, eager, knowledgeable, independent and imbued with idealism." He quotes a special university report to the Board of Regents in 1966: "eight thousand students, roughly one out of ten on all campuses, spend afternoons, weekends and vacations working in disadvantaged areas throughout California and the world."

responsibilities, but over the years her attitudes toward issues of authority have changed.

> This was the Sixties, right? I mean it was the time when everything was supposed to be relevant, so it was right in the thick of that. And I can remember some very glib remarks that Tussman made about closing the door, keeping [out] all that noise from the outside—we didn't need to concern ourselves with that stuff. I was very offended by that, and I felt like—and I still do actually—that was 100 percent wrong. If we were going to be reading *The Federalist Papers* for God's sakes, we can make them relevant, we can say, "What does this have to do with our responsibilities today?", and we didn't do that. I mean we did it in the most abstract and removed political way, which is part of academic life, academic people do things that way.

Her argument with the way the Program was conducted in this regard apparently did not have so much to do with the choice of readings, although she thought some of them "one-sided," as with how the readings were used. Although she was sure she objected to the givenness of the Program at the time, she said she would not object to it now that she sees the benefits.

> The thing that maybe mitigated this authority issue at the Program was that in effect you were doing that in the general university, too—you were having to take a lot of required courses as undergraduates in the lower division. We didn't get to shop around for these in the Program; we had to just go with what they were giving us. I didn't know [that] I cared about the Peloponnesian Wars, so I wouldn't have made the same choices. But I see that now as a great gift. Really, I mean I see that as one of the wonders of having done it this way, that somebody else knew more than I did, and made those decisions. I'm sure I wouldn't have told you that for several years after (laughs), although I liked a lot of things we were doing. We read the Bible. Lord, you know—religious education. Really!

A woman from the first cycle who may have objected at the very first to the required readings soon came to appreciate them. She said she had been brought up to question authority and thought the Program encouraged that.

> [It] ran right along those same lines [and] improved it . . . I think that this kind of program where you're taught to think for yourself was not making

cookie cutters of [us]. There has to be some authority in a program, saying, "We're going to have a paper, and it's going to be due on such and such a date and it would be nice if it was on these books." I'm willing to go along with that. [The requirements were] very fair. They were obviously a lot older than we, and—when they first gave us the reading list, I thought, "Oh, god, I have to read this or that." I realized fairly soon it was much more interesting than it might appear from the outside. It becomes amazing how few people really have sat down and read what are considered to be the classics of Western culture's literature. And later on I really realized what a privilege it is to encounter these ideas, even though at the time it seemed very difficult and maybe didn't quite make sense or you're not old enough, or whatever.

A man from the second cycle who said he had resented authority somewhat, still did not object to the requirements and wasn't "bothered by them . . . I figured there was wisdom in having chosen that curriculum. And who am I to decide that we want to read some other silly book that just came out instead of some book that'd been around for three hundred years."

A man from the first cycle had attended a private secondary school where the teachers were very close to the students, camped with them, were called by their first names, in a spirit of egalitarianism. He found the Tussman Program to be a continuation of that close faculty/student relationship and had no problem accepting that the faculty were in charge there, either. Instead of seeing the set requirements as confining, he had the opposite reaction.

It seemed like it was more your own thing than it would have been if I'd been in the regular school. My memory's probably very different from what it was, [but] I remember that it felt kind of like freedom. That it didn't feel real locked in. I didn't feel that it was unreasonable. I don't remember feeling trapped. I sort of have this memory that this is more Shakespeare than I want to read. I'm sure we had to be there at nine o'clock in the morning. It's not like I could stroll in when I felt like it. And I'm sure that papers were due on a date . . . I think the kids hate choices and I think they do better knowing what the limits are and the structures. I remember thinking it's very well defined, here's what's going to be required and here's how we're going to do it, and then there were the surprises and the uncertainty, the unknowns of the group discussions and so on.

Habits of Mind

To be grateful for having choices made for them by experts, or to be somewhat resentful of faculty uses of authority were views certainly compatible with the stages of transition in which Program students found themselves.

Participants' attitudes toward authority and toward politics were closely related and interdependent. How the Program influenced participants attitudes toward authority, and how their attitudes toward authority in turn effected their participation in the Program is taken up in the next chapter.

CHAPTER 13

Authority in the Program

The whole question of authority (including the questioning of authority) was a major one in the Program, not only abstractly because it was embedded in the curriculum and was one of the themes of the education for democracy program, but personally because students were asked to accept the set nature of its structure, curriculum, and requirements. The particular time and place in which the Program was set acted to bring issues of authority to the forefront. One second-cycle man said,

> It amazes me that [the Program] held together during that time as much as it did. Because there was a constant undermining undercurrent [in] the '60s. It was a constant barrage of stuff. If there were any cracks in the staff, kids are going to find them. And so given that, it's amazing that it was as coherent as it was over that long period of time.

His views on authority were "shaped by the Program," and he came to see the basis of authority as the "essence of democracy, that the people are the authorizers, looking at the source of authority." He said of the Program that he "both loved and hated it." And the part he hated had to do with authority.

> [It] was the sort of authoritarian arrogance, the attitude that we saw coming from some of the professors. But hate is an attachment. . . .

The Program certainly managed to capture his affect, and in spite of his conflicts with authority, he was able to come to terms with them sufficiently to realize what the Program could offer him.

> The Program became a crucial orienting place for me so I have great positive feelings about it.

Many of the participants interviewed said they had held attitudes toward authority that were far from hostile. One man from the first cycle laughingly said authority "was the only thing I agreed with Joe Tussman about." A man who had close relationships with his high school teachers viewed his teachers in the Program, as well as after the Program, as mentors who were helpful to him rather than authority figures. "You used these people who were in positions of authority, let's say, and you used them in a personal kind of way," to gain knowledge and experience. Another from the second cycle was apparently persuaded by the reasonableness of authority in the Program.

> I knew we were going to college for professors to teach us stuff and it didn't really follow—there was a theory in the air that all babies are born Buddhas and we are only fouled up by our elders, and corrupted and degenerated. Joe had some strong feelings on that subject, since babies aren't Buddhas, they're kids, and there was no telling him that freshmen in college should be on the tenure committees. I remember he asked if we would want our professors to [have been given tenure] by our parents. And we all agreed that wouldn't be right. I think authority and I got along o.k.

Another man from the same cycle who objected "a little bit" to the givenness of the requirements but "not to the point of rebelling against it," found an accommodation with authority in the Program.

> I did not reject it immediately as being bad. I was willing to work with people who were in positions of authority. [The Program] probably gave me a healthier respect for authority than I would think the regular University might have. If nothing else, Tussman's attempts to try to explain to us what is really going on, how decisions are made, why people are acting in the way they do, that there is a long history of intellectual thought behind decisions that are made [even though they] seem to us to

be arbitrary now and very much against our self interest, either as individuals or as a country.

QUESTIONING AUTHORITY

While these men allowed themselves to be persuaded of the reasonableness of authority in the Program, others changed their views about authority in the opposite direction either during or after the Program. One explained his need to accept authority while in the Program in terms of family dynamics, and describes how that need has changed over time.

> While other kids there became antagonistic toward authority, I couldn't believe that the father could be wrong, and certainly didn't want the father to be wrong, so I was not going to challenge authority for anything. I had an idea that you couldn't run a ship without any rules, and that chaos was conceivable, and that you wanted to avoid that at all costs.
> That's what I believed then, but now, I'm not convinced. Now I have other feelings about authority. Though I don't deny that you have to have some kind of order, I'm not sure how that order gets arrived at, or how people fit into that order. It's a very different idea for me now than it was then. [When I entered the Program] I believed that I had to please authority, for various reasons, and frankly, it's been a long process of coming to believe differently than that.
> [The Program] certainly reinforced the idea that you are a child, you're not entitled to your feelings, you're not—this is the bad part of the Program—you are not entitled to your own ideas, you're a slovenly, undisciplined little creature who thinks he knows what he wants, but really doesn't, and you have to listen to Daddy, or your elders, or your teachers, and so I come to question that now. I mean, there is the big fight between the individual—Antigone, let's say, and her claim that she's going to do what's right for her, versus Creon. That was really an issue, but I'm coming more to sit on Antigone's side now than I did. My attitude was, "Right, I'm with Creon, and Tussman is with Creon, and I'm going to be with Tussman and Creon," and now I'm much more willing to say, "I'm gonna side with Antigone."

Using a metaphor he learned in the Program, this man is now challenging the interpretation of authority he had accepted back then.

Several men reported learning to question authority in the Program. One from the second cycle relied on metaphors from that time to explain his changing position on authority.

> Somewhere around [the time of] reading *Paradise Lost* I felt myself more of a devil's party than of the angels (laughs). I think I began to have some rebellion against the—or I was trying to find myself. I had always been rather an obedient and good member [of society], that's how I'd been brought up, and the devil's party looked pretty attractive. I think that's where I first began to get a bit rebellious, on my own account.

A man from the first cycle also changed his views on authority while in the Program.

> In high school I not been the most obedient to authority but on the other hand, did not defy it. I guess my position was: they tell you to do it, you basically go along with the Program. But my attitude I guess did change. I don't know how the Program had an effect on it, but I'm sure it did. It happened while I was in the Program, 'cause I remember writing this in my intellectual autobiography, that I regarded laws as guidelines....
>
> The Program probably had something to do with it in the sense of what we read and my own intellectual development. I began to decide the coincidence of law with morality often was so irregular that to give laws which represent authority the kind of respect that some people think you ought to give them is more than they deserve, because they are not always right in terms of what they're trying to get me to do. That's what I meant by guidelines. In other words, they're not telling you what's really right; to the extent that they coincide with what you believe to be right, you follow them, and to the extent they don't, you don't. That didn't mean necessarily I was going to go out and break every law that I didn't like, or was going to openly defy them.

One man said his views changed after entering the Program when he learned he could challenge authority.

> [My attitude] was certainly respectful. I treated [authority] with deference. I generally assume that those in authority have earned it. That might have changed in the Tussman Program. I realized you could challenge authority somewhat. I mean, even if you weren't right you

could still challenge it, but it made more sense if you were right. At least you feel more satisfaction. I think that was a good aspect of the Program.

Other students in the Program helped one man learn how to challenge authority in a way he doesn't think could have happened in any other classes at the university.

> There were some fine minds, very challenging minds, in the Program. And the fact that I got to watch them rebelling against what they thought was being shoved down their throat[s], and I got to watch that process and kind of come up with sophisticated arguments and take on authority in a way that I don't think I would have seen develop in my [outside] classes. It was good for me, because I would tend to be more intimidated and laid back. So I'm thinking psychologically, but also intellectually . . . I liked to watch some of the people that seemed very bright and verbal and articulate challenge the views. . . .

And another first-cycle man, who came into the Program challenging authority "all the time," said the Program's effect on him was to enhance his ability to challenge authority rather than to change his views.

> It made me a more effective challenger. It didn't squelch me. . . . I think one of the missions of the Program was to create or to help educate, or motivate a group of people that would ask some really tough questions and be the anti-bodies to the brave new world. To not go along with authoritarian systems, not to bite your tongue. . . . Okay, a bunch of cynics, a bunch of educated cynics. If I were to use a single analogy about the Program, if there was any single model, they were looking to do Diogenes, wandering around with a lantern looking for an honest man.

Students could hold views on authority at different levels simultaneously. A second-cycle man said that his change in thinking did not translate into a change in behavior.

> While on the intellectual plane I think I became more accepting of it as a result of what we were studying, I think on the personal level and in day to day life, it didn't do that. I don't think I made the transfer from the intellectual and the academic understanding of authority and the reasons behind the assertion of authority, [to] the practical reality of what it meant in my life, in terms of, "Okay, I'm living within a hierarchical system, and

here's my place in it, and therefore I must accept what's going on." I might not have struggled as hard as I could against it, but on the other hand it didn't mean that I was any more accepting of it because of what I was learning about it. . . .

    I could play devil's advocate on either side of the issue and argue the case either way. For example, when we read Plato, and the concept of the philosopher-king, or reading Hobbes, or Machiavelli—I mean, all those things that we read within the course of the Program—I understood intellectually where those trains of thought came from, and where they fit in the scheme of things and the logic behind them, but that didn't make them any easier for me to accept, or make me more willing to accept it. . . .

In this process he gained what he thought was a useful skill:

[to] able to see and evaluate various arguments in a detached manner . . . in order to survive in the Program [he was the man quoted earlier who had to justify his reasons for staying in a "politically incorrect program"] . . . detaching my emotional side about an issue from the philosophical and rational, and the academic or intellectual side, being able to split those two things.

A woman from the first cycle expresses a different kind of separation between her attitudes toward authority and her behavioral response to it, and explains her typically adolescent ambivalence.

[My attitude toward authority was] to get away from it. But at the same time, I was really looking for it to be there. It's like I didn't want to engage authority but it really meant something to me that the Program was grounded with some kind of authoritarian rules and that limits were being set. I saw that as being positive.[1] If I had any objections [to the

---

    [1]The importance of rules and limits to many students, no matter how much they might rail against them, is illustrated in an anecdote reported by one second-cycle man about another student who had wanted to leave the Program in order to travel, and had therefore expected not to be able to complete the Program. When Tussman was apparently willing to relax the Program's requirements to allow him to do that and still stay in the Program, the student felt "disappointment and didn't like it. 'I'm either going to be in or out.' Because what (the student) first learned from the Program was that there are rules that shouldn't, can't be

requirements] I probably wouldn't have paid any attention because I would have simply just circumvented it. I was so very confident [that I could] be very clever and do what I wanted anyway. I never let a "no" stop me.

DIFFERENT TYPES OF AUTHORITY

Other women made the distinction between kinds of authority. One thought there was in the Program the "good kind of authority—used in good ways—a benign authority." Some women talked about being able to question authority, and test authority, in the Program. One says the Program effected her attitudes because

> authority was open to question, you could question authority, and authority was accessible. By and large, authority [in the Program] was basically . . . human and kind and reasonable. . . .

Another woman focused on testing the limits, which she found difficult to do in the Program.

> Authority was something to be feared and obeyed and you did what you had to because you were being judged by that authority. [In the Program] I was . . . testing limits and finding how far I could go without it backfiring. And I had a real hard time with them not imposing limits. In a way, it's [freedom] wasted on freshmen who have been under parental control living at home, and suddenly they have all this freedom. I think it takes an unusually mature freshman to really be able to have the self-constraint. I just think most freshmen want to see how far they could get away with things.

One "pretty rebellious" woman changed her views about authority over time. Even while in the Program her attitudes became differentiated because she was not forced to contain her anger, and was able to distinguish different kinds of authority.

---

bent." And he left. Since he never completed the Program, it is possible he needed that rule to justify his leaving it.

I was given the freedom to react to authority more than I ever had.... Maybe I was less angry at the authorities within the Program and more angry at the United States government. But now that I look back on it, people, including the TAs, were angry at some of the professors because they wanted to get rid of the TAs. I still think that was a bad decision but at the same time—we were looking at these professors as being—as the bad guys. And now I look back and boy, what kind of bad guys *were* they anyway (laughs)!

One woman was not sure enough of herself to "test authority" the way the others had.

It's probably because I was just really intimidated by these illustrious professors and intellectual TAs. If I had had more confidence, I probably would have been more questioning of what they were doing and what their motives were and where we were headed.... I do remember other students questioning and arguing, testing how we might effect what we were being told to do. I don't remember feeling that I wanted or needed to do that.

Another "pretty rebellious" woman was able to examine her attitudes toward authority while in the Program and change them to suit her changing values.

I became less [rebellious] by the time the Program was over. Maybe just being able to have an environment where you could explore that, could be rebellious, and challenge, where it was comfortable to challenge the authority. We had a lot of authority struggles as I remember, in the Program, and that was fairly well tolerated. I got a chance to explore, act that out a little bit. Explore that a little bit and see what it was like, where it led. "What are those things that I was so attracted to? Were those real issues? Was it all really that important?" A change of values, probably....

Somehow I connect the Program in the context of exploring the anti-war issues that were going on then. A lot of energy and struggle didn't necessarily mean that change took place. You weren't going to be able to change things just automatically overnight. That it was a slower process than rebellion was, to spend a lot of energy and a lot of time just on acts of rebelliousness was not very productive. I just remember going from exploring different groups that were trying to think up different ways to change policy and coming to the fact that I didn't agree with any of them and didn't think that a lot of what they were doing was very productive and that there's probably a different way that might be better.

What I finally did was just decide that I could affect me and the people around me, just for myself and people [whom] I could affect directly. Which is why I think I eventually went into social work and therapy. I felt that eventually I could put my energies toward making things better for a few people and I wasn't going to make much headway trying to change the world. I guess all through the Program the themes that we were dealing with were—times when there was a lot of change going on, or people were thinking about how life should be. I think that just the whole process of thinking about what I wanted to do with life, that came a lot from the Program.

She was another of those students who during the course of the Program and influenced to some degree by it, began training for careers that channeled their political and social concerns into professional lines. In explaining the factors involved in progressing developmentally towards the stage of commitment, Perry (1970, 35) states: "What is required is a capacity for detachment. One must be able to stand back from oneself, have a look, and then go back in with a new sense of responsibility." It appears that this woman, and other students like her, found the freedom to do that within the Program.

FREEDOM AND RESPONSIBILITY

Related to issues of authority, at least internalized authority, was the question, "What about your attitude toward 'freedom and responsibility'? Did that change in response to the Program?" Several men said they have come to understand and appreciate the meaning of the phrase only later in life, after the Program. One says he is "still finding out." Another said,

The ideas I had about freedom and responsibility were necessarily imperfect, and they are probably still developing. I find as I get older, I think more about it.

Another said,

That was another big Tussman theme. I'm not sure I really appreciated all those issues at the time. I haven't really thought about it since then, until now, really. I mean in the context of the Program.

Some men from the first cycle thought the Program played no role in how they viewed the connection between freedom and responsibility at the time. One said,

> Freedom doesn't mean license—you have to make certain choices, and you have to be responsible for those choices. [The Program did not play a role in forming that view], not at a conscious level. I developed that attitude somewhere along the way.

But another changed his views about authority after it was over:

> I don't think my attitude changed [in the Program]. Let me put it to you this way: I've heard this little tandem since I've been in school, "If you want freedom you have to realize it carries with it responsibility." The Program didn't necessarily enhance my appreciation of these two qualities going together. I always thought that one of the properties of freedom is the ability to be irresponsible. But later on I came to understand what they meant by it . . . after the Program . . . I came to realize that when you have freedom you incur responsibility, you have to be prepared to bear the consequences. . . .

Another first-cycle man was affected by the way this issue was presented by Tussman in the Program.

> I responded to Tussman's sincere and passionate interest in that question. . . . I felt Tussman really wanted us to engage the issue of our contract with society, and I think that issue basically is the issue of freedom and responsibility. I mean he really cared about those questions. And as a result, I thought about them and engaged in them during that period. And that would be a positive experience that I took out of the Program.

And for some men from the second cycle, the Program definitely did play a role in forming their attitudes toward freedom and responsibility. It did not necessarily change them, but provided a context within which to examine them. Said one,

I examined it every day during the Program because I was certainly interested at the time in my own freedom and finding out what it consisted [of], and what I could do, and I guess I'm still finding out. The Program pointed out many of these issues—the idea of freedom and responsibility and the different kinds of freedom that there are, the freedom from constraint, the freedom to engage in something, and negative freedom, and positive freedom. We talked about all these things in the Program, and I probably still formulate the issues in my own thinking in the way that we did it at the time. My basic attitude toward freedom and responsibility probably hadn't changed. I guess I always thought that responsibility sort of outweighed personal freedom in my education, and I guess I still feel that way.

For another man, the concept became elaborated rather than reversed:

it certainly became a lot more detailed, the in's and out's and being able to discuss it. It certainly got more depth to it.

Although it did not come easy to him, another man thought his attitude towards the concepts of freedom and responsibility did change in the Program.

Yeah, it's the responsibilities that enable you to be free, and freedom without it doesn't make sense. And that was a hard one, because freedom [unconnected to responsibility] was the catchword that was spreading throughout the campus. Once you take over, as Joe said, who's gonna empty the garbage (laughs), who's gonna pick up the trash? Every revolutionary, once he takes over, faces the same problems that have been there before.

One man found a framework in the Program for developing his ideas about freedom and responsibility, which reached fruition only after it was over, and which have continued to grow over time.

I had my first sense of that, those two ideas there [in the Program]. I never thought about it before. I didn't have a real clear concept of how those two things actually play out in a real, human life. I mean they were just words, concepts to me. Gradually I have come to really believe that responsibility is essential, and that freedom without it is dangerous and meaningless. I really feel that coming to accept the responsibilities of one's life, and going gratefully into them, is the way to [the] freedom we can have. So that's something in the Program that I find to be truer now even than then. It gave me a literary and theoretical background to that idea that later I began to live. I have the framework.

One man from the first cycle found his views changing dramatically during the Program.

I always thought of freedom and responsibility as one of those real broad type things, it's like apple pie and Mom, that's what America is all about. That's what I thought before I went in. While I was in it, this was the biggest burden anyone could have. I'll give you a specific example. We read the Orestean trilogy in the Program. At one point Orestes says, "Jesus Christ! My freedom to act is just . . . weighing me down." You have responsibilities because of who you are and what you represent. You realize that in a sense your freedom is only to move aggressively in the channel that's been predefined for you. To put it this way, freedom was [before the Program], "Hey, blue sky, fantastic!" Freedom in the Program was, "infinity is cold."

Sometimes the Program did not change the attitudes toward freedom and responsibility, but helped students to clarify them, as this second-cycle woman remembers.

I think I saw that more clearly as a result of the Program, that freedom needs responsibility. To have freedom you have to be able to accept the responsibilities that go with that freedom. I think I saw that connection much more clearly as a result of the Program, the responsibilities that go with any kind of freedom.

A second-cycle man was less certain about the Program's effect on his attitudes toward freedom and responsibility, but he connected it to his personal life.

I would never have tied the two together in the way the Program did, that they go hand-in-hand. Freedom is impossible without responsibility. Would I have found that through the rest of the University? I don't know. But it certainly was one of the themes I was fascinated by and accepted. . . .

> I think more was demanded of people in the Program. Part of it came from the issue of freedom and responsibility. You were given a great amount of freedom in terms of doing work that you weren't really checked on. You have to write papers showing you were familiar with what the topics were, but as many people proved, you could write papers and never have read any of the material. It was sort of a lesson. It was structured [but] you had freedom within it. You were reminded of that at times: "You are supposed to be doing things, and we're not really going to check you on these, but we expect you to be doing them." I think it was an ideal. I don't think they honestly expected everyone, or anyone, to do everything that they suggested was done.

Assigning readings and papers without the sanctions of tests and grades added to the students' responsibility to learn. The journal, a requirement that was seldom checked on by faculty, was fulfilled by some students but not by others; attendance at lectures and seminars was a requirement more easily monitored. A first-cycle man talked about freedom and responsibility as it applied to the Program's requirements.

> I remember feeling that it was a two-way street there. They gave us the freedom to do the journal or not do the journal but then there was a sense of responsibility that it really was part of it. I think we did have to come to class [lecture]. As I remember, in the regular University you didn't always have to show up in class. In the Program it was your responsibility to show up. I remember they imparted this sense of responsibility that was part of this process. You did it because it was for your benefit. After all it was your education, not theirs.

WOMEN'S ATTITUDES AS THEY DIFFERED FROM MEN'S

The question about attitudes toward freedom and responsibility drew different responses from men and women regardless of which of the two cycles they had been in in the Program. Men tended to answer the question in terms of abstractions (with a few exceptions) and women in terms of their personal experiences in the Program, although there were exceptions in both cases. Women, from both the first and second cycles, usually responded to the issue of freedom as they found it in their daily lives in the Program; a few participants did not welcome that amount of freedom. For one of the two women who said she would not repeat the Program, it was a drawback.

> I remembered there being an awful lot of freedom. Too much freedom for me, I think. Too much freedom to not participate. And the way I handled that at the time was to not participate. To participate elsewhere.

The Program thus could not capture her attention, and she might have dropped out if it had not been for another student from her high school who enrolled in the Program with her and for whom it was a more positive experience.

Other women had more favorable things to report about personal freedom and responsibility in the Program.

> I think [my attitude] changed a lot. It was a lot of freedom for me to deal with personally and as a result I think I was scattered. But at the same time, I think it was a good thing. I don't think it was a bad thing for me. I think it really made me ultimately have to focus myself and take a lot of responsibility for my own learning. Maybe I didn't take as much responsibility for my own learning as I would have liked to, but I think it made me aware that I had to do that.

Another woman thought freedom and responsibility in the Program was beneficial to her both then and now.

> I think it was good for me. I think that I learned a lot about budgeting my time and taking responsibility in the seminars without the faculty member present. I think it was good. I don't think I did as much as I could have done. Maybe having been given less freedom I might have worked a little harder, maybe not. It's hard to know. But I think I benefited from being given the amount of freedom I was given with my time.

And she has applied some of this to child rearing, so the benefits may have been passed on to her children.

> I think I'm probably a little more willing than some parents to let [her child] guide herself in her timing and in her [school] responsibilities.

Many participants, men and women, said they had difficulty separating out the influences of the Program from other influences of family and society, and from the natural course of their own maturation. One woman found both intellectual and personal freedom in the Program, although she attributes her ability to learn to handle the two to her general maturation as well as to the Program. But it has been only after the passage of time that she has been able to trace these insights into her development.

> One of my most vivid memories, particularly the first year of college, is the almost sinful enjoyment of all that freedom. Both intellectually, with the Tussman Program, and in my personal life. Being able to do anything I wanted to do, whenever I wanted to do it. It's a very liberating feeling for a young person who'd always lived at home. Now that I look back, I see the change—it's like if you began to work in a candy store, and the first few months you make yourself sick. [But] by the second or third year you realize there's really a lot more going on than just staying up all night, or whatever. I don't know that the Program influenced me just as much as my own maturation—and growing.

AUTHORITY, GROWTH, AND DEVELOPMENT

In the answers to questions relating to authority and the "givenness" of the requirements in the Program are many statements from participants about aspects of growth and development. Not only are these about the normal stages of separation and individuation that adolescents pass through on their way to adulthood, they are about that *rite de passage* as it took place during the intense politicization and radicalization of this particular generation of college students and the effects on them of the drug and sexual "revolutions." Participants expressed this in a variety of ways, sometimes related to the Program and sometimes not, usually in reference to the family. One woman spoke of the need to change in and of itself as an imperative.

> Your family structure is very important, and I had always been a person who did whatever I was told. And the hard part was changing. I did start to change, and you don't know what to do then, when you've always been brought up to believe that you should do what an authority figure tells you to do and all of a sudden you're starting to . . . hear things differently . . . I think I just *had* to change.

Another woman who began to rebel by going to protest demonstrations and going barefoot on the campus, still found comfort in the parental aspects of the Program.

It was a very, very centering influence in my life because I think I still needed kind of a parent, a little bit of a parent, a little bit of parent centering.

Another woman who was "strongly in rebellion" said the Program provided a focus for her rebellion, and spoke of the changes she went through in the course of her education.

[We had] that feeling of family or feeling like we were in on a good argument, an important place to be. I think that's healthy for education, to ask questions and to be critical, rather than to be accepting and passing. Though I also remember very strongly going to graduate school and not being in rebellion (laughs) and what a relief it was.

Changing relationships with authority, an important characteristic of the Odyssey experience, was encouraged and promoted in the Program, even as it was led by a teacher some labeled as authoritarian. Several men describe how the Program changed their attitudes toward authority in highly individualistic ways. One marked the beginning of this process with the reading of *Paradise Lost*.

I think I became less submissive, perhaps to authority, at that time [of the Program]. I know I was doing that in my personal life, and I know I was finding that in the readings. I was interested in Marx, and Freud, and Malcolm X, and all those sort of iconoclasts that we got into in the last half of the last year. And I read them very, very closely, and really took them seriously. I can't say that I'm a Freudian today, or a Marxist, or an anti-white racist (laughs) like Malcolm X, or rather a liberationist, but all those things were important. It was a really perfect passage for my two years of lower division.

It wasn't easy at all times. I was having personal difficulties, and romantic difficulties, and difficulties with my parents. Their reaction to me was [that] I was becoming a smart-mouthed unbeliever, I was becoming an intellectual, I was becoming argumentative. I was becoming all the things they had brought me up not to do—I was arguing the existence of God. And their reaction was bad while the Program was going on. I was living at home when it started and by the end of the first year I moved out—things were so bad between us that I moved to an apartment in Berkeley. I can think of no place in the Program in which you were encouraged to be rebellious, but without the Program having showed me *Paradise Lost*, I wouldn't know there was a side of the devils and a side of the angels.

FACULTY USE OF AUTHORITY

Problems with authority were frequently part of the testimony of men in the study. Several men spoke of the role that the founder of the Program played in their struggles with authority.

> I thought I got away from home. And here I got somebody just like my father, only worse.... We're in the sixties, there's people selling LSD on the streets, and marijuana. All that freedom to do whatever you want, total anarchy, and you got Tussman here who's doing the same thing we all thought was wrong with our parents. They always wanted to tell us what to do. And I'm gonna do what I wanna do. They told me I can't do this, and this is fun, so I'm gonna do it.

Nonetheless his attitude toward authority was changed dramatically by his participation in the Program. He used imagery from Milton to explain how rebellion, authority, and power took on new meanings for him.

> It ameliorated some of my hostility to it. Being raised military and Catholic, rigid Catholic, I've always had a central focus and problem with authority. Other people telling me what to do. And the Program was a place—an environment where you could challenge authority without seeming to threaten it. The whole point of it was to get you to challenge authority without—to get back to Milton—the "satanic rebellion." I mean, there's a difference between rebellion and challenging authority. You're challenging things, you gotta question them. You learn through questioning, but do you rebel? This is a place where you really had to go pretty far out to rebel. I mean, basically, the "seven deadly sins"—sloth—you had to not do any work. If you didn't turn in your papers and didn't show up at the seminars, they'd kick you out, but there wasn't a whole lot of other sanctions involved. If you called them names and argued with them, they'd argue back.
>
> It taught you the difference between authority and power . . . if you started listening to these people, they had a lot of authority. Everything that you regarded as important in argument these guys had, they had the thoughts, they had some wisdom, much as we hated to admit it, being know-it-all children. So I'd say my attitude became a lot healthier. That

eased the transition quite a bit from being a teenager to being an adult. Because you saw authority as something you could have as well.

This is a striking example of how faculty not only encouraged students to challenge their own intellectual authority but were willing to share it with them as well, treating them more as intellectual equals and easing their entry to adulthood.

The Program might have had a kind of leveling effect on its students—if their own developmental needs required them to become more independent of authority, they could; if they needed to become more accepting of reasonable authority, there were opportunities for that, too. Most importantly, the Program shortened the distance between adolescent rebellion and responsible citizenship by allowing students to view authority not as outside themselves but something they could have, too.

Another man spoke of the role that Tussman in particular came to play in his feelings about authority and gave an illustration of how crucial that issue could be for some students in helping to determine what they learned in the Program.

> My memory of the authority issue for me in the Program centered around the person of Tussman more than the subject matter. I perceived sometime within the first year that whether he was right or wrong about what he clearly knew, he knew lots and lots. . . . Plus his being thirty years older than I or whatever. . . . [But] I was distressed by what I found to be a rigidity and compulsiveness in his character and that finally overshadowed [the material]. I found it increasingly difficult to engage in the issues that he wanted us so passionately to engage in because I felt he had an axe to grind somewhere. And it bothered me. At the same time, I didn't feel motivated to confront him, and I was probably unprepared to as well. But I felt that he was the central authority issue. I wouldn't say I wrote him off because I always found him a pretty interesting guy, pretty fascinating guy. [But] I couldn't really be rejuvenated by the themes and the issues that he was trying to get us engaged in because of his personality. It's a very difficult thing to talk about, authority (laughs).

According to several participants a myth grew up among Program students about Tussman based on the role he played in the faculty deliberations concerning the Free Speech Movement that lent him a kind of liberal mystique. Some knew of his participation in the Loyalty Oath conflict at Berkeley many years before that reinforced his image of a kind of academic "freedom fighter."[2] The man quoted earlier who had been "polarized" by the response Tussman and other faculty took to Program students skipping lectures to attend the Stop the Draft Week protests in the fall of 1967 had trouble reconciling this image of a more liberal Tussman with what he believed to be Tussman's conservative reactions during that week particularly. He was left with somewhat confused and contradictory perceptions of Tussman as both authoritarian and libertarian.

Other men said their feelings about authority focused on Tussman, and one man saw him as a proponent of authority.

> Joe Tussman has this real sort of authoritarian, big brother sort of image that was prevalent through the Program. I mean, he would always give examples of why authority is good and why it's not to be resented, it's not to be scoffed at, it's a good thing, it's a creative thing, it's the right thing. And I had a lot of difficulty accepting that. And I think maybe "getting it," was reconciling yourself with authority. It was one element of "getting it" ... I got parts of it. I'm not sure I got all of it.

"GETTING IT"

Tussman's use of personal authority and the abstract concept of authority in the Program obviously became intertwined for several male participants. And for some, "getting it," getting the point of the Program, became synonymous with accepting Tussman's authority. The notion that there was something in the Program to "get," and that some students did and some didn't, came up several times in the interviews, exclusively with men. Second-cycle men talked in terms of "getting it," and of the "hidden agenda" behind the Program. One man said he thought the expectation behind the Program was

> I should be a good citizen and a good soldier. I thought we were supposed to get the message and to carry that message on.

---

[2] See David Gardner, *The Loyalty Oath Controversy* (Berkeley: The University of California Press, 1967).

Another explanation of "it" came from the man who described Tussman as authoritarian "just like his father only worse." He notes the difference between the curriculum and the "hidden agenda" of the Program.[3]

> The Program was kind of a Hawthorne experiment, where you tell people it's an experiment, and no matter what you do, it's wonderful and they make more light bulbs. Well, it's kind of the same effect here. I mean, telling us it's an experiment made us cheerful for a while. But I didn't understand it, and it was kind of mysterious. I think that probably frustrated a lot of people. I mean, what's the point of all of this other than Tussman's just making us do it . . . I didn't understand it. It just seemed to be that there was something going on then, that it was making progress and it was interesting. . . . A lot of what this program is, is basically an intangible. You try to describe it to people and they say, "Well, you just sat around and read books? Gee." Or they think of something like St. John's where great books are an end in themselves. And this wasn't a St. John's. I mean, St. John's is an elite program. This was not an elite program, if you could do it at junior college [one of Tussman's proposals].
>
> They had a hidden agenda while we were here, and they told us that "Here's the up front agenda, here's what you're going to read now." Tussman, at the end of it says, "Here's what we're really up to," and that's when he started talking about the invisible city and those sorts of things . . . the metaphor that turned up probably towards the end of our second year. It's something that stuck with us, or stuck with me, anyway. He was trying to explain the significance of the culture and the ideal. . . . The long term aspect of the Program, where they grounded you in your culture and the principles, and get you looking at that history that you've dealt with in school but never really came to grips with, you know, [not] the dates but the meaning, the importance of it. . . .

---

[3]This "hidden agenda" was quite different from the "hidden curriculum" Snyder found at MIT (1971). Snyder discovered the hidden curriculum there to be the implicit primacy the Institution placed on grades above all else, and all the devices and procedures students could develop to raise their grades, despite whatever instructions teachers might give them to the contrary about the importance of curiosity, imagination, experimentation, and the like. This amounted to a kind of "double message," whereas the Program kept its ultimate goals unexplicit until close to its end.

Authority in the Program

Tussman explained to us why it was important to focus on the ideal as opposed to what's really going on. There's a real attraction to knowing what's really going on . . . getting away from rigid, meaningless forms and rules, opposition to the Vietnam War . . . it was very easy to lose track of what was important and Tussman was trying to get us to focus on the important—the enduring—and the ideal. The idea started with Plato's cave where the images of things were displayed on the walls and they aren't real but the true believers and knowers can rise up out of the cave and go out into the sunlight and see the true things which are invisible to everybody else. And these are things which do not exist right here in the world, but which the world tries to exemplify and follow. Basic Platonic thought, in some ways. The idea was that there's something fundamental here and you have to strive for the ideal, and part of striving for the ideal is knowing that you're not in it alone, that you've got the other people you can talk to and there is that community, the city. There was a community-city theme that ran through the Program, and that kind of crystallized a lot of what we'd been going through.

Somebody accused Joe of having a hidden agenda in a conversation we were all having downstairs in the lobby and he said, "Of course I've got a hidden agenda. What I was trying to do was get you to look at this stuff and see things this way. Not that you have an ideological viewpoint where you can say, 'This action is right, this one's wrong,' but that you know that there are boundaries to discussion, that you know that there are confines, that you have obligations to other people as well as to your own conscience."

One who said that his understanding of community was the Program's major impact, also said that community was "it," and explained how he understood the point of the Program only at the end when he was asked to write the final paper.

The big lesson I learned from the Program was what I think a community is, which is what the Program's all about. I remember very clearly, there were people that didn't get it. We studied for two years all these different communities, although they never told us that [was what we were studying], or if they did, I missed that day, or it didn't register. Plato's *Republic*, the Bible, John Locke, John Milton, all of these different philosophies. And then our final paper was to write about your definition of community. And I remember getting that assignment initially and going, "What does this mean? I have no idea why I am being asked to do this." I remember this *very* clearly, that we were supposed to define your notion of a community, a working community, and why, and support it. And I realized after thinking about it for a while, that suddenly—what we had been studying over two years was different forms of community. The Bible was a community. I could never figure out why we'd read the Bible. It made no sense to me really, in the scheme of things . . . I didn't understand how it fit in with everything else.

And this final thesis, it fit, it fit for me, and I suddenly realized what I'd been doing for two years. And what I was able to do was to take bits and pieces of all those different philosophies and notions of community and society and put them together and explain what I thought a community was. I don't even remember what I said, but I remember *very* clearly knowing that I had gotten the point of the Tussman Program. . . . I don't ever remember being told specifically that what we were going to do was study a series of communities. I remember being told we were going to be studying these things and comparing Karl Marx to so-and-so, and it was interesting. We were obviously studying philosophy, we were studying political science, but it was never couched in terms of community. . . . I remember a lot of people going, "What are we doing, why are we doing this, what's the point?" And I think there are people who never got it, never really understood what was going on. And what it allowed me to do was to take what I had learned, or thought I'd learned, or not learned, but to really look at what I'd done over that two year period and evaluate it in a completely different way. I hadn't taken it as parts of a whole.

This man provides us with a remarkable example of the process of intellectual and moral development toward which Tussman and the other Program teachers were leading students, and illustrates how difficult it would have been to try to describe this "aha!" experience to students—thus the "hidden" agenda. Each student needed to combine what they had been hearing and reading in their own unique way to form their own creative intellectual interpretation. And by coming to it themselves, rather than receiving it from their teachers, even if that were possible, they could "own" it themselves—a true sharing of authority and intellectual power.

This striving for the ideal within the context of community was in a sense the culmination of the Program, and it is perhaps understandable that Program faculty felt they could not explicitly state it at the beginning, but rather, had to lead students to it gradually through readings and discussions. They must have been aware that this ideal represented a significant cognitive and moral developmental shift for college freshmen, something that could not really be explained to them at least until they had arrived at a different level in their intellectual growth. It is no wonder, then, that in the political climate of the time, some students who did not thoroughly understand the aims of the Program, led by a man who was not adverse to the use of authority, became suspicious of its "hidden agenda" and the attempts to "initiate" them into the world of the "invisible city."

For some students, that stage of commitment was still out of reach in a developmental sense, and their alternative was escape or retreat, in Perry's terms. As suggested earlier, perhaps this accounts for some of the drop-outs who left the Program, as the man quoted earlier said, with the attitude, "This is bull shit, I don't want to deal with this anymore, let me outta here," before they had had the two years necessary to put it all together.

One man from the second cycle took a class from Tussman in the philosophy department after he had completed the Program, and along with other Program graduates, had a second chance to "get it":

> There were a lot of Program people taking the class and hearing him give lectures, and reading the stuff that you had to read for that class. One got a more distilled version of what he was aiming at. Because in the Program he never came out and said, "Here's what I want to do, here [are] the themes I'm stressing, this is where I want to lead you." But in this philosophy class that he gave, you got more of an idea of what his thoughts were about, the relationship with man, the body politic, freedom and responsibility and authority, and all those things. I thought that after I'd taken that class, I understood it better. I was more sympathetic. I was also more mature. I was a year more mature, which at that time, is a lot.

And perhaps more developmentally receptive to Tussman's goals.

First-cycle men did not use the term "getting it" as frequently as second-cycle men, but they did talk about the Program's aims as they understood them. Ironically, one first-cycle man found the Program fell down precisely where its message was tied to the relevant issues of the day.

> We would start out talking about some literary issue and it seemed like a common course of events that we would digress to talking about what, in my opinion, was really uppermost to Joe's mind which was the nature of the contract, the implied contract between the individual and society. Once we got into that, the students could respond with what was going on outside the class right now . . . so the war would come up, or free speech.

> And so the seminars were problematic for me.... What happened often in the seminars was that the bridge from the concepts and the ideas or the principles that were expounded very effectively in the lectures to our daily activity, towards how we act out our lives ... was strained to say the least.

Another first-cycle man talked about the sense he got from the Program for the need for political decisions to be morally grounded, and gave examples of how society might justly deal with poverty or how the prosecution of criminals should be handled today.

> If we think it's most expedient to get rid of [Noriega] by some kind of assassination ... if we thought sanctions were the way to do it ... if we thought a coup was the way to do it ... an economic boycott ... we could do it [but] none of them has any grounding in anything fundamental, has no moral grounding.

It was the intellectual autobiography that came at the end of the two years that forced him to ask himself "these hard questions." He arrived at this understanding as it "came together" for him, in his words, only at the very end.

REJECTING "IT"

Another man talked about how he wasn't ready even at the end to accept the Program's aims. He understood Tussman's theory about how

> people should organize themselves in communities.... That was nice, but I was very aware that I hadn't developed my own [theory] fully, so to write that [in his intellectual autobiography] was premature.... I didn't like the idea that maybe you should sign on as a citizen, be given the choice of whether or not to assume citizenship.

Another man, who would not repeat the Program, rejected much of the Program's premise as he explained why he didn't get it.

> I had a different focus and a different approach, and to this day this is probably true.... I learned to respect that this is the way Tussman thought, and that he wasn't going to think my way ... there wasn't

systematic, rigorous, thorough, extensive imparting of knowledge. I think after all is said and done, part of what you have to do is to give people knowledge. Teach them to think critically, yes, but you've got to do more, that's my thought. . . .

I didn't understand at first why I wasn't getting it. It took until the beginning of the second year for me to figure that out. . . . I don't know that anybody that I talked to was as self-consciously aware that they didn't think [they were able] to learn what they wanted. . . . There were a lot of people, particularly by the second year, who just weren't focusing very much. This was 1966 and '67—a lot going on. You've got nineteen year-old kids who've got a lot of other things that were important to them. I mean, they have relationships, they have drugs, there were just any number of things that were taking up people's attention besides school those days. . . .

The first year, I started to think, "Either I'm some sort of academic Philistine who just doesn't care about what these people are talking about, or there's something here that they're all getting that I'm not." They talk in these concepts that mean a lot to them, about moral rights and stuff emanating from the material, and I thought "Where the hell is this leading? This is leading nowhere for me. . . . Let's get down to brass tacks here, let's talk about it in context." I don't think you can always talk about things in the abstract. . . . That's not where I am . . . I think to the extent you're not getting with the Program, you're reading the same stuff, you're doing it all but you're not getting it the way these people seem to want you to get it, makes you a little bit less certain about, if not your abilities, at least your level of perception. Later I just decided, "Wait a minute. I really do care about learning, about the material, but my approach to it is just far different than theirs, or from Tussman's,"

Another first-cycle man sensed a disparity between Tussman's conception of the Program and that of other Program faculty and teaching assistants, and doubted that there was an "it" to "get." He made the distinction between the Program's approach to education and "getting facts:"

If you hit the right combination of professors and peers, you would have said you got a lot out of it [but] it's possible to go through and miss a lot of the intellectual excitement, if you've been really unlucky the whole way though. You know [G] and these other people who were less exciting, more authoritarian . . . if they'd kept the TA's the second year, there would probably have been more intellectual excitement.

> Because you were not getting a lot of facts. If you're going to college to be a sponge and suck up facts, you were not getting a lot of facts [in the Program]. . . . I think we did go into a lot of depth within a framework. . . . Maybe I just wasn't getting it, what was going on with the Program, but I don't think so. I don't think there was an 'it." I think Joe had an "it." I don't think all the other professors really bought into it. I'm sure the TA's didn't. I know some of the professors didn't. It was a major topic of conversation, I think, that people weren't buying Tussman's conception of the Program. Which kind of made it harder to figure out what you were there for, what you were learning. What the point of it was and whether all the professors were doing the same thing as Tussman was doing. I think it's pretty clear that people in Tussman's section were reporting a very different experience than the people in [B's].

In spite of whether or not there was an "it" to get, he still felt he had made the right choice in enrolling in the Program and would do it again. He compared his experience in the Program with that of his dorm roommate who was in the regular lower division program.

> His life was sheer drudgery, going through the standard freshman programs. And he was not a dummy, he was a smart guy, but he was just miserable . . . an object lesson in what it was like to go through the regular freshman mill at Cal.

And even though he, too, would repeat the Program, another man from the first cycle came to object strongly to the way in which it was not set in any historical context, and to reject what he understood to be Tussman's central premise.

> Throughout the history of political philosophy, Tussman had found philosophers that said something that he liked, that built foundations or structures that he found he could use in his own philosophy. But they were spread out all over history. What he did was pick out these philosophers from wildly divergent historical, social, political, economic contexts, and somehow stuck them all together. He tended not to pay attention to these various contexts of civilization in which they had originated. He wanted to convert us to his own version. . . . I found I was increasingly annoyed all the while at the lack of attention that was paid to the specific context in which each work in itself had come into being. I

Authority in the Program

found that all this stuff was sort of jammed into a stew that, because of this lack of sorting, was very unpalatable.

His remark, "You're not getting down to the nitty-gritty, you're not paying attention to the real question, the most important question here is, 'Is he right?'" is the question he asked that I didn't consider to be valid in any way. I couldn't swallow this business of taking broad statements from wildly divergent contexts and judging their correctness out of the context. . . . I think what happened to me, and probably a lot of others who stayed in the Program, was that the first semester was a lot of fun, very enjoyable, even though it had these aspects that . . . you're disappointed in, it doesn't mean you think the whole thing is for the birds. But what was most wrong with the second term, I thought, was that we had skipped so much between the ancient Greeks and the modern English. It also began to be that I got along quite well with [B], with [D], with [C] and [H].

It is probably not accidental that these last three first-cycle men who rejected "it" either wholly or partially all became close to some faculty and at least one teaching assistant who were in opposition to Tussman, some quite openly. What is not clear, however, is whether opposing faculty at all influenced students to turn away from Tussman's underlying premise of the Program, or whether students first turned away from him and then found faculty who sympathized. From Tussman's memoirs we learn that the Program faculty in the first cycle were by no means unanimously behind him in his conception of the principles behind the Program, and that at least one faculty member and one teaching assistant were actively subversive. As has been noted several times, in view of the much more substantial agreement among faculty in the second cycle, it is likely that faculty unity was a major factor in helping students reach the goals of the Program. When active resistance on the part of several faculty members during the first cycle was reduced to just one dissenter in the second, it stands to reason the message was delivered more clearly and uniformly. Students not only encountered much less faculty subversion, there was only one second-cycle teacher offering students a different view of the Program, and that one was muted since he had removed himself from public faculty interaction. Students had virtually no examples of dissension as they did in the first cycle, and therefore did not receive the faculty permission, perhaps even encouragement, to reject Tussman's concepts of the Program that students did in the first cycle. Reading Tussman's essay, one begins to wonder if all first-cycle faculty "got it," or at least accepted it.

The seemingly mysterious nature of the "hidden agenda" at the heart of the Program—mysterious because Tussman did not believe in making explicit just where he was trying to lead them—did nothing to allay suspicions that he did, in fact, have an unstated goal in mind and a point of view that he was trying to get across to them. Some men, partly because of their psychological development in relation to male authorities especially, and partly because of the intense politicalization of the campus at the time, felt the need to resist faculty efforts to convince them of the validity of their arguments. Men from both cycles tell us that the Program's leader, at least for men, became the magnet for feelings about authority, and that authority was closely linked to the notion of "getting it"—understanding and accepting the point of the Program.

The fact that among these former students, no women mentioned "getting it," and that women sometimes spoke of authority in the Program as "good," or "benign," suggests a gender difference perhaps related to development. This should not be interpreted to mean that women didn't get the point of the Program—several women spoke of connecting what they learned in the Program to professional careers in service to others, as well as to community volunteer work and to the education of their children. (And incidentally, some men also spoke of the importance of community now in their everyday lives; some lawyers chose their profession partly for "moral" reasons inspired by the Program.) Most women in this study apparently simply did not conceive of the Program's agenda as a struggle with authority in the same intense way that many men did.[4]

---

[4] Carol Gilligan (1982) warns of the "observational bias" of psychological theorists who adopt the male developmental pattern as the norm. In her study of gender differences in moral development, she finds females come to have a more contextual and less abstract morality than males. That finding appears to be consistent with the observation reported earlier in this study that women tended to respond to questions about freedom and responsibility in personal and concrete ways while men tended to deal with the abstract concepts.

IMPLEMENTING THE PROGRAM'S AIMS

It was not Tussman's intention that there be a single message or an "it" to get in the Program; rather he aimed to develop habits of mind in the adolescent students he sees as preparing to take "their places among the guardians of civilization" (Tussman 1969, 100). In the opening paragraph of this first book about the Program he states: "The American college must rediscover and renew its commitment to its fundamental purpose . . . for society and for the individual, to develop our rational powers, to heighten sensitivity to and awareness of fundamental human problems, to cultivate and strengthen the habits and dispositions which make it possible for humanity to displace the varieties of warfare with the institutions, the practices, and the spirit of reasoning together . . . " (ibid., 3). And later: "Democracy imposes on everyone a political vocation; this vocation demands a special education (105) . . . the purpose of the first program [the Experimental College Program] is to lead the student into a broad and sustained examination of the 'moral' dimensions of the situation in which he and we find ourselves . . . and must be related to the deep controversial issues of our time" (50).

What Tussman was asking of students was to make a commitment to the political vocation; and doing so required advances in their moral and cognitive development most likely along more than one line. "Reconciling yourself with authority," as one participant put it, was certainly one developmental component; commitment to community and understanding the citizen's obligation to society were others. When participants said they got only "parts of it" they were recognizing that there were several dimensions to the Program's curriculum and aims, and demonstrating that it was not always developmentally possible for each student to achieve all of the Program's goals.

It was suggested earlier that much of the Program's great strength lay in its diversity of teaching methods and strategies and their interrelationships. Another major part lay in the way its plan fit in with, took advantage of, and enhanced the social, ego, cognitive, and moral development of its students. It offered an intimate style of learning, a family-like atmosphere, a "whole family" of mentors from which to choose, and support for resisting the emotional appeals of extremist political groups. It afforded its students a safe haven for the often rocky transition from late adolescence to adulthood, from high school to the large, impersonal university, and from the fierce and attractive distractions of the campus political scene of the day.

The one major developmental need it did not address was the vocational one. Tussman says, "What the freshman is going to become vocationally is really beside the point. He is already something that he will continue to be—a member of a society, a social individual, a center of values and awareness, a person required to act on our common state. He needs to get his bearings there so that, if he doesn't wander off, he can understand the part he is to play" (ibid., 50).

Most of the participants interviewed in this study were content to postpone pursuing the vocational interests that they might have been following had they been taking the regular lower division premajor courses. But there is evidence that a few of its students may have felt they would have been more advanced professionally at the end of college had they been taking introductory lower division courses, or if the Program had paid more attention to their eventual choice of upper division majors. Two factors mitigated against that becoming a serious flaw for most: one, the tenor of the times was decidedly against professionalism and most of the participants in the study did not feel their undergraduate majors had much to do with their eventual careers anyway; and two, for those students who made the connection, the Program helped in some ways to channel their natural, youthful idealism and tie it to future careers in law, psychotherapy, and teaching, for example. Nonetheless, completing the two years of the Program did demand a moratorium from the kind of beginning academic preparation for postcollegiate careers that vocationally oriented students might have felt they needed.

That the Program should help to advance its students along developmental lines should not be surprising since, unlike the regular lower division, it was a program that depended on development: the Program required growth and change in its students, but it also offered them the support they needed to arrive at the "political vocation" of which Tussman speaks. Through the study of "culture in crisis," Tussman proposed to "establish a ritual which will support and encourage the development of a set of intellectual habits consistent with a reasonable, effective, and continuous use of the mind" (ibid., 114). All this was aimed at engendering in students a state of mind "capable of sustaining and developing the life of a democratic society" (104).

The Program's emphasis on its intellectual and moral goals did not mean it neglected all other sides of student growth; in fact it made use of many of them. It recognized the importance of community in validating and affirming students' progression from adolescent to adult reasoning, and in helping them to establish an intellectual identity at the very beginning of their college years. Its teaching structure acknowledged the need for students to learn its moral curriculum in an intimate setting with support from both faculty and peers, factors that aided students in making the cognitive/moral leaps necessary to growth in this area. And as a byproduct of helping to meet these needs, it inadvertently became a more congenial place than the large, impersonal university for many of its students in their transitional phase from high school to college.

But at the same time the Program addressed developmental needs and opportunities for most of its students, it may have not been appropriate for some students whose particular point along their developmental progression was not congruent with what it required. In their summary of growth and change in college, Pascarella and Terenzini (1991, 628) cite evidence to suggest that "instruction interacts not only with personality but also with the student's level of cognitive development . . . not all students will benefit equally from the same classroom settings and instructional approaches." Students wanting more distance from faculty rather than intimacy, students in states of what Perry calls cognitive/moral retreat or escape, students wanting to get started earlier along career lines, students depending on charting their academic progress through exams and grades, would not be well served by such a program, to say nothing of students for whom the Program's curriculum simply held little interest or for whom the teaching styles held no appeal. What looked attractive to applicants in the one-page description of the Program may not have turned out to be what some students actually wanted or came to appreciate once they enrolled. It was fortunate that in the design of the Program there were provisions for such eventualities—an escape hatch for students who became dissatisfied allowed them to return to the regular undergraduate program at any time with a "pass" grade and most of their requirements satisfied so that their academic losses were minimal or nonexistent.[5]

Pascarella and Terenzini (ibid., 565) mention development as one of the major problems "endemic to the study of freshman to senior change," and that "the freshman to senior change during college does not necessarily reflect the impact of college. Many of the dimensions on which change occurs during college may have a developmental base . . . it is important to differentiate change from development."[6] The implications that could be drawn from these statements are that both individual development and the impact of college are separate conditions that influence change in college students. I would suggest that on the basis of the evidence presented here of what former students have said about the effects of the Experimental College Program on various aspects of their own development, the changes they underwent were connected to development; that is, the changes could not occur unless a certain degree of developmental receptivity or readiness had already been reached.

It seems quite likely that the important features of the Program that have been described here actually influenced changes in their social, moral,

---

[5]However, since drop-outs were not interviewed for this study, it is not possible to determine whether or not there were any other losses they might have experienced in transferring from the Program to the regular lower division.

[6]There appears to be a certain overlapping use of the term "development" in the literature; it is often used as if it were synonymous with change, difference, variance, shift, growth, evolution, progression. I use development here to mean an irreversibly expanded, more complex organization of experience, information, and knowledge. Examples would include the ability to accept the fact that there might be more than one answer to a given problem and the ability to take the viewpoint of others into account (Perry's change from dualistic thinking to contextual relativistic reasoning)—commonly cited as effects of college in studies of change from freshman to seniors. Maturation and age are sometimes used interchangeably as well—in their summary of Pascarella and Terenzini's synthesis of research on college outcomes, Barton and Lapointe (1995) state that the latter controlled for maturation when in fact, they controlled for age, which is not the same thing. I use maturation to mean an increase in self-confidence, self-esteem, personal responsibility, among other traits, which appear with age in young people inside or outside college, and which is not necessarily connected to development of an intellectual kind. It is possible Pascarella and Terenzini are referring to maturation as synonymous with development here.

and cognitive development of its students both during and after the Program, and what difficulty there might be in separating change from development is due to the fact that substantial change is part of development. It does not seem likely that development occurs in a vacuum—changes in intellectual ability and moral reasoning in the direction of more flexibility and more differentiated thinking cannot occur without affecting developmental levels, as well as the reverse. If, as Kuhn and Phelps suggest (1979), the most formidable obstacles to intellectual development may be the abandonment of old patterns rather than construction of new ones, and if, as Perry states and Tussman illustrates, courage is required to accomplish these changes, the Program was designed to facilitate development by encouraging and guiding students by means of the interest and close attention of faculty and the support of the entire social/academic community of faculty and peers. Growth and development require change; the Program not only required students to change if they were to "get it," to arrive at a "political vocation," the Program helped them to get there. The Program not only helped them to learn to think for themselves, it furnished them with ideas to think about, lasting well beyond the Program's end. These cognitive/moral changes students came to in the Program are in line with Perry's theories, with increases in intellectual development of students in learning communities as reported by MacGregor (1987), Moore and Kerlin (n.d.), and Tinto (1993), and with the summary of changes due to college cited by Pascarella and Terenzini. Students in the Program arrived at these changes during the first two years and could benefit from them in the latter two. And from the participants in this study, we have evidence of how they changed.

Because there are different strands, or lines, of development—psychological, social, moral, cognitive, for example—that continue into adulthood, it is not surprising that students just completing the Program would not demonstrate or be aware of all of the effects the Program had in initiating or facilitating change until later in their lives when they had reached certain other points in their maturation—marriage, family, careers, community involvement, and the like. That would account for why participants described the Program as "an intellectual net that has stretched over time"—"a seed that was planted"—"a radioactive pill that's inserted ... and ... keeps radiating," as well as why several said they could not have answered questions about its impact until many years after it was over. And because of the time involved in this process, a proper assessment of change and development cannot be accurately done at the time of such a program, or indeed, for many years after its completion.

THE LESSONS LEARNED

CHAPTER 14

Summary, Implications, and Conclusions

CRITICISMS OF THE EXPERIMENTAL COLLEGE PROGRAM AND SUGGESTED IMPROVEMENTS

As part of the interview, we asked participants what changes they would make in the Program. Some participants were virtually uncritical of the Program in its design, structure, and execution. In response to the question, "Would you change it in any way?," six of the 40 people interviewed said they would make no changes at all. For example:

> I can't offer any improvements to it. I think it was really quite effective as it was, for its purpose, for political education, education for people living in a democracy.

Several others mentioned minor changes in the form of "tinkering" or "wishful thinking," at the same time insisting they would not make any major changes:

> I wouldn't change it in any way. I think the structure was pretty good. I would have wanted the people who acted as parents [the teachers] to be different, but that's a silly wish.

Others, even though they might have been very enthusiastic about the Program and positive about its impact on their lives, suggested more substantial changes. Since suggested changes implied some criticisms, no matter how minor, and criticisms made of the Program through the open-ended interviews implied participants would like to see some changes, the two categories are here reported together.

These are general comments on the Program: criticisms, dissatisfactions, or suggested changes to specific features of the Program have been included in the sections on educational and vocational effects and the impact of the various components of the Program. General criticisms and desired changes were evenly distributed between participants in the two cycles, and between men and women, with an average of 14 comments for each group. The six people who had no criticisms or suggestions for change were evenly distributed as well. The remaining group of 34 participants offered 56 items of criticism or desired changes.

Criticisms can be grouped in the three major categories used in the section on the impact of the Program: (1) those dealing with the intellectual and curricular content of the Program; (2) those dealing with various aspects of faculty performance and educational techniques employed in the Program; and (3) those dealing with the social and personal aspects of the Program.

In the first category, comments about the intellectual content of the Program (10) centered on three issues: the need felt for more historical context within which to place the readings; the wish for an interdisciplinary approach; and complaints that the views represented in the readings represented too narrow a spectrum.

It is understandable that although the Program was never intended to provide an historical background for the ideas it presented, it might have been confusing to students to present material in chronological order but separated for the most part from any historical context. Perhaps its very lack of historical context aroused in some students an interest in history. Several of them went on to major in history in the upper division.

The "subdisciplinary" approach of the Program might also easily have been misunderstood by students. Although the Program was designed deliberately to avoid a disciplinary approach, it did, in fact, present views from a variety of perspectives, and in the case of the first cycle drew its teaching faculty from several different departments. Some students, then, believed the intent was to be interdisciplinary and felt it didn't go far enough in that direction. After many years of dividing up their schooling into discrete, mutually unrelated subjects in secondary school, it may not have been easy for some students to fully adapt to a completely adisciplinary approach. When they compared themselves to their peers in regular lower division courses who were taking history and English and chemistry in the customary academic progression, they might have felt a bit behind.

"We read Hobbes, and we didn't read Locke. We read one side, mostly," was the complaint about narrowness of the readings. It was never intended that the reading list represent a balance of different points of view, but that might have seemed biased to some students. The fact that all faculty in the second cycle were from philosophy departments may have led some students to believe they were getting only one side of things.

In the second category, educational criticisms, the greatest number of references were to the need for improved teaching and leadership from the faculty (9), and for developing better seminars, drawing out students who did not find it easy to participate (8). Examples of these comments, all from the first cycle are:

> [A desired change would be] "the training of professors to be more adept at handling eighteen-year-old students. I think a lot of these professors were used to dealing with graduate students and upper division students. I think for many of them dealing with novice college students must have been a new experience.
>
> I don't think they all knew what they were doing. I don't think they all agreed on what the Program was supposed to be, or how you teach young, impressionable college freshmen.
>
> If each of the teachers wasn't going to be responsible for teaching writing, somebody should have been. It was like they let you express your ideas but didn't necessarily tell you whether you were doing a good job at it. Not really enough feedback to change bad habits.

It is not surprising that these critical comments of faculty came from first-cycle participants in view of the dissension among faculty and the high faculty turnover in the second year of that cycle. There were fewer criticisms of faculty performance from second-cycle participants.

The need to improve seminars and draw out students was expressed by people in both cycles in equal proportions:

> There has to be a way to get people like me more a part of it. You need a seminar training course or something before you go into it.

> I wonder if there are ways to draw out students more.

> Instead of leaving the group alone to have their discussion [in the unattended seminar, it would be better] if there were a teaching assistant to lead that discussion rather than leaving you alone. But still having all the other closer contact with professors that you don't normally get otherwise. That's what makes it unique. Keep that—just inject a little teaching assistant element into it.

> Structured a little more in certain areas, like the unattended seminar—have some written account come out of it, keep minutes.

> I'd have some sanctions attached to the journals, or else have more frequent seminars and smaller seminars, just so people will talk.

College and university teachers do not always come to their work with sufficient preparation for teaching, particularly in seminars where especially vocal students can dominate to the detriment of shyer ones, since unskilled teachers are often grateful if anyone speaks up. Not only teachers but students themselves could use training in how to participate in seminars, especially in a program that emphasized seminars.

There were some other miscellaneous comments about the educational structure of the Program. A couple of people wished for more accountability in the form of tests and grades, which was purposefully left out of the Program's design. A few others mentioned the difficulty of not knowing exactly what they were learning or how they were doing. Three people thought it was hard to understand the goals of their work, particularly the papers they were asked to write. A few people from both cycles made comments to the effect that they found the second year of the Program less rewarding than the first, both in terms of readings and general rigor. One participant from the second cycle, while feeling he had gained from the first year, thinks now he might have profited from leaving the Program after the first year, as several students did, although that did not occur to him at the time. (These comments were in contrast to those mentioned earlier who thought the Program came together only near the end of the second year.)

Summary, Implications, and Conclusions

The ethnic and gender representation in the Program drew comments from four people. Two women from the second cycle wished there had been women involved in the curriculum then, either on the faculty or represented in the readings. Two people from underrepresented minority groups wished there had been more cultural diversity in the Program, although they didn't think of it then. While admitting there would have been a problem finding time for this, one says he would have liked to have had "a section on multi-cultural themes where there were separate concentrations on each of several cultures: Asian, Hispanic, Black, European."

In the third category, comments about the social and personal aspects of the Program had to do mainly with two areas, the social side of the Program, and the need for some form of guidance for beginning freshmen. In the social area, it was somewhat surprising, in view of the smallness of the Program and the opportunity for interaction among students it afforded, that a few people still felt the need for closer contact in a more structured fashion:

> I'd find more ways to get student bonding going on. . . . If people had to work, find some way through funding support for students not to have to go out to work, or work on the house, build [something] for the Program, but work *together*, not have to go work outside.[1]
>
> What really would have worked for me at that time would have been to have more scheduled things where relationships were deliberately built . . . have a stronger social program where it's not just academic, where participation was encouraged and built and developed.

And other people, who lived at home and commuted to the campus, expressed regret that they didn't have more time to "hang out with the kids," a perpetual complaint of the commuting student, but one perhaps felt more acutely by these students in the Program who were not always able to take advantage of the opportunity to socialize and study with their peers in the cozy environment of the House.

Tussman himself suggested the need for a house manager: someone on the program staff who would monitor the use of the building so that all

---

[1]This participant worked full-time on campus while in the Program; a few others worked part-time on and off campus.

students could feel comfortable there, and abuses could be prevented. The House was an ideal place to generate student sociability, yet some study participants wished for more activities planned for that purpose. More activities designed to help students get to know each other and faculty better both at the House and at retreats would help facilitate the integration of the social and the intellectual aspects which are important to student development.

The picture of the entering freshman student as bewildered and vulnerable was put forth by some people who expressed a need for more attention to their rather fragile state. A few wished for opportunities to discuss personal problems of an emotional and social nature:

> What it didn't touch on was the interpersonal, psychological stuff. We read Freud, and that was great, but its design was not to work on the emotional side, and I don't know whether that was good or bad. Relationship talk was taboo. . . . I'm ambivalent about it . . . I think it could have been addressed. I just know that the whole social, emotional part of me as a male in society growing up is sort of short-changed. The Program [could] provide the kind of atmosphere where those issues could be addressed . . . in a group situation, with discussion about personal issues . . . like drugs, family dysfunction, all could have been handled within that framework, enriching the other part of the Program.

Others wished for guidance in more practical matters, such as "a basic course in library science," or information about extracurricular activities on the campus. Some wanted more help with choosing majors: "Have people come in from other departments [to explain] what is it like to be in that field." Even though participants generally reported no major difficulties with the transition to the upper division, some said they were uneasy about not having had the usual introductory lower division courses. This could be remedied by bringing in guest lecturers, faculty or graduate students, from academic departments to describe them to prospective majors, and by allowing students to visit upper division classes. (Students in the Program were encouraged to audit outside classes; some did, but many did not.)

A few expressed the wish for career guidance, something most certainly never considered in the design of the Program:

> I would have liked the Program—I would have liked somebody in those years to have done more to have helped me be directed towards what it

was that I wanted to do when I grew up. And there was nobody, whether it was in the Program, or—I don't think I ever saw a college counselor while I was at Berkeley.

Given the nondisciplinary nature of the Program, it would have helped some students to know about the career guidance offered in the Counseling Center at UCB.

One observed the discrepancy between the inclusive, coherent organization of the curriculum and pedagogical structure of the Program and the absence of attention to the personal side of student life.

> It seemed like there's some issues of responsibility around the Program that were really unfulfilled. You know, there was a lot of thought about [how] the Program was going to be this sort of great, all-encompassing experience but I think there was only responsibility taken for certain aspects, like training people to think in a certain analytical way. And there wasn't enough thought or responsibility on the parts of the founders of the Program in terms of what was happening to the rest of these kids' lives. And I think that that could have been thought out more thoroughly.

These comments bring up an important but perhaps easily overlooked aspect of the Program: in proposing to undertake the entire education of first- and second-year students, except for the one outside course each quarter or semester, it set up expectations that it would encompass all aspects of their undergraduate lives, not just the intellectual, academic, or educational—that it would offer, for instance, the usual orientation functions most colleges and universities offer entering students during the first few weeks of the term, and would offer counseling services. The Program was in most ways self-contained and was viewed by its students as such. (They usually called it the "Tussman College" or "Tussman Tech" rather than the "Experimental College Program" or "The Program," and some wore "Tussman College" sweatshirts.) It seems logical, therefore, that some participants should believe that the kind of attention to students' extracurricular life described above naturally belonged in the Program rather than in another campus agency such as the Counseling Center.

While any special program may focus on academic issues, the student, especially the beginning student, often has needs of a more personal nature that can not be met by an academic program. As facilities designed to address these needs are regularly part of universities, students can learn about such facilities through the special programs themselves. Services such as personal counseling and a guide to using the library should not necessarily be provided by special programs, but some guidance should be provided to help students find where to go within a university the size of Berkeley for such help.

A program such as this cannot be stretched to include all the intellectual needs or desires of students, but it is natural that, having a taste of each in this program, students might want it to be both interdisciplinary and historical. Lifting students out of the ordinary kind of undergraduate education where they must pick and choose among many alternatives each term, a program like this runs the risk of being considered exclusionary if it does not include all parts of a standard lower division educational program. Some participants seemed to understand this very well, and thought the Program "did what it set out to do" and lived up to the intentions set forth in the invitational letter. Perhaps some forgot that letter in the excitement and confusion surrounding the beginning of college. Some students enrolled in the Program without ever having seen the letter. If students in a special program like this do not take part in the usual freshman orientation, they need an orientation of their own that includes both information about the program as well as about the university of which it is a part, and reminders about how the two are related and how they differ.

One positive aspect of the Program was the case of transferring back to the regular university. Such programs are not suitable for all students for a variety of reasons already mentioned—some are vocationally oriented, uncomfortable with the postponement of career choices, and want to begin a prevocational course of studies; some need grades and tests in order to measure their own progress. Flexibility in allowing students to transfer back to the regular university is essential, since they may not discover their needs until well into a program. In Tussman's program, there were no penalties in terms of lost credits, and participants thought that was important.

Overall, the question about desired changes in the Program elicited no major criticisms of the Program, beyond the various suggestions for improvement we have been discussing, and participants seemed generally content with the way it operated. However, it must be borne in mind that these participants were the students who were satisfied enough with the Program to stay the whole two years; those with major dissatisfactions presumably left before that, as well as students who liked the Program but felt they had gotten from it all they could sometime before the end of the two-year cycle.

SUMMARY OF THE PROGRAM'S EFFECTS

This completes the picture of what participants had to say about the Experimental College Program during the interviews. Reprising what has been reported in earlier chapters, they have told us what appealed to them about the Program, mostly the small size and close contact with faculty. We have learned about how they viewed the faculty, how they appreciated their availability, their diversity in teaching styles, and how and why some were judged more effective than others. Students testified to the importance of having the House, a place for almost all Program activities, and how it contributed to creating an educational community where they could learn from each other as well as from faculty. They found the readings universally popular and diverse. Diversity was also an attribute of other educational features—the reading list, lectures, seminars, unattended seminars, papers, and tutorials each judged by some to be the best part of the Program. But most importantly, the features gained effectiveness through their integration, allowing students to experience a variety of learning situations and to fit them together with the curriculum.

Almost every former participant, whether they would choose to repeat the Program or not (and more than nine out of 10 of them did repeat), felt they had gained something from it. Very often they did not realize all the benefits the Program had for them until years after the Program was over. Frequently the influences of the Program were intertwined with influences from other sources and sometimes served to reinforce previously held values.

We find testimony to the diverse effects of the Program on the lives of these 40 participants in the areas of education and work. Some felt the Program was the most significant educational experience of their lives, some that it was a model for an ideal kind of education. Some owed the motivation for attending graduate school directly to the Program. Many said the Program taught them to become independent thinkers, taught them how to learn for ideas rather than for grades, and to read critically. Several thought it nourished their creative abilities.

The jobs and careers of participants included law and teaching, medicine, the arts, business, the helping professions, public service, community organization, homemaking. Some of them found little or no effects of the Program on their work, but for the majority who did, there appeared to be more of an influence of the Program in particular fields—law, education, civil service—where some found their "callings" through the Program. The lawyers found a range of its effects in their practices, from help in writing briefs to the ability to take a long-range view of problems to an understanding of the bases of American constitutional law. Not only teachers but former participants practicing other professions found a life-time appreciation of liberal education in the Program, and an ability to look at educational issues in depth and from a wider perspective. Some found training in leadership in the Program to be useful in business; others found the respect they learned for other people's opinions useful in settings as varied as an interdisciplinary hospital support team and law practices.

The Program addressed the developmental needs of its students; the politics of the place and time affected its functioning; and the learning community it established was important to student development. We know what improvements these former students would make in the Program.

In light of all this evidence of the various successes of the Program, we can now turn back to the questions raised at the beginning of the book: Why did it end? What factors likely to affect the outcome were significant after all? Is there a place for programs like this in undergraduate education today? Summing up the evidence presented here it seems fair to conclude the Experimental College Program, while not necessarily a program suitable for all lower division students at Berkeley at the time, nonetheless had considerable merit and was a great success in the eyes of the participants interviewed for this study. It had a place on the campus. Roughly 10 percent of entering freshmen applied in 1965 and 1967 and two-thirds of its enrollees were satisfied enough to remain in the Program. Returning to the regular upper division in the university, participants reported no major difficulties in making the transition, although many felt a sense of loss at having to leave the intimacy and intellectual satisfaction they had found in the Program. Many felt the Program had "eased them" into U.C. Berkeley, that it had "bought them time," had given them a feeling of being special, and provided a kind of "safe haven" in a large, impersonal university in turbulent times. Students who completed the Program earned higher grades during the rest of their two years at Berkeley and remained to graduate in significantly higher numbers than others who were not students in the Program—perhaps, because as some testified, it had made them "stronger for the rest of the college years," providing "ballast" and an "anchor," a kind of half-way house in their progress toward independence.

The interviews provided evidence of immediate gains from the Program—gains in critical thinking, in reading, writing, discussion, and significantly, in the integration of these skills. It created an effective intellectual and educational community within which it could further its educational goals, aided by close faculty interaction with students and close faculty attention to individual intellectual development through regular tutorials and a variety of pedagogical approaches. Students found a psychological and academic identity in the small, intimate Program and a sense of confidence in themselves that eased their entry into the larger, more impersonal university. Some participants, many of them women, learned discussion skills in the Program that they could apply in upper division seminars. The Program, built around issues of political authority, engaged many students in a debate they have found rewarding and worthwhile to this day. It was developmentally appropriate and enhancing for many students, and those students for whom it was not, or for whom the Program turned out to be not what they wanted, could drop back to the regular lower division without loosing academic credit.

The Program achieved its long-range goals of education for responsible citizenship in what participants said about how it instilled in them a sense of the democratic tradition, the importance of democratic institutions and of community, and the fundamental questions it raised with which they are still concerned today.

REPLICATIONS

Affirming the efficacy of programs based on the Meiklejohn-Tussman curricular and pedagogical approach is the fact that it has been replicated—at Vico College at SUNY-Buffalo,[2] at San Jose State University, and at Malaspina College in British Columbia where it has become a two-year

---

[2]My thanks to Professor David Hollinger for bringing this to my attention.

degree completing program in conjunction with the University of Victoria.[3] Its curriculum has been adapted as the Arts One first-year program at the University of British Columbia in Vancouver, which recently celebrated its twenty-fifth year anniversary, and its pedagogical structure at Evergreen State College in Washington State, which has led to the formation of the Washington Center for Improving the Quality of Undergraduate Education, a statewide consortium emphasizing both faculty and curriculum development, which has itself given rise to its many replications, or adaptations.[4] Tussman's book about the Program, *Experiment at Berkeley*, is still being read and referred to in discussions of curricular reform. It was used recently at Carleton College in a review of their curriculum. Tussman's plan influenced administrators at University Extension at Berkeley in the design of their new Humanities Certificate program. There is even a vestige of Meiklejohn's Experimental College remaining at the University of Wisconsin in the form of Integrated Liberal Studies, begun in 1948 and reconstituted in 1981. It is an interdisciplinary program consisting of 10 related courses focused "on the great ideas and great ideals of Western civilization and their application to contemporary problems"[5] although changed and adapted, it is a direct descendant of the Experimental College. One of several learning communities on the campus,[6] and following in the footsteps of its originator, it may become residential, as was the original Experimental College at Wisconsin.

These innovations modeled after the Meiklejohn-Tussman programs may be subject to the same difficulties that faced those original programs as they run against the strong main currents of American mass higher

---

[3]Gary Bauslaugh, "Proposal for a Bachelor of Arts in Liberal Studies offered by The University of Victoria at Malaspina College," Malaspina College, British Columbia, 1990.

[4]F. Gabelnick, J. MacGregor, R.S. Matthews, and B. L. Smith, "Learning Communities: Creating Connections Among Students, Faculty, and Disciplines," *New Directions for Teaching and Learning*, No. 41 (San Francisco: Jossey-Bass, 1990).

[5]"Integrated Liberal Studies," University of Wisconsin, College of Letters and Science.

[6]See the Bradley Evaluation Committee, "End-of-Year Progress Report on the Bradley Learning Community," University of Wisconsin, Madison, August 15, 1996.

education. The modular system in place almost everywhere has made a fixture of the single course taught by individual faculty members. Relatively few teachers have the background, the training, or the desire to teach in these demanding programs, even though teachers who do so frequently find them rewarding. In research universities the attention given to research is incompatible with the commitment to teaching and the availability to students required of faculty to run these programs. Few students today hold the casual attitudes toward future jobs and careers that students did in the sixties and seventies, and they are less willing to take chances on untried, experimental, and broadly based liberal arts programs. On the other hand, the many learning communities that have sprung up in mostly smaller colleges across the nation have adopted the pedagogical methods used in the Program rather than its curricular content, are shorter in duration, are composed of related courses, and can be less demanding of faculty and administration. They would not be considered programs in the Meiklejohn-Tussman sense, but they are apparently thriving.

THE PROBLEM OF STAFFING: THE PROGRAM'S ACHILLES HEEL

Still, the tradition has survived, passing from Meiklejohn at Wisconsin to Tussman at Berkeley, who inspired Hollinger and others at Buffalo and Rowan and Marriage at the University of Vancouver who had taught in Tussman's program at Berkeley, and who in turn, inspired Bauslaugh and others at Malaspina. If the Program was a success in the views of former students, if an adaptation of Meiklejohn's first experiment at Wisconsin lives on, and if Tussman's vision of educational reform was potent enough to lead to reincarnations from Buffalo to Vancouver over a period of 20 years, some of them still thriving, why did it last only four years at Berkeley?

The first chapter suggested four factors likely to influence the outcome of the Experiment at Berkeley: the kind of educational reform that the Program represented; the campus on which it was conducted; the political implications of the particular time in campus history in which it came to life; and the places occupied by its students in their developmental progression.

Of these four factors, the last two probably worked against its acceptance by some post-FSM students at Berkeley. Its reliance on classical literature, which did not include women or many minority writers, was subject to accusations of irrelevance; its passionate, authoritative leader devoted to his vision of lower division education and his unstated goals of educating students to become better citizens made him suspect of authoritarian coercion; its appeal to reason in the long-range interests of the community, set against the prevailing mood of emotional distrust of all authority and the call for tearing down educational institutions not meeting the demands of the movement, all made the Program "politically incorrect" in the eyes of some students. The Program made demands on its students that the regular lower division did not: a kind of suspension of disbelief about its political underpinnings and a willingness to cooperate with the faculty's use of authority in insisting upon the fulfillment of the requirements of regular attendance at lectures and seminars and papers turned in on time.

On the other hand, the issues of political and civil authority and responsibility were, after all, *the* issues of the times and may have attracted many students to the Program where they found a forum through which to work through their conflicts about moral authority. Arguing with faculty face to face may have provided a natural outlet for timely developmental expressions of rebellion not possible with professors "so far away on a stage that you couldn't see them." The Program required students to grow morally and intellectually, to make commitments, to abandon old ways of thinking and perceiving society and the world. It offered them new ways of relating to authority. Developmentally it afforded them a challenge and means to meet that challenge. It stood for reason and order and commitment to community when voices on the campus told them to "throw your bodies on the machine and make it stop," "steal a book," and "tune in, turn on, and drop out." The appropriateness of the curriculum and the skill of its faculty in engaging students in important issues while wrestling with their artful forms of resistance, its collegial learning community together, and its pedagogic approach to mediated learning with close faculty attention to student development all held the Program together at a time when regular undergraduate programs were under attack. Its many advantages made it appealing enough to attract students even in that unlikely time, although perhaps those were the very qualities that many students were seeking when the university as an institution was threatened by critics both inside and outside. The political confusion and turmoil of the late sixties at Berkeley may have turned out to be precisely the setting most compelling to many

Summary, Implications, and Conclusions

students for this kind of program dealing with fundamental problems in democracy and periods of moral crises. It was both the best and the worst time to present this Program to students on the Berkeley campus.

The first two factors did not bode well for the Program. As an example of telic rather than popular reform,[7] it demanded hard work and personal commitment from students and faculty alike. And a large, prestigious research university may not be the ideal setting for any kind of crusade for undergraduate curricular reform. Tussman's mission of initiating lower division students into the responsibilities of society might have been appealing to some on the Berkeley faculty and in the administration, but Berkeley faculty were busy meeting demanding research schedules and administrators were busy keeping state legislators at bay and student demonstrators under control. After the first cycle, neither academics nor administrators were free to take up the cudgels and join Tussman in his missionary crusade to turn the wasteland of the first two undergraduate years into a coherent program with a moral purpose, even if they were so inclined. Despite all this, the Program in both cycles appealed to twice as many students as it could admit and retained two-thirds of them in both cycles. Lack of appeal to students was not the Program's undoing.

Moreover, neither the administration nor the Academic Senate disapproved of the Program. The basic obstacle to sustaining the Program lay in the faculty tenure problem. In his essay, Tussman explains how it defeated him at the end.

> In the Program at Berkeley I wanted to avoid the "second class [nontenured] citizen' problem by getting some Berkeley faculty ... and ended up in the war of the first run. For the second run I gathered a non-Berkeley faculty that did ... things brilliantly, but I could not solve the problem of turning them into Berkeley faculty.

---

[7]Even attempts at popular reform at Berkeley at the time did not always succeed. Strawberry Creek College (formally the Collegiate Seminar Program) allowed faculty to escape from regular departmental teaching and students to take politically popular alternative courses, but the courses were unrelated, no community developed, and the "College" failed to attract or retain students in sufficient numbers. Report of the Ad Hoc Committee on The Collegiate Seminar Program to the Berkeley Division of the Academic Senate, University of California, June 14, 1979.

Personal as well as institutional factors were at play in Tussman's decision not to continue the Program. While he had found willing faculty who were committed to his plan during the second cycle, he was not able to keep them at Berkeley as untenured faculty. In the last pages of his essay, he expresses his doubt and ambivalence about what it might have taken to continue the Program. He was baffled by the problem of tenure for the second-cycle faculty, an impossibility since they were members of a program and not a department, and there was no chance of getting five tenure positions in other departments in the university, especially for faculty who were recruited as good teachers rather than for their research reputations.

Beyond the Gordian knot of tenure lay another problem even more difficult to resolve. And that was Tussman's own ambivalence about tenure for Program faculty. He cited problems in the collective life of the Program, its intensity, its intimacy with other faculty and students and the lack of the "healing privacy of a course of one's own." He concluded about tenure for Program faculty: "I was not sure that I would want it or could recommend it." He candidly admits to being exhausted at the end, leaving one to wonder if the cause of his exhaustion was the work of leading and teaching in the Program for four years, his consistent battling with the administration over the tenure problem, or his underlying doubts about whether tenure was even advisable. Perhaps it was all three.

IMPLICATIONS FOR THE FUTURE

Tussman's dilemma and the demise of the Program illustrate a fundamental problem with experimental programs: they usually rest on the shoulders of one visionary and charismatic faculty member, supported by the energy, enthusiasm, dedication, and imagination of a few other individuals. When the people responsible for organizing the program leave, it has little then to hold it together.[8] (Indicative of the burden Tussman carried to make his program work, one first-cycle faculty member said that when Tussman was present in the House, the Program worked; when he wasn't, it didn't.) Are all of these experiments at educational reform,

---

[8]Vico College at SUNY-Buffalo was successful enough to last 10 years. But it disappeared after all its faculty left SUNY.

whatever their merits, bound to fail? Is it worth the time and trouble to initiate them if they are so fragile and vulnerable to the educational stamina of one or two or a few faculty, only to wither away when they leave?

Answers to these questions involve at least two factors: the first is their basic appeal, adaptability, and resilience over time. It has been almost 70 years since Meiklejohn began the Experimental College at Wisconsin, and his original model, although modified, has reappeared twice in its original home; Tussman's model is currently being reborn in British Columbia. Each replicator, beginning with Tussman, has made changes in the preceding example. Tussman himself made changes from the first to the second run of his program, and thereby made it stronger; the program at Malaspina has tried to circumvent some of Tussman's difficulties by establishing closer ties with faculty and administration right from the beginning, as well as by using already tenured faculty. The originator there has purposefully dropped back to leave the continuation of the program to others, thereby avoiding some of the problems of burn-out that Tussman experienced. The version at Evergreen State has been modified substantially, but they seemed to have solved the staffing problem by using a rotation of tenured faculty and a combination of visiting and junior faculty—just the kind of "second-class citizens" Tussman wanted to avoid. So the model is adaptable, and modified versions of it endure, even if some of the original principles must, on occasion, be sacrificed.

THE NEED FOR LONG-TERM RESEARCH

A second factor bearing on the life cycle of the Meiklejohn-Tussman telic reforms is the fact that many of their effects on students and even their major impacts do not show themselves for many years. Students graduating from such programs may appreciate the quality of their educational experiences at the time, but it is only after the passage of time that students begin to comprehend their full value, as this study of the Experimental College Program and other alumni studies have shown.[9] The resulting time

---

[9]Before enough time has passed for this kind of long-term assessment to be made, evaluations of special programs like this depend almost entirely on contemporary student evaluations and contemporary judgments of faculty and administrators that are subject to campus hearsay. For example, some observers

lag produces a kind of dormant period during which enthusiasm for the program may appear to have expired, only to spring up again in another place in another form, perhaps as another former student comes to the full awareness of the long-term value of such a program and sees an opportunity to renew it.

This tendency for special programs, indeed for colleges themselves, to produce delayed effects is an argument for more long-term research. If we expect the college experience to have a lasting impact on students, we must find ways to document and explore those changes for periods longer than the four years in college or even five to 10 years afterwards.[10] Longitudinal studies are ideal, tapping into judgments of former students about their

---

at Berkeley judged the Program to be a failure at the time because it ceased to exist and because some of the teaching assistants who had been let go after the first year of the first cycle had negative things to say about it. Even some 10 years later, Arthur Levine in the *Handbook on Undergraduate Curriculum* (1978) said the Program was "a victim of changing times" because it "permitted students little if any involvement in governing the curriculum," while this study of long-term effects indicates that students in the Program were for the most part pleased to have their curriculum chosen for them, no matter how much they may have complained at the time.

[10] A case in point exists in the files of the Educational Process Study that formed the basis of the study of first-cycle students (Suczek 1972). Five years after they had completed the Experimental College Program, participants in the Educational Process Study were sent questionnaires asking them to evaluate their experience at Berkeley. About a dozen Program graduates who later were participants in this current study were among those who answered questionnaires in 1972. Several stated in the questionnaire that they had come to appreciate their experiences in the Program, but one in particular was especially negative about its influence. Now, 20 years later, that participant gave very positive comments about the Program—he told me it had been the greatest educational experience of his life. He said that during his college years and for sometime afterwards, he'd had severe conflicts with his father, later resolved. It is quite likely this case illustrates the theories put forth in the chapter on authority about developmentally based conflicts with authority interfering with students' receptivity to the Program's purpose. It certainly illustrates the fact that recent college graduates do not always evaluate their college experiences in the same way they do later in life, and these early evaluations therefore are subject to change in the light of later experience and developmental position.

educational experiences at different points with the passage of time. But as we hope this study has shown, intensive interviews with alumni as they approach mid-life can reveal much about their mature judgments of the effects of their college experiences, even if their memories have faded.[11]

This study of the Experimental College Program did not by any means exhaust its research potential: faculty have not been systematically interviewed, nor have drop-outs from the Program. Former students who applied to the Program but were not been offer an ideal source for more comparative studies, with questions probing more deeply into differences in attitudes and behavior of the two groups.[12] And it is not impossible that another set of interviews with the same participants after more time has passed might produce even more data about what the Program has meant to them as they progress further along the life cycle. Many participants in this study enjoyed thinking about and discussing their experiences in the Program; there could be benefits to periodic symposia of graduates discussing among themselves, along with faculty, administrators, and current students, ways to capitalize on the successes of the Program as well as ways to improve it. Comparative studies of the long-term effects of other kinds of special undergraduate programs—university abroad programs,

---

[11]If their evaluations of the Program were to depend on memory alone, they would be subject to the distortion, the "rosy glow" effect of memories of those golden college years, where painful memories are often screened out or softened and mostly the pleasant ones remain. But participants were asked to make judgments about what the Program has meant to them over the years, and what it means to them now, and to try to trace its influence on their lives—quite a different task from that of remembering specific details. There is no doubt some of their memories are subject to distortion over time, and that some of the participants made an effort to look for positive effects of the Program. There may have been in some cases some minor confusion between what Spence (1982) calls "historical" truth and "narrative" truth. But not remembering names of some faculty members or just which nights they had dinner at the House or not remembering accurately how well they performed on certain assignments are not serious obstacles to recognizing the impact that the Program had on them over the years.

[12]One problem arising in doing such long-term research is finding former students after many years have passed: any special program such as this would do well to keep addresses up to date, but of course, in the case of programs such as these which have been discontinued, the machinery for doing this is lost.

honors programs, Watson fellowships, the Strawberry Creek College at Berkeley—would serve to put the Experimental College Program into a broader perspective.

Tussman has suggested the Experimental College Program would be suitable for junior college, constituting the first two years of college;[13] Malaspina College has added it as a degree-completing program to its junior college, making it the last two college years, but the gains and losses of the two arrangements have not yet been weighed. Many study participants, particularly women, thought they had not taken full advantage of the Program as undergraduates; some wished they could have another go at it at this stage in their lives. In spite of Tussman's impassioned pleas for a program to fill the wasteland of the first two undergraduate years, we need to know more about the best time in life in which to participate in this kind of program, or what kind of programs are best suited to which stages of the life cycle.

Effective programs like these need not be and are not necessarily based on the Meiklejohn-Tussman theme of education for democratic citizenship. Other topics, such as the ethical issues raised by immigration in a democratic society, the moral concerns surrounding advancing science and technology in modern society, the relationship of arts to society, are examples of subjects around which similar programs might be built.[14] These ideas need to be tested through experimentation and research. Many study participants testified to the advantages of having two years to establish the learning community that made the Program work. Yet the Arts

---

[13]The merits of this argument are that such a program might stimulate continuation in a four-year program, and that if students did discontinue their higher education after two years, they would have at least had a good start on a liberal education.

[14]As described in the first chapter, one of the most important and successful components of the Experimental College Program was the curriculum, the "rich and varied literature in which powerful minds grappled with fundamental human problems." As noted in Chapter One, Tussman called it the "concrete plan" for leading "the student into a broad and sustained examination of the 'moral' dimensions of the situation in which he and we find ourselves." Whatever the subjects of other such programs, their full efficacy in terms of intellectual and ethical development would seem to depend on a similarly deep curriculum with a moral dimension.

Summary, Implications, and Conclusions

I program at Vancouver has survived as a one-year program: a closer look at how these two programs differ and how they each accomplish or accomplished their purposes would be instructive. And now that new modes of teaching through interactive technology and distance learning are being introduced to undergraduate education, questions arise about the suitability of different types of instruction for different kinds of students, "traditional" and "nontraditional," at different times and places.

Many of the gains reported by former students in the Tussman program are similar to gains Pascarella and Terenzini found arising from attendance at four-year colleges—gains in verbal, general quantitative, oral and written communication, and in analytical skills, development of critical thinking, intellectual flexibility, and the use of reason. The Tussman program produced these same results in the first two undergraduate years, thus positively influencing retention rates and enhancing learning in the subsequent two years of college. Identifying through research the points in the usual four-year college experience associated with these gains, as sone researchers have begun to do and comparing them with the Experimental College educational trajectory could be of help in planning improvements in the four-year programs.

LESSONS FROM THE PROGRAM

This study has demonstrated again that students generally learn best when their imagination is captured and their feelings engaged, even if those feelings are somewhat negative; they tend to learn best in small groups where cooperation rather than competition is the rule; they often need encouragement to make contacts with faculty in the form of regularly scheduled appointments; they welcome cohesive course programs; many in their first two years are glad to have the sequence of their instruction laid out for them; and "ordinary" college students can master difficult material when it assumed that they can and learning takes place in a supportive community.

The results of the study have demonstrated the value to the effectiveness of the Experimental College Program of a variety of pedagogical approaches: team teaching, the use of an accumulation of students' papers over a given time period in "portfolios," individual tutorials, lectures focused on understanding of the readings rather than on imparting information, emphasis on the students' responsibility for their own education, and most importantly, the establishment of a learning community made possible through the sharing of a common curriculum as well as through faculty sharing intellectual power with students. The study has also pointed to areas where the Program could be improved: more recognition of student needs falling outside the strictly academic arena; the need for more student involvement in both faculty and student led seminars; the monitoring of more peripheral but nonetheless important assignments such as the journal.

This study was not intended to be a full-fledged evaluation of the Program as a whole, but rather a look at the short- and long-term effects as reported by former students. From what they have to tell us, it seems fair to say the Experimental College Program was successful enough to have produced both short-term gains and lasting positive effects for these participants. It has been successful enough to have spawned successors. And Tussman's failure to solve the problem of staffing the Program with either tenured or nontenured faculty may have helped others following him to avoid that pitfall.

From Meiklejohn to Tussman to Rowan to Bauslaugh, to Vico College, Evergreen State, and others (perhaps someone from Tussman's program, since a few participants did talk about starting programs themselves)—the sputtering torch continues to burn. Seventy years is not an insignificant span of time for a reform to stay alive in a system of state institutions of higher education that is hardly more than two hundred years old (if one takes as its beginnings the chartering of the University of Georgia in 1785 or the first instruction at a state university at the University of North Carolina in the 1790s). The fact that Meiklejohn's and Tussman's programs and their closest successors have mostly appeared at large, public universities is an indication of the need recurrently expressed to bring more liberal and humanistic education to these institutions that are usually focused on research rather than on teaching, and on professional rather than liberal education.

Lessons have already been learned and put into practice for surmounting the difficulties of establishing small programs like this that may go against the grain of the host institution. Using Tussman's Experimental College Program as a template, the following are some of the key characteristics of successful programs.

1. A long-range solution to Tussman's staffing dilemma, involving either enough tenured faculty from the beginning to ensure continuation

(Malaspina) or some combination of tenured, visiting, and junior faculty (Wisconsin, Evergreen State). Faculty agree about the purpose and methods of the program and meet regularly to discuss the curriculum and student progress. Tussman's experiment in communal leadership during the first cycle of his program was not successful—one person or several people take charge, even on a rotating basis.

2. A cohesive and coherent curriculum, one that is not subject to current whims and fads, reflects faculty confidence in their ability to tell students what they should be reading. This does not preclude room for occasional additions, but if the basic curricular structure is open for constant debate, as it was at San Jose State, it cannot last.

3. If the curriculum has a moral dimension, it will be more challenging and meaningful to students. It might not necessarily be the "Athens-to-America" moral curriculum used by Meiklejohn and Tussman, but if it does not advance ethical/intellectual development it will not take advantage of this time in their lives when, moving outside the moral authority of the family and striking out on their own, they are specially responsive to ethical concerns. If the curriculum is anchored in a time frame that enables students to find themselves on a point along a continuum of tradition rather than historically unfocused, it will help them see themselves and their time in "the long view."

4. A learning community in which students and faculty participate in an equalitarian mode that allows faculty to share intellectual power with students. Continuity of faculty and students over a two-year span, as in the case of Tussman's program, helps develop familiarity and trust and provides the setting for that rare experience of everyone sharing a common reading program. The absence of exams and grades allows a spirit of cooperation to take the place of competition. A stable academic environment enhances students' ability to form academic identities. A physical location for the exclusive use of the program adds significantly to the formation of that identity and allows for informal but important student-faculty interaction to take place. (Malaspina has recognized this and built a separate building in which to house its program.)

5. Individualized instruction permits students to receive the kind of faculty attention and support necessary to help them make the moral/cognitive steps required to progress to other developmental stages. This kind of teaching helps to make the curriculum accessible to all university students, not just an elite cadre of honor students.

6. Requiring undergraduate students to use original rather than secondary sources is a potent device to develop critical and independent thinking. The usual reliance of students on textbooks and secondary sources, encouraged by most faculty, interferes with their own exploration of the meaning of required readings. The message that faculty recognize the students' ability to think for themselves encourages that ability.

7. A program using a team of faculty with a diversity of teaching styles and approaches to the same coherent curriculum offers students with different interests and abilities an extended range of learning possibilities; it also presents students with a diversity of views that encourages them to sort out the differences for themselves. Students can find in this diversified approach "something for everyone."

ASSESSMENT: ANOTHER LESSON OF THE STUDY

One of the most significant findings of this study is that participants could not have adequately assessed the full effect of the Program at its end or even after they had finished college or graduate school. They were not then in a position to judge its impact on their professional and occupational lives or their family lives. An important difficulty in assessing educational experiences at the time or soon has to do with the crucial relationship of the late adolescent to authority. Now that 25 years have gone by, many have accepted the responsibilities of authority in the work place or with their families or in volunteer activities, and that leads to an entirely different relationship with authority than when they were just leaving home and beginning college.

Above all, the study has shown that graduation is not the end of the learning experience. We have found ex-students from the Program still thinking about what they learned there, still exploring the meaning of their educational experiences, still arguing with each other, and with their teachers. Participants have said about the Program in describing its lasting value: "It has given me a background in which to think about things to make decisions, whether they are day-to-day life decisions, or philosophical ones"; "It awakened me to issues that continue to be near and dear to me . . . questions of human nature and political activity, a question of natural law and moral law, and first principles . . . issues brought up in the Program seem to be still critical and still crucial. . . . It furnished me with intellectual material on which to work for the rest of my life."

Surveys of students at the time of graduation or soon after are quick, convenient, and inexpensive, but can be misleadingly incomplete if the nature of the program requires reflection for a proper assessment. This study demonstrates the value of intensive, extensive, personal interviews in revealing the long-term impacts of programs such as these. It is clear from their testimony that an educational experience as strong as the Experimental College Program continues to have significant and cumulative effects at least for the next few decades after students leave the Program, and probably, for some of them, for the rest of their lives.

THE FUTURE OF THE MEIKLEJOHN-TUSSMAN PROGRAMS

There is no longer a question of whether the Meiklejohn-Tussman program can be replicated today—it has been and is constantly reborn on campuses across the nation, cloned and copied in a dazzling variety of new forms. While more easily adapted to junior colleges and small liberal arts colleges, small programs of liberal education in large public research universities obviously fill a need, particularly for entering students. Wisconsin has repeatedly offered a version of the original Meiklejohn experiment that is still being modified.

The key to the success of the Meiklejohn-Tussman replications appears to lie in their ability to adapt to changing academic circumstances. At Malaspina, for instance, science has been added to the curriculum, helping to fulfill graduation requirements no doubt, but certainly adding to the required reading that Tussman purposely kept at a minimum. At Wisconsin, the Integrated Studies Program is not a separate college as was the original Experimental College, and students have the flexibility of taking as few or as many courses as they wish, when they wish, perhaps at the price of less coherence than in the original college. And at Evergreen, as already mentioned, the curriculum has been radically altered. These changes may seem heretical to supporters of the original plan; but if adaptations enable new programs to survive, it may be worth some sacrifice of purity in order to keep alive this tradition of curricular reform. Universities themselves may develop more receptivity to such programs as research over time makes more apparent the worth of their long term effects on students. (The difference between bringing a horse to water and making him drink is an adage applicable to educational reform: Gruber and Richard (1990, 159-60) give instances of proven effective undergraduate teaching interventions that remain unimplemented in the face of "self-satisfied tradition.") As to the "elite" curriculum, the pendulum may yet swing away from Europhobic tendencies so prevalent recently and back towards more tolerance of diversity in reading material, if the benefits to a broad range of students of a curriculum that includes "the classics" are recognized.[15]

Periodically there are calls for more emphasis on teaching in the research university. In a recent collection of essays on the research university, Adrienne Jamieson and Nelson Polsby describe a program for undergraduates at the Institute of Governmental Studies at the University of California, Berkeley (IGS), in which undergraduate students in an advanced political science course join with graduate students and research faculty at the institute in working on research problems generated by the class but of use to the research team as well. These undergraduates, graduate students, and research faculty together create a scholarly community, with benefits for all (Jamieson and Polsby 1994, 225-30). The only danger in this program and others involving undergraduates in faculty research is that they may, as supporters of Tussman-like programs would argue, run the risk of leading to premature specialization for students who have not yet had enough general or liberal education. (In a university with the resources of Berkeley, one could imagine students starting with a lower division program such as Tussman's, adding some of the superior lecture courses available in Berkeley's upper division and an apprentice course such as this one in IGS in the upper division years—truly the best of all worlds.) In another effort to improve undergraduate education at Berkeley, a program of Freshman Seminars in theory allows every freshman to attend at least one small nondepartmental seminar of 15 students during their two lower division years, no doubt a welcome respite from the usual huge introductory lecture classes, but a far cry from a coherent two-year program such as Tussman's.

---

[15]James Miller, "The Academy Writes Back: Why We Can't Close The Book on Allan Bloom," *Lingua Franca*, Vol. 7, No. 3 (March, 1997). See also Stephen Zelnick's review of *Great Books: My Adventures with Homer, Rousseau, Woolf, and Other Indestructible Writers of the Western World*, by David Denby. (New York: Simon and Schuster, 1996), in *Academic Questions* (Spring, 1997), and Edward Rothstein, "Culture Wars Go On, But the Battle Lines Blur," *The New York Times*, Tuesday, May 27, 1997.

Summary, Implications, and Conclusions

A program modeled after the Tussman College would have distinct advantages for certain types of students for whom universities currently express concerns.[16] Commuting students, for instance, would clearly benefit from having a place and a program on campus to call their own where they could meet faculty and fellow students on an informal basis. They could thus be provided greater opportunities for connecting with faculty than regular courses and on-campus housing can usually offer (although there always exists the problem that commuting students, who often have jobs, are not necessarily able to remain on the campus long enough during the day to take advantage of these opportunities). Older, re-entry students, and students coming from disadvantaged backgrounds often live at home to avoid the expense of on-campus living, and they would stand to benefit from a program such as this that affords "a home away from home" not only in the physical and psychological but also the intellectual sense. Similarly, students who come to college less well prepared academically than others, and students who are slow readers (although of average or above intellectual abilities) can benefit from this kind of individualized teaching approach and emphasis on cooperation in a learning community, which puts them on the same basis as their more advantaged peers. Unlike many other academic programs, there is no particular high school preparation necessary for such programs, other than university level competency in reading and writing. And we have seen from testimony of program participants how faculty and other students in such a learning community can serve as models for the acquisition of learning skills that then can be applied to other educational experiences.

As Tussman has demonstrated, programs like these can be funded at the cost levels of ordinary undergraduate instruction, so that they are feasible even in today's climate of budget constraints. Furthermore, Pascarella and Terenzini (1991, 592) argue that institutional prestige, material wealth, and technical resources are not related to educational quality. In discussing the wide variability in cognitive effects of different departments within colleges, they state:

---

[16]See Christina Maslach, *Promoting Student Success at Berkeley: Guidelines for the Future.* Report of the Commission on Responses to a Changing Student Body, University of California, Berkeley, 1991.

To understand between-college impacts on cognitive growth, we need to focus less on a college's resources and more on such factors as curricular experiences and course work patterns, the quality of teaching, the frequency and focus of student-faculty non-classroom interaction, the nature of peer group and extracurricular activities, and the extent to which institutional structures and policies facilitate student academic and social involvement.

These are all factors we can now recognize in the Meiklejohn-Tussman programs.

Since the tendency persists for versions of the Experimental College Program to reappear from time to time and place to place, and in view of the vigor of the learning community movement it has heavily influenced, it may now be recognized as an important predecessor to a continuing series of educational reforms. As Arthur Levine points out (1978, 376),

> the Experimental College Program illustrates the fact that a program may close but need not thereby be considered to have failed. Even though the program ceases operation, it can affect its participants for the better and serve as guidance for the future. This is no small accomplishment for anything experimental.

In light of their role in undergraduate curricular reform in different educational settings, their capacity to enhance student development well into the years following college, and their ability to meet many of the needs of undergraduates today as they face increasingly impersonal educational environments (Marchese 1998), these programs deserve to be taken seriously, to be observed and studied, particularly their long-term effects.

And the long-term effects simply cannot be overestimated—they can be truly "seeds planted over time." As an example, just as this book was going to press, a former student in the Program who had been interviewed for the study almost nine years ago called to tell me she had changed her mind about some of the things she had told me then. She had been at the time of the interview the least positive of all the informants about her experiences in the Program, but has since been reevaluating her time there in light of a renewed interest, first kindled there, in the readings. She said she had "finally understood what Joe Tussman was up to" in tracing Western political thought from its origins in Greece through to America's traditions. In spite of recently taking classes in the classics at major

Summary, Implications, and Conclusions

universities in the area, she found "no classes did what the Program did"—took the readings out of the disciplinary context of history, classics, archeology, and so forth, and introduced them directly to the students with no intervening criticism or secondary analysis, revealing the scope of "some of the greatest writing and thinking that has survived over the centuries." Even reading the Odyssey from cover to cover now in one class did not give her the context that she remembered from the Program. She explained that when she entered the Program, she was only seventeen, had just left her family for the first time, and in this socially and politically disruptive time her only "context" had been her "own personal self," which did not allow her to take advantage of what she now sees as a "brilliant" program of study.

This postscript again illustrates the importance of development during a person's lifetime in determining the assessment of the Program's worth. This former student's judgment of the Experimental College Program clearly has changed over the years as her lifetime experience has changed. Now, almost 35 years later, she is, so to speak, ready for the Program. And what could serve as a better illustration of Henry Adam's prophecy quoted at the beginning of this book? No one yet knows where the influence of Joseph Tussman, or of this Program, will stop.

The Experimental College Program was unique in its ability to address two major debates in higher educational reform today, one that centers around the curriculum, the other around pedagogy, and to demonstrate how the two are intertwined. Perhaps the overwhelming testimony presented here of the penetrating effects of such a program over the span of 20 years and more is the best evidence of the effectiveness of programs that integrate both. A program that combines team teaching and individualized teaching methods with a strong curriculum in a learning community, addresses important moral issues and deals directly with the cognitive and ethical development of its students, is capable of establishing habits of mind that can last a lifetime.

REFERENCES

Alwin, D. F., et al. 1991. *Political Attitudes Over the Lifespan: The Bennington Women after Fifty Years*. Madison: The University of Wisconsin Press.

The Antiochian. 1990. Yellow Springs, Ohio: Antioch College (Fall).

Astin, Alexander. 1993. *What Matters in College?* San Francisco: Jossey-Bass.

Axtell, James. 1985. *The Invasion Within: The Contest of Cultures in Colonial North America*. New York and Oxford: Oxford University Press, 179-364.

Barton, Paul E., and Archie Lapoint. 1995. *Learning by Degrees: Indicators of Performance in Higher Education*. Princeton: Policy Information Center, Educational Testing Service.

Bauslaugh, Gary. 1990. "Proposal for a Bachelor of Arts in Liberal Studies offered by The University of Victoria at Malaspina College." Malaspina College, British Columbia.

Berkeley Division of the Academic Senate, University of California. 1979. Report of the Ad Hoc Committee on the Collegiate Seminar Program. June 14.

Bernhardi, Robert. 1985. *The Buildings of Berkeley*. Berkeley: The Berkeley Architectural Heritage Association.

Bess, James L., ed. 1997. *Teaching Well and Liking It: Motivating Faculty to Teach Effectively*. Baltimore and London: Johns Hopkins University Press.

Beyer, Janice M. 1997. "Organizational Cultures and Faculty Motivation." In *Teaching Well and Liking It: Motivating Faculty to Teach Effectively*, ed. James L. Bess. Baltimore and London: Johns Hopkins University Press.

Bloom, Allan. 1987. *The Closing of the American Mind*. New York: Simon & Schuster.

Blos, Peter. 1969. "The Second Individuation Process of Adolescence." *The Psychoanalytic Study of the Child, XXII*. New York: International University Press.

_____. 1971. "The Child Analyst Looks at the Young Adolescent." *Daedalus*, vol. 100, no. 4, Proceedings of the American Academy of Arts and Sciences (Fall).

Bowen, Howard R. 1977. *Investment in Learning: The Individual and Social Value of American Higher Education.* San Francisco: Jossey-Bass.

Bradley Evaluation Committee. 1996. "End of Year Progress Report on the Bradley Learning Community." Madison: The University of Wisconsin. August.

Brown, Cynthia, et al. 1984. "Alternative Education: Trends and Future Implications." In *Against the Current: Reform and Experimentation in Higher Education,* ed. Richard M. Jones and Barbara Leigh Smith. Cambridge, Mass.: Schenkman Publishing Co.

Cadwallader, Mervyn. 1984. "Experiment at San Jose." In *Against the Current: Reform and Experimentation in Higher Education,* ed. Richard M. Jones and Barbara Leigh Smith. Cambridge, Massachusetts: Schenkman Publishing Co.

Cerny, Susan D. Stern. 1990. "Northside: Historic Survey of a North Berkeley Neighborhood Before and After the 1923 Wildfire." Berkeley: Berkeley Architectural Heritage Association.

Chickering, Arthur W., and Associates. 1981. *The Modern American College.* San Francisco: Jossey-Bass.

Clark, Thomas F. 1981. "Individualized Education." In *The Modern American College,* ed. Arthur W. Chickering. San Francisco: Jossey-Bass.

Cole, J., E. Barber, and S. Graubard, eds. 1994. *The Research University in a Time of Discontent.* Baltimore: Johns Hopkins Press.

Cowan, Philip A. 1978. *Piaget: With Feeling: Cognitive, Social, and Emotional Dimensions.* New York: Holt, Rinehart and Winston.

Denby, David. 1996. *Great Books: My Adventures with Homer, Rousseau, Woolf, and other Indestructible Writers of the Western World.* New York: Simon and Schuster.

Dillon, Sam. 1995. "Islands of Change Create Friction: New York's Alternative Schools." *New York Times,* May 25.

Elmen, Julie, and Daniel Offer. 1993. "Normality, Turmoil, and Adolescence." In *Handbook of Clinical Research and Practice with Adolescents,* ed. Patrick H. Tolan and Bertram J. Cohler. New York: John Wiley and Sons.

Erikson, H. E. 1968. *Identity: Youth and Crisis.* New York: Norton.

Feuerstein, Reuven, et al. 1988. *Don't Accept Me as I Am: Helping "Retarded" People to Excel.* New York: Plenum Press.

References

Gabelnick, F., et al. 1990. "Learning Communities: Creating Connections Among Students, Faculty and Disciplines." *New Directions for Teaching and Learning*, no. 41. San Francisco: Jossey-Bass.

Gamson, Zelda. 1984. *Liberating Education.* San Francisco: Jossey-Bass.

Gardner, David P. 1967. *The California Oath Controversy.* Berkeley: University of California Press.

Gilligan, Carol. 1982. *In a Different Voice: Psychological Theory and Women's Development.* Cambridge: Harvard University Press.

Gitlin, Todd. 1987. *The Sixties: Years of Hope, Days of Rage.* Toronto: Bantam Books.

Goines, David. 1993. *Free Speech Movement: Coming of Age in the 1960s.* Berkeley: Ten Speed Press.

Grant, Gerald and David Riesman. 1978. *The Perpetual Dream: Reform and Experiment in the American College.* Chicago: University of Chicago Press.

Gruber, Howard E., and Lucien Richard. 1990. "Active Work and Creative Thought in University Classrooms." In *Promoting Cognitive Growth Over the Life Span*, ed. Milton Schwebel, Charles Maher, and Nancy Fagley. Hillsdale, N.J.: Lawrence Erlbaum Assoc.

Hardy, Mary. 1997. "Historic Resources Inventory, University of California, Berkeley, 2607 Hearst, Graduate School of Public Policy." Emeryville, Calif.: Siegel & Strain, Architects, March 7.

Heirich, M. 1971. *The Spiral of Conflict: Berkeley, 1964.* New York: Columbia University Press.

Hirsch, Judi. 1989. "A study of a program based on Feuerstein's theories intended to teach high-level cognitive skills to African-American and Mexican-American junior-high school students identified as learning disabled." *Dissertation Abstracts International*, vol. 49, no. 8.

Hoelke, Larene. 1977. *The University Experience: Eight Year Follow-Up ... 1966 and 1967 Freshmen.* Buffalo, N.Y.: State University of New York at Buffalo.

Hult, A. 1990. "The Profession as Notion: An Analysis of Students' Notions within Four Higher Educational Programs." Dissertation of the Faculty of Social Sciences. Pedagogiska institutionen, University of Umeå.

Hunter, D. Lyn. 1997. "Berkeley Women at Century's End." *Berkeleyan*, vol. 26, no. 13 (November 5-11).

"Islands of Change Create Friction: New York's Alternative Schools." 1995. *The New York Times.* May 25.

Jamieson, Adrienne, and Nelson W. Polsby. 1994. "The Research University as a Setting for Undergraduate Teaching." In *The Research University in a Time of Discontent,* ed. J. Cole, E. Barber, and S. Graubard. Baltimore: Johns Hopkins Press.

Jones, Richard M., and Barbara Leigh Smith. 1984. *Against the Current: Reform and Experimentation in Higher Education.* Cambridge, Massachusetts: Schenkman Publishing Co.

Kuhn, Deanna and Erin Phelps. 1979. "A Methodology for Observing Development of a Formal Reasoning Strategy." In *Intellectual Development Beyond Childhood,* ed. Deanna Kuhn. San Francisco: Jossey-Bass.

Levine, Arthur. 1978. *Handbook on Undergraduate Curriculum.* San Francisco: Jossey-Bass.

Light, Richard. 1990. *The Harvard Assessment Seminars: First Report.* Cambridge, Massachusetts: Harvard University.

_____. 1992. *The Harvard Assessment Seminars: Second Report.* Cambridge, Massachusetts: Harvard University.

Lipset, S. M., and S. Wolin Sheldon, eds. 1965. *The Berkeley Student Revolt: Facts and Interpretations.* Garden City, N.Y.: Doubleday-Anchor.

Loevinger, Jane, Ruth Wessler, and C. Redmore. 1970. *Measuring Ego Development,* 2 vols. San Francisco: Jossey-Bass.

MacGregor, Jean. 1987. "Intellectual Development of Students in Learning Community Programs 1986-87." Occasional Paper Number 1, Fall. Washington Center for Improving the Quality of Undergraduate Education.

Marchese, Ted. 1997. "Student Evaluations of Teaching." Editorial in *Change,* vol. 29, no. 5 (September/October).

_____. 1998. "Disengaged Students II." Editorial, *Change.* (May/June).

Marton, Ference; Dai Hounsel, and Noel Estwhistle. 1984. *The Experience of Learning.* Edinburgh: Scottish Academic Press.

Maslach, Christina. 1991. *Promoting Student Success at Berkeley: Guidlines for the Future.* Report of the Commission on Responses to a Changing Student Body. Berkeley: University of California.

References

McArdle, Phil, ed. 1983. *Exactly Opposite the Golden Gate: Essays on Berkeley's History, 1985-1945.* Berkeley: The Berkeley Historical Society.

Meiklejohn, Alexander. 1932. *The Experimental College.* New York: Harper & Row.

Meyerson, Martin. 1993. Personal communication.

Miller, James. 1997. "The Academy Writes Back: Why We Can't Close The Book on Allan Bloom." *Linguafranca*, vol. 7, no. 3 (March).

Moore, Diane M., and Scott P. Kerlin. N.d. "Examining the Effectiveness of Coordinated Studies: 1990-94." North Seattle Community College.

Mussen, P. H., J. J. Conger, and J. Kagan. 1979. *Child Development and Personality.* New York: Harper & Row.

Newcomb, Theodore, et al. 1967. *Resistance and Change: Bennington College and Its Students After Twenty-Five Years.* New York: Wiley.

Pascarella, E. T., and P. T. Terenzini. 1991. *How College Affects Students.* San Francisco: Jossey-Bass.

Perry, William G. 1970. *Forms of Intellectual and Ethical Development.* New York: Holt, Rinehart & Winston.

_____. 1981. "Cognitive and Ethical Growth: The Making of Meaning." In *The Modern American College*, ed. Arthur W. Chickering and Associates. San Francisco: Jossey-Bass.

Peterson, Eric. 1969. "The Program has Helped MeKnow That I Don't Know: A Report on the Berkeley Experiment." *Mademoiselle* (August): 261.

Pritchett, V. S. 1970. *A Cab at the Door.* Harmondsworth, Middlesex, England: Penguin Books.

Reisman, David. 1993. *Abundance for What?* New Brunswick, N.J.: Transaction Publishers.

Rorabaugh, W. J. 1989. *Berkeley at War: The 1960s.* New York: Oxford University Press.

Rothstein, Edward. 1997. "Culture Wars Go On, But the Battle Lines Blur." *The New York Times*, May 27.

Rudolph, Frederick. 1977. *Curriculum: A History of the American Undergraduate Course of Study Since 1636.* San Francisco: Jossey-Bass.

Searle, John. 1971. *Campus War.* New York: The World Publishing Company.

Schwebel, Milton, Charles Maher, and Nancy Fagley. 1990. *Promoting Cognitive Growth Over the Life Span.* Hillsdale, N.J.: Lawrence Erlbaum Assoc.

Scott, Peter Dale. 1989. "Strawberry Preserved." In *Teaching at Berkeley*, University of California at Berkeley, #22, Fall.

Smelser, Neil J. 1993. "The Politics of Ambivalence: Diversity in the Research Universities." *Daedalus*, vol. 122, no. 4: 37-53.

_____. "The Odyssey Experience." Unpublished manuscript.

Snyder, B. R. 1971. *The Hidden Curriculum.* New York: Knopf.

Spence, Donald P. 1982. *Narrative Truth and Historical Truth.* New York: W. W. Norton.

Statdman, Verne. 1970. *The University of California, 1868-1968.* New York: McGraw-Hill.

Suczek, Robert F. 1972. *The Best Laid Plans.* San Francisco: Jossey-Bass.

Tinto, Vincent. 1993. *Leaving College: Rethinking the Causes and Cures of Student Attrition.* Chicago: University of Chicago Press.

Tolan, Patrick, and Bertram Cohler. 1993. *Handbook of Clinical Research & Practice with Adolescence.* New York: John Wiley & Sons, Inc.

Trow, Katherine. 1987. "The Experimental College Program in Retrospect: An Exploratory Study." Unpublished manuscript. July.

_____. 1991. "The Experimental College Program at Berkeley: Long Term Effects of an Experiment in Undergraduate Education." Occasional Paper #73. Berkeley: Center For Studies in Higher Education, University of California, January.

_____. 1992. "The Experimental College Program at Berkeley: Some of Its Long Term Effects and Implications for Educational Practice." Stockholm, Sweden: Council for the Renewal of Undergraduate Education.

Trow, Martin. 1962. "Student Subcultures and Administrative Action." In *Personality Factors on the College Campus*, ed. R. L. Sutherlan, et al. Austin, Texas: Hogg Foundation for Mental Health.

Tussman, Joseph. 1963. *Obligation and the Body Politic.* Oxford: Oxford University Press.

_____. 1962. *The Supreme Court on Church and State.* New York: Oxford University Press.

_____. 1969. *Experiment at Berkeley.* New York: Oxford University Press.

References

———. 1988. "A Venture in Educational Reform: A Partial View." *Occasional Paper #67*. Berkeley: Center for Studies in Higher Education, University of California.

———. 1989. *The Burden of Office: Agamemnon and Other Losers*. Vancouver: Talonbooks.

———. 1997. *The Beleaguered College: Essays on Educational Reform*. Berkeley: Institute of Governmental Studies, University of California.

University of Wisconsin. N.d. "Integrated Liberal Studies." College of Letters and Science.

Vico College. 1970. A Prospectus.

Waugh, Dexter, and Larry Spears. 1969. "Ethnic Studies and the Strike." *California Monthly* (April-May): 347n.

Weathersby, Rita Preszler. 1981. "Ego Development." In *The Modern American College*, Arthur W. Chickering and Associates. San Francisco: Jossey-Bass.

Yankelovich, Daniel, Inc. 1972. *The Changing Values on Campus*. New York: Pocket Books.

Zelnick, Stephen. 1997. Review of *Great Books: My Adventures with Homer, Rousseau, Woolf, and Other Indestructible Writers of the Western World*, by David Denby, 1996. *Academic Questions* (Spring).

APPENDIX A

Report of the Executive Committee, Faculty of the College of Letters and Science, 1966-67

TO THE BERKELEY DIVISION:

The Executive Committee of the College of Letters and Science transmits the following report on the Experimental Collegiate Program to the members of the Berkeley Division.

September 20, 1966

Respectfully submitted,
J. H. RALEIGH, Chairman

THE EXPERIMENTAL COLLEGIATE PROGRAM

The Experimental Collegiate Program has now been in existence for a year. While it is certainly too early to speak with any confidence of its results, an informal interim report to the Berkeley faculty seems appropriate.

I

The program is a direct spiritual decedent of the Experimental College created and conducted at the University of Wisconsin by Alexander Meiklejohn in the 1920's. Dr. Meiklejohn was, in fact, a sympathetic observer of the early stages of the development of the Berkeley variation.

A number of problems had to be solved before the program could come into operation. The University at Berkeley is a powerful, complex institution with a large, vigorous student body and a large, confident faculty. Over many years programs and patterns of study have burgeoned, reflecting many educational conceptions and needs; and general educational requirements and standards have been embodied in university legislation. A new program had not only to be approved on its academic merits but students in such a program had to come to terms with college and university requirements. The winning of academic sanction was seen from the beginning as the major problem. Unless the faculty authorized the program there would be no program.

Apart from academic sanction the problems involved teaching staff, budget, and space. Faculty members willing and eager to take part in the program had to be freed from their departmental responsibilities for one or two years. Funds had to be provided on rather short notice. And space had to be found in a situation in which space is very scarce.

In retrospect, the launching difficulties do not seem to have been very great. But since there have been rumors of war and, no doubt, some misunderstandings, a brief account may be useful.

In the late spring of 1964 (before the FSM had appeared on the scene) the proposal, in rough form, was taken informally to President Clark Kerr. He responded with friendly enthusiasm, and we were encouraged by the knowledge that there was support at the highest administrative level.

Early in the fall of 1964 the proposal was taken to Dean Fretter of the College of Letters and Science. He was sympathetic and open minded, made some helpful concrete suggestions, and sketched out the path leading to academic approval. This involved several meetings with the Dean and the Executive Committee of the College—augmented by the chairmen of several other committees. The presentation was largely oral, and we were not pressed to write out more than a brief two-page statement of the plan.

The first serious check was at the hands of the College Committee on Courses. Normally, a new course is proposed by a department, and the Committee exercises some quality and jurisdictional control. And normally a course is about something which can be stated fairly clearly and carries about three units of credit. We requested approval for a two-year program without courses, which we were calling, for accounting purposes, a 48 unit "course." It is not surprising or shocking that the Committee declined to approve such a course on the basis of the brief description provided.

It was also clear, however, that we could not, at that stage, provide more detail. The details were still to be worked out by the teaching staff which was ready to take up the work should the proposal be approved. We were in no position—nor really willing—to attempt a speculative mock-up of a sample semester.

At this point a closer look at university legislation revealed that the College of Letters and Science had been authorized by the Academic Senate to conduct experimental programs for a limited period of time simply on the recommendation of the Executive Committee and with the approval of the faculty of the College. The Executive Committee recommended approval and, at a rather sparsely attended meeting, the faculty gave its approval.

There is, however, a Berkeley Division Committee on Courses, and, out of habit, the proposal was routinely sent to it. Like its corresponding committee of the College of Letters and Science, it also was unwilling to give its approval without much more information. This appeared fatal. Spring vacation was upon us, and everything else waited upon academic authorization. It was almost too late for the fall of 1965, and a year's delay was, for various reasons, out of the question. We were rescued from this impasse by a ruling of the Committee on Rules and Jurisdiction that the approval of the Faculty of the College of Letters and Science was, under existing legislation, all the approval needed.

The legacy of the encounters with the Committees on Courses was an unfortunate one. While we were duly and properly authorized, nevertheless the fact that we had by-passed or overridden the course committees subjected us to suspicion and criticism.

With academic authorization achieved, we turned to other problems. Acting Chancellor Martin Meyerson, though heavily pressed by problems growing out of the FSM, gave us his full support. Professors Bendich, Jacobson, Ostroff, Schaaf, and Tussman were given departmental leaves; a budget was pieced together; and after almost coming to grief in the quest for space we were given the use of an old recently vacated fraternity house on the north edge of the campus.

In July, a brief description of the program was sent to all who had been admitted to Berkeley as freshmen with an invitation to apply for admission if interested. It was clearly stated that the program was not an "honors" program. We received about 325 applications and admitted 150 (75 men, 75 women) selected randomly.

During the summer the faculty planned and prepared itself for the first year's work. In September—somewhat to our astonishment—students arrived and we were off!

The lesson is fairly clear: a large, complex university can indeed be flexible and receptive to innovation. The administration proved to be, at every level, helpful and sustaining. Although its powers of initiative in this area are slight it does not see itself—and it is not—hostile to change. As for the faculty—it is, of course, the great conservative force on the educational scene. The practices of the institution largely express faculty views and attitudes. There is no doubt but that at essential points the conceptions embodied in the Experimental Collegiate Program run counter to deeply held convictions about scholarship and teaching. Realizing this, we are grateful for the patience, tolerance, and good humor with which the faculty at Berkeley has authorized us to take liberties with established practice.

II

The graduate, the upper division, and the lower division teaching situations present the University with distinctive tasks and challenges. Graduate education is, essentially, professional training; we are initiating relatively mature students into our own guilds, providing for the continuity and development of our own academic disciplines. At the upper division level we are also working close to our professional concerns. For the upper division is characterized, even dominated, by the conception of the "major." While the major is, of course, preparation for graduate work it is not, in principle, only that. We deem it an important part of the general A.B. program that a student pursues understanding under the aegis of one of the academic disciplines, in sufficient depth so that he can grasp something of the methods, the spirit, the central concepts, and the problems which characterize it. We do not consider the major as "wasted" on those who do not pursue graduate work in the field. At both the graduate and upper division levels the faculty is working "professionally" and teaches with interest and confidence. But the lower division, for which our program is designed, presents a radically different picture. Commitment to a vocational path is generally being deferred. It is, of course, a time of preparation, but it is in many ways more significantly the culmination of earlier phases of education, a time of orientation and reorientation. There is no "major" in the lower division, and we try (often unsuccessfully) to guard against premature specialization.

The lower division is the only phase of university education during which the student is not primarily under the authority of a department. Nevertheless, his education—the courses he takes—are offered by departments. And while the departments may not necessarily be overconcerned with recruiting (or seducing) for their disciplines, it is inevitably the case that lower division courses tend to be—explicitly or not—"introductions to" or "elements of" an academic discipline.

Appendices

A department, after all, represents a discipline. Faculty members are members of departments. Their status, their competence is essentially disciplinary, and the more university-like or graduate school or research-oriented the institution the more will this be the case. Faculty members are chosen for excellence or the promise of excellence in a particular field, and when they do what they do best they are working at and within the discipline. This is description, not criticism. But the result is that the lower division is the spiritual stepchild of the university. It is conducted by departments which, on the whole, have their minds on something else.

It is not our purpose here to provide another exhaustive analysis of the defects of the lower division. Everyone is aware that something goes wrong. It is not entirely the fault of the curriculum, but something we do, or fail to do, contributes to the sophomore slump, to disillusionment, to alienation and bitterness. It is widely recognized that our entering students are very good. They have been under heavy pressure and their preparation is better than it used to be. They are prepared for hard work and concerned about serious matters. The student, in short, is not the problem.

It is against this all-too-familiar background that we present this interim report on the theory and practice of the Experimental program. And we stress, at the outset, that, in addressing ourselves to the lower division situation we are taking for granted the value of the disciplinary way of life incarnated in the upper division conception of the "major." What we are trying is a different way of handling the first two years.

Stated negatively, our problem is to provide an alternative to the system of sampling introductions to the academic disciplines as the organizing principle of the first two years. We are not disciplinary; nor are we interdisciplinary. We are nondisciplinary or subdisciplinary. Our position, with all the difficulties it entails, is that lower division education need not, should not, be conceived in terms of the academic professions.

If this is taken seriously, other familiar notions get shaken. Consider "subject." A subject is something a professor has, even when he does not have problems. It is a purely academic category—a subdivision of a field over which a department holds precarious and sometimes exclusive jurisdiction. And a "course" is simply a crude administrative device for teaching a subject. Quite naturally, "taking courses" has gotten confused with "getting an education."

But apart from this passing suggestion that there may be some deep and subtle connections between "courses," "subjects," and "academic disciplines," a difficulty with courses is that the student is taking four or five of them at the same time. And it is clear that this involves a fragmentation of attention and energy and very little in the way of coherence or unity. So, taking a firm grip on the baby, we throw out the course and plan the semester (or quarter) as a whole without internal division into courses or subjects.

It is not easy to make our organizing principle explicit, although, in fact, we think it worked out beautifully. It is easy to say that each semester is focused on a particular period—5th century Greece, 17th century England—but that may suggest more historical concern than we really had. We picked these periods (and we could easily have selected others instead) because they produced a rich and varied literature in which powerful minds grappled with fundamental human problems. So that "problem-centered" is perhaps as adequate a characterization as "period-centered." But we defined the problem rather loosely, if at all. We sometimes said of the first semester that the question was "why did the Greeks destroy themselves in the Peloponnesian War?" But we really did not try to answer it in any careful or systematic way. It hovered usefully as "a brooding omnipresence in the sky." For both semesters the reading list is more revealing than any abstract statement of the organizing principle.

Educational form has two aspects: first, the formulation and development of the intellectual theme or themes; and second the development of a fruitful habit or pattern of work involving reading and writing, lecture and discussion. And just as we were breaking away from the traditional subject and course, so were we also breaking with the conventional classroom and examination pattern.

The problem was this: we had five senior faculty members working full time in the program and 150 students. This 30-1 ratio was mitigated by the addition of five teaching assistants. How could the available teaching energy be brought to bear so as best to further the educational life of the student? We expected to make use of the whole range of devices-from lectures to the entire group to individual conference although some things were clear from the start. There was a place for the lecture, but we did not dream of approaching the 10 to 12 hours a week which 12 units would normally involve. There was an important place for the individual conference or tutorial but our student-faculty ratio precluded regular or routine individual tutorial instruction. In accepting the 30-1 ratio we understood that we were not to attempt an individual tutorial system of instruction.

The formal structure for the first year was as follows:

We designated Tuesday as lecture day and asked each student to keep the hours of 10-12 and 2-4 free from outside commitments. We expected to have a rather full day-possibly two hours of lecture in the morning (staff or visitor) followed by discussions in groups of thirty from 2 to 3, reassembling at 3 for further lecture, panel, or general discussion. The first semester we also reserved Friday, 2-4, for additional lectures.

In addition, each student was to attend a seminar, in groups of 15, for a two hour period once each week.

Thus, the formal schedule for the student involved up to four hours of meeting on Tuesday, an occasional additional lecture Friday afternoon or during an evening, and a two-hour seminar. Attendance was required in principle and somewhat sporadic in practice. We expected that there would be a great deal of informal group meeting and discussion at the house.

We also planned that the student would write a paper every two or three weeks and would, from time to time, have a conference about his work with a faculty member or a teaching assistant. There was also a "term project."

The faculty members' schedule shaped up as follows: he participated in or attended all Tuesday exercises. He had two seminars each week. He read student papers, conferred with students about papers or other work, held general office hours, was sometimes available for evening discussions at the house, spent several hours in staff conference and, in addition, studied the same material the students were studying.

So far as we allowed ourselves to dream of "community" it was seen in these terms—a common intellectual enterprise, a common attempt at understanding through grappling with the same problems through the same material. There was no "course" to be given or taken. Everything turned on the students' becoming increasingly able to do sustained intellectual work with independence and enjoyment.

To say this much is already to foreshadow many questions and tensions—the different roles of faculty and student in a common enterprise, authority and freedom, the relation between the common task and individual differences in interest and bent. We were quite radical in abandoning the normal lower division structure. But we were not anarchic, or individualistic, or student-interest oriented. We had a common, completely "required" curriculum.

A common required curriculum is not, in fact, incompatible with the useful and necessary recognition of individual differences. But the common program may need to be protected and the legitimacy of its overriding demands acknowledged. We had indicated, in general terms, what the program would involve so that students who chose to enter were aware of what they were committing themselves to. Beyond that, we planned to keep the common core to dimensions which would leave time for the pursuit of related special interests; and we provided for a wide range of choice in term projects and even in the regular papers. It seems quite possible to provide adequate scope for differences while developing a common core.

If we stress the significance of the common core it is because we wish to make it clear that in avoiding the Charybdis of courses, subjects, and classes we do not seek refuge in the Scylla of "what the student is interested in." There are programs and institutions based on that principle, but ours is not one of them.

III

The First Year

We asked the students, when we notified them early in August of admission to the program, to read Herodotus before the semester began. We spent the initial three weeks of the semester on the Iliad and then a two-week period on the Odyssey, Xenophon's Anabasis, and Hesiod's Works and Days. Against this background we spent three weeks on Thucydides' History, supplemented by some of Plutarch's Lives and some Aristophanes; then a week on the Oresteia of Aeschylus, a week on the Theban trilogy of Sophocles, and a three-week period on Plato's Republic, Apology, and Crito. This brought us to the Christmas break. We suspended our normal operation for the rest of the semester, asking the student to devote the two weeks of vacation and the three following weeks to relatively independent work on a project of special interest related to what we had all been studying. Five papers were assigned during the semester and, in addition, many students wrote longer papers in connection with their term projects, although a paper was not required.

The second semester began with a 17th century best seller, the Bible (King James version), on which we spent about four weeks. This was followed by about four weeks of Shakespeare—essentially the historical plays and King Lear, about four weeks on Hobbes' Leviathan, and a final three weeks on Milton's Paradise Lost. We also asked the student to read a history of 17th century England as, for example, Trevelyan's History of England under the Stuarts. There was also a term project on which the student was to be working during the entire semester. We assigned only four papers during this semester but expected more writing in connection with the term project.

This was the general pattern. Some comments follow.

The Readings

The readings defined the work of the program in the sense that, at any particular time, the answer to "what are we doing?" was "we are reading ___."

We had to guard against the tendency to add to the basic list. We preferred a few good things handled in depth to many good things read in haste. Keeping the core small permitted intensive reading and rereading. It also gave students time to do additional reading on their own initiative in related primary or secondary materials. We felt that, generally, students are required to read so much that they can hardly read at all, or can hardly read with a sense of leisure and enjoyment.

We also preferred primary to secondary material. We wanted to read the Iliad rather than what scholars and critics said about the Iliad; or, at least, we wanted to read the Iliad first.

Obviously, we read the Greeks in translation. We apologize to everyone. But it was either the Greeks in translation or no Greeks at all. We regret that they chose to write in Greek, but we do not regret reading something like them in English.

It should be noted that "three weeks" on the Republic or on Thucydides—since that is, except for one outside course, the student's only assignment—amounts to almost a full semester three-unit course in terms of time. It is, of course, concentrated, but it provides a qualitatively unique and significant experience.

Clearly, the readings develop persistent and recurring themes. We did not, however, attempt to organize the reading about these themes—moving, let us say, from a speech in Thucydides to a section of Antidote to the Crito to develop a view about "law." We read each work as a whole, generally in temporal order. It required less orchestration.

On the whole, the reading list was the most successful feature of the program. The faculty felt increasingly justified in the selections, and the students, while responding differently to different works, found the reading rewarding and exciting.

The major challenge of the reading was, of course, to learn to read; that is, to learn to read slowly and thoughtfully, to savor the quality of character and situation, to ask fruitful questions, to follow and assess arguments, and to enjoy the process. Preoccupation with rapid reading, overlong assignments, and graded examinations have gone a long way towards destroying the art. Academic reading has become, for many students, not a mental activity but a physical ordeal. This is a real scandal.

Term Projects

Each semester, in addition to the common reading and its related writing, we provided for a special or term project. The first semester, as has been mentioned, we concluded the common reading program before the Christmas vacation and asked the students to devote the vacation and the three weeks after vacation to work on a special project. We asked that they pursue in depth some aspect of Greek life or culture that seemed to them especially interesting and significant. Thus, they might spend the five weeks reading Greek tragedy and get into secondary and critical literature; or they could study Greek politics, religion, history or art. This, we thought, would give them a chance to pursue individual interests related to the common program.

We originally spoke rather loosely of a "term paper" and it soon became clear that the problem of producing a paper—and a term paper at that—was taking some of the joy out of life and drastically modifying the shaping of the work. Since, at this point, we were more interested in having the student roam and explore we made it clear that writing a paper was optional and that we would accept a brief description of the work or reading done if the student did not write a paper.

Many of the students did a great deal of interesting work during this period, and some good papers were turned in. On the whole this break in the routine was welcome to all and the time was well spent.

During the second semester we attempted a different sort of project. Without a Herodotus and a Thucydides, the history of the first half of the 17th century in England did not receive much direct attention. And while we asked the students to read Aubrey's Lives and a standard history of the period, we thought that something more was needed. The core readings—the Bible, Shakespeare, Hobbes and Milton—were fairly cosmic in setting, and we wanted something that would, in contrast, provide an immersion in the concrete complexities of the situation. We hit on the following device: each student was to select a person whose life was significantly involved in the characteristic crises of the period—as, for example, Cromwell or Charles or Lau or Wentworth or Milton—and was to take this person as a secondary focus for the entire semester. The student was to attempt, through essentially biographical study, to understand him, his problems, his decisions. We thought that in this way the student would be getting an interesting grasp of the history of the period. Again, the writing was optional. But we suggested that the students might organize a Cromwell circle or a Milton circle, etc., to pursue the common interest together.

It was, we think, a very good idea. But nothing much happened. The circles never formed and many students never really got started. Some students picked topics which were not really in the spirit of the assignment. It should also be said that some students worked very hard and profitably at the project and are even continuing work during the summer.

Both projects were, we think, good ideas. But the second semester's was clearly a victim of underorganization.

Writing

We assumed from the very beginning that writing was an important part of the program and we expected to assign a paper every two or three weeks. This represented less a judgment about the proper amount than it expressed the conviction that the student should be steadily under the necessity of bringing his work to careful expression. Writing is, of course, an art; but we thought of it as a useful pedagogic tool—as revealing the student's mind and as providing a basis for helpful analysis and criticism. A copy of each paper is kept on file so that we have available for reference all of the student's written work.

We drifted into asking for less than we had expected to, since the writing assignments tended to coincide with reading blocs. Thus, if we were on the Bible for a month we asked for one paper on the Bible. We ended up with nine or ten papers on average, although, some students wrote more. On the whole, students turned in their papers promptly, although, of course, some did not. Again, on the whole, the assignment was taken seriously, although many papers were obviously done in a superficial, hasty, and perfunctory manner. Length varied—some students averaging 4-5 pages, others 10-15 pages. The range in quality was from unusually good to very poor. But we are in no position as yet to hazard a judgment about the general quality of performance and what it may reveal about the nature of the program.

The student's work needs prompt and careful analysis and criticism. This imposes considerable burden on the faculty, and our response may, in many respects, have been inadequate. Usually the professors read half the papers, and the teaching assistants read half. We were, in principle, to pay attention to everything—spelling, sentence structure, organization, coherence, clarity, ideas. In practice, correction, comment, and criticism varied considerably with the reader. Some of us were more practiced, with a better eye for detail and more patience than others. Some jumped hard on what others passed over lightly. Since the student is assigned to a different professor each semester he should come eventually under a wide range of critical scrutiny.

Written criticism was supplemented in many cases by discussion in conference, although we could not have a conference with each student on each paper.

We still have much to learn about the form in which writing assignments should be made. Should we simply say, "Write a paper on Thucydides?". Or should we say something much more specific and directed: "Write a speech in which you take part in the debate about Mytilene." How much choice should the student have, etc.?

Behind such questions lurks an interesting controversy about writing as "expression," as an exercise in "creativity," as something done freely and spontaneously, and writing as an exercise to be done willy-nilly, as, at worst, a "task" to be performed at a certain time and in a certain way because it is judged, by a teacher, to be an educationally useful activity. The faculty was not of one mind on this question; nor were the students. It is a fundamental problem, or at least an aspect of a fundamental problem. Everyone seems to be for "freedom"; but whether freedom is to be understood in terms of mastery and discipline or in terms of impulse, inclination and release that is the question. At any rate, some cosmic questions come to bear on the assigning of student writing and we will surely have the answer before the end of the fiscal year.

Individual Conference

We have said that, in accepting a 30-1 ratio we were, in principle, accepting an arrangement which precluded systematic use of the "individual tutorial" method of instruction. Some private institutions with ratios, of 6-1 through 10 or 12-1 can, if they wish, make the individual tutorial the rock upon which they build. But quite apart from the question of its merit—and it is a real question—it is not an option for the normal institution in the modern world. The individual conference can be invaluable. It is also very demanding and exhausting. We could not, and did not attempt to, meet all our students regularly in private tutorial session.

The trick is to keep faculty time sufficiently free so that when a student needs a conference he can have one. And this may be a session of several hours during which the student's work and his problems can be explored in helpful depth. Sometimes a student will be aware of his need for a conference; sometimes the faculty member must take the initiative as he becomes aware of the need when he reads a student's paper, or hears the student in section, or perhaps notices his absence. The problem, then, has two aspects: providing time, and sensing when a conference is needed.

Our involvement in conference varied widely. One professor, at least, tried to see most of his students about most of the papers and was clearly overworked. Some of us may not have been sufficiently available.

The individual conference can be of such crucial importance that, of course, we must have it. But, if it is done as it should be, its demands are heavy. It hardly needs to be said that the conference, however academic the initial focus, inevitably makes the faculty member aware of a frightening range of problems, most of which he is not professionally prepared to face and all of which have a hearing on the student's education. It should also be said that conferences can be utterly delightful.

The Seminar

We planned, initially, that each student would attend one seminar each week in a group of 15. It was also expected that on Tuesday, if there was no afternoon program, or even as part of the afternoon program, we would meet in groups of thirty for an hour. We had not planned that teaching assistants would conduct sections or seminars on a regular basis.

Our practice drifted in several directions. The meetings of thirty were generally found unsatisfactory and some professors split the group with the teaching assistant. In some cases the professor would also divide the seminar of 15 into two groups. Each professor handled the seminar situation as he thought best. In the general press of work the staff devoted relatively little time to discussion of this phase of the work, so that differences remain largely unanalyzed.

That the seminar had a place in the program we took for granted. It is a standard teaching institution and 15 seemed, abstractly, an ideal number. We thought of it as a discussion session, but what that is, or should be, is not always clear.

The focus for discussion was obviously to be the material we were reading. But the instructor was presented with the usual range of alternatives, including talking too much himself. Should he pose the question for the day and insist on relevance and development? Or should he throw open the door to whatever anyone wanted to bring in or up? Should he insist on universal participation, call on silent students, ration the articulate, or should he let the reins go? And so on.

Some sessions were very stimulating, and some were frustrating and disappointing. Wide open discussion seemed to some to "go nowhere"; directed discussion might go somewhere but, as likely as not, to the wrong place. There was some desire expressed for more section meetings, but the demands on faculty time were already too great. There appears to be general agreement that 15 is, in fact, not a very good number, and we have some variations in mind for next year.

Lectures

The Tuesday lecture occupies a place of special importance in the program. It is the only occasion on which we are all formally together, so that it is a college or program "assembly" as well as an academic exercise. Its potential influence on the tone or spirit of the whole enterprise—for good or for ill—is very great. We knew this and, from beginning to end, worried a great deal about Tuesday. It was, perhaps, the staff's greatest failure.

Appendices

We expected the common Tuesday program to develop and reinforce a sense of unity and involvement in a common enterprise. It is encouraging, occasionally, to see the idea in the flesh. But apart from ritual and ceremonial value, it provides an opportunity for the student to hear from professors other than the one to whom he is assigned for the semester, to be presented with a range of views and attitudes.

Our conception of the "lecture" itself was that it was primarily to sharpen and clarify the issues and problems developed by, or implicit in, the materials we were reading. We expected that there would be much disagreement and controversy which, openly expressed, would spark the program—driving us all more deeply into the material, more eagerly into discussion and argument.

It was clear, however, that we were letting ourselves in for something radically different from the normal university lecture. Usually when we lecture, we lecture on a subject in a field in which we have some professional competence, or at least an academic degree. That, of course, was not our situation. Professional competence in what was before the house was accidental or coincidental. We were drawn from literature, law, political science, mathematics, and philosophy; but we were not in the program as representing our special fields, and we were not, at this point, to fall lamely and belatedly back on ourselves and lecture on our respective specialties. Nor were we, in an amateur way, to bone up desperately on different subjects in order to give lectures which are given regularly and better in departmental courses. We were to be studying what the students were studying, and, as old hands, we were to take the lead in sharpening the issues.

The fact is, we suffered a general failure of nerve and, with some exceptions, the Tuesdays fell apart and dwindled, to revive sporadically when deliciously real faculty quarrels boiled over into public view.

Apart from the "professional competence" question a chief difficulty seems to be that we are not, in our teaching, accustomed to working with each other or even in each other's presence. An occasional irresponsible visitor is one thing, an active critical colleague is quite another; the visitor politely watches you mislead your students, the colleague observes with consternation that you are ruining his.

Vanity (more charitably, insecurity) also enters the picture. Each of us develops his own style as he adjusts to the demands of the classroom. Some deliver carefully prepared and polished lectures, some work from detailed outlines and notes, some seem to make things up as they go along. We are not reluctant to sparkle, but we don't sparkle in the same way or in the same setting. Thus, every proposal—that we do this or that next Tuesday was likely to be uncongenial to some of us. We recognized this, drifted into a system of reluctant volunteering, and were so grateful for anyone's efforts that we were hesitant to take issue or criticize.

At any rate, the Tuesday lectures by the staff were sometimes interesting and stimulating and sometimes not. The quantity tended to fall off, and we had fewer "full" Tuesdays than we had expected. The staff was generally dissatisfied and worried about the problem, and the students frequently were disappointed.

The lecture program as a whole was greatly helped by the generous response of the Berkeley faculty to invitations to speak. We had about a dozen guest lecturers during the year, invited to speak about subjects in their fields as these were relevant to the work of the program. These lectures were much appreciated by students and staff. Our usual practice was to invite an outside speaker only after we had a chance to study the material, and under these circumstances the lectures were eagerly anticipated. They gave us a refreshing glimpse of the professional at work. Requests by students for "more lectures like that" usually followed, and many students undertook, more or less systematically, to audit lecture courses outside the program.

A good deal of thought will have to go into the improving of this important feature of the Experimental Program.

The House

A physical center is essential to the program. An obvious and traditional possibility is to take over a dormitory, converting some space to office and academic use. In our search for a center we considered this possibility briefly. Space is scarce, and there is some dissatisfaction with the present structure of dormitory life, so that some form of residential lower division college within the larger university community merits further consideration. But it was not clear that we could make the necessary arrangements in time, and, in any case, we were reluctant to take on an additional set of problems.

Our needs were, we thought, adequately provided for when we were assigned the use of an old, recently vacated fraternity house at the north edge of the campus. Something needs to be said about the physical situation since it is not without its effect on the spirit.

We had the use of two floors. Faculty offices took up the top floor. The main floor provided a lovely, large, wood-paneled, befireplaced commons room or lounge, a large library or reading room, several small lounges or conference rooms, the secretary's office, and, in the old kitchen, a coffee-making machine. The offices were furnished with standard office furniture. The reading room had two long library tables with chairs for thirty or forty. There were several hundred paper-backs on the shelves, mostly contributed by publishers. Apart from a variety of collapsible or portable chairs and some tables we had virtually no furniture. A special grant of $1,000 provided a large, badly needed rug for the commons room and a hi-fi set. The Law School contributed two old sofas. The mother of one of our students sent us several dozen attractive cushions. And that was it.

The result was a combination of charm and ugliness. Visitors, charmed by the exterior, were appalled by the interior. It was probably no one's special fault, but the University's provision for the suitable furnishing of the center for its experimental program was simply a joke. And the effect of this on the use of the house is difficult to judge. Some students found the situation very attractive and even expressive of their metaphysical views about the universe and its furniture. Others found it simply unattractive and stayed away.

We expected that the house would be a beehive of activity—students eager to discuss the readings with each other and with stray faculty members, informal, ad hoc seminars, sessions with visitors, evening programs, etc., etc. We hoped that our students would generally hang out there and that the common intellectual interest would develop and flourish so that the formal seminars would only be interruptions in a continuous discourse.

Alas! These expectations were, no doubt, unrealistic. Berkeley is, for new students, at least a three-ring circus. The north edge of the campus is not where the action is, and students generally live on the south side. But whatever the contributing physical factors the explanation must be deeper. The use of the house was uneven and sporadic. For a small but active group the house was almost home; for others it was strange and even hostile territory; for most it was just there—sometimes visited, sometimes not.

For the faculty, hearing their footsteps echo in a deserted house could be a disconcerting experience. What have we done wrong? Is the program dead? And things would seem dead for a stretch of days, only to revive suddenly for no very clear reason. The house was visible—with its flaws and disorder, its dominant in-group, its absent throngs. Its condition was always a sign of something, but a sign not easy to interpret.

IV

The special quality of the program is not adequately communicated by this sketch of its formal and informal structure and practice. The first year was marked by rapidly fluctuating moods of exaltation and despair, of eagerness and weariness, of disillusionment and renewal of faith. It was a year of tension. It is difficult to say how much was due to the special problems of getting started, of breaking new ground, and how much is built into the program. But this report would be seriously incomplete without some hint of the stresses and strains.

A group of students and faculty set out, in the midst of a powerful, ongoing, somewhat turbulent institution, to develop and engage in a radically different mode of educational life. We were doing not only what we had not been doing before but what others around us were not doing. And we were a more or less conventional group of faculty members and a fairly representative group of Berkeley freshmen.

We quickly came to realize how much shelter the normal classroom situation provides for the professor. He sees his class TuTh or MWF for an hour. Students arrive, pause briefly, and depart. The professor is clearly in charge. He is on his own ground, a plenary grade wielder, protected by tradition and "academic freedom" from external and even collegial scrutiny. He is responsible for only a small fraction of the students' education and need not concern himself about what happens elsewhere or about what it all adds up to. He faces a collection of individuals who are generally strangers to each other and who have only the slightest transient identity as a "group." Only extremely good or extremely bad teaching can transform a class into a community capable of developing and asserting the power of its own peer-group culture. And the subject, defined in disciplinary terms, permits the formulation of issues or problems in ways appropriate to the special perspective of the discipline and the professor. The standard mood is academic.

In our program, however, the faculty was without its usual insulation. We were exposed to each other at the point of the exercise of the art of teaching. And we were in contact with students in a radically different way. We were aware that we were almost entirely responsible for the students' education. The core problems—war and peace, freedom and authority, order and chaos—were problems with which they were vitally concerned, and the stakes were not merely academic tokens and counters. Moreover, the students came to know each other and to develop something of a sense of themselves as a group with interests which called for expression and assertion.

Conflict was not unexpected; although it is somewhat surprising that there was so little conflict or tension between the program and the outside world and so much that was generated internally—between faculty members, between students, and between faculty and students. Our foreign relations were amicable, our domestic life troubled. It was all very healthy and interesting—"all passion spent"—but it would be impossible as well as inappropriate to detail our family quarrels to even a friendly world.

It is impossible for the Berkeley faculty to be unaware of the deep-seated disaffection of large numbers of students. Youthful rebellion or generational conflict is, of course, old stuff. But it is always a real problem, and we face it in an aggravated form and from a fairly vulnerable position. Education involves initiation into the ongoing enterprises of a culture. But initiation is not a blind or mindless process; things must make sense. And, not without cause, large numbers of intelligent, sensitive, moral young men and women have come to doubt the sanity and integrity of their elders. We ask them to commit themselves to our democratic procedures and institutions as the best way to serve the ideals of peace, justice, freedom, equality. They see these procedures leading us into the morass of brutal war with, at best, shaky moral credentials. They see racial injustice yielding only reluctantly to direct and even "illegal" action. They are not captivated by the sterile quality of consumer life offered by our affluence. They find, or think they find, the betrayal of all ideals by tired, old, conventional hypocrites. They are not ready to join us.

Education in the context of the program is directly relevant to these concerns. The path is not easy nor the outcome assured. But at least we are involved in the great battles of the age. It should come as no surprise that conventional political categories—liberal, radical, conservative, left or right—were altogether unimportant. The issues are deeper, posing a challenge to the very notion of civilization and "order" and even to the value of rationality, coherence, and clarity. In this situation even questions of how to read and write tend to become ideological or metaphysical.

There were several "confrontations" during the year. Some students felt that the student body should have a share in the shaping of the curriculum, and while there was some discussion of the curriculum—formally and informally—the faculty reserved the right and power of decision to itself. We have a required curriculum, and students who commit themselves to the program must accept the authority of the faculty to determine the course of study. We have neither an internal elective system nor student determination of the structure of the common program. Given the temper of the current student generation, this is inevitably a fighting point.

In the same "authoritarian" spirit the faculty rebuffed a student move to attend or sit in on regular faculty meetings. And, toward the end of the year, having decided not to renew teaching assistant appointments, the faculty held to this decision in spite of a student petition requesting that the teaching assistants be given the option of continuing in the program. There were bruises and hard feelings all around.

In spite of (because of?) everything, the program not only survived the pains and crises of the first year but managed to end the year in high spirits.

There is no simple answer to "how is the program going?" It has been, in many important ways, an exciting, fruitful, and significant experience for both students and faculty. Our faith in the fundamental educational conception is strong and unshaken. In fact, the idea is so sound that it triumphs over shortcomings and failures in execution at any point and even at every point. Contrary to rumor, we are not about to fold. We will take the first class through its second year and hope to take on the second freshman class in the fall of 1967.

The crucial, overriding problem is that of the availability of faculty. It is an important part of the conception of the program that it be staffed by regular members of the faculty on leave from their departments for one or two years. We do not want a separate lower division faculty set apart to teach in the program on a permanent basis—although it would be relatively easy to recruit a faculty of able mavericks eager to come to Berkeley for this purpose. This may be a dogma worth re-examining, but the reasons are obvious to anyone familiar with the structure of faculty life in a large university. However, we wish not only to avoid the negative aspects of a separate "teaching faculty" but to make a positive point of the value of allowing or encouraging faculty members to take part, now and then, in radically different teaching programs. While this creates problems of stability, it also insures freshness and could prevent an enterprise which goes dead from prolonging its physical existence through the operation of vested interests.

When we consider that a dozen faculty members could keep the program going at its present scale, admitting a new class each year, the difficulties do not appear to be too great. But they may prove formidable. There is a great deal of teaching energy and imagination in the nontenure ranks. However, the pressures for professional achievement and departmental service are so great at this stage that it is hazardous for nontenure faculty to participate in the program. At tenure ranks half the faculty seems either to be on leave or to be going on leave the next year, and the quarter system may add complications. And there are research projects, books and articles with deadlines, graduate program demands, and departmental teaching responsibilities which have to be considered by even that relatively small proportion of the faculty which is interested in novel educational ventures in general and this one in particular. It is hoped that this report will evoke expressions of interest in possible participation in the program. It is becoming clear that, for institutional as well as important pedagogic reasons, the greatest hope lies in interesting relatively senior professors in the possibilities of participation.

All other problems are minor and manageable. Staffing is the serious problem. If we can solve that we can continue the program on a trial basis until the University, in due course, assesses its work and determines its fate.

Appendix

A Technical Note on Academic Bookkeeping

At the end of two years the student enters the regular program of the College of Letters and Science as a junior. In semester terms the program carries 48 units of credit. A single outside course each semester would bring the total to sixty or over.

The program is considered as satisfying the social science and humanities breadth requirements and the reading and composition requirement. Students who have not satisfied the foreign language requirement when admitted must take a language course as their outside course. Normally, the language requirement will be satisfied by the end of the first year. This leaves only the science requirement which can be satisfied during the upper division years or through the outside course during the sophomore, or, in some cases, the freshman year. Thus, students in the program are not excused from normal requirements; what the program itself does not reasonably fulfill is satisfied by regular courses.

Preparation or prerequisites for the major poses some problems. It is hoped that the outside course during the second year and, in some cases, summer session work, will be sufficient, without asking that departments waive their usual prerequisites. We intend, however, to explore with some departments the degree to which the program will be regarded as providing some preparation for the major in lieu of some regularly recommended or required freshman or sophomore courses. Obviously, students who look forward to science careers or majors will not be able to take our program unless they are prepared to take an extra year.

It is recognized that the program does nothing in the way of integrating science with the social sciences and humanities. We leave the two-culture problem for wiser men to solve. In this respect, however, our students are neither better nor worse off than others.

Students who transfer out of the program before the two years are completed are given 12 units of credit for each semester's work.

In spite of some pressure, we have generally held, and will continue to hold, that a student may take only one course outside the program. Under the quarter system the point of this is even more obvious. One outside course provides a change of pace, maintains contact with the traditional course life, and helps in satisfying requirements. More than a single outside course would, we think, have subtle but significant and adverse effects on the whole conception of the program. Of course, auditing lectures and any other use of the resources of the University is encouraged. Our students should live a normal, varied, active student life.

After much uncertainty, the grade situation has been clarified. We did not—could not, since legislation was necessary—announce "pass-not pass" grading as a feature of the program. It quickly became apparent that adoption of such a system was highly desirable, and we deferred grading until legislative action by the Berkeley Division made adoption of the "pass-not pass" system possible. The student is given an option. He can indicate, at the beginning of the semester, whether he wishes to be graded on the "pass-not pass" or on the conventional letter grade system. During the first year all but a handful chose "pass-not pass." We will be interested to see whether this changes.

There are problems connected with "pass-not pass." What about scholarships, prizes, honors? transfer to other institutions? admission to graduate and professional schools? draft board? employers? parents? Since we keep a file of each student's work and know him quite well we are able to write letters where that is acceptable. And we are quite willing, at the request of the student, to do so. But we do not yet know the full dimensions of the problem. We do not want to drift into a double grading system—"pass, but if pressed, B." "Pass-not pass" may be coming into more general use, but it is not without complications.

We have been uncertain about what to do in a number of "marginal" cases. Our procedure is a great break from the student's normal high school work pattern. We expected that there would be some difficulty in adjusting, and that in some cases a good deal of time would be required. Our inclination is to stay with a student, to ride out some storms, to wait and see (and hope), rather than to make life easier for ourselves by quickly dropping our problems or resorting to disciplinary grading techniques. Toward the end of the first semester, about 14 students indicated that they were transferring out—for a variety of reasons. No students (remaining or transferring) were given "not-pass" for the first semester, and we were quite aware that reasonably strict grading standards were not being cooly applied. Students were aware, however, of our judgment of the quality of their work. During the second semester, some of the marginal performers improved and some did not. A number, aware that they were not working well, decided to transfer out and subject themselves to the more familiar discipline of the regular program. In some cases, we advised transferring; and a review of the work this summer may well lead to more advice of this kind and even to some involuntary transfers.

The whole problem of grades and discipline is troublesome, and we are not yet clear about what to do. A premature resort to grades, or to expulsion, as a means of providing discipline and motivation can easily destroy the possibility of developing a different kind of—and a deeper—motivation. But abandoning the traditional prods and checks also poses problems. We will need to watch this situation closely.

JOSEPH TUSSMAN

APPENDIX B

The Reading List

Calendar for First Year, Readings*
(Three 10-Week Quarters)

Fall Quarter

1. Homer's *Iliad*
2. *Iliad*
3. Homer's *Odyssey;* Zenephon's *Anabasis;* Hesiod's *Works and Days*
4. Thucydides' *Peloponnesian War* (supplemented by selected lives from Plutarch and comedies by Aristophanes)
5. *Peloponnesian War*
6. *Peloponnesian War*
7. Aeschuylus' *Oresteia*
8. Sophocles' *Three Theban Plays*
9. Euripides' *The Bacchae*
10. Plato's Apology and *Crito*

Winter Quarter

1. Plato's *Gorgias*
2. Plato's *Republic*
3. *Republic*
4. *Republic*
5. Bible (Selections from the King James version)
6. Bible
7. Bible
8. Shakespeare's *King Lear*
9. Machiavelli's *The Prince*
10. (Short Quarter)

Spring Quarter

1. Milton's *Paradise Lost*
2. *Paradise Lost*
3. Hobbes's *Leviathan*
4. *Leviathan*
5. *Leviathan*
6. J. S. Mill's On *Liberty*
7. On Liberty
8. Arnold's *Culture and Anarchy*
9. *Culture and Anarchy*
10. General Review

Readings for Second Year

(This list is tentative, and probably incomplete. The sequence is subject to change.)

Fall Quarter

Henry Adams	*The U. S. in 1880*
The Flag Salute Cases	U.S. Supreme Court
The Federalist Papers and The Constitution	
McCulloch V. Maryland	(John Marshall)
Calhoun	*Disquisitions On Government*
Edmund Burke	*Selections*

Winter Quarter

Supreme Court cases on church and state, conscience, freedom	
Thoreau	(selections)
Meiklejohn	*Political Freedom*

Spring Quarter

Marx (selections)
Freud (selected works)
The Education of Henry Adams

Appendices

The Autobiography of Lincoln Steffens
The Autobiography of Malcolm X
Meiklejohn   *Education Between Two Worlds*

---

*From *Experiment at Berkeley*, 137-39. This list is for the second cycle. Suczek (1972) gives a list for the first cycle, first semester (182-83), which also includes Xenophon, Plutarch's *Lives of the Noble Greeks*, Aeschuylus' *Oresteia*, Kitto's *The Greeks*, Bacon's *Essays*, Aubrey's *Brief Lives*, Trevelyan's *Brief History of the Seventeen Century*. The second semester list includes Locke's *Second Treatise* and *Letter of Toleration*, Burke's *Reflections on the French Revolution*, Paine's *Rights of Man*, Kenyon's *The Anti-Federalist*, Solberg's *The Federal Convention and Formation of Union*, Tussman's *Supreme Court on Church and State, Supreme Court on Racial Discrimination*, De Tocqueville's *Democracy in America*, and Dostoyevsky's *The Brothers Kamarazov*.

APPENDIX C

Time Table of Major Political Events Before and During the Time of the Experimental College Program*

1957—formation of Slate, a student political party, supporting candidates for the ASUC and publishing the "Supplement to the General Catalog."

1957—Clark Kerr becomes president

1960—House Un-American Activities Committee (HUAC) hearings in San Francisco; student demonstrations and arrests; some faculty organize a student defense fund

1962—Regents vote to make ROTC voluntary after Slate, the Academic Senate, and the university administration oppose compulsory enrollment

Spring 1964—Professor Joseph Tussman begins discussing his proposal for the Experimental College Program with university and campus administrators

September, October 1964—Beginnings of the Free Speech Movement: the first sit-in in Sproul Hall, the police car entrapment in Sproul Hall Plaza

December 1964—student takeover of Sproul Hall: mass arrests; Kerr meets with 16,000 students in the Greek Theater, Mario Savio seized by police, 10,000 students rally at Sproul Hall and reject Kerr's political proposals; the Academic Senate adopts the FSM platform

January 1965—Chancellor Strong is replaced by Acting Chancellor Martin Meyerson

March 1965—"filthy speech" rallies

Spring 1965—The Experimental College Program approved by the College of Letters and Science

May 1965—marathon 33-hour Vietnam Day teach-in

July 1965—Acting Chancellor Martin Meyerson is replaced by Chancellor Roger Heyns

July 1965—invitational letter describing the Program sent to all admitted Berkeley freshmen

September 1965—first cycle of the Program begins

October 1965—antiwar marches from Berkeley to Oakland Army base

February 1966—Vietnam Day Committee Rally

March 1966—Charter Day walk-out and more antiwar rallies

September 1966—Berkeley changes from semester to quarter system

December 1966—strike against Marine Corps recruiters in the Student Union; 5,000 students boycott classes, 89 students disciplined, and 3 arrested

Fall 1966—change from semester to quarter system goes into effect

January 1967—Kerr dismissed by the Regents

February 1967—thousands of students march to Sacramento to protest budget cuts and the threat of tuition

Fall 1967—second cycle of the Program begins

October 1967—Stop the Draft Week; 300 students arrested, 81 students disciplined

November 1967—Dow-CIA protest against the use of napalm, 34 students disciplined

November 1967—Sproul Hall mill-ins protesting university discipline over Stop the Draft Week protests; 41 students disciplined

January 1968—Charles Hitch chosen by the regents to replace Clark Kerr

October 1968—Sproul Hall sit-in; 117 students arrested

October 1968—Moses Hall takeover; 76 students arrested

January to March 1969—Third World Liberation Front strike, 99 students arrested; Wheeler Hall gutted by arson

May, June 1969—People's Park disturbances and riots, 285 students arrested, Berkeley under military occupancy for two weeks

June 1969—end of Program; last of Program students "graduate" to UC upper division

---

*Compiled from Stadtman (1970) and Rorabaugh (1989).

APPENDIX D

Invitational Letter

UNIVERSITY OF CALIFORNIA
COLLEGE OF LETTERS AND SCIENCE, BERKELEY

July, 1995

To Entering Freshmen:

The College of Letters and Science at Berkeley has authorized an experimental program for entering freshmen, which is to begin in the fall of 1965. The purpose of this letter is to describe the program and to give you an opportunity to apply for enrollment in it.

The program, which will involve 150 students and five regular members of the Berkeley faculty drawn from a variety of disciplines, is planned as a two-year sequence. Its essential structural feature is that it abandons the course system and, instead, organizes the educational life of the student around the study of significant themes and problems. Each semester will focus on a single period—the first semester, Greece during the Peloponnesian Wars; the second, 17th-century England; the third, the period of the adoption of the U.S. Constitution; and the fourth, contemporary America. Studies in each period will involve a wide range of material, a great deal of reading, writing, and discussion, and the flexible use of lecture, seminar, and tutorial.

The program departs rather sharply from the traditional pattern of lower-division work and will demand much of faculty and student alike. The work will be hard, the program flexible, the spirit informal. The work of the program will be facilitated by its physical location in a converted fraternity house on the edge of the campus. This center will contain faculty offices and conference rooms, a library-reading room and a large commons-room. Much of the work of the program will be carried on at the center, although, of course, all of the resources of the University—general libraries, lectures and concerts, auditing privileges, gymnasia, etc.—will be available to the student.

Participation in the program will constitute the student's full program except for one regular "outside" course each term. The student is expected to remain in the program for the two-year period and upon successful completion of the program and outside courses will achieve junior standing.

Technically, the program itself carries 48 units of credit and, upon completion, the student will be regarded as having satisfied the following College of Letters and Science requirements: reading and composition, social science, and humanities. This leaves the foreign language and natural science requirements to be satisfied outside the program. *It is expected that the student will use his outside course to pursue his foreign language studies* and, probably in his second year, to satisfy prerequisites for his upper-division major.

This program, considered as liberal education, is not designed especially or exclusively for those who plan further work in the social sciences or humanities. it may, in fact, be particularly suitable or appropriate for students who intend to pursue work outside these areas. It is obvious, however, that the program will occupy most of the student's time for the first two years, and it will be impossible for him to prepare himself for certain major programs—for example, physics or music—which make heavy demands on the student's time during his freshman and sophomore years. Consequently, the student who is interested in this experimental program should consider whether it is compatible with his subsequent educational plans. Generally, there will be only minor problems, if any, for students not planning to major in one of the sciences. But prospective science majors will need to consider the adequacy of their high school preparation and the need for supplementary work in summer sessions or an additional semester.

It should be emphasized that this is an experimental program, and all such programs offer risks as well as rewards. Problems will, no doubt, arise which will call for imagination and flexibility. You are not expected to apply for admission unless—all things considered—you are willing to devote yourself to work in the program for the next two years.

This is not considered an "honors" program. We hope for a representative group of students. We cannot, however, admit students to the program who have not met the Subject A requirement or who do not pass the Subject

Appendices

A examination and who, therefore, are required to take the noncredit course in English composition.

If you wish to apply for admission to this experimental program, please fill out and return the enclosed form by August 1, 1965. We hope to be able to notify you about admission and about any further action which may be necessary well before the beginning of the fall semester.

(signed)
William B. Fretter
Dean, College of Letters and Science
University of California Berkeley

Enclosure

July, 1995

I wish to apply for admission to the Experimental Collegiate Program.

    Name
    Age: Sex:
    Residence:

    High School:
    High School grade-point average:
    S.A.T. scores (if any):
    Present plans, if any, for major or career:

Return by August 1, 1965, to:

Experimental Collegiate Program
4102 Dwinelle Hall
University of California
Berkeley, California 94720

APPENDIX E

Interview Questions

1. What has been the major impact of the Program on your life?
2. How did you come to apply to the Program? What appealed to you about it?
3. Where did you go to high school?
4. Did anyone support your entering the Program?
5. Did anyone try to discourage you or have any objections?
6. How well did you feel your high school background prepared you for the Program?
7. Do you think that having been well or poorly prepared increased the value of the Program for you? Do you think you would have benefited more if you had been better or less prepared?
8. Did you experience any kind of "culture shock" when you first entered the Program? Did you see entering the Program as taking a kind of risk? (Were you anxious or worried about anything? What? When did that end?)
9. How was the Program similar to what you expected, and how was it different?
10. At the time, how did you feel about the various features of the Program?

Lectures	The intellectual biography
Seminars	Individual conferences with faculty
The "unattended seminar"	Relationships with faculty
The readings	Relationships with other participants
Papers	The House
The journal	Retreats

11. Have your views on any of these changed over time?
12. Did you experience a sense of community in the Program? Elsewhere in the University?
13. Were there any rewards or benefits to you of participation in the Program? What were you getting out of it at the time?

14. What would you have said you were learning at the time? Now?
15. Were there any real costs or disadvantages to you of being in the Program—either that you felt at the time or since?
16. When you first entered the Program, did you ever worry about having made the right choice? Did you ever consider dropping out? Do you believe now you made the right choice?
17. While you were in the Program, could you describe your predominant feeling about it: boredom, fear, excitement, enthusiasm, anger, indifference?
18. Did you strongly identify with the Program; or was it just another way to complete your lower division requirements; or did you feel rather alienated from it?
19. Did you identify with or greatly admire any of the faculty? Have you stayed in touch with any of them?
20. How important to your education were other students in the Program? Did you often talk with any of them about the readings, seminars, issues, etc.?
21. Have you stayed in touch with any of them over time?
22. What about relations with other U.C. students? Personally and intellectually?
23. What was your judgment of your academic abilities as a high school graduate?
24. Did participation in the Program change the way you felt about yourself academically?
25. Did that change or remain the same in your upper division years?
26. Did you ever feel you were part of any and of intellectual "elite"?
27. How do you think being in the Program had an effect on your ability to write? Your reasoning skills? Your ability to argue effectively?
28. There was a great deal of political activity on the campus during your time there. Were you involved in any way? Did your membership in the Program affect your participation in politics, on or off the campus, at the time?
29. Can you recall the most important changes you were undergoing during your time in the Program (changes in your intellectual or academic interests or goals, your political interests, in your maturity, etc.). And do you think the Program had any part in those changes?
30. There were apparently some themes important to the Program. I am interested in your attitude toward them then, and now. What was your

Appendices

attitude toward "authority" when you entered in the Program? Did you object to the "givenness" of the requirements? Did the Program have any effect on your attitudes toward authority at the time? And now, at this time?

31. What about your attitude toward "freedom and responsibility"? Did that change in response to the Program? And over time?
32. Can you say something about the relationship of the Program to the rest of your university life? What was the transition like when you entered the upper division (classes, faculty, grades, papers, examinations, peers)?
33. Did you have problems of any kind switching from the Program to the regular University?
34. When you entered the upper division, did you feel prepared for the academic work?
35. How did you compare yourself with other upper division students who had not been in the Program?
36. What did you decide to major in?
37. How did you come to make that decision? When?
38. Was your experience in the Program a factor of any importance in your choice?
39. Had your choice of major changed over time?
40. Can you think of any major life decisions you have made, say about your career, family life, political commitments, religious affiliation—do you have any sense that the way you learned to think in the Program had any bearing on the way you made this decision, or was it pretty much irrelevant?
41. When did you graduate?
42. Do you remember your G.P.A.?
43. What did you do after graduation? And up to now?
44. What work do you do now?
45. Has your work been any different as a result of your having participated in the Program?
46. Have you gotten anything from the Program in subsequent years that you haven't mentioned so far?
47. Has the Program had any effect on other parts of your life (cultural interests, social, civic and political participation or attitudes)?
48. Because of your participation in the Program, did you feel there was something special expected of you? Was there some kind of ideal you

felt you should live up to? And do you still feel that way? Did you feel you achieved that ideal?
49. Do you have any regrets about having been in the Program?
50. Would you do it again?
51. Would you change it in any way?
52. How has your life been different as a result of being in the Program?
53. What was the most significant intellectual experience you've ever had?
54. Do you have anything you want to add?
55. Are there any other questions you think I should be asking?
56. What did you think of the interview?

APPENDIX F

Methodology and Survey Findings

The Pilot Study and the Larger Study

In order to test the viability of the project reported in this book, I undertook a pilot study of the long-term effects of the Program on its participants. Professor Tussman lent support to the idea of a follow-up study, opened his files to me, and was available to answer questions. He provided a list of four names of former participants who he knew lived in or near Berkeley. Those former students, two men, two women, from both of the two-year cycles of the Program, were quite willing, and some of them eager, to talk about the Program, their experiences in it, and what it had meant to them over the years. While they did not always remember in detail every aspect of the Program, their overall memories of it and its various features were often vivid and revealing. Although the information and insights gained from these four interviews were enlightening, no generalizations could be made from such a small number of participants. On the basis of that pilot study (K. Trow 1987), a larger study seemed feasible and promising. With the help of a grant from the Fund for the Improvement of Postsecondary Education at the U.S. Department of Education, I developed a study of the effects of the Program on the lives of its former students, expanding the number of interviews to a total of 40.

How Participants Were Chosen

A list of students who had completed the Program was obtained from files in Professor Tussman's office and given to the Alumni Records Office, which supplied addresses (a practice still permitted at that time). Professor Tussman supplied names and addresses for the four former students interviewed for the pilot study and who were included in the larger study. Some additional names were supplied by participants during the interviews. Only Program graduates with addresses in the Bay Area were chosen to be interviewed.[1] Only people who had completed the Program were interviewed in order to include in the study people with enrollments of equal and maximum duration.

Since the entering class of each of the two Program cycles were divided equally between men and women, I decided to keep the same ratio in the interviews. Twenty men and 20 women, half from each of the two cycles, agreed to be interviewed. (After each of these four categories were filled, the list of graduates from the Bay Area was virtually exhausted; three graduates who actually lived out-of-town but whose original addresses were given to be in the Bay Area were also interviewed in order to make the categories even.) A letter explaining the study was sent to each prospective interviewee (Appendix H); a follow-up phone call was made to them to set up appointments.

The specific question of the representativeness of the group interviewed was addressed by gathering additional survey data from other comparable populations: (1) the questionnaire described above, which was sent to an additional 19 graduates of the Program who lived outside the greater Bay Area, (2) the College Attitudes Questionnaire sent to 45 respondents who had applied to the Program but not been admitted, and also completed by the participants who were interviewed; (3) a large survey of approximately 1,700 entering Berkeley freshmen during the same period, administered by the American Council on Education. A comparison of the 40 participants who were interviewed intensively for this study with these other groups does not suggest that the interview group was dissimilar from any of these three populations on any important demographic characteris-

---

[1]Since participants were chosen purely on grounds of their proximity to Berkeley, they did not represent a true sample of all Program participants, but rather a geographical cohort. However, this group of 40 participants did amount to 20 percent of the two hundred former students who completed the Program, and therefore constituted a large enough segment of the total to give weight to their responses. Additionally, a questionnaire composed of nine of the major questions from the longer interview schedule of 55 questions was sent to 19 former students who had completed the Program but who lived outside of the Bay Area and were unavailable to be interviewed. These responses were consistent with the others in their assessment of the value of the Program: for example, only one of the 19 would not repeat it (see Chapter 6). We could see no evidence, therefore, of a Bay Area vs. an out-of-Bay Area bias.

Appendices

tics. (The questionnaire is reproduced in Appendix G; the results are discussed more fully later in this appendix.)

Demographic Characteristics and Occupations of Participants

At the time participants were interviewed in 1989 they ranged in age from 38 to 42. The average age of the 1965 entrants at the time of the interviews was forty-one and a half; the average age for 1967 entrants was thirty-nine and a half. Of the 40 participants, two were Asian, one black, one Hispanic (two men and two women), all from the first cycle. Over half of the participants were married; 10 percent had been divorced; the rest were either single or single people living with partners in long-term relationships. Half of them were parents; a few mentioned planning to have children in the near future. Only two of them had not graduated from college, one man and one woman from the first cycle; otherwise there were no differences between men and women or between people from the first or second cycle on these demographic characteristics.

When asked about their grade point averages at graduation, answers from those who could remember ranged from two point something to close to four point, averaging a little above three points (a B average). (They were not asked about collegiate honors, but one mentioned she had been elected to Mortar Board, the senior women's honorary, and one man had been elected to Phi Beta Kappa.) Several said they had graduated a quarter or two or even a year early. Twenty-nine of the 40, almost three-quarters, had done some graduate work. Twenty-six had received advanced degrees: 13 of those, just about one-third of the total number of 40 participants, had received master's degrees and two of those were close to earning Ph.D.s. Another third of the total had received Ph.D.s, M.D.s, or J.D.s.[2]

The occupation of the greatest number of participants was law—a total of eight had become lawyers, including one woman. The next most

---

[2]Since this group of participants in the study does not represent a true sample of the entire Program enrollment, these distributions cannot be viewed as necessarily representative of the entire group of Program graduates, but simply as descriptive of the group of participants. However, they may be seen as suggestive of the educational attainment and occupational distribution of the larger group of Program graduates.

common profession of participants (seven) was teaching, from kindergarten through university. That number increased to 12 when including people in other professions (biology, law, business, economics) who currently taught or had taught in the past part-time at the graduate level in areas related to their major profession. Only one participant was a full-time college teacher at the time, in the humanities. Three women gave their occupations as mother and homemaker; all three of them planned to return to the labor force eventually. Ten of the women combined motherhood and work. Two women were librarians. Six participants, both men and women, worked in business, and most of those owned their own businesses, singly or with others. Four participants were psychotherapists: two psychiatrists, one psychologist, one social worker. Three participants worked in the field of communications. Four were in various branches of the arts—photography, film making, design, music. Other occupations included speech therapist, optometrist, community organizer, stock broker, fund raiser, economist, minister. A few spoke of wanting to change jobs, and some appeared to be still struggling to find their places professionally, but all in all, the occupational outlook they conveyed was one of enthusiasm and creativity.

The Interviews

Interviewees were given a choice of locations in which to be interviewed: their homes or offices; restaurants convenient to them; in the Graduate School of Public Policy, which now occupies the House where the Program had been conducted; or my home in Kensington. With only one exception, all Program graduates who were chosen agreed to be interviewed; many were enthusiastic about having an opportunity to talk about the Program. With permission of the participants, all interviews were taped and transcribed.

A spirit combining liveliness, sincerity, and earnestness typified the interviews. While answers were sometimes witty and humorous, none of the participants approached the interviews frivolously. The interviews, begun in the spring, lasted through the autumn of 1989. Participants seemed pleased to have a chance to talk about their experiences in the Program and their thoughts about it. Many said the interview stimulated them to think about certain aspects of the Program and its effects for the first time. Significantly, several said they could not have accurately answered some of the questions about the Program and its effect on them 15 or even 10 years ago, and certainly not during or immediately after completing it. Although not anticipated and therefore not included in the interview schedule, this was one of the most important findings of the study.

The interview schedule (interview questions) from the pilot study was adapted and expanded for the larger study (see Appendix E), and the original four participants interviewed a second time to bring their interviews up to date with the newer ones. The interview schedule, open ended for the most part, was designed so that answers could be compared while at the same time providing as much information as possible about how participants viewed their own unique experiences in the Program. My purpose was to get them to tell me in their own words what the Program had meant to them, and how they viewed it and their experiences there after 20 years had passed. All identifying information from the interviews was kept confidential so that participants would feel free to speak openly.

The first question asked, what had been the major impact of the Program, usually drew a kind of summary statement about the Program in response. Other questions asked were about how participants had come to apply to the Program; how their high school preparation had affected their experiences in the Program; how they felt about its various features; what the transition to upper division in the regular University was like; what majors they chose; what they did after graduation; whether their participation in the Program affected their careers, family life, politics; whether they had any regrets about having been in the Program and whether or not they would do it again.

Some participants began talking about the Program at length even before the first question could be asked. Many had thought about the Program over the years, some hardly at all. Some had prepared for the interview by imagining what kind of questions they would be asked; some had not thought about the interview beforehand. Some interviews were extensive, running to four hours or so and had to be conducted in two sessions; the average interview lasted two hours. (Interviews with men tended to last longer than with women—their tapes and transcripts were about one-third longer than women, in both cycles.) As in the case of the initial four pilot interviews, participants did not always remember each aspect of the Program in detail, but they did remember their feelings and judgments about it and its various features. While there were many common themes running throughout the interviews, each one offered a unique glimpse into the meaning of the Program for each participant, and were not repetitious in any sense.

Survey Findings

In order to obtain comparable data on the representativeness of this group of participants, a questionnaire called the College Attitude Questionnaire was developed. It included questions from the National Surveys of Higher Education carried out by the Carnegie Commission on Higher Education in 1969, and from the American Council on Education (ACE) freshman survey of Berkeley undergraduates from 1966 and 1967. The main purpose of the questionnaire was to determine if students who had applied to the Program were different in background from the other entering freshmen in 1966 and 1967. The data also offer some information on differences between those who completed the Program and applicants who were not admitted, as well as some information on differences between Program participants who entered in 1965 and those who entered in 1967.

Three groups of participants filled out the questionnaire. One was the group of 40 former students who had completed the Program and who were interviewed. The second was a group of 19 former students who had completed the Program but were unavailable to be interviewed because they lived too far from the Bay Area—this group answered on paper some of the questions asked in the interview, and also filled out the College Attitude Study questionnaire. In analyzing the survey data, the results from this group were added to the first group of 40 people who had completed the Program and had been interviewed. The third was a group of 45 former UC, Berkeley students who had applied to the Program but had not been admitted in the random selection process—this group filled out the College Attitude Study questionnaire. Some questionnaire responses from all three groups were compared with information of the same kind gathered from other entering freshmen at UC Berkeley during the years 1966 and 1967 in the ACE survey of freshmen. (There were no data for freshmen for 1965.)

In summary, the data tell us that students who applied for entry to the Program, whether or not they were accepted, were on the whole a somewhat more confident, academically better prepared group than their classmates who entered the "regular" university. Program applicants were somewhat more likely to have gone to a private school than the other UCB freshmen (19 percent vs. 11 percent); more likely to have had an A- or better grade point average in high school (58 percent vs. 38 percent); and had mothers who were college graduates or had gone to graduate school (45 percent vs. 32 percent). And as we know from the literature, the education of parents, and especially of mothers, is a decisive factor in how much and what kind of formal education children have. (Indeed, it is worth noting how well educated the parents of Berkeley entrants were in the mid '60s: fully 70 percent of the fathers of the regular Berkeley entrants, and 80 percent of the fathers of Program applicants, had had some years of college.)

There are few other demographic factors that would distinguish the Program applicants from ordinary UCB freshmen. One is religious background: where only 13 percent of ordinary entering freshmen came from Jewish backgrounds, nearly a third of Program applicants were Jewish, a pattern duplicated in the self-selection to other innovative and challenging educational programs in the United States and abroad.

Satisfaction with Undergraduate Education

In comparing the Program applicants with the other entering freshmen at UCB, we were restricted to a small number of comparable questions. But when we compare the Program attendees with the Program applicants who were not accepted, we are comparing their responses to the same questionnaire, which gives us a somewhat larger range of comparisons. And here the most striking findings are the assessments by the two groups of aspects of their lower- and upper-division education at Berkeley. For example, when asked how satisfied they were with their undergraduate education at Berkeley, with an opportunity to reply separately for the lower and upper divisions, the effects of the Program are clearly visible more than 20 years later. Half the Program attendees report that they were "very satisfied" with their lower-division experience, as compared with only 21 percent of non-Program attendees. By contrast, only 22 percent of the Program participants said that they had been "very satisfied" with their upper division experience at Berkeley, as compared with fully 42 percent of non-Program people.

Program attendees were not only more satisfied with their lower division in the Program than the others were outside it, but also were less likely to be satisfied with their upper-division experience, almost certainly by contrast in their minds with their special and intense experience in the Program. Non-Program students made the same comparison between their upper- and lower-division experience to the advantage of the upper division; the more focused curriculum and closer student-faculty relations in their major fields must have looked good after their two years in the lower division clearing away their "breadth" requirements. No finding could be more revealing of the special impact of the Program on its participants.

Relations with Faculty

We see further confirmation of these findings in questions that asked about the students' experience with faculty members in the lower and upper divisions. For example, students in both groups were asked if there had been any professors at Cal "whom you felt free to turn to for advice on personal matters." When speaking of the lower-division experience, Program participants were more likely than nonparticipants to answer this question "yes" (38 percent vs. 21 percent), reflecting the closer links that at least some students had been able to forge with faculty members in the Program. By contrast, there was less difference in their replies regarding the upper division—20 percent vs. 28 percent—with the non-Program group more likely to have such contact with a faculty member at that level.

Looked at another way, the Program participants were twice as likely to have found such a faculty member in the Program than in the upper division. By contrast, the non-Program students were somewhat less likely to have such a relationship in lower division than they were in upper division when they were already embarked on their majors. This, and other evidence from the interviews, suggests that in some respects the Program gave students the kinds of access to faculty, and the opportunities for closer connections with them, that many students found only when they had entered their majors. (It still needs to be noted that overall relatively few students—only about a quarter—found such relationships with faculty in the upper division.)

More evidence along the same lines is provided by responses to a related question asking if "there were any professors at Cal who took special interest in your academic progress." On this question over half (53 percent) of the Program attendees said "yes" with regard to the lower division (i.e., the Program), as compared with only a third (34 percent) who answered similarly with regard to the upper division. Again, by contrast, slightly more of the non-Program group found such a faculty member in the upper division than in the lower division (38 percent vs. 32 percent).

Looked at another way, the Program group were distinctly more likely to have found such an interested faculty member in the lower division than the non-Program participants (53 percent vs. 32 percent), and a little less likely to have found such a person in the upper division (34 percent vs. 38 percent).

Other Attitudes Toward Education

Another small cluster of findings suggests the impact of the Program on attitudes towards education. For example, the questionnaire asked both groups whether they thought "undergraduate education would be improved if grades were abolished." Students who had been through the Program, where grades had been abolished, were much more likely to agree with that statement as compared with the non-Program students who had applied but not been accepted to the Program: 47 percent of the former as compared with only 14 percent of the latter.

The Program participants had clearly been persuaded of the importance of a broad liberal education, as compared with specialized studies at Cal. A quarter of a century after going through the Program, they were distinctly more likely than non-Program people to reply "not important" to the question, "How important was it to you to get a detailed grasp of a special field when you were at Cal?": (58 percent vs. 36 percent). When a similar question is asked in the present tense, "would you agree" that "undergraduate education would be improved if there were less emphasis on specialized training and more on broad liberal education," 86 percent of the Program group as compared with 67 percent of the non-Program group agreed. Since both groups had applied to the Program, they were probably disposed toward the values of liberal education from the beginning; but experience in the Program clearly had an influence on these attitudes independent of their earlier sentiments and leanings.

Something of this impact comes through in responses to questions about "How important was it to you to get along with other people when you were at Cal?" and "How important was it to you to formulate the values and goals of your life when you were at Cal?" With respect to getting along with other people (probably an important consideration in the small intense environment of the Program), only 17 percent of Program participants replied "not important" as compared with more than twice that many (38 percent) of non-Program people. On the question of formulating goals and values, something the Program stressed both explicitly and implicitly, only seven percent of the Program participants replied "not important" as compared with three times as many non-Program participants (21 percent).

Politics

Finally, an intriguing set of answers to the questions "How would you characterize yourself politically while at Cal?" and (in a separate question) "Now?" Both groups of respondents remember themselves as left or liberal while at Cal: 90 percent of Program and 84 percent of non-Program people put themselves in one of those two categories (perhaps not surprising, considering the years when they were at Cal). The real difference between the two groups is in the proportions who remember themselves as "left" rather than "liberal" or anything else: 44 percent of Program participants as compared with 26 percent of non-Program participants would put themselves in that category while at Cal. Referring to current politics, both groups show movement away from the category "left" (though not from "liberal," still the most popular position). Even now, Program participants are twice as likely to refer to themselves as "left" than are nonparticipants (29 percent vs. 14 percent). But they also are now a bit more likely to hold moderate or conservative views: (32 percent vs 26 percent). Perhaps both of these are effects of the Program, which, as its participants know, had both radical and conservative dimensions, a combination at the heart of its intellectual challenge.

APPENDIX G

College Attitude Study Questionnaire

1. From what kind of secondary school did you graduate? (check one)

    ____Public ____Private (denominational)
    ____Private (nondenommational) ____Other

2. What was your average grade in secondary school? (check one)

    __A or A+   __B+   __B-   __C

    __A-   __B   __C+   __D

3. What were the major sources of financial support during the first of your undergraduate education? (check as many as apply)

    ____Personal savings and/or employment   ____Scholarships or grants
    ____Parental or other family aid   ____Other
    ____Repayable loan

4. What was the highest level of formal education obtained by your parents *at the time you entered U.C.?* (check one in each column)

	Father	Mother
Grammar school or less	____	____
Some high school	____	____
High school graduate	____	____
Some college	____	____
College degree	____	____
Post-graduate degree	____	____

5. What is the highest academic degree you now hold?

    Degree_____ Major or field_____ Year earned_____

6. (Please indicate the extent of your agreement with each item below by writing the appropriate number next to it.)
   1. Strongly agree
   2. Agree with reservations
   3. Disagree with reservations
   4. Strongly disagree

   Undergraduate education would be improved if:

   ____ All courses were elective.
   ____ Grades were abolished.
   ____ Course work were more relevant to contemporary fife and problems.
   ____ More attention were paid to the emotional growth of students.
   ____ Students were required to spend a year in community service in the U.S,
   ____ There were less emphasis on specialized training and more on broad liberal education.

7. Taken all in all, how satisfied were you with your undergraduate education at Berkeley? (check one in each column)

	Lower Division	Upper Division
Very satisfied	____	____
Satisfied	____	____
Neutral or mixed feelings	____	____
Dissatisfied	____	____
Very dissatisfied	____	____

8. When you entered UC Berkeley, how well prepared did you feel you were compared to most other students in your classes? (check one)
   ____ Better prepared than most
   ____ About as well prepared as most
   ____ Not as well prepared as most

Appendices

9. And when you entered the upper division at Cal? (check one)
   ____Better prepared than most
   ____About as well prepared as most
   ____Not as well prepared as most
   ____Did not enter upper division

10. Were there any professors at Cal: (check "yes" or "no")

	Lower Division		Upper Division	
	Yes	No	Yes	No
Whom you felt free to turn to for advice on personal matters?	___	___	___	___
Who took special interest in your academic progress?	___	___	___	___
Who had a great influence on your academic career?	___	___	___	___

11. (Please indicate the importance to you of each item below by writing the appropriate number next to each.)
    1. Essential
    2. Fairly important
    3. Not important

People want different things from college. How important was it to you to get each of the following when you were at Cal?

   ____A detailed grasp of a special field.
   ____A well-rounded general education.
   ____Training and skills for an occupation.
   ____Learning to get along with other people.
   ____Formulating the values and goals of your life.

12. How would you characterize yourself politically while at Cal and now? (check one in each column)

	While at Cal	Now
Left	_____	_____
Liberal	_____	_____
Middle of the road	_____	_____
Moderately conservative	_____	_____
Strongly conservative	_____	_____

13. When you graduated did you feel you had been in charge of your own education at Berkeley, or that were more or less part of an educational "machine"? (check one)

    ___I felt I had been in charge of my own education.
    ___I felt I had been part of an education "machine".
    ___In between; some of both (explain).

14. What is your birthdate? ___ ___ ___
                                            month date year

15. What is your occupation?

16. What is your ethnic background?

17. What is your religious background?

18. Your gender? ___Male ___Female

19. Finally, can you describe briefly your most significant educational experience?

APPENDIX H

Interview Invitational Letter

Dear (prospective participant):

The Experimental College Program that Professor Joseph Tussman created in the sixties on the Berkeley campus of the University of California was unique even for its time. It was, as you know, a radical departure from the conventional curriculum and traditional modes of teaching, and represented one of the most significant curricular experiments in recent decades.

University records show you as a member of the Experimental College Program. And that means that you can help us learn something potentially very useful: how did this particular experimental program of intensive study and interaction affect the subsequent education and lives of those who went through it? Did it have any discernible effects that participants like yourself were aware of and recall now?

The Program and its participants give us a rare opportunity to study aspects of higher education ordinarily closed to research. This Program occupied a large enough part of the education of its participants to have made a real difference to them. And if it did make a real impact, we might now be able to study the long-term effects of this intensive kind of undergraduate education in ways that are almost never done.

The study will be carried out mainly through individual interviews with a selected sample of students who were accepted to the Program for each of the 1965 and 1967 entering years. Names were picked at random from lists of students according to gender and year of entrance, so both entering classes and males and females would be represented equally.

We are asking you to give about an hour or so of your time to talk with Katherine Trow, the project director, about your experiences in the Program and your reflections on those experiences. We will arrange a time and a place convenient to you.

All information you provide will be held completely confidential. Your identity will be known only to the interviewer: interview results will be coded according to gender and year of entry. We are not interested in identifying individual students for any purpose, but only in looking at patterns that shed light on the long-term effects of higher education.

In addition to the interviews, questionnaires will be sent to a similar sample of former students who applied to the Program but were not admitted, and to another sample of former students who entered UC Berkeley at the same time as Program applicants but who did not apply to the Program. This will help to establish the degree of comparability among the three groups. You will be asked to fill out this short questionnaire at the time of your interview.

The study has the support and cooperation of Professor Tussman. It has been given support by the Fund for the Improvement of Postsecondary Education (FIPSE), a federal agency which will help disseminate any useful findings of the study. The study will be housed and administered by the Center for Studies in Higher Education, a research institute on the Berkeley campus.

We plan to publish the results of these surveys in scholarly journals, and in a report to FIPSE. In addition, we will prepare a summary for general distribution. If you are interested in receiving a copy of this summary, you can let us know at the time of the interview.

We and others believe that this unusual study of the long-term effects of the Experimental College Program's impact on its students could help make undergraduate education, at Cal and elsewhere, more rewarding for students and faculty alike. Thank you for cooperating with us.

Sincerely yours,

(signed)
Katherine Trow M.A.
Project Director

(signed)
Martin Trow Ph. D.
Principal Investigator

KT: ge

P.S. I look forward to meeting with you soon. K. T.

INDEX

Academic self-esteem, 188-98
Accountability, 134, 267
Alwin, D. F., 21
Antioch College, 30, 291
Authority, 16, 17, 26, 45, 49, 55-57, 203, 277-78, 282, 286, 348-84
Barton, Paul E., 382
Bernhardi, Robert, 78
Bloom, Allan, 168
Brown, Cynthia, 7
Carleton College, 398
Cerny, Susan D. Stern, 77, 78, 95
Clark, Thomas F., 292
College Attitude Questionnaire, 47, 51-59, Appendix G
Commuters, 78, 79, 301, 303, 391
Conger, J. J., 299
Cost of the Program, 37, 38, 286
Cowan, Philip A., 287, 339
Criticism and changes, 387, 395
Curriculum, 2, 4, 8-13, 15, 17-18, 27, 28, 32, 33, 47, 53, 62, 83-90, 151-52, 159, 175-78, 209, 263-65, 268, 290, 295, 307, 312, 318, 321, 324, 342, 344-47, 349, 370, 381, 398, 400, 404, 406, 409-12
Dartmouth College, 12n
Debates and arguments, 42-52, 62, 63, 68-71, 93, 94, 95, 204-05
Denby, David, 412
Differences between men and women in the Program, 33, 46, 60, 88, 106, 177-79, 192-93, 363-65, 369, 378
Diversity within the Program, 59, 73, 83, 391, 394-95, 410
Elitism, 184-88, 194, 289

Elmen, Julie, 242, 244
Erikson, Eric, 255, 314, 339
Evergreen College, 13, 306, 398, 403
Exams and grades, 11, 31, 34, 41, 48, 54, 64, 134, 141, 149, 191, 194-95, 197, 205, 265-70, 273, 390
Feuerstein, Reuven, 290
Franke, Sigbrit, 21
Free Speech Movement (FSM), 1, 8, 14, 18, 220, 340-42, 368
Future research, 113, 333, 403, 407
Gabelnick, Faith, 306
Gardner, David, 369
Gender differences, 33, 46, 60, 88, 106, 177-79, 192-93, 363-65, 369, 378
Gilligan, Carol, 378
Gitlin, Todd, 14
Goines, David, 419
Graduate school, similarities of the Program to, 202, 204, 300
Grant, Gerald, 13, 17
Hardy, Mary, 77
Heirich, Max, 14, 15, 322
Henrico College, 12n
High school preparation, 106, 192, 199-200, 223, 413
Hoelke, Larene, 21
House, the, 16, 22-24, 43, 49, 75-81, 247
Hult, A., 21
Hunter, Lyn D., 178
Integration of pedagogical features and methods, 95-96, 128-29, 157

Intellectual controversy and argument, 42-56, 62-63, 68-71, 93-95, 204-05
Invitational letter, 14, 15, 27-29, Appendix D
Jamieson, Adrienne, 412
Journals, 11, 96, 103, 118-23
Kagan, J., 299
Kerlin, Scott P., 307, 383
Kuhn, Deanna, 383
Lapoint, Archie, 382
Learning communities, 79, 80, 81, 263, 306, 317, 318, 319, 409
Lectures, 2, 10, 11, 38, 53, 54, 58, 62, 64, 66, 68, 90-98, 100-01, 145, 233
Levine, Arthur, 404, 414
Light, Richard, 272
Lipset, S. M., 14
Long-term effects, 44, 51, 84, 86, 109, 122, 137, 162-65, 167-70, 172-74, 182, 184, 190, 231-35, 312, 318, 327-30, 338, 348, 361-62, 403, 405, 414-15
MacGregor, Jean, 306, 307, 383
Malaspina College, 397-98, 409, 411
Marchese, Ted, 414
Maslach, Christina, 413
Matthews, R. S., 306
Meiklejohn, Alexander, 7-9, 13, 22, 51, 75, 306, 398-399, 403
Miller, James, 412
Moore, Diane M., 307, 383
Mussen, Paul H., 299, 339
Newcomb, Theodore, 21
Offer, Daniel, 242, 244
Papers, 11, 107-13, 265-66
Pascarella, E. T., 381, 382, 383
Pedagogical features and methods, curriculum, 2, 4, 8-13, 15, 17-18, 27, 28, 32, 33, 47, 53, 62, 83-90, 151-52, 159, 175-78, 209, 263-65, 268, 290, 295, 307, 312, 318, 321, 324, 342, 344-47, 349, 370, 381, 398, 400, 404, 406, 409-12; examinations and grading, 11, 31, 34, 41, 48, 54, 64, 134, 141, 149, 191, 194-95, 197, 205, 267-69, 270-73, 390; integration of, 95-96, 128-29, 157; intellectual controversy and argument, 42-56, 62-63, 68-71, 93-95, 204-05; lectures, 2, 10, 11, 38, 53, 54, 58, 62, 64, 66, 68, 90-98, 100-01, 145, 233; primary vs. secondary sources, 69, 89, 136, 137, 155, 156-57, 176, 410, 415; seminars, 10, 65, 96, 98, 101-07, 165, 192, 198, 208, 234, 338, 389-390; student led seminars, 10, 97, 102-07, 364; students' writings, intellectual biography, 123-28, 150; students' writings, journals, 11, 96, 103, 118-23, 150; students' writings, papers, 11, 107-13, 265-66; students' writings, portfolios, 208, 407; tutorials, 11, 113-18, 264-65
Perry, William G., 284, 287, 307, 315, 319, 382, 383
Peterson, Eric, 2
Phelps, Erin, 383
Polsby, Nelson W., 412
Portfolios, 208, 407
Primary vs. secondary sources, 69, 89, 136, 137, 155, 156-57, 176, 410, 415

Index

Reform, neo-classic telic and popular, 13, 17
Riesman, David, 13, 17
Risk taking, 33-35, 161, 186-87, 189, 284, 287, 334
Rorabaugh, W. J., 14
Rothstein, Edward, 412
Science, 28, 39, 215, 217, 221-22
Scott, Peter Dale, 2
Searle, John, 14
Seminars, 10, 65, 96, 98, 101-07, 165, 192, 198, 208, 234, 338, 389-390; student led seminars, 10, 97, 102-07, 364
Smelser, Neil J., 257-62, 317
Smith, Barbara Leigh, 306
Snyder, Benson R., 21, 370
Spears, Larry, 347
Spence, Donald P., 405
Stadtman, Verne, 341
Staffing, 37-38, 51, 57-58, 62, 399, 401-03, 408-09; teaching assistants, 46-50, 56, 58, 93, 358, 375-76
Strawberry Creek College (Collegiate Seminar Program), 20, 401, 406
Students' writings, intellectual biography, 123-28, 150; journals, 11, 96, 103, 118-23, 150; papers, 11, 107-13, 265-66; portfolios, 208, 407
Suczek, Robert F., 20, 195, 250, 404
Terenzini, P. T., 381, 382, 383
Tinto, Vincent, 307, 383
Tussman, Joseph, 2, 7-10, 12-16, 19-20, 38, 52-53, 62, 73-74, 89-91, 107, 116, 118, 227, 231n, 283, 286, 289, 397-98, 401, Appendix A

Trow, Martin, 317
Tutorials, 11, 113-18, 264-65
University of California, Berkeley, comparisons of Program with, 91, 109, 110, 114, 116-17, 150, 159, 189, 198, 206, 207-12, 217, 246, 248-49, 270, 275, 279, 280-81, 296-98, 300, 309, 311-12, 316, 334, 349, 352, 355, 362, 376, 400; courses outside of the Program, 27, 28, 92, 110, 196, 206, 215, 216-18; junior year abroad, 214, 258; requirements, 27, 28, 92, 215, 331, 381-82, 394; Subject A course, 28, 39-40, 111, 185, 199, 289; transition from Program to upper division, 205, 208
University of Victoria, B.C., 397, 398
University of Wisconsin, 398, 411
Vico College, SUNY-Buffalo, 1, 397, 402
Waugh, Dexter, 347
Weathersby, Rita Preszler, 261
William and Mary College, 12n
Zelnick, Stephen, 412

ABOUT THE AUTHOR

Katherine Trow was born in Cleveland. She received a B.S. in education at Ohio University, and an M.A. in child development from the University of California, Berkeley, with an emphasis on cognitive development. She has held research positions at the Fels Research Institute for Human Development at Antioch College and the Survey Research Center at the University of California, Berkeley, and has been an associate at the Center for Studies in Higher Education at Berkeley.

Trow has maintained a private practice and consultancy in the treatment of learning problems of children and young adults, and taught for many years in the Graduate Clinical/School Psychology Program at San Francisco State University. Her interests lie in the psychological and developmental aspects of learning and the ways in which schools and colleges can promote student development.

Trow has presented papers on her research at the National Council for Studies of Higher Education in Stockholm, the University of New England in Australia, Malespina College in British Columbia, and the annual Fund for the Improvement of Postsecondary Education Project Directors meeting in Washington, D.C. She is currently a research fellow at Berkeley's Center for Studies in Higher Education.